The Continent
of International Law

Explaining Agreement Design

BARBARA KOREMENOS
University of Michigan

CAMBRIDGE
UNIVERSITY PRESS

University Printing House, Cambridge CB2 8BS, United Kingdom

Cambridge University Press is part of the University of Cambridge.

It furthers the University's mission by disseminating knowledge in the pursuit of education, learning and research at the highest international levels of excellence.

www.cambridge.org
Information on this title: www.cambridge.org/9781107561441

First published 2016

Printed in the United Kingdom by Clays, St Ives plc

A catalogue record for this publication is available from the British Library

Library of Congress Cataloguing in Publication data
Koremenos, Barbara, author.
The continent of international law : explaining agreement design / Barbara Koremenos.
Cambridge, United Kingdom : Cambridge University Press, 2016.
LCCN 2015042444 I ISBN 9781107561441 (paperback)
LCSH: Treaties.
LCC KZ1301 .K668 2016 I DDC 341.3/7–dc23
LC record available at http://lccn.loc.gov/2015042444

ISBN 978-1-107-12423-3 Hardback
ISBN 978-1-107-56144-1 Paperback

*In memory of George Koremenos (1920–1997),
whose unwavering work ethic, creative and calculated
risk-taking, and unconditional love continue to inspire
and sustain me.*

Contents

Figures

Tables

Acknowledgments

The research for this book, especially the data collection, was funded primarily by a National Science Foundation CAREER Award, "Designing International Agreements: Theoretical Development, Data Collection, and Empirical Analysis" (SES-0094376), and by a National Science Foundation grant, "The Continent of International Law: Theoretical Development, Data Collection, and Empirical Analysis" (SES-0801581). Both UCLA and the University of Michigan have been especially generous in almost matching my NSF grants through various funding opportunities and thereby allowing me to undertake data collection at the level I desired in terms of breadth and depth. The Christopher Browne Center for International Politics at the University of Pennsylvania, the Center of International Studies at the University of Southern California, the American Academy in Berlin, and the University of Mannheim all hosted me for extended periods, thereby allowing me to focus on my research program.

This book has been a long process and would not have been possible without the support of many individuals. I know I will forget to mention some who have contributed and for that I apologize.

I want to begin by acknowledging my students, starting with my first undergraduate class at UCLA. Since I always present work-in-progress, the lively class discussions and course papers, usually on particular international agreements, have been appreciated and useful.

The data collection aspect would not have been possible without my dedicated set of undergraduate coders at UCLA and Michigan, who painstakingly worked to understand and document the details of the international agreements. Anthony Ambroselli, Caitlin Antos, John Costello, Stephanie Huang, John Lister, Laura Mowry, Leigh O'Dell, Leslie Padilla, Jessica Perszyk, Amin Ramzan, Boris Sigal, Abe Tabaie, and Jaisha Wray were with the project for sustained periods and greatly increased the reliability of the data set. The coders never eschewed the countless meetings reconciling differences. One coder in particular,

Tim Reid, worked with me 24/7 before the expiration of the computing end of the project at UCLA. I am especially indebted to my managers, Sherol (Michaeli) Manavi and Peter Wennerholm, who kept the coders, coding, inter-reliability reports, and meetings organized. Because they were able to keep track of broad theoretical categories as well as details, they often noticed and raised intricate coding issues with me; their intellectual contributions are thus reflected in the resulting data set. The supportive phone conversations with my friend and colleague, Ron Mitchell, who was addressing some of the same challenges of major data collection in his own project, were invaluable. I thank former students Daniel Chardell, Ewan Compton, Eleni Gouvas, Jennifer Herstein, Alexis Juncaj, Nora Sandvik Ling, Jonathan Mansker, Victoria Noble, Raya Saksouk, Gabriel Shea Vanloozen, and Logan Trombley for other valuable research assistance, including help with case studies. I owe a special debt of gratitude to Christian Spreitzer at UCLA for designing and managing the international agreements database.

I have worked with graduate research assistants that are kind, mature, and talented from Jana von Stein at UCLA to Michelle Allendoerfer, Vincent Arel-Bundock, Papia Debroy, Jennifer Kavanagh, Paul Poast, and Johannes Urpelainen at Michigan. I thank Kevin Cope for his expert assistance in the first round of copyediting. Ji Won Kim volunteered to help with the book while at Michigan Law, and her expertise and excellent research and writing skills proved valuable. I owe a special debt of gratitude to Timm Betz, who helped with the coding of the cooperation problems, managed the data set, conducted the analyses, and gave me insightful comments. As he transitioned from being my student to one of my colleagues, his professionalization in organizing and documenting the data set so that others could replicate the results went above and beyond the call of duty. Mi Hwa Hong conscientiously, skillfully, and efficiently redid all of the tables and figures with the final data set so that I could meet my publication deadline. I have been fortunate to have a research associate these past two years, Julia Gysel, who is professional, organized, and thorough. Her skills and friendship allowed me to be much more productive during the final push to publication. Likewise, my sister Annie's love and support and her keen eye and intelligence in proofreading have been priceless during this stage.

I am indebted to numerous colleagues for their valuable input into the COIL project, including the articles that gave rise to this book.

In particular, I received valuable feedback from Matt Baum, George Bunn, Jack Child, Jerry Cohen, Kevin Cope, Paul Diehl, Jim Fearon, Charlie Glaser, Andy Kydd, Cliff Morgan, Jim Morrow, Brian Portnoy, Eric Posner, Bob Powell, Lee Sigelman, Beth Simmons, Al Stam, Randy Stone, Alan Sykes, and Daniel Verdier. Richard Bilder inspired my dissertation and has always been available to talk to me about whether my models capture a real negotiator's thought process. I thank Jeff Smith for many stimulating discussions over the years and detailed comments on many article drafts that preceded this book. Jeff has also been an invaluable go-to guy with every statistical question I have had over the years, and he could practically teach an IR class by now.

I am lucky that Duncan Snidal is my friend and colleague. When my brain aneurysm ruptured in 1998, I called Duncan. When I needed timely and incisive comments on my first and last chapters this past summer, I emailed Duncan. Both times and many others, he came through.

In the year 2000, at an extremely busy APSA meeting given he was delivering his presidential address, Bob Keohane took the time to meet with me to discuss my NSF Career Award. Ever since, Bob has been supportive of the project and of me personally, taking the time to give me advice when I most need it.

In addition, a set of people played an especially large role in this book by commenting on the whole manuscript, large sections of it, or single chapters, including four excellent reviewers for Cambridge and Princeton. While all these colleagues greatly improved the work, I am responsible for any errors or omissions.

To begin, I am beholden to Jeff Dunoff and Mark Pollack for organizing a book conference in the spring of 2013 at Temple University Law School. I wrote my first book draft for that conference and received pivotal feedback from the organizers and the attendees. Specifically, I thank Rachel Brewster, Robert Brown, Sarah Bush, Orfeo Fioretos, Jean Galbraith, Erin Graham, Leslie Johns, Ian Johnstone, Yon Lupu, Ed Mansfield, Abe Newman, Jessica Stanton, Ed Swaine, and David Zaring. The interdisciplinary dialogue was enormously valuable and shaped in significant ways the subsequent draft that I submitted for publication.

The University of Chicago's Program on International Politics, Economics, and Security (PIPES) was the most formative part of my graduate school experience. Through PIPES I learned about the cutting-edge debates in the field, how to write and present original papers, and the art of constructive criticism. Hence going back to PIPES in the spring of 2013 to present parts of my manuscript was a terrific experience on multiple dimensions. I thank Charles Lipson for that opportunity. Charles' comments and those of David Benson, Robert Braithwaite, Anne Holthoefer, Jack Jacobsen, Jide Nzelibe, Emilia Powell, John Stevenson, Alana Tiemessen, and especially Felicity Vabulas, who served as my discussant, were both provocative and tremendously useful.

Likewise in spring 2013, Lawrence Broz, David Lake, Peter Gourevitch, and Christina Schneider, gathered at the University of California, San Diego to give me feedback. They helped me particularly with issues of framing. In his written comments, David, who was a terrific mentor during my days at UCLA, asked me all the hard questions. The book is vastly improved as a result of these colleagues.

In spring 2014, Christina Davis, Dan Kelemen, Bob Keohane, Jeff Kucik, and Andy Moravcsik devoted a large part of a day to discuss my revised manuscript. I am very grateful to them for their instrumental comments and to Helen Milner, director of the Niehaus Center for Globalization and Governance at Princeton University, for providing financial support for the workshop.

I thank participants at workshops sponsored by Cornell University Law School and Government Department, New York University Law School (special thanks to Ryan Goodman), the Mershon Center at Ohio State University, Princeton University, and the University of Illinois.

Jeff Dunoff read the manuscript so very carefully, and his comments have been detailed, provocative, and thoughtful. Erik Voeten, one of my reviewers, provided great food for thought, and I took his comments seriously. Jonas Tallberg has been supportive for years, and as a reviewer for Cambridge, he encouraged me to broaden the connections with other work and put my book in perspective. I am indebted to him for his stimulating comments. While all these colleagues made this book better, I want to give special thanks to two: Alex Thompson and Mark Pollack.

Alex Thompson, a friend and colleague since our Chicago days, has been a source of intellectual and emotional support for years and has made me laugh a lot along the way. Perhaps because of our shared background, he understands where I'm coming from intellectually better than anyone (other than Duncan) and thus often suggests better ways for me to communicate my ideas. Lucky for me, Alex was a reviewer for Princeton and gave me extensive and brilliant comments on topics ranging from the broad framing down to my footnotes.

In terms of this book, my greatest intellectual debt is to my friend and colleague, Mark Pollack. The Temple Law book conference offered the first occasion for Mark to provide comments so insightful and helpful that I would refer to them regularly as I revised the first book draft into the version I submitted for publication. I was extremely fortunate that John Haslam asked Mark to be a reviewer for Cambridge. While not having quite as much to say given how seriously I took his first-round notes, on this second occasion, Mark essentially gave me my final chapter-by-chapter to-do list, with comments on both substance and style. At both junctures, with his overall summary statements and critique, Mark not only catapulted me to think hard about how I was framing my argument; he provided a detailed mark-up of the entire manuscript.

Loch Macdonald, twice my neurosurgeon and now a friend, has continued to follow my case regularly and carefully, reading and interpreting test results and giving me the peace of mind to focus on my family and my work. From my very arrival at UCLA, Victor Wolfenstein was a tireless and wholehearted supporter of me both personally and intellectually. I miss him dearly. Eric Crahan, senior editor at Princeton University Press, gave me some very useful and smart advice, and I appreciated his patience while I made my publication decision. Working with John Haslam at Cambridge University Press has been an absolute pleasure as he has been both supportive and efficient during the entire process. I also thank Carrie Parkinson, Christofere Fila, and David Mackenzie at Cambridge and Sri Hari Kumar Sugumaran at Integra.

I, like so many others in our community, lost a treasured friend and mentor last year: George Downs. We met because he really liked a paper of mine (an early version of my 2001 *IO* article) that he saw in the "paper room" at the San Diego ISA meetings. I was only a third-year PhD student so, of course, that meant the world to me. Our relationship quickly evolved into a deep friendship. We never lived in the same city but kept in touch by phone and over wonderful dinners in New York and Santa Monica, whenever he would visit that coast. During the time my dad was stricken with Alzheimer's, the first thing George would do was ask about him. His love and devotion to his own dad connected us. When I saw him last in November of 2013, he wanted to know all about my mom and daughter. His priorities were always honorable. I hope this book meets his high standards.

Finally, and most important, I thank my family. I have been blessed with extremely loving, smart, creative, and supportive parents who always let me know how proud they are of me. Given I am a first-generation college graduate, my parents and I navigated this new path together, looking up whether Phi Beta Kappa was a good thing to join my junior year and discovering what Brookings was when I was invited to apply there. My dad figured out earlier than anyone else that I was destined for an academic life. I dedicate this book to him.

My mom, Frances, has accompanied and supported me my entire life through all kinds of ups and downs – in the latter case, smoothing the path for me to continue working on a project that she did not completely understand and simply having faith that over a decade of work would turn into this book. Her baklava has followed me to the Brookings Institution (where it was tasted by Alice Rivlin) to the University of Chicago (where it was enjoyed on multiple occasions by the incomparable Charles Lipson) to UCLA (where then Chancellor Albert Carnesale devoured it). Perhaps that is one explanation for all my invitations!

My husband, George Tsebelis, named the project as we were on one of our many drives along Pacific Coast Highway to visit the edge of our continent. Our romantic life began along that edge, and George's support has been profound and steadfast in every facet of my life. Way before that, George was a wholehearted devotee of my work, reading that same paper George Downs did and eagerly trying to hire me at UCLA. He is as excited about my work as I am, and read and improved multiple versions of my introduction and conclusion.

Finally, I thank God for my daughter and best friend, Selene Koremenos-Tsebelis, the petite girl with the big vocabulary, who makes everything easier and more pleasant, including the final push on this book. I am blessed each day by her joyfulness, playfulness, affection, patience, creativity, and lovely voice among what feels like a million other sweet attributes. As Leonard Cohen writes, "I used to live alone before I knew you."

1 | *(Re)discovering the continent*

Every year, states negotiate, conclude, sign, and give effect to hundreds of new international agreements. In 2013, 500 separate agreements officially entered into force;[1] an additional 248 agreements were modified. All told, a substantial body of international law was enacted or changed to adapt to the evolving needs of international cooperation. Adding these new pieces of international law to the body of pre-existing agreements, the total number of international agreements and agreement updates now in force approaches 200,000.[2]

These numbers will surprise many, as most international observers focus on just a small fraction of these agreements. Indeed, the media, the public, and even many international law and relations scholars pay heed to the largest agreements and the major international organizations they create, including the United Nations (UN), the European Union (EU), the International Monetary Fund (IMF), and the World Trade Organization (WTO). But these well-known agreements and their organizations are just the tip of the iceberg: Tens of thousands of agreements actually govern day-to-day international cooperation. All of this law is developed to address the significant problems plaguing the international realm, problems that transcend national borders and whose solutions require joint action by states. The subject matter of all of this law ranges from the most important security issues, like nuclear weapons, to human rights to environmental problems to diverse economic issues – essentially to nearly every facet of international life.

[1] To put that figure in perspective, during the four-year period from 2011 to 2014, the US Congress enacted just under 148 laws per year on average. Available at www.govtrack.us/congress/bills/statistics [Last accessed July 11, 2015].
[2] The data referenced in this paragraph consist of agreements registered with the United Nations Treaty Series and can be accessed here: https://treaties.un.org/pages/Publications.aspx?pathpub=Publication/UNTS/Page1_en.xml [Last accessed July 11, 2015].

What's more, the success of these tens of thousands of cooperative agreements depends not only on their substantive provisions; their *design/procedural provisions matter*, too. When chosen correctly, the detailed institutional design provisions of international law help states confront harsh international political realities, thereby increasing the incidence and robustness of international cooperation in each of these subject matters. The study of these institutional provisions and why and how they matter is the subject of the Continent of International Law (COIL) research program.

This book maps the *vast and shrewd variation* in international law with respect to design provisions, including those for duration, monitoring, punishment, escape, and withdrawal, and *ultimately shows its order*. While international law develops under anarchy, states design this body of law rationally, in ways that make sense *only if* they are seeking to solve their joint problems and to stabilize these solutions. They do not neglect its details as they would if law did not matter in their calculus. Nor do they simply follow a uniform normative template because it is the "correct" way to make law. They astutely tailor the law to their cooperation problems. The design of law is consistent with the goal of effectiveness in the face of harsh political realities.

Furthermore, I explain law covering diverse issue areas (economics, environment, human rights, and security) with varying membership (bilateral and multilateral), including differentiated regime types over various geographic regions under one theoretical framework. In other words, there is a strong underlying logic unifying these seemingly diverse instances of law. In this sense, bilateral investment agreements and multilateral human rights agreements are on the same *continent of international law*. Through the theory put forth in this book, I explain the variation we see in details like the kind of monitoring provisions incorporated or the notice period stipulated in a withdrawal clause. Scientific testing confirms the theory.

What does this variation look like? If one examines the random sample of United Nations Treaty Series (UNTS) agreements across the issue areas of economics, environment, human rights, and security that is featured in this book, about half of the agreements have dispute resolution provisions, while the other half are silent on the issue. And while less than a third of environmental agreements have dispute resolution provisions, about twice as many human rights agreements do. Moreover, there is great variation regarding the form of dispute resolution within the half of agreements that mention it, ranging from the friendly negotiations encouraged by some agreements to the mandatory adjudication stipulated by other agreements.

In this same random sample, the typical agreement has a finite duration, a statistic that seems to fly in the face of the conventional wisdom in international relations that tying one's hands leads to credible commitments.[3] The issue area variation is also impressive, with just over half of environmental agreements calling for a finite duration, whereas over 80 percent of economic agreements consciously give a termination date to the cooperative endeavor.

Monitoring and punishment provisions also display variation both across and within issue areas. Just over half of the agreements have monitoring provisions, ranging from self-reporting to delegated monitoring or even both. For instance, 63 percent of disarmament agreements formally involve intergovernmental organizations (IGOs) in the monitoring process, a finding that contrasts markedly with other security agreements, less than a quarter of which rely on IGOs. Regarding punishment, although at times the provisions call on member states to handle noncompliance, punishment is usually delegated to a pre-existing IGO. Almost half of the agreements in the issue areas of economics and human rights contain formal punishment provisions, whereas the share is much lower for environmental and security agreements.

While the average international agreement is somewhat precise,[4] the average economics agreement is far more precise than the average human rights agreement. Likewise, while the average agreement had no reservations added to it at the time of entry into force,[5] only 1 percent of economics agreements had reservations attached at that

---

[3] Such duration provisions could also be viewed as deliberate modifications of the default indefinite duration of international law implied by Customary International Law (CIL) as codified in the Vienna Convention on the Law of Treaties (VCLT) (UNTS Reg. No. 18232). VCLT Article 56 (1) codifies a presumption against the right to withdraw or denounce a treaty that contains no clause regarding termination, denunciation, or withdrawal. (See both Christakis 2006: 1958f. 1973 and Giegerich 2012: 986 for arguments that VCLT Article 56 (1) is indeed CIL.)

[4] Details regarding the coding of this variable are found in Chapters 3 and 6.

[5] A reservation is "a unilateral statement, however phrased or named, made by a State, when signing, ratifying, accepting, approving or acceding to a treaty, whereby it purports to exclude or to modify the legal effect of certain provisions of the treaty in their application to that State" (VCLT Article 2 [1] [d]).

time, while an astounding 32 percent of human rights agreements had them attached.

Such interesting and often surprising descriptive statistics are practically endless: For instance, the average agreement contains a withdrawal provision, does not contain an escape clause, and does not call for the creation of an intergovernmental body.

I argue that all this variation in the design provisions of international law matters. In fact, the variation we see is a sign that *states* care, which is why they take the time and effort to negotiate specific treaty provisions that fit the demands of the situation. Because the set of *cooperation problems states are attempting to solve* with their international agreements vary in interesting and important ways and because the *characteristics of the states* solving these problems also vary greatly, the design of international law is characterized by considerable and meaningful variation, a glimpse of which was showcased above.

This book accordingly makes two distinct contributions. First, I present a positive theory of international law design, explaining differences across the multiple dimensions of international law highlighted above, like the rules governing duration, monitoring, punishments, disputes, and even withdrawal. I do so in terms of a set of logically derived and empirically testable hypotheses.

Second, I present a data set featuring a random sample of agreements across the issue areas of economics, environment, human rights, and security. This data set, because it is a random sample, lends itself to testing both my theory of international law design as well as other theories that focus on international cooperation and institutional design.

The central thesis

There are a multitude of opportunities and problems in every issue area that transcend national borders and require some sort of joint action by states to realize or solve. States attempting to cooperate to realize joint interests or solve problems often face a set of common and persistent obstacles. These obstacles to cooperation, which I call "cooperation problems," can make otherwise beneficial agreements difficult to achieve. For instance, fears that one's partner in cooperation might cheat on an agreement might make certain states unwilling to go forward with cooperation, despite the gains that could potentially be realized. Likewise, uncertainty about whether cooperation will be beneficial in all possible future conditions might make states forego current cooperation and the long-term gains it could bring. These obstacles or cooperation problems often transcend issue area and the particulars of the states involved. Although these obstacles are present in varying degrees and combinations, these "cooperation problems" are general, recurrent, and challenging.

The COIL theoretical framework starts from a very basic premise: *The underlying cooperation problems states are facing and character-istics of those states in the aggregate* (e.g., their number, heterogeneity, and power asymmetries) *are fundamental to understanding interna-tional institutional design.* This does not mean that other factors are irrelevant.[6] It does imply, however, that any analysis that does not start with or least pay significant attention to cooperation problems and state characteristics, like relative power, is problematic.

Drawing on contract theory and game theory, I link *cooperation problems*, like uncertainty about the future or uncertainty about beha-vior, to *dependent variables of institutional design*, like finite durations or centralized monitoring provisions, through a series of *hypotheses*.[7] Consider the following examples: When there are incentives to defect from an agreement, as in particular environmental agreements for which free-riding off of others' cooperation is the dominant strategy, one can imagine that a third party could play a useful role in arbitrating disputes and setting punishments. *Ex ante*, all parties would agree to such centralization or delegation in the face of the enforcement problem since that is one way to ensure Pareto-superior[8] mutual coop-eration rather than mutual defection. In contrast, if the issue addresses technical standards, there is likely a distribution problem over which standards to choose, but once resolved, parties do not face incentives to defect. Therefore, we would expect centralized punishment provisions to feature in agreements designed to address enforcement problems, but not distribution problems.

---

[6] Cooperation problems themselves can and should capture factors ranging from historical relations to the institutional context, if any, under which the international agreement is being negotiated.

[7] Many of these conjectures are found in the "Rational Design of International Institutions" (Koremenos, Lipson, and Snidal 2001b), discussed later.

[8] If an outcome makes at least one actor better off and no actor worse off relative to the status quo, it is considered Pareto superior.

I also link *characteristics of states in the aggregate*, like whether there
are power asymmetries among the actors or whether the set of potential
cooperators is characterized by great regime or interest heterogeneity
or even by large numbers, to dependent variables of institutional
design, like voting rules, precision, and centralization. For example,
in a cooperative endeavor that relies on the resources or power of large
states but that includes small states as well, it is not surprising that
powerful states would require asymmetric procedural rights before
they were willing to disproportionately fund or otherwise implement
the cooperative mandate. Likewise, large numbers of states that wish to
cooperate will often find it cost-effective to rely on some kind of
centralization to coordinate their exchanges in place of a large set of
bilateral exchanges.

Thus, self-interested states, while not wanting to give up control for
no reason at all, will usually impose mutual self-constraints through
international law when it helps them solve their problems. If creating
and then delegating to an international organization helps states realize
their goals, they are likely to do so. At the same time, they tend not to
lose themselves in these institutions, but rather they incorporate provisions that insure themselves against unwelcome outcomes. If they are
among the most powerful in the subject matter being covered, they might
give themselves weighted voting to better control institutional outcomes
or impose one-sided monitoring. If they fear uncertain outcomes, more
often than not they leave open the possibility of renegotiating, escaping,
and/or completely withdrawing from their agreements, depending on the
specifics of the outcomes they fear. And if they are worried about states
failing to comply with or opportunistically interpreting international
law, they tend to design delegated monitoring and/or dispute settlement
mechanisms.

Why international law?

As recently as a decade-and-a-half ago, the thesis that the design
provisions of international *law* matter tremendously by helping states
confront harsh international political realities would have seemed provocative at best, and downright ill-advised at worst. International
relations (IR) scholarship had "evolved" to the point where international law was foreign! As Stein (2008: 202) states: "Ironically, the key
victim of the [postwar] realist shellacking of idealism was not the study

of international organizations, but rather the study of international law. What had been part of the core curriculum in international relations before the Second World War, the study of international law, was relegated to law schools and was systematically ignored by political scientists for more than half a century."

Likewise, Dunoff and Pollack, who themselves have bridged the international law–international relations divide both individually and collaboratively, state: "Legal scholars sought to emphasize law's autonomy from politics, and focused on identifying, criticizing, or justifying specific legal rules and decision-making processes. For their part, political scientists seldom referenced international law as such, even when their topics of interest, such as international cooperation and international regimes, overlapped in clear ways with international law" (2013: 3).

One reason that IR ignored international law for so many decades is that considerable attention was given to what is truly distinct about IR, at least compared with the fields of American politics, comparative politics, and law: anarchy. Indeed, the significance of anarchy has been trumpeted to such a degree that IR is (to a great extent voluntarily) isolated from these other fields.[9]

This view of IR, however, ignores the vast array of international agreements I call attention to in the first paragraph of this book that prescribe, proscribe, and/or authorize specific behavior and sometimes impose sanctions for deviant behavior (just like domestic law). Moreover, the institutional variation among the separate pieces of international law is tremendous, as the statistics above showcased, with differences ranging across multiple dimensions, including the rules governing membership, voting, disputes, and escape. Hence, as the title of this chapter signals, it is imperative to (re)discover this enormous and interesting continent.

This variation, and the hard inter-state bargaining that leads to it, cries out for explanation, particularly among those who assign international law no causal force. I therefore ask the following: How can we explain the variation in state choices about international law? Does anything on this continent resemble the landscape in other fields? Other fields find institutions worthy of study and have developed a set of tools, mostly rooted in economics, to explain them. If we want to

---

[9] See Lake (2010) for a compatible view.

understand the institutional realm of IR, is a paradigmatic shift necessary (because no overarching, authoritative international government
exists as in the domestic sphere), or can we be creative in applying the
rational choice paradigm already proven in these other fields?

As this book demonstrates, states typically behave rationally when
they design international law. International agreements therefore
obey *law-like* regularities and are designed to regulate international
interactions in lasting and successful ways, just as institutions and laws
do in other realms of study.

I also zero in on international *law* as opposed to international
cooperation more generally, or even international institutions as manifested in IGOs, because the conventional focus on IGOs is too narrow,
as I elaborate in Chapter 3. At the same time, a focus on the concept of
regimes is too broad. "Regime" provided a valuable catchall concept
in the 1980s when scholars were first theorizing and examining the
general role of international institutional arrangements – and trying to
escape the confining conception of formal international organizations
prevalent in law scholarship and prior IR research.[10] However, such
a broad concept that includes "implicit or explicit principles, norms,
rules and decision-making procedures" (Krasner 1983) also provides
little specific guidance for theoretical or empirical work; it seemed
that almost anything could be and was called a regime. A focus on
international *law* introduces the greater specificity essential for tight
theorizing and rigorous empirical work.[11]

In legal scholarship, international law is composed of treaty law,
customary international law (CIL), and "general principles." I focus on
treaty law in great part because, as articulated above, the systematic
testing of hypotheses is central to this research, and it is very difficult to
disaggregate CIL or general principles into the measurable dimensions

---

[10] Interestingly, as Chapter 3 demonstrates, in the study of IGOs many scholars
have gone back to a very restricted definition of "international institution."
[11] Regarding the latter, Lake (2002: 141) finds the failure to "operationalize our
variables" one of the key impediments to progress in many areas of IR. He cites
the problems of measuring "cooperation" as an example. Lake argues that,
although Keohane's (1984) definition of cooperation as "mutual adjustment in
policy" was reasonable at the time, "the concept of 'adjustment' remains
ambiguous." Lake (2002: 142) states: "How much cooperation occurs? How
has the level evolved over time? How does it vary across issue areas? Without
answering such basic questions, most theories of cooperation cannot be tested."

required for comparative institutional analyses.[12] At the same time, theorizing and quantifying the design of international treaty law provides a useful baseline for those who want to study the relationship between custom and treaty or even the relative importance of one over the other depending on the issue area.[13]

COIL's broad foundations

A focus on international *law* also makes sense given the evolution of IR scholarship over the past fifteen years. In the early 2000s, attention was shifted from the possibility of cooperation to an examination of specific institutional details: Why are agreements designed the way they are? The Goldstein et al. (2000a) special issue of *International Organization*, entitled *Legalization and World Politics* (Legalization), identifies Legalization as a particular kind of institutional design – one that imposes international legal constraints on states.[14] The authors make great advances in variable conceptualization, defining three dimensions of Legalization – precision, obligation, and delegation – and make these dimensions come to life by giving numerous empirical examples from well-known agreements.

Another *International Organization* special issue by Koremenos, Lipson, and Snidal (2001a), *The Rational Design of International Institutions* (Rational Design), also appeared around the same time, building directly on the early institutionalist literature (e.g., Keohane 1984; Oye 1986).[15] The theoretical framework is grounded in a game-theoretic perspective, and states are thus assumed to behave rationally as they pursue joint gains from cooperation. However, unlike the earlier institutionalist literature, which focuses on whether cooperation is possible or whether institutions matter, Rational Design asks what

---

[12] As Goldsmith and Posner (1999: 1114) state: "It is unclear which state acts count as evidence of a custom, or how broad or consistent state practice must be to satisfy the custom requirement. It is also unclear what it means for a nation to follow a custom from a sense of legal obligation, or how one determines whether such an obligation exists."

[13] For a creative, game-theoretic based analysis of CIL regarding immunity, see Verdier and Voeten (2015).

[14] The special issue article, "The Concept of Legalization," by Abbott et al. (2000) provides a detailed definition of the concept and its components.

[15] The introductory article by Koremenos, Lipson, and Snidal (2001b) lays out the general framework of this special issue of *International Organization*.

forms of institutionalized cooperation emerge to help states solve problems. In other words, institutions and their specific attributes become part of the game, and Rational Design sets out to explain why states choose a specific design among the many options they have available. Thus, by deriving the design of international institutions from underlying cooperation problems, Rational Design moves away from the abstract nature of the early institutionalist literature. Both Legalization and Rational Design bring international *law* into the mainstream IR literature. Interestingly, a full decade earlier Abbott (1989) called on international law (IL) scholars to take a more IR approach to their subject.

Raustiala (2005), coming from both the IR and IL perspective, can be viewed as a complement to both the Legalization and the Rational Design frameworks. Raustiala distinguishes between legality (whether an agreement is legally binding), substance (the degree to which an agreement deviates from the status quo), and structure (monitoring and punishment provisions). In particular, Raustiala considers how these three categories relate to each other, and assesses the implications for the effectiveness of international institutions.

The COIL research program builds on Rational Design but extends and refines it substantially both theoretically and empirically. In doing so, COIL trades some parsimony for more accuracy. First, there is a refinement and unpacking of the relatively broad dimensions of design in the original Rational Design formulation: In particular, centralization and flexibility, and to a smaller extent control and scope, are carefully disaggregated, as elaborated in Chapter 2. This disaggregation is important because, for example, as Part II on flexibility mechanisms makes clear, each separate flexibility mechanism considered is driven by a unique set of underlying cooperation problems. The mechanisms are not substitutes for each other; rather, they solve different problems and are analytically distinct. I also leverage the COIL framework to begin the investigation of what might be best left informal – that is, it might be optimal to leave some provisions implicit within formal international law.

Additionally, COIL features a broader set of cooperation problems than did Rational Design. Specifically, commitment/time inconsistency problems, coordination (which too often has been conflated with distribution problems), and norm exportation are added. Many of the broad conjectures of Rational Design are also refined or even corrected.[16] COIL also examines interactions among cooperation problems and, in doing so, implements further refinements of the original Rational Design conjectures. In all these ways, COIL extends the intellectual agenda of Rational Design. The book also begins to fill the gap articulated by the Legalization authors (Goldstein et al. 2000b) that institutionalism has failed to identify when legalization should occur.[17]

The empirical contribution is a data set featuring 234 randomly selected agreements across the issue areas of economics, environment, human rights, and security, and it includes the careful definition and operationalization of the cooperation problems so that they can be identified across the sample. With two separate sets of coders for the cooperation problems (the independent variables) and the hundreds of design dimensions (the dependent variables) to preserve the integrity of the project, the data set allows the testing of both the COIL hypotheses as well as other theories regarding international agreement design.

One of COIL's main attributes in this regard is its consistent operationalization of variables across cases, which is desirable because it broadens the comparisons that can be made in the study of international cooperation. Chapter 3 details this aspect of the project, but it is worth mentioning here that the empirical foundation is now laid for analyses that transcend issue area, number and kinds of parties, and regions, among other things.

COIL *and alternative approaches*

The COIL framework embraces an *actor-oriented perspective*: States form institutions, like international law, to further their interests. The assumption of *rational, self-interested* states does not imply that states cannot have as one of their goals the realization of human rights abroad or other such nonmaterial interests; it simply requires that they systematically seek to maximize whatever interests they have. Rational, self-interested behavior also implies that when designing international law, states consider both costs and benefits of particular institutional

---

[16] For instance, Chapters 7 and 9 demonstrate that centralization is not necessarily an institutional answer to problems of uncertainty about the actions of one's partner.
[17] I return to this theme in the concluding chapter.

design solutions: For example, states will not create and/or delegate dispute resolution authority when it is not likely to be needed; but if delegation helps states solve their collective action problem and reach a Pareto-improving cooperative outcome, they (even the most powerful among them) will delegate authority.[18] Finally, even though state characteristics like regime type are featured in certain hypotheses, the COIL framework *does not explicitly include domestic politics.* COIL takes preferences as exogenous and looks instead at how international law should be designed given a set of preferences. COIL is thus easily complemented by studies that look to domestic level considerations as the primary explanatory variables of preference formation, including liberalism.

COIL thus shares common ground with some general theories of international law articulated by international law scholars, including those in *How International Law Works* (Guzman 2008) and *The Limits of International Law* (Goldsmith and Posner 2005). Both books share my fundamental conviction that one cannot entertain a positive theory of international law without considering international politics, in particular, how power and self-interest matter for both the design and enforcement of international law.[19] At the same time, many of the implications drawn from the COIL theoretical framework and the empirical analyses testing its predictions differ from these important scholarly works, in particular, from Goldsmith and Posner's very skeptical view of international law. I highlight some of the differences in the concluding chapter.

Constructivist IL scholars, too, tend to take international law seriously. Their focus is on how international norms influence state behavior. These scholars tend to focus more on the compliance side of cooperation than on design, but their underlying assumptions have implications for the design of international law.

Specifically, many constructivists believe that the key cause of compliance is not that compliance is in the best interest of individual

---

[18] I include "sovereignty costs" in the category of costs. For an excellent discussion of sovereignty costs that is consistent with the COIL framework, see Abbott and Snidal (2000).

[19] Both books articulate a general and positive theory of international law and share COIL's basic assumption that states are the main actors in "global governance" and pursue their self-interest. Guzman also builds on the early institutionalist literature in his book, and both books ground their assumptions in rational choice.

states[20] or that compliance-promoting liberal domestic institutions exist; rather, compliance stems from a socially *constructed* identity of respect for and adherence to international norms. In other words, through interaction with international society, states come to believe that commitment and compliance are appropriate actions for them as sovereign states. They develop a "culture of compliance" (Franck 1990; Henkin 1995a) as they come to see international law as a legitimate source of authority. Over the last two decades, scholars working within this broad framework have sought more specific explanations for how compliance identities come to be constructed. For example, Franck (1990: 25) believes that states obey an international rule because "they perceive the rule and its institutional penumbra to have a high degree of legitimacy" or "right process." Chayes and Chayes (1993) view the making of international law as itself a persuasive endeavor. By taking part in the discourse that accompanies the treaty-making process, states gravitate toward compliance (Chayes and Chayes 1995). Therefore, the primary mechanism for promoting compliance is "an iterative process of discourse among the parties, the treaty organization, and the wider public" (Chayes and Chayes 1995: 25).

As Chapters 7 and 8 in particular demonstrate, I argue that compliance will be forthcoming only if the design of an agreement corresponds to its underlying cooperation problems and its members' characteristics. If the underlying structure of the cooperative endeavor can be described as a prisoners' dilemma (in which a state would find it best to cheat while its partner cooperated), without an appropriate dispute resolution or punishment provision, states will not comply. Leaving out punishment provisions and relying instead on the pull toward compliance is not sufficient. The design provision itself makes a difference. In fact, I go so far as to argue that without the correct design provisions, states will often not even ratify the agreement, regardless of how heavily involved they were in the discourse leading to it.

---

[20] Compliance might be in the best interest of states because the agreements originate in the first place to solve problems that transcend national borders and because even short-run losses are usually worth tolerating so as not to upset the overall benefits a state gains from such cooperation. That is the logic of this book.

My state-centric theory also differs markedly from Avant, Finnemore, and Sell's (2010) assessment in their edited volume that nonstate actors are active agents that make and change rules in global governance. In Chapter 10 on voting, I find that experts are often chosen to constitute the bodies created in certain human rights agreements. Chapter 9 delves into the informal authority granted to NGOs with respect to monitoring international agreements. Nevertheless, the underlying premise is that states grant this authority to such nonstate actors. In this vein, my view is comparable to that of Tallberg et al. (2013).

Another approach to the design of international law emphasizes processes of diffusion. Börzel and Risse (2012) examine such an approach in their study of whether the structure and institutional outcomes of the EU influence other institutions. There is evidence that the EU model has diffused not just within Europe, but to different regional integration systems across the globe, though the extent and method of that diffusion varies considerably based on several factors (Börzel and Risse 2012).

COIL emphasizes how institutional design is affected by the particular characteristics of the actors cooperating and by the underlying cooperation problems, rather than by existing institutional models, as do Börzel and Risse (2012). Yet it appears that the two perspectives are not entirely at odds. Importantly, much of Börzel and Risse's analysis focuses on the EU's influence on new EU states and accession candidates. One of the very purposes of the EU supranational institutions is to foster homogeneity in member states, and many EU policies facilitate those changes directly. The agreements in the COIL data set arise far more independently of each other;[21] generally speaking, they are not strictly dependent on each other for their existence. Nor, by-and-large, is there evidence that COIL agreements *are designed to* promote their own structure in other, later-developing institutions, as is the EU framework.

Finally, the design of international institutions is at the center of a normative debate about legitimacy in international (or global) governance. Under that view, actors adopt particular design features because they are legitimate or because they promote democratic

---

[21] Moreover, agreements forming regional integration institutions are a small subset of treaties overall.

principles, not because they are efficient solutions to the problems being solved. I return to the discussion of legitimacy as a driver of institutional design in the concluding chapter.

Organization of the book

This book is organized in three parts, in addition to the introduction and conclusion. Part I (Chapters 2–3) lays out the theoretical framework with its focus on cooperation problems and the data set featuring a random sample of UNTS agreements. Parts II (Chapters 4–6) and III (Chapters 7–10) focus on the broad design dimensions of "flexibility" and "centralization, scope, and control," respectively.

Specifically, Chapter 2 presents COIL's theoretical framework and elaborates the primary theoretical building blocks of COIL: the cooperation problems and characteristics of state actors in the aggregate. I also present the design dimensions, bringing them to life with examples from domestic law. I then present the theoretical conjectures, which are refined and tested in later chapters. I expound on the idea of *equilibrium institutions* and discuss some of the insights gained by COIL's game-theoretic underpinnings, including how certain international law provisions are useful even if we rarely, if ever, see them employed in practice.

Chapter 3 introduces and showcases the data dimension of COIL. I first briefly review the theoretical motivation for the COIL data set and discuss the unique questions it can answer. I highlight some of the main features of the data collection, especially those that might distinguish it from other data sets in existence. I then locate COIL on the spectrum of other international cooperation data sets and discuss complementarities among them. I exploit the COIL data set to get leverage on the following questions: When designing agreements to solve their cooperation problems, how often do states create a new intergovernmental body? How often do states delegate to an existing intergovernmental body? The simple descriptive statistics and a few straightforward analyses unveil a new set of puzzles that researchers can explain.

Chapter 4 focuses on finite duration provisions as a way of accommodating uncertainty regarding the distributional implications of a cooperative endeavor, what I call "Uncertainty about the State of the World." The non-trivial nature of this institutional design choice is made explicit in the case study of the Nuclear Non-Proliferation Treaty (NPT). This chapter makes clear that under conditions of high uncertainty about the consequences of international cooperation, a finite duration is a necessary condition for an international agreement to come into being; without such a design provision, states often find cooperation too risky to enter into.

Chapter 5 presents analyses of escape clauses and withdrawal provisions. With respect to escape clauses, their nuanced sub-provisions, including whether states are required to give proof of extenuating circumstances, are argued to affect the robustness of cooperation. Withdrawal provisions, which are dismissed by some as final clauses written without much thought, are shown to be strikingly meaningful and systematic in terms of both the length of their notice period as well as the time stipulated before they can be invoked. The analyses in this chapter also highlight the complementarity of broad flexibility provisions with sub-provisions featuring centralization or hands-tying mechanisms.

Chapter 6 brings the focus to (im)precision and reservations. This chapter highlights the usefulness of the COIL framework in explaining all four issue areas covered in this book, including human rights. I argue that the vague language and reservations that many believe make human rights agreements distinct and meaningless are deliberate, rational choices that imply these agreements are intended and expected to influence state behavior. In fact, once I control for the COIL theoretical variables, human rights is no different in this regard from the other issue areas.

Chapter 7 not only explains one of the statistics featured earlier (i.e., that around half of international agreements contain dispute resolution provisions); the chapter also explains the variation between informal and formal (delegated) dispute resolution. The chapter showcases surprising descriptive statistics, such as the fact that 80 percent of the agreements with formal procedures explicitly encourage informal settlement as well, with more than half of these agreements imposing time limits on the dispute resolution process. This chapter also argues that we need to distinguish carefully between the use of dispute settlement mechanisms and their effectiveness.

In Chapter 8, I provide a theory of punishment provisions, a form of scope increase. The descriptive statistics alone belie much of the conventional wisdom in realist scholarship about the absence of such provisions. Additionally, I show that most of the time when a punishment provision is needed to stabilize the cooperative equilibrium, the necessary provision is indeed formally incorporated into the agreement – that is, scope does increase in the presence of incentives to defect. I also present a set of hypotheses about whether any needed punishments will be formalized or not. This theory gives rise to a two-part empirical analysis conducted on the COIL data set.

Chapter 9 brings the focus to monitoring provisions, including looking at the interaction of uncertainty about whether one's partner in cooperation is complying or not (what I call, "Uncertainty about Behavior") and incentives to defect. The chapter highlights how this interaction affects the specific design of monitoring provisions – specifically, whether to delegate monitoring to a third party or to rely solely on self-reporting. New research on NGO monitoring of the agreements in the COIL sample finds that such monitoring tends to be layered on top of the formal monitoring called for in many agreements.

Chapter 10 looks at asymmetric design rules, including voting rules, and power. I first present some descriptive statistics about how often the provisions of the agreements in the COIL sample reflect the underlying distribution of power. Interestingly, I find asymmetry in monitoring and punishment is common in the presence of underlying power asymmetries among the states cooperating, but weighted voting is not. I then present three case studies (using agreements from the sample) that illustrate some of the themes of this chapter as well as generate some interesting questions for future research. I draw attention to a number of factors that might confound any conclusions drawn from a simple look at the correspondence between power and rules.

Chapter 11, the concluding chapter, underscores the book's main theme that both international law and international politics matter. Both the scholarly and policy implications of the project are discussed. Particular attention is paid to what sorts of conclusions can and cannot be drawn both from this book and other scholarship in the area; in this way, some of the leading international law scholarship is challenged to explain what COIL uncovers, in particular how law-like or systematic international agreements are in reality.

Appendix 1 lists the agreements in the COIL sample. Appendix 2 briefly describes the coding of high or low for the cooperation problems. I also explain how actor characteristics are measured. Appendix 3 considers the question of selection effects that might plague data sets like COIL's that focus on observed, ratified agreements. It is designed for a broad audience, with examples, for instance, of what failed cooperation between the United States and Cuba over the last 50+ years implies for data sets like COIL's that rely on agreements that have entered into force.

Concluding thoughts

The COIL theoretical framework can explain why, when the Strategic Arms Reduction Treaty (START) expired in 2009 and no longer governed United States–Russian nuclear arms control, the United States' inability to monitor effectively Russian nuclear forces through on-site inspections implied losing "the holy grail," according to many experts.[22] COIL can explain why bargaining over the (ultimately finite) duration provision of the NPT was long and hard, with the United States and the Soviet Union on one side of the battle, and eventually compromising their position, and the non-nuclear weapon states on the other. COIL can also explain why the immense debate over the right to life provision when the Organization of American States (OAS) negotiated its human rights agreement, the American Convention on Human Rights, was resolved only when the phrase "in general" was added before the phrase, "from the moment of conception," thereby rendering it less precise.[23]

In each of these examples, particular cooperation problems and particular characteristics of the states involved suggested specific institutional design solutions. The presence (or, in the case of START's expiration, absence) of these design solutions in international law tilted

---

[22] Washington Post, "START expiration ends US inspection of Russian nuclear bases." August 17, 2010. Available at www.washingtonpost.com/wp-dyn/con tent/article/2010/08/16/AR2010081605422.html [Last accessed June 17, 2015]. The inability to monitor each other's nuclear arsenals lasted for over a year until the New START Treaty, with its meticulous monitoring provisions, came into force.

[23] See Forbes, Amber. 2006. "Institutionalizing the Right to Life in the Americas." Unpublished student paper. University of Michigan. Article 4 (1) reads: "Every person has the right to have his life respected. This right shall be protected by law and, in general, from the moment of conception. No one shall be arbitrarily deprived of his life."

the balance between Pareto-improving, stable solutions to international political problems and the absence of such solutions. Down to its last details, in these three contexts, international law mattered to states.

By widening the net sufficiently to include international law but not making it so unwieldy that the dependent variable cannot be measured in a reliable way, the thesis of this book can be confirmed: There is systematic variation in the world of international law, as the rest of this book will demonstrate.

By not selecting on issue area or on a particular state or region or on IGOs or multilaterals, we can see that the continent of international law is remarkably unified as well and can be explained by a common framework. There is no need for separate theoretical lenses to explain the design of human rights agreements versus economic agreements, to explain cooperation that includes superpowers versus cooperation that is between two small developing states, or to explain cooperation that results in the IMF versus that which results in a two-page, year-long agreement on fighting locusts.

Just as important, COIL does not prejudge importance and leave out particular cooperative endeavors because they are deemed trivial. It is not the role of the scholar who seeks to articulate a positive theory of international cooperation to leave out a bilateral agreement between two poor states in his/her analysis. That bilateral agreement could in principle be raising the standard of living for hundreds of thousands of citizens, while an almost universal agreement in a hot issue area could in principle be changing behavior very little. The COIL research program acknowledges all international treaty law with impartiality. In this way, it can also be used as a yardstick against which to measure any particular agreement if a researcher has a hunch that the agreement in question is an exceptional case. That is, the theoretical framework can be leveraged to gain insight into the agreement's design, and the data can be exploited to see if the agreement is or is not exceptional.

Many interesting findings emerge when considering this entire continent of international law. For instance, some kind of flexibility characterizes 96 percent of the sample. Moreover, flexibility provisions are not the "softening" mechanisms that some scholars label them to be; rather, the provisions are quite nuanced to prevent opportunistic behavior and in this sense "harden" the obligations through complementary centralization or hands-tying sub-provisions. Variation in such subtleties, such as whether *approval is needed* to utilize an escape clause and the *notice period* in withdrawal clauses, buttress one of the overall arguments of the book: Nuanced design provisions are necessary for international law to stabilize cooperation. Consider another example: Centralized (delegated) dispute resolution is necessary in the presence of underlying prisoners' dilemma-like incentives to defect and/or time inconsistency problems; decentralized (i.e., informal) dispute resolution helps solve uncertainty about others' actions. When these problems are absent, so are these provisions.

The COIL research program elaborated in this book will allow researchers to study and analyze the design of international law regardless of the issue area, the parties involved, their relative power, and whether or not an IGO is created, and it will do so in a consistent way. In the chapters that follow, a theoretical framework based on game-theoretic underpinnings unites the various analyses; the scientific data set allows empirical corroboration of the theory in many different issue areas, ranging from disarmament to human rights.

Thus, in this book, the Convention on the Elimination of Discrimination against Women (CEDAW) shares important underlying characteristics with the Agreement for Environmental Cooperation between Denmark and Oman. CEDAW also shares different, but equally important, characteristics with the Chemical Weapons Convention. The important differences across these agreements are also clarified through the COIL lens. The goal is a rigorous, generalizable theoretical framework that is brought to life and tested with rich and diverse empirical data. As stated, the framework relies on two main building blocks: the underlying cooperation problems plaguing states at the negotiating table and certain characteristics of those states in the aggregate. These building blocks, the independent variables, are combined and used to explain and unite diverse and complicated pieces of international law.

The detailed design provisions of international law matter for phenomena that scholars, policymakers, and the public care about: when and how international cooperation occurs and is maintained. The implications of the research program are that international law will be neither ignored nor automatically followed. It will enable and sustain cooperation when it is rationally designed. The data reveal that, far more often than not, international law *is* rationally designed. And this international law is as rationally designed in human rights as it is in security; it is as rationally designed for powerful states as it is for the less powerful. Most significant, this rational design implies that states are more concerned about solving joint problems than they are in retaining full sovereignty or control over outcomes.

All in all, the framework and testing lead to a very simple but consequential discovery: Taking into account the vagaries of international politics, international cooperation looks much more law-like than anarchical, with the detailed provisions of international law chosen in ways that increase the prospects and robustness of international cooperation.

COIL's building blocks: theory and data

Introduction to Part I

Part I introduces the theoretical framework and empirical component of the COIL research project. Part I thereby sets the stage for the analyses of flexibility, centralization, scope, and control provisions that follow in Parts II and III.

Chapter 2 briefly positions COIL among other scholarly work by elaborating its main assumptions. COIL's basic theoretical premise is that international agreement design and comparison across agreements begin by understanding the underlying cooperation problem(s) that the agreements are trying to solve. COIL identifies eight distinct and recurrent cooperation problems that states potentially face alone or in various combinations, depending on the particular characteristics of the underlying environment in which cooperation occurs. I thus give considerable attention to the concept of underlying cooperation problems, given its centrality in the COIL research program. I also identify some characteristics of state actors in the aggregate that have implications for agreement design. I then briefly present the four broad dependent variables analyzed in the rest of the book: Flexibility, Centralization, Scope, and Control.

A set of theoretical conjectures linking the independent variables (cooperation problems; state characteristics) to broad dimensions of institutional design are presented and discussed. Distinct cooperation problems call for nuanced agreement design solutions. In this way, institutions (i.e., pieces of international law with specific design features) are explicitly incorporated as options in the game – *equilibrium institutions.* This chapter concludes first by examining the implications of considering international law as an equilibrium institution, and second by briefly highlighting COIL's theoretical connections to other subfields of political science.

The empirical contribution of the COIL research program, which features a random sample of agreements across the issue areas of economics, environment, human rights, and security, is presented in Chapter 3. I first describe the data collection effort, including its empirical foundations and the main COIL attributes, many of which get beyond common selection problems in other data collection efforts, like those that select on agreements with particular members or on multilateral agreements. I place COIL on the spectrum of other data sets featuring international agreements, highlighting differences and complementarities. I elaborate the background research that went into coding the underlying cooperation problems of a particularly puzzling agreement in the COIL sample: The Agreement for Environmental Cooperation between Denmark and Oman signed in 1993. This example serves as an illustration of the kind of research that went into the coding of the cooperation problems underlying every agreement in the sample. (The coding of the cooperation problems is described more fully in Appendix 2.)

Descriptive statistics and a simple analysis of delegation to existing IGOs are presented, showcasing one of the analytical benefits of focusing on international agreements as units of analysis as opposed to focusing on bodies themselves. Looking at IGOs alone ignores the fact that the amount of cooperative activity supported by an IGO may change dramatically over time, as many new agreements delegate tasks to existing IGOs. According to the COIL sample, the IGOs that gain authority through this delegation are predominantly those that play a role in dispute resolution.

The theoretical and empirical portions of COIL are integrated: the COIL data speak directly to the comparative static predictions the theoretical framework generates. The theoretical framework preceded and greatly informed the data collection, but importantly, as I make it clear in Chapter 3, the project maintained a complete separation of coders for the independent and dependent variables. At the same time, the data should prove useful to those working outside of the institutionalist tradition. Many of the variables can potentially inform network-type analyses as well as serve as a baseline for those who hold quite different beliefs about the design and role of international law.

2 | *Theoretical framework*

There is little room for trust among states. Although the level of fear varies across time and space, it can never be reduced to a trivial level. . . . States are often reluctant to enter into cooperative agreements for fear that the other side will cheat on the agreement and gain a relative advantage.

(Mearsheimer 1994–5: 11, 13)

Trust but verify.

(President Reagan's oft-repeated phrase when negotiating arms control cooperation with General Secretary Gorbachev)

There is no doubt that cooperation problems such as incentives to cheat, uncertainty about other states' true intentions, and struggles for power pervade the international system. States have different, often dramatically divergent, interests and seek advantage over one another. States also want to capture the benefits of cooperation, but, as the Mearsheimer quote makes clear, the obstacles (what I call "cooperation problems") are severe.

This book argues that international law can solve these kinds of problems. More to the point, the fine-grained design provisions of international law, when chosen optimally, help states solve such problems in the international environment – problems that, if unheeded, could diminish international cooperation or prevent it altogether. Straightforward design provisions like on-site inspections to monitor compliance with a treaty's terms, or escape clauses to allow states to deal with unpleasant surprises, allow states to realize common interests and achieve a Pareto-improving cooperative outcome.[1]

Still, in the words of Krasner (1991), winding up somewhere on the "Pareto frontier" can involve tough bargaining. That is, depending on

---

[1] As mentioned in Chapter 1, if an outcome makes at least one actor better off and no actor worse off, it is considered Pareto improving.

the circumstances, states may fight hard over both substantive and design provisions before reaching the Pareto-improving outcome. Indeed, choosing the detailed design provisions of treaties is often a form of political interaction in which states maneuver and bargain for their interests. Why? Because international agreements *and their design provisions* are consequential.

COIL's basic theoretical premise is that the key to understanding international agreement design and to making comparisons across agreements, including across issue areas, is a focus on the underlying *cooperation problem*(s) the agreements are trying to solve and the underlying *characteristics of the states* involved in the cooperative endeavor – that is, properties that describe the set of actors in the aggregate. For example, some issues, like trying to ban chemical weapons or trying to encourage the rights of women, pose huge information obstacles: How can one state know what other states are doing? Such *Uncertainty about Behavior* is absent in issue areas like the settlement of a bilateral debt for which behavior is quite transparent. Some issues, like the stationing of military bases, involve actors of very different size and power, like the United States and Greece. This *Asymmetry* is absent in issues of arms control between the superpowers.

Cooperation problems such as these, as well as state characteristics, often have a dynamic element. For instance, unpredictable changes in bargaining power may leave states in a situation of being bound to agreements whose division of gains no longer reflects their relative bargaining power. If their power has fallen, states will not complain; but if it has risen, they might. Indeed, they might go so far as to renege (or cheat) on an agreement whose gains have become too small relative to their bargaining power.[2]

COIL argues that such problems can be confronted and solved through the design of international law. Specifically, by drawing on contract theory, COIL links cooperation problems (like uncertainty about the future) and characteristics of the actors (like asymmetry of power) to dependent variables of institutional design (like renegotiation provisions and one-sided monitoring rules, respectively). Therefore, the often harsh actualities of international politics

---

[2] Such "power transitions" are, according to one school of thought, one of the major causes of war (Organski 1958).

are incorporated into the theory itself, resulting in a project grounded in reality and not situated in ideal worlds where international law reigns simply because it is international law. Empirically testable comparative static predictions regarding agreement design are presented in this chapter. These predictions are refined and tested in later chapters. "Trust but verify" and many other institutional design solutions are explicitly incorporated into the theoretical setup – in other words, as *equilibrium institutions*.[3] Simply put, without the verification or monitoring that is part of the treaty design, arms control treaties between the superpowers would not have made both parties better off. Both states would prefer to not cooperate on this issue at all than to cooperate without verification of the other's activities. The monitoring itself is thus what makes this cooperation a stable outcome to which each party has an incentive to adhere. Both the substantive terms *and the monitoring* are necessary for the treaty to be an equilibrium institution.

This chapter begins by briefly elaborating the main assumptions underlying the COIL framework. I then give considerable attention to the eight cooperation problems, given their centrality in the COIL research program. I also identify some properties of the set of actors in the aggregate: the total number of cooperators, their relative power, and the degree of homogeneity or heterogeneity with respect to their level of democracy and overall interests. I introduce the broad design dimensions of COIL, the dependent variables, and introduce the refinements employed in the analyses that follow in Parts II and III. I then present a series of conjectures linking cooperation problems to elements of institutional design.[4] I highlight some insights that come from using a framework with game-theoretic foundations[5] and conclude with a brief discussion of how this book connects to the broader political science literature.

---

[3] This concept is explained in detail at the end of the chapter.

[4] This chapter reproduces some of, and builds on, "The Rational Design of International Institutions" (Koremenos, Lipson, and Snidal 2001b). COIL introduces a number of additions and refinements to Rational Design, but does not depart from its premises or overarching variables.

[5] For a brief review of the history of cooperation as a dependent variable in international relations and the evolution of 2 × 2 games, see Koremenos (2013a).

Underlying assumptions

First, *states* are, and for the foreseeable future will be, the main actors in global governance.[6] That is not to say that other actors, like NGOs or transnational civil society, are not influential. Nonetheless, such actors are not the major force behind global order. And at the core of global cooperative activity are states exercising their power and realizing their interests through international law. The theoretical framework is thus very much in the spirit of Keohane's *After Hegemony* (1984), in which he accepts the twin realist assumptions that state power and interests matter and shows how and why institutions are more than epiphenomenal and, in fact, rather effectual and enduring components of international relations.

Still, just because powerful states influence both the substantive and procedural aspects of international law in no way undermines the importance of international law, nor reduces state relations to anarchy. Rather, the fact that the details of international law square well with the configuration of power and interests makes the body of law a stable equilibrium outcome and one that informs and influences greatly the day-to-day behavior of states. Furthermore, because international law reflects the interest of powerful states, their long-term interest in its survival explains the non-trivial number of times that they obey it, even when it imposes net costs.[7]

Second, states are *rational* actors that pursue their self-interest when facing cooperation problems. Following the tenets of rational choice theory, no assumption is made about the sources or the substance of state preferences. As the rest of the book will demonstrate, states can care about increasing their wealth, making themselves more secure, protecting the environment, and seeing their human rights standards embraced by others.[8] This broad set of goals is not inconsistent. Nor do

---

[6] Given my assumption of the primacy of states, I rarely use the phrase "global governance" but instead employ phrases like "international cooperation." But see Chapter 9 for a discussion of NGOs, which are part of the global governance structure.

[7] In Chapter 10, I briefly illustrate this point by looking at the behavior of the United States in the last of the series of International Coffee Agreements to which it belonged.

[8] Steinberg (2013: 149) states: "Other than the assumption that states seek survival, realism does not require a commitment to any particular assumption about the content of state interests. . . ." Still, compared to most scholarly work in the realist tradition, Rational Design and COIL are less dogmatic about state

we find states acting "less rationally" in some issue areas or "more rationally" in others.

Finally, when designing international law, states pursue *Pareto-improving agreements with minimum cost*. For example, states will not delegate monitoring authority when compliance behavior is already readily observed. But if centralizing monitoring helps states solve their collective action problem and reach a Pareto-improving cooperative outcome, they (even the most powerful among them) tend to delegate such authority.

It is worth noting that the "states as unitary actors" assumption is employed in the formal models underlying many of the conjectures that are presented in this chapter and that are refined in later chapters. One can assume there exists some aggregation mechanism at the domestic level in most states most of the time that yields a state preference at the international level. Thinking about states as unitary actors is without a doubt a fruitful theoretical assumption but not one that necessarily yields a complete empirical picture. Still, as the large-n analyses corroborate, treating states as unitary, rational actors is not only parsimonious; the COIL theoretical framework has great explanatory power when it comes to the subject of this book: the design of international law.[9]

Independent variables: Cooperation problems and actor characteristics

Most political scientists, policymakers, and ordinary citizens would argue that international politics is all about questions of enforcement, distribution, commitment, and struggles for power and influence, all of which are exacerbated by multiple kinds of shocks, uncertainties, and distrust. Even the most optimistic among us would have to admit that

---

preferences and assume greater capacity for convergent state interests than most realists would concede. As Steinberg very clearly points out, what realists say is different from what realism as a paradigm has to say about this issue. In any event, in his conclusion Steinberg (2013) points out that, without being complemented by other approaches, realism cannot explain how, why, and when international law works.

[9] Domestic politics informs the coding of the cooperation problems, serving, for example, as the driving force for both the inclusion and operationalization of the Commitment/Time-inconsistency cooperation problem.

international political interactions are characterized by some subset of
these problems at least some of the time.

In this section, I identify and bring to life a set of distinct and
recurrent cooperation problems that states face either in isolation or,
more typically, in various combinations when they attempt to realize
the gains of cooperation. That one must understand the cooperation
problems before making sense of design may sound obvious, but it
is overlooked with great frequency in the policy community. For
instance, many NAFTA (North American Free Trade Agreement)
specialists lament the fact that NAFTA does not resemble the EU.[10]
In their book chapter, "Whither NAFTA: A Common Frontier?"
Hufbauer and Vega-Cánovas argue that NAFTA should be further
developed into a "Common Frontier" and should address "border
management," "defense alliance," and "immigration" (2003: 129).[11]
Likewise, Grinspun and Kreklewich argue that NAFTA is "institution-
ally deficient" (1999: 18). The first question that must be asked is
"Should NAFTA look like the EU?" The cooperation problems
Europeans were facing when the institutions of the EU began to form
in post–World War II were far more dramatic than those facing
North America. While trade issues involve incentives to defect and
hence that cooperation problem is a common one, Europeans faced
a problem with Germany that could be characterized as either significant Uncertainty about Preferences (i.e., Could Germany be trusted?
Was Germany a peace-loving state or would it end up going down the
same path that brought about two world wars?) or a Commitment
problem (i.e., it is just a matter of time before some future German
leader follows the same destructive path). Given that the Europeans
had to solve either an Uncertainty about Preferences or Commitment
problem, the institutional design of the EU would likely be more
elaborate than that called for by the pre-NAFTA environment. Put
simply, before we can ask, "What is the optimal design of a given
agreement?" we need to ask a logically prior question, "What kind of
problem(s) is the agreement aiming to solve?"

---

[10] For an exception, see Mace and Bélanger (2004), who analyze NAFTA using the
lens of Rational Design and come to a very different conclusion.
[11] Hufbauer and Vega-Cánovas continue: "In our view, the Common Frontier
should be the analogue of the 1980s concept of a European Economic
Space–designed to link the European Economic Community (EEC) and the
European Free Trade Area (EFTA)" (2003: 129).

I also elaborate a set of actor characteristics – that is, *properties that describe the set of actors in the aggregate.* For example, the most straightforward measure is Number: How many states are involved in the cooperative endeavor. As IR theorists started to address problems of cooperation in more complex and realistic settings, they started with noise (the inability to observe behavior perfectly – what Rational Design and COIL label as Uncertainty about Behavior) and *large numbers.*[12]

The rationale for two separate categories, cooperation problems and actor characteristics, is simply descriptive. Although the original Rational Design conjectures (and COIL's sometimes refined and/or more complicated versions of them) feature more cooperation problems than actor characteristics, one category is not prima facie more important theoretically.

The cooperation problems

The COIL cooperation problems capture *interests* (traditionally encapsulated through underlying enforcement and distribution problems but also engaging more altruistic interests like promoting norms as well as challenges posed by time-inconsistent preferences) and *constraints* (posed by underlying uncertainties about the state of the world, behavior, and other actors).

I now showcase the full set of cooperation problems. This aspect of COIL is significant because, as noted, scholars have been talking about "games of cooperation" for decades. Nonetheless, quantifying what these games might look like beyond a few paradigmatic cases and thus gauging their prevalence in real international cooperation has heretofore not been attempted, despite their centrality in our theories. One main challenge is the enumeration of cooperation problems such that the list covers most of the themes prevalent in both scholarship and real cooperative endeavors but is not overly cumbersome.[13] The challenge

---

[12] On noise, see Downs and Rocke (1990); on large numbers, see Oye (1986) and Pahre (1994).

[13] When thinking about the kinds of problems that ought to be included in COIL's theoretical framework, the cooperation problems identified in Rational Design (Koremenos, Lipson, and Snidal 2001b) are an obvious place to start, especially because they build on some of the foundational scholarship in international cooperation theory (i.e., Oye 1986).

of empirically coding the cooperation problems is covered in Chapter 3.

Before I elaborate the cooperation problems, I simply list them. Most of them should be familiar given their significance in much of the existing research. I have highlighted those that did not appear in the Rational Design volume. The problems best captured in the "interests" category are Enforcement problems (a.k.a., prisoners' dilemma), Distribution problems, *Coordination problems, Commitment problems (time inconsistency), and Norm Exportation.* The problems best captured in the "constraints" category are Uncertainty about Behavior, Uncertainty about Preferences, and Uncertainty about the State of the World.

Perhaps the cooperation problem that has garnered the most attention over the past three decades is the Enforcement problem, the predicament at the center of prisoners' dilemma and public goods problems.

Enforcement problem: *An Enforcement problem is present when actors have individual incentives to defect from cooperation while others cooperate – that is, a situation in which free-riding off of others' cooperation is optimal.*

Even if a cooperative arrangement makes everyone better off, some or all actors may prefer not to adhere to it because they can do better individually by cheating, so long as all or most of the other actors continue to cooperate. Issues are characterized by Enforcement problems when actors find unilateral noncooperation so enticing that they may risk sacrificing long-term cooperation.

Enforcement problems can be found in all four of the issue areas featured in COIL. Whether the subject is nontariff barriers in trade, limits on pollutants like carbon monoxide emissions, or limits on nuclear weapons, many states would be better off if they could cheat while their partner(s) cooperated – the so-called "free rider" problem. Even the issue area of human rights is sometimes characterized by an underlying Enforcement problem. Consider the 1925 Convention Concerning Equality of Treatment for National and Foreign Workers as Regards Workmen's Compensation for Accidents. An Enforcement problem is present given the prisoners' dilemma structure of the payoffs: A state wants its workers to be treated well in other states, but would prefer not to spend resources on foreigners working within its borders.

Of course, in many issues, before cooperation can even commence, Distribution problems must be addressed.

Distribution problem: *A Distribution problem captures the divergent preferences states have over the substantive terms, and hence the distribution of costs and benefits, of a potential cooperative agreement.*

None of the issue areas featured in COIL are exempt from Distribution problems. In trade, states often disagree on which tariffs to lower. Regarding disarmament, disagreements over which weapons to ban or reduce are often severe. Some environmental sub-issue areas have a zero-sum game quality to them, like the allotment of quotas for fishing. Even the issue area of human rights is fraught with distribution problems. Just as issues like the death penalty, abortion, and torture ignite major debates among parties domestically, these same issues animate international human rights negotiations regarding which rights to include, which to prohibit, and even how to define the rights themselves.

As an example of an agreement with an underlying Distribution problem, consider the 1971 Agreement Concerning the Compensation of Netherlands Interests between Egypt and the Netherlands. Egypt owed the Netherlands some compensation because Egypt had nationalized private assets. The issue was how much compensation, which is essentially a Distribution problem.

Even if states solve the Distribution problem during the negotiation stage, they at times need to be conscious of commitment or time-inconsistency problems within some subset of the member states.

Commitment problem: *A Commitment problem refers to a domestic commitment problem or a time-inconsistency problem – that is, a situation in which an actor's best plan for some future period may not be optimal when that future period arrives.*

In other words, while complying with the terms of an agreement may be in a state's interest today, noncompliance may be in this same state's interest in the future, perhaps because of a change in government like a dictator replacing an elected official. Put differently, what might be best for a state's long-term interests may not be beneficial in the medium run or in particular future periods. The payoffs of cooperation are inconsistent over time. The most popular example of this kind of problem is a government's policy toward inflation. It is optimal for the government today to promise low inflation in the future, but when the future arrives, it is politically difficult to lower inflation because unemployment will most likely go up. The US government solves this problem by delegating inflation policy to an independent central bank because high inflation is not in the United States' long-run interest.

The 1980 Agreement for the Promotion and Protection of Investments between the United Kingdom and Bangladesh is characterized by an underlying Commitment problem. Given its tumultuous political history, including military coups in the 1970s, Bangladesh has a credibility problem regarding the safety of outside investments. Hence, it needs to tie its hands in the present so that it will not cave in to possible future pressures to nationalize or expropriate foreign investment. This hands tying is especially important given outsiders' perception of the likelihood of a regime change in Bangladesh; thus potential investors are unlikely to invest without some credible commitment on the part of Bangladesh to uphold its promise.

With this particular cooperation problem, COIL specifically incorporates themes typically found in liberalist approaches to international cooperation (e.g., Moravcsik 2000, 2008, 2010[14]). As Moravcsik (2000: 220) famously argues, international human rights agreements are "a tactic used by governments to 'lock in' and consolidate democratic institutions, thereby enhancing their credibility and stability." Here the time inconsistency is being driven by, for instance, a newly democratic government's uncertainty regarding how long it (and democracy more generally) will survive in a particular state. Future preferences may not be consistent with current ones. The problem is still one of time inconsistency or domestic Commitment.

While all agreements require "coordination" on agreement text, COIL has a very specific definition of a Coordination problem.

Coordination problem: *In situations characterized by underlying Coordination problems, actors must coordinate on exactly one outcome to be better off cooperating. The worse it is to "miss" some specific solution, the more severe the coordination problem.*

---

[14] Moravcsik, Andrew. 2010. "Liberal Theories of International Relations: A Primer." Unpublished manuscript. Princeton: Princeton University. Available at www.princeton.edu/~amoravcs/publications.html [Last accessed June 25, 2015].

Traditionally, (e.g., Stein 1982, Snidal 1985) a Coordination problem exists if states are better off matching policies – coordinating on either a movie or a ballet, for example. Because the overall purpose of codifying law is to coordinate policies at least loosely, COIL has a higher threshold for a Coordination problem: The policy matching has to be almost exact if states are to be better off cooperating; otherwise, they prefer unilateral action to cooperation.[15] It is important to note that traditional 2 × 2 game representations fail to note the exact nature of the Coordination problem. Coordinating on an exact movie (or ballet) is not mentioned as a necessary condition of one of the Pareto outcomes of the Battle of the Sexes. Most would agree that, in such a situation, coordinating on different movies is worse than no coordination at all, especially if one prefers ballet!

As explained more fully in Chapter 6, a COIL Coordination problem does not imply a Distribution problem: the former can exist without the latter (and vice versa).[16] That is, a scenario can make exact agreement on some policy critical, but there may be different policies – that is, different equilibria – on which to coordinate; the two actors may have divergent preferences over these policies (i.e., a Distribution problem) or may not have divergent preferences (i.e., no Distribution problem).

---

[15] In terms of utility functions, a Coordination problem exists when the utility from coordinating on one exact outcome is much higher compared with that of just missing that outcome by failing to coordinate exactly. In other words, the marginal benefit of strict agreement is large, making the attainment of such an agreement paramount. The severity of the Coordination problem can be measured by the difference in utility between coordinating exactly on an outcome and the utility from not coordinating exactly.

[16] Stein (1982) conceptualizes Coordination problems slightly differently than does COIL. What Stein calls a "dilemma of common aversions" is similar to COIL's Coordination problem, but appears to presume a Distribution problem as well: "[C]oordination is difficult to achieve when, although both actors least prefer the same outcome [(often, noncooperation)], they disagree in the choice of preferred equilibrium" (Stein 1982: 313–14). Snidal (1985) also describes Coordination problems, acknowledging that they may but need not include Distribution problems: "Sometimes coordination is presented simply as the problem of two or more actors matching policies where they are indifferent about where they match . . . ." (Snidal 1985: 931). Notably, unlike Snidal's understanding of Coordination problems in macroeconomic agreements, in which "coordination is not an all-or-nothing problem and there is no need to meet exactly" (Snidal 1985: 932), COIL's conceptualization of a Coordination problem requires that the parties do meet exactly at a single policy point in order to be better off cooperating.

Most of the famous Coordination problems are coupled with Distribution problems: dividing territory, cooperating on technical standards, even the quotas decided upon by the Organization of the Petroleum Exporting Countries (OPEC) states. But as not all Coordination problems go hand-in-hand with Distribution problems, not all Distribution problems are Coordination problems.

Consider a human rights agreement that calls for the abolition of child labor. If some states define a child as someone under 18 years of age and act accordingly even though others define a child as someone under 15 years of age, as long as both are reducing child labor, however they define it, both are better with the agreement than without it. Of course, the state that defines a child as anyone under the age of 18 would prefer the other state to act in a similar fashion, but it still prefers the other state's elimination of child labor for those under 15 years of age to no reduction at all.

International human rights agreements raise another cooperation problem, one not limited to that issue area by any means: the exportation or reinforcement of norms.

Norm Exportation: *The cooperation problem of creating or spreading norms is one in which one state or set of states wants to create or spread its norms in another state or states.*

I assume there is no need for direct material benefit to the state that wants to export its norms. By adding Norm Exportation as a cooperation problem, COIL links to constructivist scholarship (Finnemore and Sikkink 1998). Norm Exportation is of clear relevance to states and deliberately encouraged in some international agreements – yet this idea is not incorporated in much of the institutionalist literature. At a basic level, one state or group of states is trying to change the preferences of another state or group of states over time.

The Agreement on Environmental Co-operation between Denmark and Oman is coded as having an underlying cooperation problem characterized by Norm Exportation. Denmark entered into this agreement with Oman in October of 1993 and then signed five similar agreements with other developing and noncontiguous states in June 1994. These agreements, which offer no material benefit to Denmark, were concluded after the Earth Summit in Rio de Janeiro in 1992, in which environmental development was discussed at length.[17]

The goal of Norm Exportation underlies many cooperative endeavors in human rights. As Simmons (2009) compellingly argues, many (usually relatively powerful, democratic) states do not need to change their policies at all to be in compliance with certain multilateral human rights agreements; at the same time, there is a set of states for whom the norms embodied in these agreements have not yet taken hold and for whom the agreement can lead to behavioral change.[18] Some disarmament agreements are put in place to solve immediate problems, like those of Enforcement, but have as a longer-term goal the internalization of norms like nuclear disarmament.

Finally, moving from the "interests" to the "constraints" category of cooperation problems, *uncertainty* in the international realm makes realizing joint gains from cooperation even more challenging. COIL, like Rational Design, distinguishes among three kinds of uncertainty: Uncertainty about Behavior, Uncertainty about Preferences, and Uncertainty about the State of the World.

Uncertainty about Behavior is probably the type of uncertainty most discussed in the institutionalist literature. Reciprocity as a strategy to induce cooperation works only if an actor can identify the behavior of its partner in cooperation.

Uncertainty about Behavior: *Uncertainty about Behavior refers to uncertainty regarding the actions taken by others.*

Often it is simply difficult to know what other states are doing – in particular, if they are cooperating or defecting. Consider weapons of mass destruction. Whatever a state may say publicly, it is very difficult for others to ascertain whether it is pursuing technologies associated with the development of biological or chemical weapons.

Particular sub-issues within the area of human rights are also subject to Uncertainty about Behavior given that sub-state actors are the ones whose behavior is relevant. For instance, not only is it difficult to see

---

[17] The SusNordic Gateway. 2008. "Denmark's International Engagements: Development Co-Operation." Available at www.sum.uio.no/susnordic/den mark/national_policies/international.htm [Last accessed March 30, 2009].

[18] And like in all attempts at cooperation, both domestic and international, there exists a set of actors for whom compliance may never be forthcoming – what Simmons (2009) calls the "insincere ratifiers."

whether certain human rights laws are being enforced in any particular state; if reliable data on noncooperation are readily available, one still cannot be sure whether it is the government who is violating human rights or soldiers in the field not following orders.

The 1997 multilateral Convention on Human Rights and Biomedicine is an example of an agreement whose underlying cooperation problem is characterized by Uncertainty about Behavior. It is very difficult to see whether particular laws regarding access to health-care and medical research are actually being enforced, and hence it is difficult to tell whether states are cooperating or not.

Statements about the level of risk in the international environment sometimes hinge on not trusting the intentions of one's potential partner(s) in cooperation, what I call, Uncertainty about Preferences.

Uncertainty about Preferences: *Uncertainty about Preferences refers to uncertainty regarding what one's partners in the potential cooperation really want out of the deal.*

State A may want to try to solve a particular problem with State B, but State A may be unsure about what exactly State B wants. I assume states know their own preferences, but may or may not know the motivations or intentions of other states. For example, a key problem underlying arms competition (and therefore attempts at arms control) is determining whether another state is simply seeking its own security or is greedy and expansive. Is India's nuclear testing a result of its desire to aggrandize itself against Pakistan, or is it a defensive reaction against China? As another example, a few EU members are unsure of Turkey's true nature and are therefore hesitant about EU expansion in that direction. Of course, a major problem in determining states' prefer-ences is that states may have incentives to misrepresent them.

The Security Treaty between the United States and Japan is an example of an agreement whose underlying cooperation problem is characterized by Uncertainty about Preferences. After the Second World War, the prime minister of Japan used a strategy of double talk while communicating with the Japanese public and the US government, often making contradictory statements to the two sides. While he would publicly reject rearmament of the Japanese military and oppose the idea of allowing long-term US bases in Japan, he would also try to convince the United States that there was a secure foundation for security cooperation between the two states. This strategy created confusion and frustration within the American administration and made it difficult to build an alliance between the two states (Swenson-Wright 2005: 57).

Finally, states may want to solve a particular problem but be uncertain about the future consequences of their own actions, the actions of other states, or the actions of international institutions – including the institutions they create. This kind of uncertainty, with its frequent distributional implications, is Uncertainty about the State of the World.

Uncertainty about the State of the World: *Uncertainty about the State of the World refers to uncertainty regarding the consequences of cooperation.*

The uncertainty can be scientific and technical or it can be about politics or economics. Consider the dispute over the Spratly Islands, which lie off the southern coast of China and have been claimed by a number of states. This dispute has taken on a special urgency now that the area appears to hold significant oil deposits and China has attempted to restrict access to the surrounding waters and airspace, which include key trade routes. However, no one is sure how much oil is actually there, or its future value, and China's intentions surrounding access to the waters and airspace remain unclear. Thus if cooperation were attempted now, it would be characterized by Uncertainty about the State of the World because the true distribution of benefits (i.e., who actually wins most, who loses most) could not be known until the future.[19]

Uncertainty about the State of the World can be present in the absence of shocks that change either the distribution of benefits or the total benefits. That is, absent any shocks, there can still be uncertainty about how an agreement will work in practice, especially in more complex issue areas. This is akin to an "experience good" in economics: The true nature of the good can only be known with experience, that is, time. Thus the uncertainty is sometimes, but not always, about the "future" state of the world. [20]

---

[19] The subject matter is also characterized by underlying Uncertainty about Preferences regarding China.

[20] Uncertainty about the State of the World can be present regarding the total benefits or effectiveness of an agreement, absent any distributional consequences, although this poses less of a cooperation problem since states would be in agreement about the correct course of action.

The 1969 multilateral International Convention for the Conservation of Atlantic Tunas (with Final Act and Resolution adopted by the Conference of Plenipotentiaries) is an example of an agreement characterized by underlying Uncertainty about the State of the World. This was a relatively new issue at the time the convention was being negotiated in 1966. Technology was becoming so advanced that some fisheries were in danger of being over-fished. The states involved were not sure of the sustainable yields of the fisheries, the correct methods to prevent over-fishing, or the net costs or benefits of such measures. In other words, they were not sure how best to care for this common resource at the time or how their cooperation might affect the fisheries and their own economic well-being.

These eight cooperation problems are obviously not an exhaustive list. There is no doubt, however, that future scholars would build on this list, not replace it, as these eight problems in numerous interesting combinations (as Chapter 3 shows) underlie real international law.

Characteristics of states in the aggregate

Characteristics of actors most certainly play a role in the design of international law. As I mentioned earlier, that the simple *Number* of actors involved in the cooperative endeavor can affect international cooperation has been noted for some time. Bilateral cooperation is likely to be different than multilateral cooperation given the straightforward challenges that larger numbers pose even for relatively simple tasks like communication.

The original Rational Design formulation included Number as an independent variable, and Number captured broadly both the actual number of actors and asymmetries between or among them. Here I continue to use Number of states as an explanatory variable and, as a separate variable in many of the chapters, I operationalize asymmetry.

Asymmetries among actors, in particular *Power Asymmetries*, matter for international cooperation. Some agreements bring together states with roughly similar levels of power, whereas others bring together states with vastly different power levels, for example, the United States with a small state like Jordan. Cooperation that features Russia and the set of former Soviet states has a very different quality to it than cooperation among the permanent members (P5) of the United Nations Security Council (UNSC). Both military power differentials and/or economic power differentials can, under conditions elaborated in Part III of the book, manifest themselves in the design provisions of international law. *Domestic Regime-type Asymmetries*, for example, democratic versus authoritarian systems of government, also could matter for international cooperation. States might find the challenges of cooperation more easily solved when cooperating with like-minded states with respect to how democratic they are.

Finally, heterogeneity with respect to state interests, *or Preference Heterogeneity*, might affect efforts at international cooperation. As I elaborate in Chapter 4, it is reasonable to assume that states would be relatively more concerned about unanticipated changes in the distribution of gains from cooperation when dealing with partners with very different preferences; in contrast, if a partner with similar preferences gains more, it can be more safely assumed that the gains will be used for shared priorities.

These actor characteristics, while not occupying the noticeable place that cooperation problems do, are important variables in the analyses in the rest of the book. In fact, Asymmetries among actors are the main explanatory variables in Chapter 10 and explain what is left informal in Chapter 8. Actor characteristics also speak to a variety of theories, including realism (power), institutionalism (number), and liberalism (domestic regime type).

The design dimensions of international law

Rational Design focused on five broad dimensions of international institutions – the dependent variables: membership rules, scope of issues covered, centralization of tasks, rules for controlling the institution, and the flexibility of arrangements. These are certainly not the only significant institutional dimensions, but they offer several advantages for systematic research. To begin, they are all substantively important. Negotiators typically focus on them, and so do analysts who focus on institutions in other realms of study. Second, they can be measured, allowing comparisons across institutions and within an institution over time. Third, they apply to the full array of international law, from the most complex (like the agreement creating the IMF) to the simplest (like a bilateral legal arrangement governing reindeer fences). Some might argue the simplest solution would be a single measure, one that describes institutions as (say) "stronger" or "weaker." Unfortunately, such measures are misleading. What they really do is collapse several important institutional design features into one overly simple statement that obscures more than it clarifies.

In this book, I engage the dimensions of *flexibility, centralization, scope, and control* and offer both theoretical and empirical refinements in Parts II and III of the book.[21] In what follows, I define the four dimensions and list the sub-dimensions used later in my analyses. I bring these refined categories to life with examples of institutional variation from the real world, including universities, firms, domestic government, and, of course, families. (In terms of how these sub-dimensions manifest themselves in international law, I define each sub-dimension and bring it to life with examples from the random sample in the relevant chapters in Parts II and III.) These dimensions reflect age-old concerns for scholars studying institutions and practitioners designing them.

Flexibility: How easy is it to modify rules and procedures or even obligations under the agreement? How easily can different positions at the outset of cooperation or during the implementation stage of cooperation be accommodated? Included in this are not only things like *duration provisions* and *escape* and *withdrawal clauses*, but also the degree of *precision* of an agreement's substantive terms and *reservations* added to agreements.

Many academic appointments start out finite but are extendable if tenure is earned after enough learning has ensued about the true benefits and costs of employing the assistant professor. In fact this logic of finite but extendable appointments is the same as that of the NPT elaborated in Chapter 4. Similarly, sunset provisions in domestic law dictate that a law will no longer be in effect after a certain date unless legislative action is taken to extend its duration. On the other hand, marriages are of indefinite duration, but in most places

---

[21] For an excellent analysis of membership that is very much in the spirit of Rational Design, see Thompson and Verdier (2014) who focus on the choice between bilateralism and multilateralism.

a complete exit or withdrawal is possible under what are usually extraordinary circumstances. Many syllabi contain escape clauses for students in the event of a personal emergency; in such a case, individual obligations can be postponed or temporarily suspended. Sometimes the emergency must be proved or verified by an expert. Driving laws are often very precise, as when a speed limit is posted. Laws about public indecency are often extremely vague. In Ann Arbor, Michigan, what is prohibited is engaging "in any indecent or obscene conduct in any public place." Finally, reservations or opt-out clauses in contracts and arbitration agreements allow for signatories to "opt out" of certain provisions. Prenuptial agreements can be understood in part as a means of opting out of a state's family and community property laws in order to craft a more customized/individualized agreement.

Centralization: What, if any, tasks will be delegated to a single focal entity? Among the tasks that might be centralized are *monitoring, dispute resolution,* and *punishment.*

In the domestic context, dispute resolution is often decentralized and informal, but centralized dispute resolution venues always lurk in the background. A dispute in a university might first be addressed through a friendly conversation; if that fails, non-binding mediation with the help of a peer might be attempted and finally, if necessary, delegation to a centralized university authority. Monitoring of professors' classroom performance is often accomplished through student evaluations. Employees in some contexts self-report their hours to confirm they are in compliance with the requirements stipulated in their employment contracts; in other contexts, a centralized mechanism like an administrator or a time clock monitors hours worked. Performance reviews completed by a designated person in an office can also ensure employees are fulfilling their obligations. Sometimes, independent bodies audit companies to determine if their accounts are maintained correctly under the law. Similarly, routine health inspections of restaurants ensure they are in compliance with food and health regulations. With respect to punishment, a course syllabus will warn students of the consequences should they fail to submit an assignment on time (e.g., a deduction of one letter grade for each day an assignment is late). The threat of punishment can also be implicit, as is sometimes the case in employee codes of conduct. Acts of misconduct are typically defined in explicit terms, but the course of disciplinary action should an employee commit such an act is not always specified. Employers will merely indicate which behaviors "will not be tolerated" or which behaviors an employee should/should not engage in.

Scope: What is the range of issues covered in the agreement? Are *rewards* or *punishments* linked to the behavior prescribed and/or proscribed by the agreement?

Linkage to other issues to reward and thus encourage good behavior and to punish and thus deter bad behavior is universal. The choice between these two simple tools varies by situation even with the same actors. Any parent knows that bribes, like dessert, tend to be used in restaurants to encourage good behavior; the public location renders the threat of immediate punishment not credible.[22] At home, taking away television is cheaper for the parent, and no one is around to hear the crying that could prevail. The promise of a good letter of recommendation or the threat of a mediocre one is often enough to encourage research assistants to do timely and good work. In the effort to encourage the use of alternative fuels and renewable energy sources, some state and federal laws offer subsidies to producers and consumers of environmentally friendly technologies (often in the form of tax credits or exemptions from federal fuel taxes).

Control: How is *control* over the institution allocated? Does it vary by task? What kind of rules characterize *decision making*?

In the US Senate, where states have equal representation, a bill requires a simple majority of votes to pass (51 if all 100 senators are present and voting). The House of Representatives also requires a simple majority (218 votes if all 435 representatives are present and voting), but the number of representatives (and, consequently, the number of votes) in each state is determined in proportion to its population. Families or couples often do not specify decision-making rules, but informal rules may exist. These rules may vary depending on whether the context requires particular expertise or what is at stake: choice of school or choice of movie?

---

[22] Of course, the typical child's time horizon precludes the usefulness of a threat of future punishment.

The broad conjectures

In what follows, I reproduce a subset of the conjectures presented in the Rational Design special issue.[23] These conjectures are anything but ad hoc. They are all derived from a consistent theoretical framework and are those for which formal theory can help the most in explaining a great deal of the interesting and important empirical phenomena across a wide range of substantive issues in international law. In fact, my co-authors and I were very careful when elaborating the Rational Design framework not to include any conjecture that did not have a sound basis, no matter how intuitively correct it seemed.[24]

These conjectures preceded the data collection. In fact, the data collection project was not even contemplated at the time the Rational Design special issue was drafted. Further, because they have logical underpinnings and are broad, the conjectures have stood the test of time. They serve as the foundation for both my refinements and quite a bit of other scholarship in international relations and international law.[25]

Each conjecture addresses the expected effect of a change in a particular independent variable, such as the severity of the Enforcement problem, upon one of the dependent institutional design variables, like whether centralization is incorporated into the agreement. Thus the logic is that of comparative statics: How does a change in an independent variable affect the equilibrium institutional design? If Uncertainty about the State of the World is high, for example, should we expect states to include more or less flexibility in an international institution? For each conjecture, it is assumed "everything else remains constant."

---

[23] This section follows directly from "The Rational Design of International Institutions" (Koremenos, Lipson, and Snidal 2001b: 782–95), with some phrases, sentences, and even paragraphs copied word-for-word.

[24] See Koremenos, Lipson, and Snidal (2001b: 783–95) for the full set of relevant citations to the scholars working in the rational choice tradition on whose work the individual conjectures are based.

[25] See Koremenos (2013b) for a summary of some of the international law and international relations scholarship using the Rational Design framework. See Poast (2012) for empirical corroboration of the conjecture *Issue scope increases with the severity of the distributional problem* and Poast (2013) for empirical corroboration of the conjecture *Issue scope increases with the severity of the enforcement problem;* both analyses focus on the sub-issue area of alliances.

I also present additional conjectures, elaborated in Parts II and III, based on some of the cooperation problems added to the COIL research program but not included in Rational Design. Specifically, the conjectures about Commitment problems follow the logic articulated in the Legalization volume; the conjectures about Coordination problems follow the logic of the spatial model presented in Chapter 6. Overall, twelve conjectures are presented here and refined and tested in Parts II and III. The few Rational Design conjectures not included are those that implicate the design variable membership and those that are not relevant to procedural provisions, the subject of this book.[26] (I number the twelve conjectures simply for presentational purposes. Four conjectures implicate the flexibility design dimension; five conjectures engage centralization; two conjectures engage scope; and one conjecture implicates control.)

The chapters in Parts II and III go into much greater detail regarding the logic of the conjectures, paying particular attention to how each conjecture operates in the context of the refined design dimension being presented and analyzed. Here I simply offer a sense of the broad conjectures, similar in spirit to the general framing found in Rational Design.

Conjectures about flexibility

Uncertainty about current or future states of the world presents states with a dilemma. Locking into an institution may result in unanticipated costs or adverse consequences. But by not making a bargain, states might pass up significant benefits from cooperation. The possibility of adjusting the agreement to deal with adverse shocks allows states to capture some of the gains from cooperation without tying themselves to an arrangement that may become undesirable when the state of the world changes or if and when states discover its true nature.

Specifically, states may know that a given agreement will yield substantial benefits in the current state of the world but would impose substantial losses in other possible future states of the world. Downs and Rocke (1995) show formally that, in such cases, it may make sense

---

[26] See, for example, fn. 29 regarding two Rational Design conjectures on issue scope.

to incorporate in advance sufficient flexibility into the agreement. Now states can temporarily "turn off" the agreement in circumstances where it no longer generates benefits. WTO escape clauses illustrate how multilateral cooperation can incorporate flexibility to allow member states to deal with domestic political and economic shocks.

Similarly, states may be uncertain about the distribution of benefits and costs of particular aspects of an agreement. Koremenos (2001) develops a model in which states plan in advance to renegotiate all or part of the agreement after enough time has passed for them to learn about which states benefit or lose the most from it in practice. The probability of renegotiation (relative to one long agreement) increases with uncertainty about the distribution of gains. Koremenos (2005) generalizes this model to the case of persistent Uncertainty about the State of the World.

The following conjecture captures this logic:

1. When *Uncertainty about the State of the World* is high, *flexibility* is more likely to be incorporated into agreement design.

Chapters 4 and 5 refine and test this conjecture by causally linking the following:

Uncertainty about the State of the World and finite duration
Uncertainty about the State of the World and escape clauses

In both cases, the broad conjecture is found to hold; in the case of escape clauses, the conjecture is refined such that Uncertainty about the State of the World is interacted with Enforcement problems. Chapter 5 explains this interaction in detail.[27]

Flexibility has also been demonstrated to help solve Distribution problems. Consider the argument in Fearon (1998), in which distributional problems, represented by bargaining costs, depend on the length of an agreement. As the intended duration gets longer, as it may when states lengthen the shadow of the future in order to solve Enforcement problems, distributional concerns become more and more severe. States bargain harder because the results of the bargaining will affect them for a longer period. In this case, states may seek to reduce

---

[27] This conjecture also passes the test of controlling for the inherent selection problem in the analysis of Uncertainty about the State of the World and finite duration. See Appendix 3.

distributional problems, and hence bargaining costs, by adopting a more flexible agreement structure. One such structure, considered in Koremenos (2002) and (2005), consists of a series of shorter agreements with renegotiation in between. A series of shorter agreements often still embodies the shadow of the future required for enforcement while avoiding the bargaining costs associated with a single, long agreement as in Fearon's (1998) model. The following conjecture captures this logic:

2. When *Distribution problems* are high, *flexibility* is more likely to be incorporated into agreement design.

This conjecture is refined in Chapter 6 by considering how interactions among cooperation problems condition the usefulness of certain kinds of flexibility in the presence of Distribution problems. Specifically, Chapter 6 refines and tests this conjecture by causally linking the following:

Distribution problems and imprecision
Distribution problems and reservations

In both cases, the conjecture is refined to consider the interaction of Distribution and Coordination problems. Only when the latter problem is absent is flexibility a rational solution to the Distribution problem. Thus the following broad conjecture, not in Rational Design, is also explicated in Chapter 6 and confirmed:

3. When *Coordination problems* are high, *flexibility* is less likely to be incorporated into agreement design.

Flexibility has another downside. Renegotiation of treaty terms, for example, is costly. And renegotiation provides an opportunity for states to "hold up" the cooperative bargain in an effort to increase their own share. Such incentives become greater as more states are party to an agreement. And, even without these strategic considerations, as more states become involved, modifying institutions becomes more difficult and time-consuming. Thus we would expect commodity agreements involving forty or so states to be renegotiated significantly less often than monetary agreements involving the G7. This reasoning leads to the final conjecture:

4. When the *Number of states* attempting to cooperate is high, *flexibility* is less likely to be incorporated into agreement design.

Nonetheless, some forms of flexibility do not impose "renegotiation-like" costs on members, like the degree of imprecision in an agreement's substantive terms. In fact, given bargaining difficulties, this type of flexibility is predicted to increase with number (see Ehrlich and Posner 1974).

Chapters 4 and 6 refine this fourth conjecture by causally linking the following:

Number of states and finite duration
Number of states and imprecision

In the first case, the conjecture holds. In the second case, the relationship is statistically insignificant.

These conjectures form the theoretical basis of Part II. In all three chapters, the dependent variable of flexibility is refined to consider duration, escape, withdrawal, imprecision, and reservations in separate analyses. In some cases, the Uncertainty about the State of the World variable and the Distribution problem variable are interacted with other cooperation problems to refine the conditions under which they hold. These refinements in no way undermine the general logic of the original Rational Design conjectures; in particular, the underlying assumptions are stable, and in no case is evidence found that refutes any of the three conjectures. Rather, the refinements are in the spirit of what Koremenos, Lipson, and Snidal hoped would follow from the Rational Design volume. More important, the refinements themselves are theoretically anchored, they precede the empirical analyses that test them, and they can serve as the basis for even further refinements consistent with the original assumptions and framework.

Part II, specifically Chapters 5 and 6, also recognizes that certain flexibility devices could be used opportunistically. That is, while a flexibility device might be incorporated into an international agreement to ameliorate the challenges of, say, Uncertainty about the State of the World, these very devices could be exploited for one member's gain at the expense of other members. This is most likely to occur when states face underlying Enforcement or Commitment problems. Chapter 5 demonstrates how states protect themselves from such opportunistic behavior with the nuanced sub-clauses of their flexibility provisions, including requiring other members' approval to invoke an escape clause, or requiring a notice/wait period before withdrawing from an agreement. Similarly, while reservations as a flexibility device are more likely when Distribution problems are high, reservations are also less likely when Enforcement problems are high so that overall cooperation will not be reduced. Chapters 5 and 6 explicate the full arguments.

Conjectures about centralization

International law can be characterized by several different forms of centralization. A body created by the agreement may have centralized information-gathering capacities, for example, without having any centralized adjudicative or enforcement capacities. Or it may gather information and adjudicate disputes but still have no capacity to enforce judgments. Although Rational Design recognized centralization as a broad variable, the following five conjectures serve as excellent bedrocks.

Consider first the standard "folk theorem" result: When states interact over extended periods, they can achieve cooperative outcomes on a decentralized basis through strategies of reciprocity. But when states are *uncertain about others' behavior,* they cannot achieve the same mutually beneficial outcomes. The greater the noise, the lower the joint gains they can achieve (Kreps 1990). Centralized information can reduce Uncertainty about Behavior so that (otherwise) decentralized cooperation can be more fully effective (Axelrod and Keohane 1985). The law merchant model illustrates the value of centralization in promoting cooperation when agents are uncertain about each other's past behavior (Milgrom, North, and Weingast 1990). This reasoning leads to the following conjecture:

5. When *Uncertainty about Behavior* is high, *centralization* is more likely to be incorporated into agreement design.

Chapters 7, 8, and 9 refine this conjecture by considering various forms of centralization as well as the interaction of Uncertainty about Behavior with other cooperation problems.

Specifically, the following relationships are elaborated and tested:

Uncertainty about Behavior and delegated dispute resolution
Uncertainty about Behavior and punishment provisions[28]
Uncertainty about Behavior and delegated monitoring

---

[28] Almost all punishment provisions (over 90 percent) involve centralization.

In all three cases, and as predicted by COIL, Uncertainty about Behavior *alone* does not lead to any form of centralization. Instead, states rely on informal dispute resolution and monitoring based solely on self-reports. Only when Uncertainty about Behavior is combined with other cooperation problems, like Enforcement and Commitment (considered in the following two broad conjectures), does it lead to these forms of centralization.

With respect to Enforcement problems, if the payoff from unilateral defection is significantly greater than that from mutual cooperation, concern for the future may not be enough to guarantee reciprocity-based, self-enforcing cooperation. In such contexts, states may find it optimal to delegate power to a third party to adjudicate and enforce mutually beneficial agreements.

The ability of organizations like the World Bank to withhold resources gives them significant leverage over weaker states. And the informational capacities of such organizations to publicize states' behavior can influence the activities of even the most powerful states by imposing international reputational costs or domestic audience costs. This reasoning leads to the following broad conjecture:

6. When the degree of the *Enforcement problem* is high, *centralization* is more likely to be incorporated into agreement design.

Chapters 7 and 9 refine this conjecture by considering various forms of centralization as well as the interaction of Enforcement problems with Uncertainty about Behavior.

Specifically, the following are causally linked:

Enforcement problems and delegated dispute resolution
Enforcement problems and delegated monitoring

In both cases, the broad conjecture is found to hold; in the case of centralized monitoring, the conjecture is refined such that Enforcement problem is included in a variable called "Incentives to Defect" and interacted with Uncertainty about Behavior. Chapter 9 explains this interaction in detail.

Following the Legalization volume, hands tying through some form of delegation is often a good solution for an underlying Commitment problem. For example, if a new regime wants to renege on the commitments made by the previous one, centralized dispute resolution or punishment provisions provide recourse for other actors to punish deviations from the state's original plans, altering the incentive structure faced by the new regime. This logic leads to the following conjecture (which is not found in Rational Design):

7. When the degree of the *Commitment problem* is high, *centralization* is more likely to be incorporated into agreement design.

Chapters 7 and 9 refine this conjecture by considering various forms of centralization as well as the interaction of Commitment problems with Uncertainty about Behavior.

Specifically, the following are causally linked:

Commitment problems and delegated dispute resolution
Commitment problems and delegated monitoring

In both cases, the broad conjecture is found to hold. In the case of centralized monitoring, the conjecture is refined such that Commitment problem is included in a variable called "Incentives to Defect" and interacted with Uncertainty about Behavior. Chapter 9 explains this interaction in detail.

Similarly, when states face *Uncertainty about the State of the World*, all may benefit from joint efforts to gather and pool information. Scientific activity on Antarctica is coordinated, and international economic organizations have substantial research capacities so that states can share the costs of collecting necessary information. Uncertainty about the State of the World can also lead to outcomes worse than expected by a particular state, perhaps generating incentives to defect from cooperation. This logic leads to the following conjecture:

8. When *Uncertainty about the State of the World* is high, *centralization* is more likely to be incorporated into agreement design.

Chapters 7 and 9 refine this conjecture by considering various forms of centralization as well as the interaction of Uncertainty about the State of the World with Uncertainty about Behavior.

Specifically, the following are causally linked:

Uncertainty about the State of the World and delegated dispute resolution
Uncertainty about the State of the World and delegated monitoring

In the first case, the conjecture does not hold. In the case of centralized monitoring, the conjecture is refined such that Uncertainty about the

State of the World is included in a variable called "Incentives to Defect" and interacted with Uncertainty about Behavior. Chapter 9 explains this interaction in detail.

Finally, as Numbers increase, centralized bargaining reduces transaction costs by replacing a large number of bilateral negotiations – or even a cumbersome multilateral negotiation – with an organizational structure that reduces the costs of decision making (Keohane 1984; Martin 1992). Centralization also allows states to coordinate their operational efforts to achieve economies of scale and to ensure that they do not duplicate or work against each other. NATO provides these advantages through a centralized command structure that allocates tasks (Abbott and Snidal 1998).

Centralization of information can also be increasingly valuable with larger numbers. Calvert (1995) shows how, with increasing group size the shadow of the future may not be sufficient to support cooperation. Multilateral communication allows states to achieve decentralized cooperation through an equilibrium outcome where noncooperation is punished by all other states, not just the one that was directly harmed. Because communication is costly, however, this mechanism can be substantially improved upon by a centralized arrangement where a "director" serves as a clearinghouse of information. Indeed, the director can even be viewed as "a third-party enforcer ... [who] in effect pronounces a sentence on the deviant player, a sentence that will then be carried out by rational players" (Calvert 1995: 70). The International Coffee Organization plays exactly this role in collecting and aggregating reports by importing countries on coffee shipments by exporting states. This logic leads to the following broad conjecture:

9. When the *Number of states* attempting to cooperate is high, *centralization* is more likely to be incorporated into agreement design.

Chapters 7, 8, and 9 refine this conjecture by causally linking the following:

Number of states and delegated dispute resolution
Number of states and punishment provisions
Number of states and delegated monitoring

In all three cases, the broad conjecture holds. Centralization alleviates the challenges to cooperation posed by larger numbers of actors.

Conjectures about scope

When the incentives on an issue are insufficient for decentralized enforcement, linkage to other issues can provide enforcement (Bernheim and Whinston 1990; Hardin 1982; McGinnis 1986).[29] The logic is the same as that of repeated games and the idea of the shadow of the future except that it works across issues rather than over time. The United States might be unable to resist domestic pressures to impose tariffs on European wine, for example, were it not for the realization that such action would invite retaliation from the Europeans on American beef. This reasoning leads to the following broad conjecture:

10. When the degree of the *Enforcement problem* is high, *scope increase* is more likely to be incorporated into agreement design.

Given the book's focus on design provisions, Chapter 8 refines and tests this conjecture by causally linking the following:

Enforcement problems and punishment provisions

The broad conjecture is found to hold. In the presence of Enforcement problems, formal punishment provisions are far more likely to be incorporated into international agreements.

Similarly, for states that have not solved the credible Commitment problem through domestic institutions, changes in the political support base of a government, for instance, may make it harder to comply with international commitments and thus trigger violations. Punishment provisions, whose negative consequences offset such political pressures, may then deter violations. As Goldstein et al. (2000b: 393) state, "Governments and domestic groups may also deliberately employ international legalization as a means to bind themselves or their successors in the future. In other words, international legalization may have the aim of imposing constraints on domestic political behavior." This leads to a second conjecture (one not found in Rational Design):

[29] Two Rational Design conjectures on issue scope are not engaged in this book: *Issue scope increases with greater heterogeneity among larger Numbers of actors* and *Issue scope increases with the severity of the Distribution problem.* Both of these conjectures stem from bargaining theory (see, e.g., Sebenius 1983; Tollison and Willet 1979; Raiffa 1982) and hence primarily address the *substantive* provisions of the agreement.

11. When the degree of the *Commitment problem* is high, *scope increase* is more likely to be incorporated into agreement design.

As in the aforementioned case, Chapter 8 refines and tests this conjecture by causally linking the following:

Commitment problems and punishment provisions

The conjecture is found to hold. In the presence of Commitment problems, formal punishment provisions are far more likely to be incorporated into international agreements.

Conjecture about control

The voting rules within an international agreement are another important element of institutional design. Rational Design featured this broad conjecture:

12. When the *Asymmetry of Power among participants* is high, *asymmetric control* is more likely to be incorporated into agreement design.

This conjecture follows from an intuition about how the importance of an actor to an institution translates into greater control over how it operates. This intuition corresponds to cooperative game-theoretic solution concepts such as the Shapley value, which relates what an actor (potentially) brings to different coalitions to the payoff it receives. When certain states contribute more to an institution than others – perhaps because they pay more dues or because their behavior is vital to the institution's success – they will undoubtedly demand more sway over the institution. Conversely, other states will want to give them this control in order to ensure their participation – as the UN granted to the permanent members of the UNSC, whose military and financial support was expected to be essential to the enforcement of resolutions (Winter 1996). This control is typically formalized in some way, as it is in the membership and voting rules of the UNSC and in the weighted voting in the IMF and other large financial institutions.

Chapter 10 of Part III considers this conjecture in the context of power asymmetries and institutional design. The chapter looks not only at voting rules as a type of control but other kinds of procedural asymmetries that could favor more powerful actors. Thus Chapter 10 refines and tests this conjecture by causally linking the following:

Asymmetry of Power and procedural asymmetry
Asymmetry of Power and power-based decision rules
Asymmetry of Power and unanimity requirements

Only the first conjecture is supported by the COIL data. The other two find no support in the data.

These conjectures about centralization, scope, and control form the theoretical basis of Chapters 7–9 of Part III. The bottom line that emerges from all the analyses, especially when taken together, is that *distinct combinations of cooperation problems* call for *different nuanced agreement design solutions.*

Part III also introduces the concept of informal design provisions within formal international law. As before, these refinements in no way undermine the general logic of the original Rational Design conjectures.

Benefits of a framework with game-theoretic underpinnings

Equilibrium institutions

The COIL framework recognizes the importance of anarchy and finds that employing a game-theoretic framework is an ideal way to incorporate the anarchical international setting into an analysis of international law. My basic strategy, following Rational Design, is to treat international law as a rational response to the problems states face. In the language of game theory, international law is an equilibrium institution. What does that mean? It means we consider not only the consequences of any particular international agreement for states; we consider why, given the underlying environment and the features of the states, they created the international agreement in the first place and why they have incentives to adhere to the agreement, even in the presence of shocks. This is an especially apt way of thinking about international law given there is no overarching central authority to enforce it as there is in most domestic settings. In other words, international law must be self-enforcing. Treating international law as an equilibrium institution has several important implications for the analysis.

To begin, the detailed agreement provisions must be "incentive compatible" such that actors create, change, and adhere to international law because it is in their interests. Consider an institution that can be sustained only through sanctions and whose members must apply these sanctions themselves rather than relying on some centralized institution. This is an equilibrium institution only if the members who are supposed to apply sanctions actually have sufficient incentives to do so. If there are such incentives, members considering defecting from cooperation know that doing so will likely cause other members to punish them. In that case (so long as the cost of receiving punishment outweighs the utility gained from defection), defection will not occur. In the jargon of game theory, defection is now *off the equilibrium path.* That is, members have no incentive to switch from cooperation to defection, and as a result, sanctions are rarely if ever imposed. Yet the mere threat of sanctions is what keeps states *on* the equilibrium path – that is, behaving in a way that allows them to achieve a Pareto-improving cooperative outcome.

The enforcement mechanism of the 1962 International Coffee Agreement[30] (ICA) is an ingenious example of an agreement with a sanctioning strategy (see Article 36) that is credible and thus likely to keep defection off the equilibrium path. According to the ICA, each coffee-producing state has its own export quota. Each state's quota represents a share (a proportion, not an absolute level) of the total annual export quota established by the ICA treaty body, the International Coffee Council. The importing states police the agreement by requiring a certificate of origin for all imported coffee. This information is then forwarded to the International Coffee Organization. If the data demonstrate that an exporter has shipped more coffee than it should, the organization deducts from its next quota the amount of the excess shipment. If this is repeated, double the amount can be deducted. If an exporter breaks the rules a third time, it can be expelled from the agreement with a distributed 2/3 majority Council vote. This punishment strategy is part of the equilibrium institutional design even though we do not expect it to be exercised. It is in the interest of all member states to carry out the punishment against the violator. The quotas of the remaining exporting states would be increased, and the importing states would simply

---

[30] UNTS Reg. No. 6791

receive their coffee from a slightly different mix of exporters – which presumably would leave them just as well-off. The punishers can thus credibly commit to punishing, and the potential defector will be deterred. Without the credible punishment strategy, defection would be part of the equilibrium, as it was in many failed attempts at a coffee cartel that did not include importers and thus lacked a credible punishment strategy.

Still, "incentive compatibility" does not mean that members always adhere to rules or that every state benefits at all times from the set of international agreements to which it belongs. It does mean that, over the long run, states expect to gain by participating in their international agreements; if they did not, they would neglect, avoid, or abandon them.

Another implication of equilibrium analysis is that the specification of independent and dependent variables requires special care. An equilibrium is a statement of consistency among its elements. For example, an international agreement with centralized dispute resolution may be consistent (in the sense that states will create and maintain it) with a certain pattern of state preferences and with characteristics of the environment and the set of states in the aggregate (which are integrated into the COIL framework). Rational Design and COIL's approach seeks a causal understanding that says, "When states have certain types of problems, they create institutions with particular characteristics." Decomposing an equilibrium into causal statements connecting independent and dependent variables requires looking beyond the equilibrium itself to the sequence.

An example that will be covered in depth in Chapter 4 might be illustrative. I argue that when Uncertainty about the State of the World is high, states will sign onto an international agreement only if its duration is limited; that way, if the agreement turns out badly for them, they are not tied to it forever. In this model, the uncertainty is a causal (independent) variable driving states to incorporate a finite duration (the dependent variable). The elements of the equilibrium are the level of Uncertainty about the State of the World and the duration of the agreement. But the model specifies a causal mechanism in terms of which elements are exogenous (the uncertainty) and which are endogenously determined (the duration).

Significantly, given the uncertainty in the environment and certain characteristics of states, *the finite duration is a necessary condition* for the agreement to be an equilibrium outcome. It can be shown, for instance, with a wide set of reasonable parameters, that when Uncertainty about the State of the World is high, not having any agreement at all is preferable to an agreement with an indefinite duration (see Koremenos 2001). Only when a finite duration provision is incorporated into the agreement is the agreement itself the equilibrium outcome.

There is no doubt that one of the major organizing principles of international cooperation and the avoidance of international conflict is self-interest and power exercised through international law. The thesis of this book rests on that fact that not just any international law will suffice. Rather, international law helps states confront harsh international political realities and increases the incidence and robustness of international cooperation if and only if the key provisions of the international agreement correspond to the particular configuration of the underlying cooperation problems the states are facing as well as to their own characteristics in the aggregate. Only then is international law an equilibrium institution. The details of international law matter.

Design features matter – even when they are not used

As just stated, the argument is that, if international law is going to provide any order for international politics, the law itself must be *self-enforcing*; that is, it must be in the interests of states to create and adhere to international law. This way of thinking about international law also provides insight into what, if any, conclusions can be drawn from the use or nonuse of international law provisions about the effectiveness of those provisions.

Sometimes states do not make use of the flexibility provisions (e.g., withdrawal clauses) or centralization provisions (e.g., dispute resolution) that they include in their international agreements. It is tempting to draw immediate conclusions about the nonuse of provisions and argue that they have no effect in promoting international cooperation. That line of argument seems especially common when it comes to the nonuse of international dispute resolution bodies. What the COIL framework calls attention to is the importance of the underlying model in predicting whether the design provision in question will be used on or only off the equilibrium path (see also Drezner 2003;

Thompson 2009). That is, the game-theoretic framework takes into account players' beliefs about what will happen in each potential stage of the game, even stages never reached in reality. These beliefs, in turn, affect states' choices.

An example from the well-known issue area of deterrence theory might prove useful. Suppose a state is contemplating whether to invade another state. In its decision calculus, it considers what would happen if it invaded and what would happen if it did not invade. Suppose further that the state that is to be invaded is part of a long-standing military alliance with great capabilities. We can imagine the following thought process by the state considering invading, "If I invade, there is an extremely high probability that the alliance will counter my invasion and impose great costs on me, precluding the possibility of my acquiring any additional territory. If I do not invade, I am left with the status quo." Given the assumptions about the military alliance, no invasion will occur. No one would counter the idea that the very existence of the military alliance and beliefs about its likely course of action had a major impact on the decision not to invade and for the status quo to continue. The fact that the alliance was not engaged does not make it ineffective. Quite the contrary, its existence and beliefs about what would happen if an invasion occurred kept that very invasion from occurring.

The same logic holds for many international law provisions. If the design provision is a renegotiation provision, put in place at least in part to solve uncertainty about future bargaining power, we would indeed expect states to renegotiate the agreement – that is, to see the agreement provision employed. Such is the case in the series of international coffee agreements: the 1962 distribution of quotas was altered in 1968, 1976, and 1983[31] (Koremenos 2002). But if the design provision is a withdrawal clause, its very incorporation into the agreement might make withdrawal less likely since optimally designed withdrawal notice and waiting periods preclude opportunistic withdrawal (see Koremenos and Nau 2010 as well as Chapter 5).

Specifically, agreements whose goal is to solve underlying Enforcement problems may include institutional design features like

---

[31] In 1989, the provisions regulating exports and imports were suspended and have yet to be reinstated.

rewards and punishments or dispute resolution provisions to try to change the short-term incentives of states to defect. Still, there remains the possibility that a "quick withdrawal" from cooperation could offer a strategic advantage to the withdrawing state, in the same way that a "sneak attack" offers an advantage to a state at war. It can be assumed that the withdrawing state knows that it wants to withdraw before it announces it. If it could withdraw immediately, it could have a strategic advantage by surprising other states with the announcement since other states would not have had time to adapt to this action. This is equivalent to the high payoff a defecting state receives in a prisoners' dilemma game when others cooperate while it defects. Even though withdrawing is lawful and not equivalent to defecting in that sense, strategically, in many cooperative settings, withdrawing has the same effect as defecting: The state that is no longer abiding by the terms of the agreement gains, but the states left cooperating lose. In a sense, including a withdrawal notice period levels the playing field for all states, mitigating the fear that the remaining states would be taken advantage of and eliminating the advantage to withdrawing. States contemplating withdrawal, not because of foundational changes in their interests in the cooperative endeavor, but because they want the strategic advantage that comes from ceasing to cooperate while others continue cooperating need only look down the game tree, so to speak, and see that their withdrawal will be matched by a complete unraveling of the cooperative endeavor as other states withdraw as well. They will thus be deterred from withdrawing in the same way the state in the example earlier was deterred from invading.

Chapter 7 makes similar arguments about dispute resolution provisions. Making the leap from unused to ineffective dispute settlement procedures overlooks the strategic interaction among and anticipative behavior of states. In fact, infrequent recourse to dispute settlement procedures may just as well indicate the effectiveness of this institutional design choice. If states anticipate the rulings of a dispute settlement mechanism and the associated punishment, they may refrain from a violation in the first place.

To recap, in the case of renegotiation provisions, their regular use is part of the institutional equilibrium; in the case of withdrawal provisions, their much less frequent use is itself the institutional equilibrium because the inclusion of nuanced withdrawal provisions alters the relative incentives to withdraw from a treaty while at the same time making states more comfortable subjecting themselves to an international commitment. The main point is that we cannot jump to immediate conclusions about the nonuse of particular international law provisions without considering whether they are used on or off the equilibrium path.

Connections to other subfields in political science

The study of institutions transformed the study of American politics quite some time ago and, more recently, it has transformed the study of comparative politics.[32] Rational Design and COIL's focus on institutional design bridges the gap between IR and these other subfields. While some of the conjectures are novel, many of them pull together insights from the international cooperation literature, whereas others translate insights developed in game theory, contract theory, and other areas of political science into the IR realm. The findings thus augment, enrich, and connect to the more general institutionalist research program.

It is enlightening to consider this book's place in the intellectual history of the study of institutions more generally. While institutions have been designed, used, and analyzed for centuries in settings ranging from ancient democracies to papal elections to the American founding fathers to the work of Lewis Carroll (author of *Alice's Adventures in Wonderland*), modern analyses of institutions can be dated from the path-breaking work of Arrow (1951) and his impossibility theorem. Arrow proved that a series of highly desirable properties of aggregation rules (like transitivity, non-dictatorship, etc.) could not be simultaneously satisfied. Arrow's theorem shook the world of social scientists and refocused the study of institutions as a means to avoid the perverse outcomes and even "chaos" generated when strategic interactions are not properly channeled and constrained.[33]

Institutions were thus viewed as regulating the options available to different players, including the sequence of their moves and the information available to them when they were making a choice. As a result, institutions were understood as shaping the strategies of the different players in an interaction and determining the prevailing equilibria.

---

[32] See, for example, Tsebelis (1990) and Cox (1997).
[33] The actual "chaos theorem" was introduced by McKelvey (1976).

Shepsle (1986) used the term "institutional equilibria" for these kinds of outcomes, although we now understand that there are no other kind of equilibria.

Game theory was perfectly designed for the study of equilibria given its focus on how institutions determine the choices of players. Moreover, game theory conceived of institutions as *independent* variables: particular institutions produce specific outcomes. But the *emergence* of specific institutions out of particular situations, conditions, and/or interactions is much less studied. In other words, our understanding of institutions as *dependent* variables remains limited.[34] In fact, some institutional theorists, like Riker (1980), argued that institutions are unknowable. Using his results regarding "the rarity and fragility of majority rule equilibria" as a starting point, Riker claims "just what combination of institutions, tastes, and artistry will appear . . . is as unpredictable as poetry" (1980: 445).

The Continent of International Law takes important steps in studying institutions as dependent variables, as products of the problems they are designed to solve and of the actors solving them. It argues not only that international institutions manifested through international law can be more than temporary equilibria, but that their specific design features are what make them stable equilibria. These features vary in systematic and consequential ways. Putting forth an explanation of how design features vary – that is, considering them as dependent variables – is a necessary step forward for international cooperation theory and the institutionalist research agenda more broadly.

---

[34] There are notable exceptions. For instance, Bednar (2011) analyzes the institution of federalism as an independent variable with respect to its potential to improve outcomes, like security, and as a dependent variable with respect to its design in terms of the distribution of authority between national and state governments. The latter is explained by a system of institutional safeguards, including judicial, structural, political, and even popular (e.g., public perception). See, too, Bednar (2014), which examines how subsidiarity principles promote the robustness of federalist systems.

3 | *The COIL sample*

This chapter introduces the data dimension of COIL. COIL's empirical focus is on the tens of thousands of extant international agreements (international treaty law) that govern day-to-day international cooperation. Each piece of international law can and should be studied as an institution. Together, this set of institutions, which truly is a "continent," is theoretically interesting and empirically diversified.

Our intuitions about international cooperation often follow from a few well-studied agreements. Often, the conventional wisdom about international cooperation is shaped and "tested" by these relatively few agreements. The multitude of studies that focus on the WTO as the canonical economics agreement often gives false confirmation that an underlying prisoners' dilemma-like structure is omnipresent in economic cooperation. Likewise, disproportionate focus on a select few multilateral human rights agreements, like the Convention on the Rights of the Child (CRC), falsely suggests that the prisoners' dilemma is absent in the whole of the human rights issue area.

In reality, however, international cooperation is far more diverse than these cases would suggest, both across and within issue areas. COIL aims to showcase and harness this diversity. The COIL data set is thus composed of a random sample of international agreements registered with the UN across the broad issue areas of economics, environment, human rights, and security. The data set features bilateral and multilateral agreements, with members representing almost every kind of regime and every part of the world. Some of the COIL agreements are short; some are extremely long. Some call for the creation of multiple intergovernmental bodies, while some create none at all. For each agreement in the sample, hundreds of institutional design variables are coded. Several of these serve as the dependent variables in the analyses in Parts II and III that follow.

In this chapter, I first briefly review the theoretical motivation for the COIL data set and discuss the unique questions it can answer. I highlight some of the main features of the data collection, especially those that might distinguish it from other data sets in existence. I then locate COIL on the spectrum of other international cooperation data sets and discuss complementarities among them. Some of the conventional wisdom is challenged by the first large-n, systematic operationalization of the cooperation problems underlying real international agreements. Finally, I exploit the COIL data set to get leverage on the following questions: When designing agreements to solve their cooperation problems, how often do states *create a new intergovernmental body*? How often do states *delegate to an existing intergovernmental body*? What kinds of tasks are delegated either internally to a new body or externally to an existing body? The simple descriptive statistics and a few straightforward analyses unveil a new set of puzzles that researchers can explain. I also compare my results using COIL to some of the results obtained using IGO data sets.

Creation of the COIL data set

Empirical foundations

For researchers studying international conflict, comprehensive data sets have existed for some time – in particular, the Correlates of War (COW).[1] Consequently, there has been a proliferation of empirical analyses over the past decades. Until recently, the empirical side of the field of international cooperation consisted mostly of case studies. Thus, we had lots of information about how certain variables operate

---

[1] There are many data sets; I describe only two here. First, the most comprehensive and widely used conflict data set is the COW project: Correlates of War Project. 2015. Data sets. Available at www.correlatesofwar.org) [Last accessed January 16, 2016]. COW actually features multiple data sets, with perhaps the most widely used being the Militarized Interstate Disputes data set, which covers the period 1816–2001 and includes a range of actions from threats to all-out war (Palmer et al. 2015). Second, Huth's Territorial Dispute data set covers post-World War II (1950-1990) territorial claims and disagreements and is characterized by a systematic and theoretically driven system for coding onset, conclusion, and variation in territorial disputes. Available at https://dataverse.harvard.edu/dataverse/phuth [Last accessed January 16, 2016].

in specific cases but little information about how those variables operate over the range of cases that international cooperation presents. We therefore knew much about specifics but little about averages. Simultaneously, game theory was revolutionizing the way we think about international cooperation, but without data, we were unable to test the implications systematically. This is no small matter, as the process of confronting models with data should discipline the evolution of modeling.

There were notable exceptions. A few authors embarked on systematic studies focusing not on international agreements but on the much smaller set of intergovernmental organizations (IGOs) – that is, entities with hallways and bathrooms. Some of these studies were theoretically driven; some were not. Wallace and Singer (1970) undertake a purely descriptive analysis, in which they count the number of IGOs in the global system from 1815 to 1964. To be included, an IGO must consist of at least two qualified members of the international system, hold regular meetings, and have a "permanent secretariat and some sort of permanent headquarters arrangement" (1970: 246). They conclude by stating: "we have tested no hypotheses, confirmed no models, and demonstrated no statistical or causal relationships between intergovernmental organization and other phenomena" (1970: 284).[2] Cox and Jacobson (1973) undertake an impressive, theoretically driven study of IGOs. They examine decision making and influence in eight IGOs, focusing on three independent variables: the stratification of state power, the economic and political characteristics of states, and world patterns of alignment and conflict.

Fortunately, things have changed. Multiple scholars have refined and extended the COW IGO data, and a host of new data sets focusing on international agreements now characterizes the field. I address these developments later in the chapter.

Theoretical motivation

In a nutshell, the COIL data set was created because of two theoretical convictions. The first originates in the Rational Design of International Institutions (Koremenos, Lipson, and Snidal 2001a) ("Rational

[2] This is the famous COW IGO data set that Pevehouse, Nordstrom, and Warnke (2004) have extended; the latter are used fairly frequently.

Design") and Legalization and World Politics (Goldstein et al. 2000a) ("Legalization") projects. These projects take the design of international law seriously, arguing that design provisions can help states confront international and domestic political challenges and thereby further international cooperation.

In particular, Rational Design argues that because the cooperation problems states are attempting to solve with their international agreements vary in interesting and important ways and because the characteristics of the states solving these problems also vary greatly, the design of international law is characterized by tremendous and meaningful variation. For example, underlying prisoners' dilemmas are solved by mechanisms like centralized or delegated dispute resolution; uncertainty about the state of the world is solved by flexibility mechanisms like finite durations.

The second conviction has to do with the power of underlying cooperation problems and state characteristics to explain agreement design *across issue areas*. COIL goes so far as to argue that law covering diverse issue areas (economics, environment, human rights, and security) with varying membership (bilateral and multilateral), including differentiated regime types/power configurations over various geographic regions can be explained under one unified framework. The theory can explain variation in details like flexibility, centralization, and control mechanisms.

Both the Legalization and Rational Design projects also changed the common unit of observation in empirical analyses: each piece of international law can and should be studied as an institution. The Legalization project went even further to include various forms of soft law (Abbott and Snidal 2000) – for instance, declarations that would not be considered legally binding. Thus there was both a narrowing from the broad idea of regimes and a widening from the narrow conception of an IGO with staff and physical headquarters.

Nonetheless, in both cases, testing is necessary to confirm theory. In fact, the Rational Design volume's reliance on case studies was criticized by Duffield (2003) for this reason.[3] Koremenos and Snidal

---

[3] Duffield (2003) also criticized the broad conceptionalization of some of the Rational Design variables. The theoretical component of COIL addresses this issue.

(2003: 437–38, 440–41), in their response to Duffield's criticisms, state that indeed the technology of case studies is itself limited, but attacking the Rational Design case studies is not particularly warranted. Koremenos and Snidal also agree that the cases do not go far enough and that the international cooperation field needs a large data set with consistent operationalization of key variables, which could enable true testing.

With that in mind, the empirical portion of the COIL project was designed. COIL not only aimed to create a scientific sample; given the debates about the supposed uniqueness of certain issue areas (e.g., Wendt 2001), COIL aimed to transcend issue area to shed light on such questions. COIL thus features a random sample of international agreements registered with the UNTS conditional on the issue areas of economics, environment, human rights, and security. COIL does not cover all forms of soft law articulated by Abbott and Snidal (2000); the agreements in COIL are always considered legally binding. Still, international agreements that are soft because they are imprecise and/or fail to delegate are featured in COIL.

COIL's population of cases

As mentioned, the COIL sample of 234 agreements comes from the UNTS. According to Article 102 of the UN Charter, "every treaty and every international agreement entered into by any Member of the United Nations after the present charter comes into force shall as soon as possible be registered with the Secretariat and published by it." Agreements that have not been registered as such cannot be invoked before any organ of the UN.[4]

Given the almost universal membership of the UN and its stature among international organizations, its list of international agreements is the most comprehensive to be found.[5] All international agreements registered or filed and recorded with the Secretariat since 1946 are

---

[4] The predecessor of Article 102 is Article 18 of the Covenant of the League of Nations.

[5] Problems of inference might arise by focusing on agreements that already exist. In Appendix 3, I confront this potential criticism directly and offer a user-friendly discussion of this issue in the context of COIL.

published in the UNTS; the UNTS also includes many agreements dating back to the League of Nations era.[6]

The UNTS Internet site provides a range of subject terms that can be used in searching for international agreements. There are approximately 300 of these terms. Although the terms are not mutually exclusive, there is very little overlap. For COIL, agreements in four different issue areas are sampled: economics, environment, human rights, and security. The economics issue area is composed of agreements categorized under four UNTS subject headings: "Monetary matters," "Investment," "Finance," and "Agricultural commodities." The environmental issue area is composed of agreements categorized under the UNTS heading "Environment." The human rights issue area is composed of agreements categorized under "Human rights," while the security issue area combines agreements under "Security" and under "Disarmament."[7]

In order to generate a random sample of agreements in each of the four issue areas, separate lists of all the international agreements within the UNTS subject heading just identified were first generated. Then using a random number generator, the agreements were reordered. Finally, each agreement was carefully examined to determine whether or not it met the inclusion criteria. These criteria are elaborated in Koremenos (2013a). The great majority of excluded agreements, that is, agreements that did not meet the inclusion criteria, are between one

---

[6] The Internet address is https://treaties.un.org. Overall, the UNTS database currently contains over 200,000 agreements and subsequent actions, where an agreement may be an original agreement, a protocol, or a renegotiated contract. To date, there are nearly 4000 registered original multilateral agreements, with over 3000 accompanying subsequent actions. Bilateral agreements and their accompanying actions comprise the remainder of the set. Notable omissions from the UNTS database include agreements registered with various regional organizations such as the African Union and agreements negotiated among Middle Eastern states and African states, more generally. Finally, an anonymous journal reviewer once stated that China and Russia tend to underreport their agreements as well, although these states are quite well-represented in the sample according to Figure 3.1; still, they may not register the same proportion of their international agreements as, for instance, the United States.

[7] The UNTS database is far from perfect in its labeling of international agreements. For instance, at some point after the year 2000, the UNTS put "social security" agreements into the "security" category, while this had not been done in the late 1990s. Such social security agreements, after being examined, were not included in COIL's security sampling. No other issue area has been found to be subject to such systematic errors; rather, the UNTS subject categorization appears to contain only infrequent, seemingly random errors.

state and an IGO.[8] In every large-n, multivariate empirical analysis in the chapters that follow, issue-area indicator variables are included[9] to address the stratified sampling in COIL, which is necessary because in some issue areas, like human rights, the population of agreements is quite small.[10] The sample of agreements is listed in Appendix 1.

COIL's coding instrument

A coding instrument with ten sections was used to record the details of the agreements. The questions cover, among other things, underlying cooperation problem(s); main prescriptions and proscriptions; whether there are annexes or appendices; membership criteria; and centralization, control, and flexibility provisions.

Specifically, the coding instrument features over 500 questions in ten sections, with 375 of these questions resulting in variables that can be used immediately and the rest composed of fill-in questions for which coders describe features of the agreement that are not easily captured in a multiple-choice question. Section 1 records basic information about the agreement, while Section 2 details the substance of the agreement, including the main prescriptions, proscriptions, and authorizations. Section 3 gathers information such as whether the agreement includes a preamble, annexes, appendices, protocols, and references to other international agreements. Section 4 addresses issue scope, while Section 5 details the membership provisions of the agreement, including membership criteria, the number of states needed and/ or the necessity of particular states to ratify the agreement before it enters into force, and the rights/responsibilities of nonstate actors. Compliance provisions, including monitoring and dispute resolution, are recorded in Section 6. Section 7 records the number of bodies the agreement creates, capturing details about membership, procedures for

---

[8] COIL was developed primarily to test theories about interstate cooperation, and thus agreements between an IGO (like a development bank) and a state are excluded.

[9] I vary which issue area indicator variable is the excluded category randomly across the analyses, except for Chapter 6, in which I want to call attention to the issue area of human rights.

[10] COIL oversamples economic agreements because the population of economic agreements dwarfs the population in every other issue area and, given this fact, the within-issue-area variation in economics in terms of cooperation problems is substantial.

making decisions, and other details about the functioning and purpose of these bodies, in particular, delegated tasks. It also codes delegation to existing third parties. Section 8 delves into information exchange, while the budgeting process is recorded in Section 9. Flexibility provisions constitute the substantive portion of Section 10 with questions about reviews, duration, extension, renegotiation, amendment, escape and withdrawal clauses, and termination procedures as well as reservations and declarations.

The member states' COW codes for the year the agreement was concluded are also recorded so that other characteristics of the parties (e.g., wealth) can be easily merged with the data.

The coding process

The reasonableness and consistency of the coding are very important issues in any data collection effort. Coder training was a nine-month process. Every agreement in the data set was coded independently by *at least* two coders. An intercoder reliability report was generated that highlighted disagreements between coders for the 375 questions for which there is a categorical answer (multiple choice, yes/no, etc.). In cases of disagreement, the responses were examined, and the disagreement was resolved by the author in consultation with the coders. The average coded agreement was characterized by disagreement on approximately 15 questions, or 4 percent of the quantitative questions, although rarely if ever was every question on the coding "survey" instrument implicated in any given agreement.[11]

Coding proceeded agreement by agreement. This approach (labeled *all variables for each observation* (AVFEC) by Mitchell and Rothman[12]) was used rather than a scheme that codes each variable across agreements at the same time.[13] The AVFEC process has the benefit of efficiency, as it helps coders understand the detailed context of an

[11] For instance, if there were no dispute resolution provisions in an agreement, the questions regarding the details of dispute resolution were precluded.

[12] Mitchell, Ronald B., and Steven B. Rothman. 2006. "Creating Large-N Datasets from Qualitative Information: Lessons from International Environmental Agreements." Presented at the American Political Science Association Meeting, Philadelphia, p. 43.

[13] Some have criticized the AVFEC approach for reducing empirical regularity. With respect to the COIL coding, this critique was addressed by generating intercoder reliability reports.

agreement, which, in turn, empowers them to better ascertain the meaning of ambiguous provisions.

Additionally, before certain data were used/released, a third coder checked particular variables across all agreements. For example, as a check on the coding of *precision* (which, unlike many variables, requires a judgment call), a third coder looked at the entire set of agreements, focusing only on precision, with international law experts weighing in on those agreements in their area of expertise.

Design variables

Each design variable analyzed in Parts II and III is defined and brought to life in the relevant chapter. Examples from the COIL sample are often featured to illustrate the range of variation in the design variable.

Given the multitude of variables, an online glossary is displayed on the COIL website,[14] with the main entries being the key terms in the instrument. Drawing on well-known international agreements, examples of the variables are provided. This glossary is important for three reasons. First, to ensure intercoder reliability, coders must be operating with precise definitions. Second, some terms have never been succinctly defined. Third, given the relationship between IL and IR scholars, comparison of their respective definitions should prove useful.

While coders relied first and foremost on the agreement text, domestic law and other international agreements were used to inform the coding if and only if the agreement in question refers to them. So, for instance, some agreements (including many bilateral mutual security agreements) expressly implement a domestic law that provides a finite duration term. In those cases, agreements whose texts facially contain no duration provision are coded as having a finite duration.

Cooperation problems

A crucial part of COIL is the coding of cooperation problems. Chapter 2 features a detailed definition and example of each problem. It is important to note here that in the actual coding more than one cooperation problem can be chosen for each agreement, thus circumventing the problem of forcing real-life issues into 2 × 2 games.

---

[14] The Continent of International Law (COIL) Project Website. Available at http://www.isr.umich.edu/cps/coil/ [Last accessed December 25, 2015].

Additionally, the states involved in any particular agreement are not assumed to be identical with respect to underlying cooperation problems. Many bilateral investment treaties (BITs) and human rights agreements, for example, feature some members with domestic Commitment problems and some members without such problems. As long as one state in a BIT is characterized by a Commitment problem, the agreement is coded as having an underlying domestic Commitment problem; the same is true of human rights agreements. Similarly, in certain disarmament treaties, some members (perhaps even the majority) have prisoners' dilemma-like preferences, but not all do. Many sign on to such agreements to help codify the norm embodied in them or to regulate states that are interested in the weapons in question. Such agreements are coded as having an underlying Enforcement problem.[15]

Each particular agreement is characterized by the presence (coded as high or 1) or absence (coded as low or 0) of each possible cooperation problem. In reality, all situations are characterized by almost all cooperation problems to some degree, but COIL codes them as existing if they are present in high as opposed to low levels. For example, Uncertainty about Preferences always exists to some degree in any interaction, but a situation has to be characterized by high Uncertainty about Preferences (e.g., Soviet Union and United States during the Cold War *for some issues,* as opposed to United States and Canada during the same period) for it to be considered present.

In making the decision to code cooperation problems as either high or low, replicability and consistency of coding were decisive factors. For instance, one alternative would be a numerical scale. Consider the cooperation problem of Uncertainty about Behavior. Suppose it could take on values from 1 to 5, with 1 reflecting a situation of great transparency when it comes to compliance and 5 reflecting one with the most severe uncertainty. Given that scholars often disagree with each other on how to code a set of five cases in case study work that is rich in detail, it is unlikely that we would each independently choose the same number when coding the Uncertainty about Behavior inherent in, say, ensuring that women have equal rights. Furthermore, scholars may

---

[15] Thus, according to COIL, the agreement must be designed for the "lowest common denominator" in this sense. Domestically, too, many rules are in place for the very few who have incentives to break them.

have very different opinions about whether the uncertainty in the aforementioned human rights sub-issue area is higher compared to the sub-issue area of chemical weapons (for which compliance is also difficult to observe from afar), lower, or the same. Yet, it is quite likely they would agree on a binary sorting: Both sub-issue areas have high as opposed to low Uncertainty about Behavior underlying them. For each and every agreement in the sample, a justification is given if the underlying cooperation problem is coded as passing the threshold from low to high.

Measuring cooperation problems and quantifying their prevalence in real international agreements has not yet been attempted, despite their centrality in our theories. Obviously, the cooperation problem questions are not nearly as straightforward as those pertaining to design. An inference must be made from the agreement to the cooperation problem(s). Nonetheless, some factors should alleviate concerns.

To begin, the inference came by looking at relevant background information. Sometimes, the political history of the states had to be examined in the decade(s) before the agreement was signed to determine whether the agreement may be attempting to solve a domestic Commitment problem – as Moravscik (2000) argues regarding newly democratized states and human rights agreements. In a bilateral agreement, the relationship of the dyad in the decade(s) before the agreement was signed was examined.

Research was also done on the general problems of the sub-issue area at the time to determine whether the sub-issue area is characterized by Uncertainty about Behavior (technological and other obstacles to using national means to determine the compliance behavior of others) and/or Uncertainty about the State of the World (sub-issue areas like agricultural commodities are prone to exogenous shocks that can alter the benefits or distribution of benefits from cooperation).[16] In some sub-issue areas, like that of environmental regulation or certain human rights standards, domestic actors within states are those whose behavior is being regulated, and their incentives may be different than the government's incentives. Such factors are taken into account in the coding.

---

[16] Koremenos (2005) details the coding of Uncertainty about the State of the World.

Importantly, only the substantive goals of the agreement, not the design aspects, were considered in the coding of the underlying cooperation problem(s). This separation is critical to the COIL research program, which focuses on the nexus between cooperation problems and design aspects of international agreements. In fact, there were two separate sets of coders for the cooperation problems and the design variables to safeguard the integrity of the COIL data set.[17] Thus, although the COIL theory is quite parsimonious, the empirical work that goes into the coding of each underlying cooperation problem draws on materials like memoirs, historical analyses, and the parties' institutional history.

In what follows, I expound on the background research that went into the coding of a particularly puzzling agreement in the COIL sample: The Agreement for Environmental Cooperation between Denmark and Oman signed in 1993. The agreement substantively covers solid and hazardous waste disposal and noise pollution. Given the distance between Denmark and Oman, the common explanation for many environmental agreements, which is that they solve the enforcement or free-riding problem that arises in part from the generation of negative externalities in this issue area, is not satisfying. Neither state will benefit in any material way from less waste or noise pollution in the other state. Moreover, if the benefits of minimizing this kind of pollution in Oman were so advantageous to Denmark, why had Denmark not agreed to similar agreements with other, geographically closer states? Oman itself had not signed a single environmental agreement in the decade before with any state. Why then did these two states decide to cooperate in this issue area?

Research on the issue area and on these two states led to a couple of interesting discoveries. First, Denmark signed five substantively similar bilateral agreements with Slovakia, Belarus, Ukraine, Bulgaria, and Poland in 1994. As in the case of Oman, these five states were at the time far less wealthy and developed than Denmark, not contiguous to Denmark, and, with the exception of Poland, without any history of making environmental agreements. Second, these bilateral agreements closely followed the 1992 Earth Summit in Rio de Janeiro at which environmental development was discussed at length. Given the importance of international environmental protection to the Danish, which

---

[17] Multiple examples of the coding of underlying cooperation problem can be found on the COIL website. See fn. 14.

was also documented, coders concluded that one of the underlying cooperation problems was Norm Exportation.[18]

This example is indicative of the kind of thought and research that went into the coding of each agreement. Appendix 2 briefly describes the coding rules for the other seven cooperation problems and the data used for the measures regarding characteristics of state actors in the aggregate. It is worth repeating that the separation of coders for the cooperation problems and the design variables helped to ensure that the former were not inferred from the latter.

Sample parameters: Coverage, time period, and number

Geographic coverage

Figure 3.1 displays the geographic coverage of the COIL sample. The legend works as follows: Those states that are almost white are barely represented in the COIL sample. The areas that are darkest, like North America, Europe, and Russia, are heavily represented in the COIL sample. The United States is the state most represented, with 75 agreements (almost one-third of the sample).

While the coverage is far-reaching, the figure also makes clear that some parts of the world are far less represented than other parts. It is not clear whether this is a function of these states making fewer

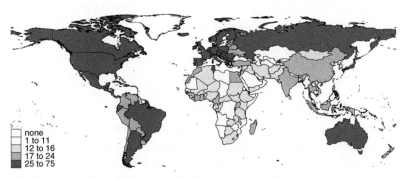

none
1 to 11
12 to 16
17 to 24
25 to 75

Figure 3.1 Geographic coverage and density of COIL sample

---

[18] This agreement is also coded as having an underlying Uncertainty about the State of the World given that the costs and benefits of the proposed collaboration were quite unpredictable at the time.

international agreements, or their not registering the agreements they do make with the UN. Most likely, it is some combination. In any event, scholars interested in areas of the world not well represented should investigate these possibilities and supplement the COIL data before any conclusions are drawn.[19]

Time period

With respect to signature dates, the agreements in the sample range from 1925 to 2004, with the oldest agreement being the Convention (No. 19) Concerning Equality of Treatment for National and Foreign Workers as Regards Workmen's Compensation for Accidents, signed in 1925, and the newest one being the Memorandum of Understanding Between the Ministry of Interior of the Republic of Turkey and the Ministry of Internal Affairs of the Republic of Belarus on Cooperation in the Field of Combating Trafficking in Human Beings and Illegal Migration, signed in 2004. Most agreements (about 68 percent of the total sample) were concluded between 1970 and 1999.[20]

Bilateral versus multilateral

International cooperation as manifested through treaty law is overwhelmingly bilateral. Multilateral agreements represent a mere 5 percent of the total number of agreements in the UNTS. Here the COIL sample, for which 31 percent of the agreements are multilateral, differs from the population it draws from mainly for two reasons. First, as mentioned, bilateral agreements between states and IGOs are excluded. Second, the COIL sample is conditional on issue area, and

---

[19] To elaborate, the fact that African states register far fewer UNTS agreements than the United States does could be a function of their producing fewer legal instruments more generally – both domestic and international. Fewer laws, in turn, may result from African states' relatively small populations and less diverse economies. In this sense, it would be akin to smaller US states, like Maine, producing fewer laws than larger, more diverse ones, like California. Alternatively or in addition, the relatively fewer registered African agreements could stem from African states' generally low levels of economic development, which may affect their capacity to build legal infrastructure, including the conclusion and/or registration of international agreements.

[20] The COIL sample drew from UNTS agreements with registration dates through 2006.

Table 3.1 *Bilateral vs. multilateral by issue area*
           (percentage of each issue area)

Issue area	Bilateral (%)	Multilateral (%)
Economics	89	11
Environment	60	40
Human rights	27	73
Security	68	32
Total	69	31

N = 234

Table 3.2 *Bilateral vs. multilateral by sub-issue area*
           (percentage of each sub-issue area)

Sub-issue area	Bilateral (%)	Multilateral (%)
Agricultural	83	17
Finance	81	19
Investment	95	5
Monetary	100	0
Environment	60	40
Human rights	27	73
Disarmament	11	89
Security	82	18
Total	69	31

N = 234

the human rights issue area is more likely to be characterized by multi-lateralism than bilateralism. Tables 3.1 and 3.2 present the descriptive statistics.

In the sample itself, agreements have about 11 members on average; membership ranges from 2 to 165 states. The modal agreement is bilateral. The average number of member states in agreements in the issue area of economics is about 6, while agreements in the issue area of human rights have about 25 members on average. Table 3.2 also shows that disarmament agreements are likely to be multilateral. This sub-issue area, too, thus influences the COIL sample on this dimension.

The spectrum of other similar data sets

Here I describe some of the new data sets characterizing the field of international cooperation, enabling researchers to see the similarities and differences among them and between them and COIL. First, impressive new IGO data sets that build on the COW data are now allowing researchers to test refined questions about cooperation through IGOs. For instance, Blake and Payton's data set (2014) is designed to test hypotheses relating the design of voting rules (unanimity, majoritarian, and weighted) to four state objectives: control (states are reluctant to give up sovereignty and therefore seek rules that give them the greatest possible influence on IGO decisions); effective membership (IGOs need a membership profile that allows them to function effectively); compliance; and responsiveness (which is akin to COIL's flexibility to respond to changes in the environment). The data set captures voting rules in IGOs founded between 1944 and 2005. Likewise, the Hooghe and Marks international organization data set (2014) aims to include the entire population of IGOs that meet a set of fairly demanding robustness criteria (e.g., at least 50 permanent staff), resulting in a total of 72 organizations. The primary goal is to test the authors' conjecture that the authority of IGOs is associated with the size of their membership and the scope of their policy profile. The Tallberg et al. (2013) data set is driven by theoretical questions regarding the institutional access that IGOs give to *transnational actors*.[21] The researchers are interested in formal access, as set forth in "treaty provisions, rules of procedure, ministerial decisions, policy guidelines, or equivalent" (2013: 10). The authors thus sought to identify a representative sample (via a stratified random sampling strategy) of 50 of the world's most significant, independent, and active IGOs. The Tallberg et al. data set is unusual and important among IGO data sets given that it identifies and catalogues organizational bodies *within* IGOs.

All three of these data sets focusing on IGOs code some of the same things covered in the COIL data set: voting rules, delegation, and

---

[21] "Transnational actors" denotes the "broad range of private actors that operate in relation to international organizations." These include "nonprofit actors such as NGOs, social movements, party associations, religious organizations, philanthropic foundations, labor unions, and scientists and profit-oriented actors, such as multinational corporations, business associations, and employer organizations" (Tallberg et al. 2013: 25).

formal transnational access (as codified in the original treaty). Importantly, all three go beyond what COIL does in different but significant ways. Both Blake and Payton (2014) and Hooghe and Marks (2014) code a different set of independent variables that are important to their theoretical concerns. Tallberg et al. (2013) code not only initial documents like COIL, but items like ministerial decisions, thereby allowing the authors to capture changes in transnational access over time.

Numerous issue-specific data sets exist that use international agreements as their unit of analysis. For instance, Leeds et al.'s (2002) Alliance Treaty Obligations and Provisions (ATOP) project collects data on the provisions of formal military alliance agreements in order to explain design variation in such cooperative security agreements. The data set includes treaties concluded between 1815 and 1944 and provides detailed data on the nature and content of these military alliances.[22] The ATOP data set is in some ways similar to the COW Annual Alliance Membership data set, which also contains records of military alliances (Gibler 2009). According to Leeds et al., "If the COW alliance data focus upon *who* and *when*, the ATOP data focus attention on *what* and *how*" (2002: 238). The alliance negotiation data set developed by Poast (2012) builds on the ATOP dataset of Leeds et al. (2002). Because of its narrow issue area focus, the alliance negotiation data set is able to operationalize variables like "scope of issues covered," which elude most other efforts.

In the environmental field, Ronald Mitchell has assembled a database that seeks to code the universe of past and present international environmental agreements (IEAs), going back to 1800.[23] As of 2014, the database contained 1598 bilateral treaties, 1248 multilateral treaties, and about 250 "other" agreements. Though Mitchell's database contains a massive number of agreements (about 70 times as many environmental treaties as COIL) and spans over 200 years, the coding captures only the most fundamental aspects of each treaty, including features like membership, signature date, and secretariat

---

[22] The most recent version of the data featured on Leeds' ATOP homepage includes treaties through 2003. Available at http://atop.rice.edu [Last accessed December 27, 2015].

[23] Mitchell, Ronald B. 2002–2015. "International Environmental Agreements Database Project (Version 2014.3)." Available at http://iea.uoregon.edu/ [Last accessed June 24, 2015].

title. Researchers can use the treaty text, which is available on the online database for many of the treaties, to draw their own observations about many other agreement features. Still, having assembled the closest thing to the population of environmental agreements is a massive public good in itself. Green (2013), for instance, draws on the database for her work on the role of private authority in global environmental governance.

Investment and trade agreements are also of particular interest to IR scholars, and several researchers have developed specialized data sets of BITs or trade agreements. One of the earliest of these data sets is Smith's collection of regional trade pacts (2000). Its purpose is to explore the factors that predict when these treaties will contain legalistic mechanisms for dispute resolution and enforcement. The data set includes all trade pacts arising between 1957 and 1995, provided they feature both: (1) reciprocal (not unilateral) liberalization; and (2) liberalization with fairly comprehensive scope. The data set consists of 62 bilateral and multilateral agreements (Smith 2000: 151). Likewise, Allee and Peinhardt developed a BIT data set designed to test hypotheses about the relationship between BIT dispute resolution clauses and parties' internal and external characteristics (2010). The data set includes 1473 BITs concluded between 1966 and 2010 (2010: 14–15). Blake recently created a smaller BIT data set comprising 342 BITs signed between 1960 and 2006 (2013: 811). The data are intended to test the conjecture that a longer time horizon (i.e., a government's expectation of remaining in power) is associated with a state preference for more flexible treaty arrangements in terms of policy autonomy. One of the main advantages of both Allee-Peinhardt's and Blake's data is, rather than focusing just on agreements, they include ample data on the member states.

Powell (2013) tackles the following research questions: How do domestic legal traditions structure the beliefs and expectations actors have about particular international legal entities, like the International Court of Justice (ICJ)? Powell's data set codes detailed characteristics of Islamic states' domestic legal institutions, both past and present. Powell consulted over 100 sources to build the data set, including official constitutions, statutes, and news articles (2013: 210). This is a terrific example of a narrower but deeper data set than COIL in terms of the amount of evidence gathered for a set of questions covering a specific set of states.

Unlike COIL, the nature of these specialized data sets requires that they represent only a small fraction of international agreements; moreover, these data sets do not approach COIL's breadth in terms of design variables. However, their narrow focus often allows them to explore their agreements in significant depth and/or cover a significantly longer timeframe than COIL. Additionally, in some of the data sets, there is sometimes an attempt to code the entire population of agreements within a specific issue area over a particular time frame (just as the COW IGO data set, from which many data sets draw, aims for the population of IGOs). COIL does not even attempt to approach the population of UNTS agreements. Still, although more power (in the statistical sense) is always preferred to less, and the larger the sample size, the larger the power, power does not increase linearly with sample size. Marginal increases in sample size have a decreasing marginal effect on the variance of estimators.[24] For COIL, the judgment was made to cover a large number of variables and invest heavily in both intercoder reliability and the separation of coders for independent and dependent variables, with the tradeoff of covering fewer agreements. It is worth mentioning that in work using the COIL data set, there has been enough power in the sample to make inferences – that is, statistically significant results are obtained and marginal effects are impressive.

Most of the data sets discussed and many others are, like COIL, motivated primarily by questions pertaining to institutional design – that is, how the institutions' features are a function of characteristics of their members or of the pertinent underlying cooperation problems, etc. Such is the case for Hooghe and Marks' data set of key IGOs (2014), both Allee and Peinhardt's (2010) and Blake's (2013) data sets of BITs, and Smith's (2000) data on regional trade treaties. Likewise, Haftel and Thompson (2006) tackle the independence of IGOs by conceptualizing and then measuring this important dimension. They proceed to explain the variation in independence among 30 regional integration agreements. In contrast, a few data sets, including that created by Tallberg et al. (2013), are focused on measuring how institutional arrangements affect institutional behavior or performance. Finally, data sets may be geared both to the study of design and the policy consequences flowing from that design. For example, the

[24] I thank Jeffrey Smith for clarification on this point.

ATOP data set was created to "help scholars investigate the causes and effects of variance in the design of cooperative security arrangements" (Leeds et al. 2002: 238).

The actual cooperation problems underlying the COIL sample

As Chapter 1 makes clear, one of the benefits of focusing on cooperation problems is the ability to see past issue area and gain insight into more general phenomena, some of which unite otherwise disparate issue areas. Table 3.3 provides descriptive statistics on the underlying cooperation problems for the COIL sample.

As the last column of Table 3.3 demonstrates, Uncertainty about the State of the World is the most common cooperation problem: 60 percent of the agreements attempt to solve it.[25] The pervasiveness of such uncertainty is not surprising, given the numerous potential international, domestic, and technological shocks that may affect international cooperation. Nonetheless, while the great majority of economics agreements are subject to such shocks, the opposite is true of human rights agreements, for which the future distribution of benefits and costs is not nearly as vulnerable.

In contrast, Uncertainty about Preferences is perhaps a great strategic obstacle to initiating negotiations, with not even 10 percent of agreements attempting to solve it. The human rights issue area is the exception here, too, with a third of the agreements characterized by this problem.[26] Future research should address whether the low incidence of this problem, other than in human rights, results from clear preferences (as is probably the case in economics) or from such uncertainty posing too risky an obstacle to cooperation – a topic addressed in Appendix 3.

Enforcement problems are important, but perhaps not as all-important as previously thought, with just over one-third of the agreements characterized by that underlying problem. Somewhat consistent with the conventional wisdom, the prisoners' dilemma/free-rider

---

[25] This is consistent with the findings of the Rational Design volume where the conjecture *Flexibility increases with Uncertainty about the State of the World* garners the most case study support. See Koremenos, Lipson, and Snidal (2001c: 1055).

[26] See Simmons (2009) for a justification of this coding.

Table 3.3 *Cooperation problems by issue area*
(percentage of each issue area)

Cooperation problem	Economics (%)	Environment (%)	Human rights (%)	Security (%)	Total (%)
Enforcement problem	37	42	27	26	34
Distribution problem	18	19	56	26	27
Commitment problem	38	2	34	2	24
Coordination problem	30	14	5	45	26
Norm Exportation	2	33	83	13	24
Uncertainty about Behavior	2	44	46	43	26
Uncertainty about Preferences	0	2	34	15	9
Uncertainty about the State of the World	78	67	27	45	60
N	103	43	41	47	234

problem is most prevalent in the issue areas of economics and environment. Still, some human rights agreements, like those bilateral agreements governing reciprocal rights for workers, are indeed characterized by a prisoners' dilemma-like payoff structure and hence coded as having underlying Enforcement problems. For example, a state wants its workers to be treated well in other states but would prefer not to spend resources on foreigners working within its borders.

Human rights is the issue area most likely to be characterized by an underlying Distribution problem. When sitting down at the table to negotiate human rights agreements, states can disagree about a number of things – most principally, what rights should be included and how those rights should be defined. This Distribution problem may arise from ideological differences, cultural differences, or the gap between a state's current practice and the proposed standard. Since many of the human rights agreements address topics that are enshrined in constitutions or other domestic laws, this issue area dominates with respect to this cooperation problem. Distribution problems as defined here need not center on matters of a material nature. Quite the contrary, just as the non-material aspects of issues like freedom of choice for women, gun control, and immigration ignite ferocious ideological battles domestically, the same is true internationally.[27] A lot of the economics agreements in the sample, on the other hand, involve bilateral aid or the rules governing investments (BITs). While an underlying Enforcement problem characterizes BITs, the Distribution problem in terms of what substantive provisions should be included is *relatively* low. Put differently, Distribution problems always exist, but given the range of issues in the COIL sample, agreements like BITs do not score high on this cooperation problem. Agricultural commodity agreements that impose quotas do meet the threshold for Distribution problems.

The human rights issue area, however, unlike the classic examples of subject matters characterized by Distribution problems (e.g., conflicts over territory or technical standards), rarely poses a Coordination problem, one of the issue area's unique features.[28]

---

[27] In fact, the domestic distributional problem is one reason the United States has not yet ratified the Arms Trade Treaty, which entered into force in 2014.

[28] Chapter 6 looks closely at whether human rights agreements are rationally designed to solve this Distribution sans Coordination problem.

The security issue area, on the other hand, which features some alliance agreements and agreements governing classified information, is the most likely to be characterized by underlying Coordination problems.

The notion that international law can be used to solve domestic problems finds support in the 24 percent of agreements that solve Commitment problems. Still, while domestic Commitment problems underlie many of the agreements in the economics and human rights issue areas, these problems rarely underlie the agreements in the issue areas of the environment and security.

Norm Exportation is most common in the human rights issue area. Nonetheless, even though the prevalence of Norm Exportation seems to make the issue area unique, many disarmament agreements also attempt to export norms as do agreements in the environmental issue area. Denmark's apparent attempts, discussed earlier, to export environmental norms using bilateral treaties is an archetypical example of the latter.

Finally, Uncertainty about Behavior underlies every issue area except economics. It is very difficult to see if human rights standards are being upheld in schools, offices, and prisons without on-the-ground monitoring. Likewise, it is difficult to see what individual firms are doing with respect to pollution controls. Both of these issue areas are characterized by the two-level problem: the behavior being regulated is often subnational. And, finally, in security agreements limiting or prohibiting certain kinds of weapons, noncompliance is quite easy to hide without third-party intervention.

Although human rights agreements tend to be characterized by both Distribution problems and problems of Norm Exportation, these two independent variables are only weakly positively correlated in the sample overall with a correlation of 0.32. Similarly, although many of the stylized facts about international cooperation and institutions assume both Uncertainty about Behavior and Enforcement problems, these two cooperation problems are, too, only weakly positively correlated with a correlation of 0.24.

Creating a new IGO or delegating to an existing IGO

As discussed, many data collection enterprises have focused on IGOs, and often only on the more robust IGOs (i.e., those that meet criteria like at least 50 permanent staff).[29] Yet when states are attempting to solve problems that call for some kind of centralization or delegation, whether to create a new intergovernmental body or to delegate to an existing intergovernmental body (or both) is an important choice at the agreement design stage.[30]

Consider the following quote from the 1968 Hearings regarding the NPT before the US Senate Foreign Relations Committee:

> The safeguards capabilities of the International Atomic Energy Agency [IAEA] will have to be expanded to meet the need. Its staff of trained inspectors will have to be increased. The IAEA is an existing organization with much experience to build on. We believe it capable of handling the job better than any new organization which might be set up.[31]

Because the COIL data set does not select on one or the other of these choices, an analysis of the choice itself becomes possible. Additionally, depending on the researcher's question, some of the existing IGO data sets are useful in supplementing and enriching the COIL data set.

What are the simple descriptive statistics regarding creation versus delegation? Let us begin with creation. One of the questions on the COIL coding instrument is whether the agreement in question creates a body or multiple bodies. Most IGOs are created at some point with an international agreement and thus this question captures whether such a body is created. However, *COIL's definition of a body does not impose any of the criteria that the COW IGO data set imposes* (or that the data sets drawing from COW described earlier impose). So an agreement body may or may not have a secretariat, it may or may not have physical headquarters (which is a question that does not even appear on the coding instrument), and it may include only two members. For example, multiple bilateral arms control agreements between the United States and Russia have used commissions authorized to make technical interpretations concerning the treaties' implementation. The New START Treaty, for instance, uses a body called the

---

[29] This section draws on Koremenos (2008).

[30] See Jupille, Mattli, and Snidal (2013) for an in-depth treatment of the topic. For a related question concerning changing an existing institution or creating a new one, see Morse and Keohane (2014). See also Hawkins et al. (2006).

[31] Statement of Hon. William C. Foster, Director, US Arms Control and Disarmament Agency. US Congress. Senate. Committee on Foreign Relations. 1968. *Nonproliferation Treaty*, 90th Congress, 2nd Session, July 10, 11, 12 and 17, p. 8.

Bilateral Consultative Commission (BCC), which has no permanent staff and is required to meet in Geneva twice yearly. This versatility thus allows individual researchers to use the data and more narrowly define the term "body" or "organization" however they see fit, depending on their research questions. Thus IGOs narrowly defined are a subset of my "agreement body," notwithstanding the absence of a headquarters question.

Based on this definition, 44 percent of the agreements in the sample call for the creation of an intergovernmental body composed of some subset of member states. Some agreements create more than one body. Specifically, 102 agreements create a total of 159 bodies. The breakdown is as follows: 76 agreements create 1 body; 12 agreements create 2 bodies; 7 agreements create 3 bodies; 2 agreements create 4 bodies; 1 agreement creates 5 bodies; 3 agreements create 6 bodies; and 1 agreement creates 7 bodies. For those 26 agreements that create multiple bodies, Tallberg et al. (2013) suggest how a researcher might decide which bodies are worthy of more focused attention. They use several subjective criteria to select key bodies representing different policy functions, including all those mentioned in the IGOs' constituent documents (2013: 59–60).

Some interesting findings emerge just from the descriptive statistics. First, according to the first column of Table 3.4, security agreements are least likely to create some kind of intergovernmental body, whereas both environment and economics agreements are above the average on this dimension. Still, as the first column of Table 3.5 reveals, the sub-issue area of investment is the driving force behind this result in the

Table 3.4 *Creation of new body vs. delegation to existing body by issue area*
          (percentage of each issue area)

Issue area	Creation of new body (%)	Delegation to existing body (%)
Economics	50	52
Environment	53	47
Human rights	41	71
Security	21	30
Total	44	50

N = 234

Table 3.5 *Creation of new body vs. delegation to existing body*
          by sub-issue area
          (percentage of each sub-issue area)

Sub-issue area	Creation of new body (%)	Delegation to existing body (%)
Agricultural	17	25
Finance	27	35
Investment	93	93
Monetary	18	0
Environment	53	47
Human rights	41	71
Disarmament	44	67
Security	16	21
Total	44	50

N = 234

issue area of economics. Almost every BIT creates an ad-hoc arbitration tribunal to help resolve disputes. Specifically, the parties must submit their dispute to an arbitral body if they cannot settle it diplomatically. The (typically three) members of this body are selected by the disputing parties: each side selects one member, and the two approved arbitrators then select a third; if the parties cannot find mutually-acceptable members, the selection process is turned over to an external source – this is thus captured in the delegation column.

Additionally, a focus on IGOs as defined by COW might understate the importance of cooperation through intergovernmental bodies in human rights because human rights agreements do not create IGOs with physical headquarters. So CEDAW, the CRC, the International Covenant on Civil and Political Rights (ICCPR), and the Convention against Torture and Other Cruel, Inhuman or Degrading Treatment or Punishment (CAT) create intergovernmental bodies like the Committee on the Elimination of Discrimination Against Women, the Committee on the Rights of the Child, the Human Rights Committee, and the Committee Against Torture, respectively.[32] These treaties and almost

[32] United Nations. Office of the High Commissioner for Human Rights. "Monitoring the Core International Human Rights Treaties." www.ohchr.org /EN/HRBodies/Pages/TreatyBodies.aspx [Last accessed July 11, 2015].

all the other human rights agreements are not represented in the COW IGO data set. Neither are many major security treaties, such as the Chemical Weapons Convention (CWC) and the Mine Ban Treaty,[33] which create agreement bodies according to COIL's definition.[34] For example, the Organisation for the Prohibition of Chemical Weapons (OPCW), which monitors state parties to the CWC and which won the 2013 Nobel Peace Prize for "its extensive efforts to eliminate chemical weapons"[35] is not part of the COW IGO data set. These four human rights agreements and these two disarmament agreements are part of the COIL sample.

Blake and Payton's (2014) findings regarding voting rules in IGOs can be tested against the COIL data set with its broader definition of a body and with its inclusion of many human rights bodies not found in the COW IGO data set. They find unanimity voting rules are more likely in the security realm, more likely over time, and less likely with greater Number of members. The authors also imply that the flexibility associated with Uncertainty about the State of the World necessitates something more responsive than unanimity. On the other hand, in monetary and commodity IGOs, some kind of weighted voting tends to be present.

Using the COIL sample, I find *no relationship* between unanimity and the security issue area, time, Number, or Uncertainty about the State of the World. *These null results might be due to the fact that all of these variables predict whether new bodies are created in the first place.* Thus it is quite likely that selection effects (discussed in Appendix 3) complicate efforts to draw inferences about any of these variables with respect to voting rules since they also predict the creation of the bodies that have voting rules.[36] With respect to Blake and Payton's results on

---

[33] The official name of the treaty is the Convention on the Prohibition of the Use, Stockpiling, Production and Transfer of Anti-Personnel Mines and on Their Destruction.

[34] It is important to note that the COW IGO data set includes organizations such as the OAS, which itself includes important treaty bodies such as the Inter-American Commission on Human Rights and the Inter-American Court of Human Rights.

[35] The Nobel Peace Prize 2013. www.nobelprize.org/nobel_prizes/peace/laureates/2013/ [Last accessed July 11, 2015].

[36] Thus, the Rational Design conjectures *Control decreases with Number* and *Control increases with Uncertainty about the State of the World* are not adequately tested and hence no conclusions can be drawn. Future work will address this question.

weighted voting, although very few agreements in the COIL sample have weighted voting, three of the four that do are agricultural commodities agreements; the fourth is an environmental agreement. Decision making in bodies created in monetary agreements, however, does not reflect power in this way.

While 44 percent of the agreements in COIL sample call for the creation of a new intergovernmental body, 50 percent delegate tasks to a pre-existing IGO.[37] The second column of Table 3.4 points to the astounding importance of pre-existing IGOs and also reveals a dynamic aspect of evolving authority that is hard to ascertain in the initial coding of an IGO. Even though this delegation is far more likely in human rights than in the security issue area, even the latter is characterized by a non-trivial amount of this kind of delegation.

The second column of Table 3.5 breaks down this delegation by sub-issue area. The difference between monetary and investment agreements is striking. As mentioned, most BITs delegate dispute resolution to a pre-existing IGO if the dispute is not solved by other means. Another striking finding is the difference between disarmament and security treaties. The former are also much more likely to be multilateral, and thus such delegation is also efficient from a transaction cost point of view.

In fact, Hooghe and Marks (2014) find that the degree of delegation to newly created IGOs is positively associated with the size of their membership and with the scope of their policy profile. While COIL cannot provide any quantitative measure of the scope of the policy profile, both delegation to a new body and delegation to an existing body increase with Number in the COIL sample.

Tables 3.6 and 3.7 show the results of analyses examining whether Number explains delegation. The log of Number is used given skewness in the variable. *An increase in participants is associated with a bigger increase in the probability of delegation to an existing body than of creation of a new body.*[38] With respect to the issue area

---

[37] The same agreement may both create a new body and delegate to an existing body.

[38] The area under the receiver operating characteristic (ROC) curve is 0.674 for the model used in the first column and 0.819 for the model used in the second column. For the second model, for instance, the ROC compares the fraction of agreements with delegation that are (correctly) predicted to have delegation (true positives) with the fraction of agreements without delegation that are

Table 3.6 *Creation of new body and delegation to existing body*

	Creation of new body	Delegation to existing body
Number (logged)	0.32***	0.84***
	(0.09)	(0.20)
Economics	0.73**	0.46
	(0.28)	(0.34)
Environment	0.67**	−0.08
	(0.30)	(0.30)
Security	−0.30	−0.67**
	(0.30)	(0.34)
Constant	−1.01***	−1.11***
	(0.30)	(0.41)
N	234	234

Note: Probit results, robust standard errors in parentheses.
*** *significant at 1 percent;* ** *significant at 5 percent;* * *significant at 10 percent*

indicator variables, an interesting finding emerges: The probability that an agreement delegates to a pre-existing body decreases by almost 20 percentage points when the issue area of the agreement shifts from non-security to security.[39] When it comes to creation, economic and environmental agreements are more likely than both security and human rights agreements to create a new body.

Table 3.7, which displays predicted probabilities, is informative as well. The probability that an agreement calls for the creation of a new body increases by almost 20 percentage points when the Number of participants increases from the minimum of 2 to the sample mean of 11. The empty dots in Figure 3.2 illustrate the increase in the predicted probability of creating a new body as Number increases. The probability that an agreement delegates to a pre-existing body increases by almost 48 percentage points when the Number of

(incorrectly) predicted to have this design feature (false positives). The second model has good predictive value, while the first does not.

[39] Technically, the difference is with respect to human rights, but the economics and environmental issue areas are not significantly different from human rights, the omitted issue area variable.

Table 3.7 *Predicted probabilities and average predicted effects*[40, 41]

	Creation of new body	Delegation to existing body
Minimum Number (logged)	0.36	0.33
Mean Number (logged)	0.55	0.81
Change predicted prob.	*0.20****	*0.48****
Non-economics	0.32	0.42
Economics	0.57	0.56
Change predicted prob.	*0.25****	*0.14*
Non-environment	0.39	0.50
Environment	0.63	0.48
Change predicted prob.	*0.24***	*−0.02*
Non-security	0.45	0.53
Security	0.35	0.33
Change predicted prob.	*−0.11*	*−0.20***

Note: All predicted probabilities in this table are significant at the 1 percent level.
*** significant at 1 percent; *** significant at 5* percent; ** significant at 10* percent

participants increases from 2 to the sample mean of 11. The solid dots in Figure 3.2 illustrate the dramatic increase in the predicted probability of such delegation as number increases: Delegation to an existing body becomes practically a sure thing for agreements that reach 33 participants.[42]

Table 3.8 lists all the tasks that can be potentially delegated and the percentage of agreements that delegate to a new body and the percentage that delegate to a pre-existing body. Thus, for example, 25 percent of the agreements in the COIL sample create some kind of intergovernmental body tasked with dispute resolution, 32 percent of the agreements in the sample delegate dispute resolution to a pre-existing body, and 46 agreements (almost 20 percent) delegate this task of dispute resolution both internally to the body created and

---

[40] Predicted effects are also known as *first differences* or *discrete differences* (Hanmer and Kalkan 2013).
[41] Throughout the book when calculating the relevant predicted probabilities and marginal effects, all other variables, except the independent variable of interest, are set to the values observed for each observation (Hanmer and Kalkan 2013).
[42] This corresponds to 3.5 on the horizontal axis.

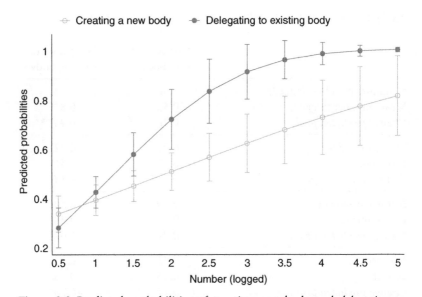

Figure 3.2 Predicted probabilities of creating new body and delegating to existing body as the number of participants (logged) increases
Note: Dots show the estimates of predicted probabilities, and vertical line segments associated with dots show the 95 percent confidence intervals. The corresponding number of participants for 1.5, 2.5, 3.5, and 4.5 on the horizontal axis are 4, 12, 33, and 90, respectively.

externally to a pre-existing body. Indeed, dispute resolution is by far the most popular task delegated, with compliance monitoring ranking second. A similar design choice is in place for overseeing complaints and punishments. No agreement gives power to any body, whether new or existing, to veto rules or decisions. A surprising descriptive statistic regarding monitoring is how many more agreements delegate this task to a pre-existing body as opposed to taking care of it internally.

It is worth noting that the two pre-existing IGOs that are most popular for the task of dispute resolution are not in the COW IGO data set: the ICJ and the International Centre for the Settlement of Investment Disputes (ICSID). Though it operates largely independently, the ICJ is connected to the UN; perhaps it is not in the data set for that reason. ICSID is an autonomous international institution established by an international agreement. Like the ICJ, ICSID was

Table 3.8 *Creation of new body vs. delegation to existing body (percentage of agreements)*

Tasks delegated	New (%)	Existing (%)	Number of agreements that delegate same task to new and existing
Figurehead	–	–	0
Secretariat/administrative duties	8	10	5
Financial administration	9	3	3
Representing the IGO in interactions	7	–	0
Collection of information	7	9	6
Collation of information	10	8	9
Analysis of information	14	6	9
Dissemination of information	15	11	13
Making rules/laws	7	0.4	0
Amending the agreement	7	7	2
Implementing rules/laws	18	12	9
Vetoing rules or decisions	–	–	0
Presiding/setting the agenda	6	2	2
Deciding which members may join	3	1	0
Granting exceptions under escape clause	1	5	0
Monitoring compliance	**13**	**31**	**15**
Soft procedures to encourage compliance	6	3	1

Table 3.8 (*cont.*)

Tasks delegated	New (%)	Existing (%)	Number of agreements that delegate same task to new and existing
Overseeing complaints and punishments	21	24	39
Dispute resolution	25	32	46
Redistributing property rights	0.4	0.4	0
Assigning new property rights	–	–	0
Addressing new, non-redistributive issues	–	–	0
Residual control	0.4	0.4	0
Other	9	9	4
Not specified	0.4	–	0

N = 234

created under the auspices of an IGO, the World Bank, and for that reason may be missing from the IGO data set.

In sum, IGOs do indeed evolve by taking on new tasks. Their authority increases over time with respect to agreement coverage. By focusing on agreements instead of IGOs, this finding is possible, especially given that many IGO data sets are selective in what they count as an IGO.

At the same time, by supplementing the COIL data with IGO data, a richer, more comprehensive picture can be attained with respect to many of the questions researchers might find most important. For instance, consider Blake and Payton's (2014) data set on the voting rules of IGOs. Their finding about the design of voting rules in IGOs can be examined with respect to delegation to IGOs: Do agreements with powerful states delegate to IGOs in which the powerful states have representation? Are powerful states more likely to choose IGOs that have either unanimity or weighted voting rules? When designing certain economic and security agreements, do states choose to delegate to IGOs for which unanimity is required?

Careful case study work along the lines of Tallberg et al. is also useful for looking at the evolving authority of IGOs as new tasks are delegated or as different (perhaps powerful) states start using them to perform tasks. Again, the evolution of the IAEA is informative in that regard, as the NPT seems to have been the impetus that catapulted that organization to what it is today. The following two quotes from 1963 and 1969, respectively, illustrate this evolution:

At present the IAEA is still weak, with no apparent direction. It is not the mechanism envisioned by President Eisenhower on December 8, 1953, for effecting a diminution of "the potential destructive power of the world's stockpiles" nor "a new channel for peaceful discussion." If the Agency's members want to develop it for that purpose, they must impart to it more vitality than is now evident (Kramish 1963: 77).

In recent months, the IAEA has in fact started to gear up for the greater responsibilities it will have in connection with the treaty: It is planning for the requisite expansion, setting budgetary goals, and has begun stepped-up recruitment and preparations for negotiating the implementing agreements contemplated in the NPT.[43]

---

[43] US Congress. Senate. Committee on Foreign Relations. 1969. *Nonproliferation Treaty,* Part 2, 91st Congress, 1st Session, February 18 and 20, p. 310.

Conclusion

The real change in the IR literature resulting from the data collection is that it allows for the testing of theories of international cooperation, given that the sample is the first random sample in the field of international cooperation and law that transcends issue area and that does not select on particular kinds of IGOs. While COIL allows for the testing and refinement of rationalist theories, it also can shed light on questions of interest to scholars working in other traditions. For instance, questions about references to other agreements and organizations, both international and domestic, allow scholars to probe the architecture of international agreements in the sense that the term is used in sociological studies of networks. Why do some agreements get referenced often in other international agreements and others hardly at all? Are there a few key sets of agreements that get referenced so often that we can think of them as the center of a "regime"?

And as Part III of the book illustrates, although COIL consists of formal international agreements, it can be exploited to study some types of informalism as well – that is, by examining the formal law, we can get a sense of what is missing and potentially left informal. Of course, although COIL broadens the available data on international cooperation, completely informal cooperation is not covered. Scholars working on compiling data on precisely that kind of informal cooperation (see, e.g., Vabulas and Snidal 2013 on completely informal IGOs) will soon broaden the empirical scholarship on international cooperation even further and in an important direction. Likewise, CIL is also extremely important in governing cooperation among states; new work by scholars like Verdier and Voeten (2015) on particular CIL provisions illustrates how to begin to quantify that kind of law, which is the first step towards more empirically rigorous scholarship on CIL.

Flexibility provisions in the design of international law

Introduction to Part II

One of the underlying tenets of international relations is that the effects of uncertainty are particularly dramatic in the international context given there is no authority to ensure state survival. Suppose that states cannot anticipate whether a cooperative endeavor will benefit them or whether the benefits, in particular the distribution of benefits, will be stable over time. Cooperation might be precluded if the uncertainty is great and the states involved do not particularly trust each other's long-term intentions. Domestic shocks that affect international cooperative endeavors are also quite common, whether they be economic shocks that affect particularly important interest groups or security-related shocks like internal strife. Can states use institutional design to internalize or contract around the effects of such uncertainty? Contracting around uncertainty may not only make more cooperation possible. Uncertainty is also a major source of reneging in the international realm. It follows that agreements designed to accommodate uncertainty are less likely to be reneged upon than are those not designed that way. Thus institutional design might also affect the robustness of cooperation.

Part II of this book addresses this theme by focusing on the institutional design tool of flexibility as a way of accommodating various forms of Uncertainty about the State of the World as well as Distribution problems. Duration provisions, escape clauses, withdrawal clauses, imprecision, and reservations are examined. In each chapter, the descriptive statistics and empirical analyses challenge some of the conventional wisdom. Chapter 4 on finite duration provisions shows the prevalence of this type of hands tying and explains how it can actually increase the credibility of commitment. Chapter 5 on escape and withdrawal clauses first presents surprising descriptive statistics about the types of agreements that allow escape as well as the vast variation even within issue areas on this dimension; with respect to withdrawal provisions (dismissed by some as examples of those final treaty clauses that are written without much thought), I find them to be strikingly meaningful and systematic in terms of both the length of their notice period and the time stipulated before they can be invoked. Chapter 6 argues that vague language and reservations are deliberate, rational choices, which implies that agreements incorporating such design tools are intended and expected to influence state behavior. Overall, each chapter converges on an important theme: Flexibility provisions are hardly softening. They increase the incidence and robustness of cooperation through international law. They indeed help states contract around the problems of Uncertainty about the State of the World and Distribution.

Recall the original Rational Design conjectures that implicate flexibility: Flexibility increases with Uncertainty about the State of the World and with Distribution problems, and decreases with the Number of actors involved in the cooperative endeavor. In the chapters that follow, these broad conjectures are refined in the following way. Flexibility that comes from a finite duration and an escape clause does indeed increase with Uncertainty about the State of the World; both types of provisions allow states to adjust to shocks that alter the benefits and costs of cooperation. While withdrawal clauses are, in the most general sense, a response to extreme uncertainty (which cannot even be modeled), sub-provisions like notice and wait periods ensure these clauses are not used opportunistically in the face of Enforcement and Commitment problems, respectively. Imprecision and reservations are the forms of flexibility best suited to resolve Distribution problems.

With respect to Number, the basis of the original Rational Design conjecture was Koremenos (2001), which featured a formal model of the choice between indefinitely long agreements and agreements with finite duration provisions that could then be renegotiated. Renegotiation provisions do indeed become more costly with a greater Number of actors, hence the hypothesis that finite duration agreements are less likely as Number increases. But, importantly, this logic does not extend to other flexibility provisions like those for escape or withdrawal or even imprecision and reservations. In fact, imprecision is likely to increase with Number given, everything else equal, bargaining problems increase with a larger Number of actors.[1]

A significant sub-theme of Part II is the following: *Without detailed variation, law would not be a stable equilibrium* – that is, law would not be robust to perturbations in the environment, whether international or domestic. This is perhaps nowhere better illustrated than in the discussion of escape clauses. While the flexibility provided by such clauses make it more likely that states will join cooperative endeavors, the nuanced sub-provisions of these very clauses affect robustness. To foreshadow Chapter 5, when an underlying Enforcement problem characterizes the cooperative endeavor, states are required to give proof of extenuating circumstances before they can escape, thereby greatly reducing the potential for opportunistic behavior that flexibility might introduce – opportunistic behavior that could lead to the unraveling of cooperation. Part II also begins the discussion of on and off the equilibrium path behavior with respect to design choices.[2] Escape clauses should indeed be invoked on the equilibrium path, but not with any particular pattern, whereas the use of withdrawal provisions to exit a treaty should be a much less frequent event.

Overall, Part II illustrates that different flexibility provisions solve different problems. Thus the variation in these provisions is tremendous and systematic. The chapters bring the theory to life through both large-n empirical analyses and examples from real-life negotiations.

---

[1] See Ehrlich and Posner (1974). See also Barbara Koremenos. "An Economic Analysis of *International* Rulemaking." Presented at the American Society for International Law Research Forum, Los Angeles, California, November 4, 2011.

[2] See Chapter 2 for an explication of these issues.

4 | *Duration provisions*

We all know that future generations will have to live, even on a strictly technological level, in a setting very different from the present one. To imprison them in an iron corset, which could not be adjusted to the changing conditions of history, would in our opinion expose that corset to the danger of bursting. We therefore prefer a steel corset which, being more flexible, could more effectively assure the continuation of the treaty.

(Statement issued by Italian Representative Caracciolo with regard to the proposed Nuclear Non-Proliferation Treaty)[1]

Looking at the COIL random sample, 60 percent of the agreements are characterized by a finite duration.[2] While economic agreements are significantly more likely to be of finite duration than human rights agreements, almost 30 percent of human rights agreements are explicitly not indefinite. These statistics contradict the conventional wisdom regarding hands tying as the surest means to a credible commitment.

Furthermore, Article 54 (b) of the VCLT stipulates that a treaty can end at any time if all of the parties agree to the termination. Why then would over half of the agreements in the sample stipulate a particular end date?[3]

The answer can be found in the politics of international law. International law often has non-trivial distributional consequences; that is, there are winners and losers. At the time a treaty enters into force, member states expect they will benefit; otherwise, they would not join. However, the distributional consequences of a new agreement

---

[1] US Arms Control and Disarmament Agency (ACDA). 1967. Documents on Disarmament 1967. Washington, D.C.: ACDA: 528.

[2] Much of the material of this chapter first appeared in Koremenos (2001) and (2005).

[3] Whether the provisions in the VCLT ought to be considered CIL is the topic of debate among IL scholars. See, for example, Christakis (2006) and Giegerich (2012), both of whom write about termination and withdrawal. Unilateral denunciation is the topic of Article 56 of the VCLT and of Chapter 5.

may not be known with certainty at the time the agreement is first negotiated. For example, if an agreement establishes a new institution or a new pattern of trade, the effect of this innovation on the GNP or on the security of each of the parties to the agreement may be known only approximately in advance.[4] States will not want to tie their hands indefinitely until they determine how the agreement actually works in practice. Thus, while all states initially believe they will benefit, after some time, some states may conclude that membership in the agreement generates a net loss (or at least a smaller gain than some different arrangement). Alternatively, over time, there may be shocks to the distribution of benefits, with the result that some states find themselves to be relative winners while others find themselves to be relative losers. In both contexts, winners would not want to renegotiate the agreement's terms.[5] Put differently, an *ex post* renegotiation of the initial bargain will always be vetoed by the winner. In both of these situations, states that find themselves on the losing side will likely renege on the agreement if it is indefinitely long. Cooperation would thus cease.

Nonetheless given that *ex ante* states are under a partial "veil of ignorance" as to how the true distribution of gains will unfold, states may find it in their collective interest to limit the duration of the initial bargain and then renegotiate its terms, thus making the cooperative endeavor less brittle and thereby enhancing the credibility of the initial commitment. Of course, renegotiation can be costly. Hence, the incorporation of this design provision is more likely when the underlying cooperation problem of Uncertainty about the State of the World is high.

In what follows, I first showcase the extent of this kind of flexibility in the random sample. I then put forth a theory regarding whether states are likely to incorporate finite duration provisions into their agreements and, if so, whether the duration of the agreements is likely to be long or short. I test this theory against the COIL data. The original

---

[4] Young (1991: 288–89) identifies this type of uncertainty when he states: "none of the stakeholders will be able to make confident predictions at the outset regarding the incidence of the benefits likely to flow from alternative institutional arrangements." Young does not, however, consider the possibility that such uncertainty might make states nervous about tying their hands.

[5] One needs only to contemplate the empty calls for a "renegotiation" of the terms of the UNSC to see the relevance of this argument in real international law.

Rational Design conjectures that *Flexibility increases with Uncertainty about the State of the World* and *Flexibility decreases with Number of actors* are confirmed. Additionally, I bring in Preference Heterogeneity as another predictor of finite duration. The theoretical discussion features examples from the actual negotiation of the NPT to establish that real-life negotiators thought about cause and effect in the same way my theoretical model stipulates, albeit with very different rhetoric as the Caracciolo quote that begins this chapter makes abundantly clear![6]

Definitions and descriptive statistics

A duration provision specifies how long an international agreement will "remain in force" – that is, how long it will last. Agreements tend to fall into one of three categories: they are explicitly finite; they are explicitly indefinite; or they are implicitly indefinite. If an agreement is silent on the dimension of duration, I assume it is indefinite. There is one important caveat to this third category. Some agreements are silent on duration, but they refer to another agreement or even to a domestic law that they are implementing. As Chapter 3 elaborates, if an agreement in the sample refers to another agreement or a domestic law, that agreement or law is taken into account in the coding if appropriate. So, for instance, a number of bilateral agreements in the COIL sample implement either the US Economic Security Act or the US Mutual Security Act. The duration of these agreements is finite and *contingent* on US legislation.

Some finite agreements have extension provisions that allow the agreement to be renewed, either for another finite period, a series of consecutive periods, or indefinitely. Other finite agreements specify that there will be renegotiation after the agreement ends. Some finite agreements call for both, whereas some are silent on the issue. For example, according to Article 71 of the 1962 International Coffee Agreement, "Parties . . . either decide to renegotiate the Agreement, or to extend it for such period as the Council shall determine." Renegotiation differs from extension in that renegotiation specifically contemplates changing some or all of the terms of the agreement. A renegotiation also differs from an amendment provision since

---

[6] See Koremenos (2001) and (2002) for full case studies of various agreements.

Table 4.1 *Duration provisions by issue area*
(*percentage of each issue area*)

Issue area	Indefinite (%)	Finite (%)	Finite and contingent (%)	Average duration of finite agreements (years)[7]
Economics	17	83	27	10.9
Environment	44	56	2	6.2
Human rights	71	29	5	8.1
Security	57	43	26	7.6
Total	40	60	18	9.3

N = 234

amendments are not "forced" or inevitable because of the conclusion of a finite agreement; rather, amendment provisions are found in both finite and indefinite agreements and are characterized by tremendous variation in terms of how often amendments can occur, who can put them on the agenda, whether they are binding on those states that do not accept them, etc. As my theory of duration provisions elucidates, the terms of an agreement must be finite to solve the problem of high Uncertainty about the State of the World; otherwise, *ex post*, some states will not want to renegotiate or amend an agreement's terms.

Table 4.1 displays descriptive statistics on whether agreements are finite or indefinite, whether they have a contingent finite duration, and finally, the average duration of the agreement in years if they are finite and not contingent. The first two columns of Table 4.1 reveal that the majority of agreements are finite. Still, the proportion of finite and indefinite agreements differs considerably by issue area. Both economics and environmental agreements are more likely to be finite than indefinite, whereas the opposite holds for human rights and security agreements. Almost a fifth of all agreements have contingency provisions; such provisions are especially common among bilateral security and economics agreements and exceptionally rare

[7] Finite agreements with contingent durations are, of course, excluded in the calculation of years.

Table 4.2 *Duration provisions by sub-issue area*
(percentage of each sub-issue area)

Sub-issue area	Indefinite (%)	Finite (%)	Finite and contingent (%)	Average duration of finite agreements (years)
Agricultural	0	100	42	17.0
Finance	42	58	42	11.0
Investment	17	83	10	10.2
Monetary	0	100	27	3.3
Environment	44	56	2	6.2
Human rights	71	29	5	8.1
Disarmament	89	11	0	5.0
Security	50	50	32	8.0
Total	40	60	18	9.3

N = 234

in human rights and environmental agreements. The duration of finite (non-contingent) agreements also differs vastly. The shortest agreement has an intended duration of less than a year, whereas the longest agreements are designed to expire after a full forty years. On average, finite agreements in the sample last about nine years and four months.

Table 4.2 displays the same descriptive statistics on duration across sub-issue areas. A number of interesting findings emerge. First, agreements governing monetary matters, like exchange rates, or trade in agricultural commodities are always finite. Moreover, agreements in monetary matters are the shortest on average at 3.3 years. Agreements in the sub-issue area of disarmament are the most likely to be indefinite, with only 11 percent being of finite duration, and none having a contingent duration. Interestingly, the small set of finite duration disarmament agreements has the second shortest average duration across sub-issue areas: five years. Environmental agreements and human rights agreements rarely have a finite and contingent duration, with the great majority of human rights agreements being indefinite.

As I argue later, the variation across agreements in these provisions is not random; rather, it results from the considered choices of the parties

to each agreement, in light of their own characteristics and the underlying agreement context – that is, the cooperation problems.[8]

Explaining duration provisions

In an international environment often so unpredictable that rational
states might understandably prefer to avoid commitment, how is
cooperation possible? States often have large amounts of information at their disposal when initiating cooperative activity, and they
often use it wisely to set the terms of cooperation and to manage its
evolution. Inevitably, though, events occur that could not have been
foreseen and cannot be controlled. Why do states commit themselves
to cooperation in the first place if they expect circumstances might
reduce their anticipated benefits? Not only do states cooperate, but
they also codify their cooperation through countless international
agreements forming a significant body of international law. How is
this possible?

One answer is that perhaps cooperative efforts only are undertaken in
the areas and among states for which uncertainty is less pronounced.
Does this imply that countless other cooperative possibilities go unrea-
lized because states cannot "insure" themselves against the unanticipated negative consequences that uncertainty might bring? Or should
we entertain the possibility that states can somehow protect themselves
in situations of high uncertainty?

Koremenos (2001) and (2005) argue that uncertainty in the international environment – uncertainty that is of varying forms and

---

[8] It might be argued that the international law doctrine of *rebus sic stantibus*
(treaties cease to be binding when basic conditions change) addresses precisely
the issue I am raising in this analysis. However, as international law scholars are
quick to point out, states rarely, if ever, invoke that doctrine because it is
considered to be very controversial. Writing about revision clauses in treaties,
Wilson (1934: 904) argues that such clauses are important because they allow
states to withdraw from burdensome obligations "without invoking the *rebus sic
stantibus* – or as it has sometimes been called, the 'notorious' – clause." Similarly,
Kunz (1939: 41) writes: "It is particularly important to insist on the complete
difference, from a juridical point of view, between the *clausula rebus sic stantibus*
and the problem of revision." More recently, Jackson (1992: 339) states:
"The traditional doctrines, such as *rebus sic stantibus* ... do not begin to
accommodate the type of evolution, innovation and step-by-step change of
circumstances that must be addressed by both national and international
'legislation.'"

degrees across issue contexts – can indeed be mitigated through the design provisions of international agreements. Specifically, high Uncertainty about the State of the World leads states to choose particular duration provisions. These provisions, in turn, affect state behavior regarding whether or not to conclude international agreements and whether or not to renege on them. Both articles feature a formal model from which the comparative static hypotheses presented later are derived.[9]

The key factors affecting the choices of duration and renegotiation provisions in agreements are Uncertainty about the State of the World (formally, the variance of the expected distribution of gains from an agreement), renegotiation costs (which increase with the Number of states involved in the cooperative endeavor), and the degree of Preference Heterogeneity among the states, which affects the degree to which any shocks to the outcome affect states' utility.

Suppose states determine that there are potential gains from cooperation and decide to negotiate an agreement. With respect to duration, they have two options in a given agreement context:

1. An agreement of indefinite duration (an inflexible agreement)
2. A finite duration agreement that can be renegotiated (a flexible agreement)[10]

The advantage states derive from concluding a finite duration agreement that can be renegotiated rather than one agreement of indefinite duration is flexibility: the division of gains can be *reset* to the initial level either once or at regular intervals. States choose to reset the division of gains to its original level because, I assume, bargaining

---

[9] The formal models assume risk-averse states, an extremely common assumption in the IR literature.

[10] I exclude the alternative of a completely contingent agreement. Most international agreements are either multidimensional or characterized by gains that are not directly monetary or both; hence it is a complex process to assign a value to all possible contingencies and combinations. Given this complexity, once a shock has occurred, often some kind of meeting among the member states is necessary to bring together and analyze all of the information each has individually gathered. Such a meeting will enable comparisons across the agreement's multiple dimensions regarding who really won and lost. Given the complexity of some of the issue areas, third party "neutral" expertise is also often solicited. For example, in the environmental issue area, experts are sometimes invited to testify at meetings of the member states.

power and other factors that influence the division do not change over time. Nothing in the model precludes the states from changing the initial division to reflect changes in bargaining power, as Koremenos (2002) illustrates.[11]

The planned readjustment to the division of gains that occurs under a finite agreement greatly reduces the chance that either state will want to renege or be forced to endure an unsatisfactory division of gains for long periods. Put differently, for risk-averse states,[12] the opportunity to reset the distribution of gains increases the *ex ante* value of a finite agreement relative to a single indefinite agreement. In fact, as Koremenos (2001) shows, in the presence of great Uncertainty about the State of the World, no cooperative agreement at all trumps an indefinitely long agreement with respect to the states' expected utility: *The finite duration provision is a necessary condition for the agreement to be an equilibrium institution;* otherwise, states are better off not cooperating.[13]

I now present empirically testable comparative static hypotheses about states' choices regarding whether to conclude a finite duration agreement and, if so, its relative duration.

(H4-1) Other things equal, agreements that are characterized by underlying Uncertainty about the State of the World are more likely to include finite durations than those not characterized by underlying Uncertainty about the State of the World.

(H4-2) Other things equal, if the parties conclude finite agreements, if the environment is characterized by underlying Uncertainty about the State of the World, the parties will choose to make their agreement(s) shorter than they would if Uncertainty about the State of the World does not characterize the underlying environment.

An increase in Uncertainty about the State of the World (H4-1) makes the parties value flexibility more. More specifically, the underlying uncertainty increases the variation in realized outcomes under

---

[11] In Koremenos (2002), states choose duration and renegotiation provisions in an environment in which there are persistent shocks to relative bargaining power. The issue facing the potential parties to an agreement is that the optimal distribution of gains, defined as the division that reflects the relative bargaining power of the parties, changes randomly each period due to exogenous factors.

[12] See fn. 9.

[13] Likewise, in certain situations where bargaining power changes, international law will be stable only if terms are renegotiable.

an indefinite duration agreement, which makes it less attractive relative to the alternative. With respect to (H4-2), the value to the parties of renegotiating either sooner or more often to undo the shocks to the distribution of gains increases; hence, they conclude shorter agreements.

(H4-3) Other things equal, as the Number of actors increases, the probability that the parties will choose finite, renegotiable agreements decreases.

(H4-4) Other things equal, if the parties conclude a finite duration agreement, as the Number of actors increase, they will choose to make their agreement(s) longer.

An increase in Number increases renegotiation costs (H4-3) and thus raises the costs of choosing a finite duration agreement relative to an indefinite duration. With respect to (H4-4), as Number increases, the costs of renegotiation increase while the benefits of renegotiation remain unchanged; thus the parties will renegotiate less frequently by making the initial agreement or each agreement in the series longer.

(H4-5) Other things equal, as the Preference Heterogeneity of the parties increases, the probability that they will choose finite, renegotiable agreements to adjust for shocks increases.

(H4-6) Other things equal, if the parties conclude a finite duration agreement, as the Preference Heterogeneity of the parties increases, they will choose to make their agreement(s) shorter.

In (H4-5), as the interests of the parties diverge, they increasingly value some form of flexibility in their agreement to reduce the variation of the realized outcomes. It is reasonable to assume that states would be relatively more concerned about unanticipated changes in the distribution of gains from cooperation when dealing with partners with very different preferences; in contrast, if a partner with similar preferences gains more, it can be more safely assumed that the gains would be used for shared priorities. In the case of (H4-6), the intuition is that, as the level of Preference Heterogeneity increases, so do the costs of putting up with an agreement whose distribution of gains has moved from that originally agreed upon. As renegotiation costs are constant, states will choose to renegotiate sooner or more often so that the variance in the realized outcomes falls.

The case of the Nuclear Non-Proliferation Treaty

The case of the Nuclear Non-Proliferation Treaty (NPT) brings to life the variable of Uncertainty about the State of the World with respect to the true distribution of gains from an agreement. The uncertainty in this case was quite one-sided in the following sense. The existing nuclear-weapon states (NWS) were not being asked to forego nuclear weapons. On the other hand, Article 2 of the NPT places obligations on the non-nuclear-weapon states (NNWS) not to receive or manufacture nuclear explosive devices. The NNWS thus composed the group most uncertain about the treaty's true benefits, and this Uncertainty about the State of the World extended to the security, political, and economic realms.

Uncertainty in the security realm

If the NWS really did reduce their nuclear stockpiles as Article 6 commits them to do, would the extended deterrence they provide to their allies who were required to remain NNWS become less credible?[14] What about the longevity of NATO? The following exchange from the 1968 NPT Hearing before the US Senate Committee on Foreign Relations highlights this particular uncertainty:

That is, the government of West Germany – 'expects the United States to make a binding public statement in one or two months. In such a statement the United States would undertake the nuclear protection of present NATO territory as it does now even if the NATO Treaty should end prematurely.' (Senator CASE, quoting "a wire service report of a story from the West German papers dated July 4")[15]

Now it is also true that nonnuclear countries concerned about their own security are interested in the status of these alliances, because some of those who are allied with us look upon the alliance as their principal protection against nuclear attack and nuclear blackmail. (Secretary Rusk, answering Senator Case)[16]

---

[14] Jenson (1974: 2) content-analyzed speeches made during a 1968 General Assembly debate on the proposed treaty in an effort to ascertain and categorize reservations. He reports that 62 percent of the speakers expressed concern regarding security guarantees, wondering how NNWS would be protected under the NPT.

[15] See Chapter 3, fn. 31: 42.   [16] Ibid., 42–43.

Senator CASE. Now, Mr. Secretary, not only the West German paper but the New York Times and I am sure other papers in this country carried stories a day or two ago. Here is the July 6 story in the New York Times, 'Bonn Seeks United States Guarantee Against Soviet Atom War.'

This question then is not just one of a German newspaper's interpretation of its Government's concern. It is apparently something quite real, and my question is again in no hostile vein at all.[17]

Uncertainty in the political realm

Would the political terms of European integration be altered if Germany and Italy committed to a non–nuclear status while France and the United Kingdom kept their nuclear weapons, as the treaty allowed? How would treaty adherence influence the political power and prestige of the NNWS? The future sources of prestige were ambiguous. Prestige could follow from the acquisition of nuclear weapons or it could follow from a state's willingness to accede to the treaty. As Jenson (1974: 38) states: "if there is general acceptance of the NPT, the few states refusing to join are likely to be just that much more criticized." Only time would tell how universal the treaty (and the norm embodied in it) would become.

Uncertainty in the economic realm

Would the treaty restrict the NNWS's ability to exploit nuclear energy, given that a line would have to be drawn between the use of nuclear energy for peaceful, civilian purposes and the use of nuclear energy for military purposes? In fact, speaking before the Bundestag in 1967, German Foreign Minister Brandt declared that his "government and others are also seeking to insure that the nonproliferation treaty does not further widen the already existing technological gap between the nuclear powers and the non-nuclear countries."[18] The following quote from the 1968 NPT Hearing is also instructive: "There were concerns expressed by several countries during the negotiations that the application of IAEA safeguards might serve to place the nonnuclear weapon states at

---

[17] Ibid., 46.   [18] See fn. 1: 49.

a commercial disadvantage by compromising their commercial secrets or by interfering with the operation of the facilities involved."[19]

Debate and solution

Given this one-sided uncertainty, choosing the duration and renegotiation provisions of the NPT provoked an intense debate. The treaty negotiations lasted from 1962 to 1968. As late as 1967, the United States and the Soviet Union (the original drafters of the treaty) were pressing for a treaty with an unlimited duration, while the Germans and the Italians, representing the NNWS, were emphasizing the impossibility of accepting such a duration. Reacting to the proposed indefinite duration, a Swiss aide-memoire stated:

To subscribe to such a commitment seems hardly conceivable in a field where development is as rapid and unpredictable as that of nuclear science and its technical, economic, political and military implications. Consequently it would be preferable that the treaty should be concluded for a definite period, at the end of which a review conference would decide about its renewal.[20]

There is no question that choosing such detailed provisions of treaties is a form of political interaction in which states maneuver and bargain for their interests. In the end, the NPT was concluded for an initial 25-year (finite) duration, after which there would be a review conference to decide whether to extend it or not and if so for another 25-year period or indefinitely. The interval of 25 years was also viewed as a learning period. Recall the trepidation of the NNWS about safeguards and being put at a commercial disadvantage because of them. As Glenn T. Seaborg, chairman of the Atomic Energy Commission stated during the 1968 NPT Hearing before the Senate Committee on Foreign Relations, "I am certain that once the safeguards under this treaty are in operation, those states that expressed some reservations will understand why we have been so confident on this matter."[21]

[19] See Chapter 3, fn. 31: 100.   [20] See fn. 1: 573.
[21] See Chapter 3, fn. 31: 100.

Empirical testing

In this section, I test the predictions articulated earlier using the COIL sample. With respect to the explanatory variables, while Uncertainty about the State of the World and Number have already been explained in Part I of this book and are available from the COIL data set, Preference Heterogeneity as a variable merits some discussion. I rely on a measure based on voting records from the UN General Assembly. The assumption is that the similarity of state preferences can be deduced in part by examining voting positions in this body.

Bailey, Strezhnev, and Voeten (2015) calculate ideal points for country-years based on these voting records. The measure of Bailey, Strezhnev, and Voeten (2015) has the advantage of being available for each state individually, not just for dyads, as was the case with previous measures; the new measure also takes into account shifts in voting patterns over time.[22] On the other hand, one weakness of this measure is that there are no issue-specific measures of ideal points – that is, the same measure would be used in, for instance, two 1975 bilateral agreements between the United States and the Soviet Union in the issue areas of security *and* human rights, despite the fact that while preferences on disarmament might be similar between these two states, their preferences on human rights might differ significantly. I use the standard deviation in ideal points among participants to measure Preference Heterogeneity; similar results are obtained when using the maximal difference in ideal points.

With respect to the design variables, I code an agreement as infinite when either it has an explicitly indefinite duration or when it does not explicitly provide for a limited duration and it is not contingent on another piece of legislation. The duration of finite agreements is coded in years, unless it is contingent.

Table 4.3 reports the coefficient estimates from the model. As expected, Uncertainty about the State of the World is associated with a higher likelihood of finite duration agreements (H4-1). The coefficient is both positive and statistically significant. Also as the results show, the coefficient on the logged Number of participants has the expected negative sign: more participants are associated with

---

[22] Voeten provides a more detailed discussion: Voeten, Erik. 2012. "Data and Analyses of Voting in the UN General Assembly." Available at SSRN http://ssrn .com/abstract=2111149 [Last accessed June 14, 2015].

Table 4.3 *Finite duration*

Uncertainty State of the World	1.04***
	(0.21)
Number (logged)	−0.32***
	(0.09)
Preference Heterogeneity	0.20
	(0.14)
Economics	0.54*
	(0.31)
Environment	0.03
	(0.32)
Security	−0.22
	(0.30)
Constant	−0.31
	(0.31)
N	212

Note: Probit results, robust standard errors in parentheses.
*** *significant at 1 percent;* ** *significant at 5 percent;* * *significant at 10 percent*

a lower probability of a finite duration (H4-3); this result is statistically significant. The Preference Heterogeneity measure, despite its weaknesses, behaves as expected in terms of its sign (H4-5), but does not reach statistical significance. The area under the receiver operating characteristic (ROC) curve is 0.835; a model without predictive power would yield a score of 0.5 and a perfect fit would yield a score of 1.[23] Finally, as in Koremenos (2005), a joint Wald test of the coefficients on all three variables suggests that they are jointly statistically significant (with a p-value of 0.0000).[24]

Table 4.4 shows that the effects of these variables are substantively quite large. Uncertainty about the State of the World is associated with a much higher probability of finite agreements. Uncertainty about the State of the World increases the probability of a finite agreement by

[23] The ROC compares the fraction of agreements with finite durations that are (correctly) predicted to have them with the fraction of agreements without finite duration that are (incorrectly) predicted to have them.
[24] This is a test of the joint null that all three variables have zero coefficients, rather than a test of each of them one by one. I use a two-tailed test, which is conservative given that my alternative hypotheses are in fact one-sided.

Table 4.4 *Predicted probabilities and average predicted effects*

	Finite duration
No Uncertainty State of the World	0.38
Uncertainty State of the World	0.72
Change predicted prob.	*0.34****
Minimum Number (logged)	0.64
Maximum Number (logged)	0.22
Change predicted prob.	*−0.42****

Note: All predicted probabilities in this table are significant at conventional levels.

*** significant at 1 percent; ** significant at 5 percent; * significant at 10 percent

almost 34 percentage points, from about 38 percent to 72 percent. Similarly, an agreement with the minimum Number of participants is almost three times as likely to be finite than an agreement with the maximum Number of participants in the sample. This result lends support to the idea that transaction costs in the form of renegotiation costs matter for agreement design; as transaction costs increase with larger Numbers, the formation of agreements of indefinite duration becomes more attractive to participating states. As in Koremenos (2005), adding control variables like a variable indicating whether a superpower is a member or not of the agreement does not change any of these results; in fact, the superpower variable is insignificant.[25]

Table 4.5 considers whether the same factors that predict whether agreements are indefinite or finite are related to the duration of finite agreements, as Hypotheses 4–2, 4–4, and 4–6 predict. As noted in Koremenos (2005), simply estimating a linear regression model in which the dependent variable is the intended duration is problematic because the intended duration of some agreements is indefinite. If I limit the sample to those agreements with a finite intended duration, I am selecting on the dependent variable, possibly resulting in biased and inconsistent estimates. I therefore set the intended duration of indefinite

---

[25] The results with the superpower variable are available upon request. Additionally, Koremenos (2005) uses three measures of risk aversion, one of which measures Preference Heterogeneity. After careful consideration, the Preference Heterogeneity measure is the only one I have confidence in from a theoretical point of view, and this is reflected in the change from 2005.

Table 4.5 *Intended duration (in years)*

Uncertainty State of the World	−53.82***
	(14.47)
Number (logged)	16.98**
	(6.82)
Preference Heterogeneity	−12.98*
	(7.78)
Economics	−24.98
	(21.10)
Environment	−18.04
	(21.20)
Security	29.85
	(23.79)
Constant	111.79***
	(23.00)
N	177

Note: Tobit results, robust standard errors in parentheses.
*** *significant at 1 percent;* ** *significant at 5 percent;* * *significant at 10 percent*

treaties as being longer than the longest agreement in the data set; for the results shown in Table 4.5, I set them to 100 years. Because the data are now effectively right-censored, I estimate a Tobit model, which takes into account this upper bound on the dependent variable.[26]

The results in Table 4.5 mirror those in Table 4.3 on the choice between finite versus indefinite agreements. Uncertainty about the State of the World leads to shorter agreements, supporting H4-2. A large Number of participants is associated with longer agreements, supporting the conjecture that higher negotiations costs lead to longer duration agreements (H4-4). And greater Preference Heterogeneity is associated with shorter duration agreements (H4-6). Moreover, based on a Wald test, the three coefficients are jointly significant, with a p-value of 0.000. This result suggests that the three variables together are significantly related to the expected duration of agreements.

[26] Appendix 3 considers issues of selection and explains and recommends various methods to address such problems, including formal sensitivity analysis. Following the general discussion, I perform a sensitivity analysis to test the robustness of the results in this chapter, given the likely selection problem.

Table 4.6 *Predicted duration (in years)*

No Uncertainty State of the World	77.33
Uncertainty State of the World	47.75
Change predicted duration	*-29.58****
Minimum Number (logged)	53.97
Maximum Number (logged)	87.08
Change predicted duration	*33.10****
Minimum Preference Heterogeneity	66.82
Maximum Preference Heterogeneity	42.94
Change predicted duration	*-23.88*

Note: All predicted probabilities in this table are significant at the 1 percent level.

*** *significant at 1 percent;* ** *significant at 5 percent;* * *significant at 10 percent*

The predicted effects of these variables are also substantial, as Table 4.6 illustrates. Both Uncertainty about the State of the World and higher Preference Heterogeneity are associated with a substantial drop in the predicted duration of agreements: An agreement with low Uncertainty about the State of the World is predicted to be about 60 percent longer than an agreement with a high degree of such uncertainty; similarly, an agreement for which all participants have almost identical ideal points with respect to UN voting is predicted to have an intended duration about 56 percent longer than an agreement with the greatest differences among ideal points. On the other hand, and as expected, moving from the sample minimum to the sample maximum Number of participants increases the duration of agreements by almost 60 percent. These results demonstrate that the choice of finite agreements and the intended duration of such agreements are affected by Uncertainty about the State of the World, the Number of actors, and Preference Heterogeneity.

What happens over time?

The excerpts showcased earlier from the NPT negotiations illustrate not only the main causal mechanism the theory articulates – Uncertainty about the State of the World causes the finite duration;

the NNWS made it clear that a finite duration provision was necessary if they were to join the regime. In other words, this detail of international law is what makes the law itself an equilibrium institution.

While this book focuses on explaining variation in these details of international law and their importance in making international cooperation through international law an equilibrium institution, taking a look at what happens over time can also be useful. In the case of the NPT, two points are important. First, finite duration provisions are often employed on the equilibrium path. That is, we should see some agreements coming to an end pure and simple; some agreements being extended; and some agreements being renegotiated. Examples of all three of these exist in the random sample, with the NPT illustrating the second.[27] Second, looking at the dynamics of the NPT review conferences reveals that the parties themselves saw these conferences as exercises to learn about how the treaty was working in practice and to resolve their uncertainty about the true distribution of benefits resulting from the treaty. Referring to the Third Review Conference, Hon. Lewis A. Dunn, ACDA, stated:

The main task at the Review Conference will be an article-by-article review of the operation of the Treaty. Woven throughout that review and ensuing debate, there will be five major questions. First, has the Treaty strengthened the security of the parties by helping prevent the further spread of nuclear explosives? Second, how well has the Treaty facilitated cooperation in the peaceful uses of nuclear energy? Third, what has been done to bring the nuclear arms race to an end? Fourth, what can realistically be done to strengthen the NPT? And most important of all, weighing each of these considerations, has the NPT been a success?[28]

---

[27] Additionally, membership changes in response to the unfolding of events are also made possible with limited-duration agreements. The Treaty on Collective Security (CST) came into force in 1994 for a period of five years and included an extension provision. In 1999, when the treaty's original term expired, Azerbaijan, Uzbekistan, and Georgia chose not to renew. The treaty was transformed into the Collective Security Treaty Organization, without these three states, and the CST ceased to exist.

[28] US Congress. House of Representatives, Committee on Foreign Affairs. Subcommittees on Arms Control, International Security and Science and on International Economic Policy and Trade 1985: *Third Review Conference of the Treaty on the Non-Proliferation of Nuclear Weapons.* 99th Congress 1st Session, August 1, p. 65.

The evidence indicates that the uncertainty about many aspects of the true distribution of gains persisted years after the NPT was signed. At the 1980 Review Conference, the debate centered on Articles 4 (which focuses on technological exchange) and 6 (which focuses on arms control). Disagreements between the NWS and the NNWS regarding how these articles were working in practice prevented the conference participants from agreeing on and hence issuing a final document. In other words, the parties had not yet been able to determine the true distributional effects of the NPT. By 1985, much more of the uncertainty regarding Article 4 had been resolved, as the following statement by Dunn illustrates:

Since the 1980 Review Conference: – all new or amended agreements for cooperation with non-nuclear weapon states entered into by the United States have been with parties to the NPT or the Treaty of Tlatelolco;[29] – virtually all US exports of enriched uranium ... were to NPT parties; ... – all of US-funded IAEA "Footnote A" (extrabudgetary) technical assistance projects – 111 projects for more than $4.5 million – have been for developing state Non-Proliferation Treaty parties;[30]

Essentially, the passage of time resolved much of the uncertainty over the distribution of economic gains from the NPT. Regarding the issue that raised so many concerns during the original negotiations, the parties successfully separated the civilian and military uses of nuclear technology so that trade in legitimate nuclear materials flourished under the NPT within a network of IAEA safeguards agreements. In practice, there has not been discrimination against the NNWS regarding technological progress in nuclear energy. Under the regime that eventually emerged, it was clear that the NNWS that joined the NPT would not suffer economic harm along this dimension.[31]

In addition to the concerns that played a major role at the review conferences, many other aspects of the uncertainty surrounding the distribution of gains from the NPT were largely or completely resolved during the initial trial period. In terms of security, the NPT greatly reduced the spread of nuclear weapons relative to what it likely

[29] The Treaty of Tlatelolco establishes Latin America as a nuclear-weapons-free zone.
[30] See fn. 28: 69–70.
[31] Nye (1981) presents additional examples of learning and uncertainty resolution in his discussion of policies relating to the nuclear fuel cycle and attempts to control aspects of the cycle related to nuclear weapons development.

otherwise would have been. During the trial period, membership in the NPT increased to the point of being almost global.

In terms of the distribution of political gains (and losses), it became clear that concerns that the NPT would prevent European integration were groundless. What turned out to matter for European integration was not Britain's bombs but Germany's GNP. Time also rendered moot Japan's worries about its ability to react to a broad US pullout from Asia.

In 1995 after four review conferences, the 163 parties to the treaty gathered in New York to decide the future of the NPT. Essentially all of the parties came to the conference favoring extension, a fact which itself provides powerful evidence of learning. Debate centered on whether extension would be indefinite or for a series of 25-year periods (Welsh 1995). The distributive bargaining that occurred at the 1995 conference mirrored the initial asymmetry concerning the Uncertainty about the State of the World, with the NNWS pressing for additional fixed periods and the NWS pressing for an indefinite duration. In the end, a consensus resolution extended the NPT indefinitely. The NWS had gained what they expected to in terms of maintaining their power and influence while the NNWS had learned how the NPT worked for them in practice.

Concluding thoughts

One way that states transcend uncertainty to achieve cooperation is to incorporate flexibility into their agreements. An important tool for doing so is to limit the duration of agreements. Thus, the underlying cooperation problem of Uncertainty about the State of the World is predicted to lead states to incorporate finite duration provisions into their international agreements. Indeed, the COIL data support this prediction, as well as the predictions about Number of actors and, to some extent, Preference Heterogeneity;[32] the variation in duration provisions is wide and systematic.

---

[32]   As noted, in Appendix 3, I submit these variables to a sensitivity analysis to control for the selection effects that come from the same variables being used to predict finite duration and the length of that duration. All three variables are robust to selection effects for the choice of finite versus indefinite duration. However, once one controls for selection, Number of participants and Preference Heterogeneity, although encouraging a finite duration agreement, have no effect on the length of that agreement.

The evolution of the NPT showcases this phenomenon. At the treaty's outset, many participants were deeply skeptical of the utility that the agreement would yield, and this manifested in a relatively short-term arrangement. In 1995, 25 years of fairly stable, favorable outcomes relieved many of these concerns. Uncertainty about future benefits had diminished, and the parties agreed to extend the NPT indefinitely.

The NPT is just Exhibit 'A' in the case for how parties strategically control the length of agreements to optimize their long-term utility from cooperation. And importantly, the mere availability of limited durations as a design option has likely allowed many treaties to arise – and to flourish – in environments of uncertainty and diverging preferences.[33] Without that design option, it appears that many of those agreements might never have existed at all.

---

[33] Koremenos (2001) marshals evidence that a similar dynamic occurred during the Antarctic Treaty negotiations.

5 | *Escape clauses and withdrawal clauses*

The function of a system of international relationships is not to inhibit this process of change by imposing a legal straitjacket upon it but rather to facilitate it: to ease its transitions, to temper the asperities to which it often leads, to isolate and moderate the conflicts to which it gives rise, and to see that these conflicts do not assume forms too unsettling for international life in general. *But this is a task for diplomacy,* in the most old-fashioned sense of the term. *For this, law is too abstract, too inflexible, too hard to adjust to the demands of the unpredictable and the unexpected.* (Emphases mine.)

(George Kennan 1951: 95)

In the COIL sample, 19 percent of agreements have escape clauses and 70 percent of agreements have withdrawal provisions. When we layer this type of flexibility on top of the finite duration and renegotiation provisions discussed in Chapter 4, international law does not appear to impose the "legal straitjacket" George Kennan ascribes to it. Quite the contrary, the escape clauses discussed and analyzed in this chapter are incorporated precisely "to temper the asperities" of the tumultuous world of international politics, and the withdrawal clauses also discussed and analyzed in this chapter allow states "to adjust to the demands" of the completely "unpredictable and the unexpected." Especially noteworthy is the fact that only 13 agreements in the COIL sample (around 6 percent of the sample) have neither escape clauses nor withdrawal provisions nor a limited duration.[1]

Still, while the detailed flexibility provisions of international law allow rather than inhibit change, these same provisions are also designed to help the agreements themselves serve as stable equilibrium outcomes. Put differently, these provisions are not the "softening"

---

[1] Of those 13 agreements, however, three are vaguely worded and one has reservations attached, two forms of flexibility discussed in the next chapter. Thus a mere 4 percent of the agreements in the sample are without at least one of the five kinds of flexibility discussed in Part II of this book.

mechanisms that Guzman (2008) labels them to be;[2] rather, these provisions themselves are quite nuanced to prevent opportunistic behavior. In fact, the sub-clauses of such flexibility provisions ensure that the provisions are not used in ways that disrupt the cooperative equilibrium states achieved in the first place through international law. The analyses of variation in such subtleties – such as whether *approval is needed* to utilize an escape clause and the *notice period* in withdrawal clauses – buttress one of the overall arguments of this book: Nuanced design provisions are a necessary condition for international law to be an equilibrium institution.

Furthermore, in making this argument, it becomes clear that CIL provisions regarding such things as withdrawal are too crude to accomplish the task of stabilizing international cooperative outcomes. Rather, given the tremendous diversity of cooperation problems characterizing international relations, variation in the subtle design of treaty law on dimensions like those governing escape and withdrawal is absolutely necessary.[3]

Escape clauses

Definitions and descriptive statistics

An escape clause is a provision that permits a member state (usually in the event of adverse circumstances) to be temporarily exempt from

---

[2] When presenting his "3 Rs" of reciprocity, retaliation, and reputation as the main variables that explain why treaties are designed the way they are and why these treaties are enforceable, Guzman (2008) finds enforcement through retaliation and sanctioning too costly (but see Thompson [2009] for a critique). Guzman thus argues that states try to reduce instances of violations by softening their agreements through, for example, monitoring provisions, escape and exit clauses, and reservations.

[3] Most modern treaties operate against a backdrop of the suspension/withdrawal provisions contained in the VCLT. In other words, treaty law contains "built-in flexibility," which applies even when parties do not affirmatively include their own flexibility provisions. Specifically, the rules in VCLT Part V, Section 3 (Articles 54–64) speak to the conditions under which withdrawal and suspension are permitted under different circumstances. Many of these VCLT rules are generally considered to reflect CIL. But recall the quote in Chapter 4, fn. 8 by Jackson (1992: 339): "The traditional doctrines, such as *rebus sic stantibus* ... do not begin to accommodate the type of evolution, innovation and step-by-step change of circumstances that must be addressed by both national and international 'legislation.'"

a requirement of an international agreement or to change its obligations or to avoid liability for nonperformance under certain conditions. Escape clauses sometimes provide that voting rights or other rights arising from the agreement are suspended during a member's "escape." An escape clause differs from a withdrawal clause (discussed later) in that the former is temporary and may be employed on a partial, selective basis, while the latter is a permanent and comprehensive exit from membership.

Escape clauses, unlike renegotiation or amendment provisions, do not allow adjustment of the agreement; rather, they allow states to temporarily escape cooperation and then return to an unadjusted agreement. Escape clauses are thus usually conceived of, and rightfully so, as responses to Uncertainty about the (future) State of the World with potentially *domestic* political implications, even though the source of the "shock" may be international.

For example, states may agree to particular terms of cooperation but then suffer shocks, like a civil war or a natural disaster, that make these terms difficult to implement in their particular states. What states require is a temporary relief from their obligations. The wording of some escape clauses suggests this purpose: "extraordinary circumstances that jeopardize extreme national interests."

For instance, the 1962 International Coffee Agreement contains an escape clause in Article 60:

(1) The [International Coffee] Council may, by a two-thirds distributed majority vote, relieve a Member of an obligation which, on account of exceptional or emergency circumstances, *force majeure*, constitutional obligations, or international obligations under the United Nations Charter for territories administered under the trusteeship system, either: (a) constitutes a serious hardship; (b) imposes an inequitable burden on such Member; or (c) gives other Members an unfair or unreasonable advantage.
(2) The Council, in granting a waiver to a Member, shall state explicitly the terms and conditions on which and the period for which the Member is relieved of such obligation.

This particular escape clause contains a sub-provision found in some but not all escape clauses: Before a member state can escape its obligations, it must secure approval; the body granting this approval will also outline both the timeline and the particulars of the escape.

The ICCPR is an example of a human rights treaty that features what most would call a derogation clause, which fits within my definition of an escape clause. Approval by a third party is not necessary in this instance. Specifically, Article 4 (1) of the ICCPR states, "in time of public emergency which threatens the life of the nation ... [states] may take measures derogating from their obligations under the [agreement] to the extent strictly required by the exigencies of the situation". If a state does take advantage of this clause, it must simply inform other state parties through the Secretary-General of the UN and detail "the provisions from which it has derogated and of the reasons by which it was actuated" (Article 4 [3]).

Table 5.1 shows the incidence of escape clauses across the four broad issue areas. About one-fifth of the agreements contain escape clauses. Economics agreements contain significantly more escape clauses than agreements in other issue areas, but human rights agreements contain significantly more escape clauses than environmental or security agreements.

This descriptive statistic regarding human rights agreements as well as the example of the escape clause in the ICCPR help make a point emphasized throughout this book: The same rational choice framework can explain the design provisions in all issue areas, even human rights, which some scholars argue are governed by a very different logic and thus would not incorporate instrumental clauses like those for escape (see Wendt 2001).[4]

Table 5.1 *Escape clauses by issue area*
        (percentage of each issue area)

Issue area	No escape clause (%)	Escape clause (%)
Economics	69	31
Environment	95	5
Human rights	83	17
Security	94	6
Total	81	19

N = 234

---

[4] In complementary scholarship focusing on the use of escape clauses in human rights agreements, Hafner-Burton, Helfer, and Fariss (2011: 675), too, adopt a rationalist framework and argue, "derogations enable governments facing threats at home to buy time and legal breathing space to confront crises while, at

In fact, interestingly, even in the issue area of human rights, in which one state's derogation or escape rarely imposes direct externalities on other states, there is considerable debate and conflict over which rights to include in an escape clause. For instance, according to Becker (2015: 56), during the drafting phase of the ICCPR, 14 rights were proposed as non-derogable, and 9 of those were ultimately adopted as non-derogable in the final draft, thereby balancing state interests. Similar disputes over escape clauses were present during the negotiations of the European Convention on Human Rights and the American Convention on Human Rights.[5]

Table 5.2 looks at the incidence of escape clauses by sub-issue area. Rosendorff and Milner (2001) argue that escape clauses are among the

Table 5.2 *Escape clauses by sub-issue area*
    (percentage of each sub-issue area)

Sub-issue area	No escape clause (%)	Escape clause (%)
Agricultural	96	4
Finance	96	4
Investment	29	71
Monetary	100	0
Environment	95	5
Human rights	83	17
Disarmament	89	11
Security	95	5
Total	81	19

N = 234

the same time, signaling to concerned domestic audiences that rights suspensions are temporary and lawful."

[5] See Becker, Monique. 2015. "An Escape from the Perceived Rationalist-Constructivist Binary: A Look into Derogable International Human Rights Agreements." Senior Honors Thesis. University of Michigan. During the negotiation of the American Convention on Human Rights, representatives of Mexico, Ecuador, and Costa Rica were against *any* limitations from derogation (Becker 2015: 74). Becker quotes the Mexican delegate in the following: "the Government of Mexico has always used, with extreme prudence, the faculty to declare this suspension and cannot admit the restrictions that are imposed by [Article 27 – the escape clause]." Ultimately, the Mexican, Ecuadorian, and Costa Rican views did not prevail.

most common and controversial features of trade agreements. Rosendorff and Milner imply that nearly all trade agreements have such provisions, and that they allow states to wriggle out of specific commitments when faced with heavy domestic pressures. While almost all BITs incorporate escape clauses (in fact, it is clear that the sub-issue area of investment is the category that drives the result regarding the economics issue area presented in Table 5.1), trade agreements in the sub-issue area of agricultural commodities certainly do not. Rosendorff and Milner's work is indicative of most scholarly work on escape clauses, which is focused on large international trade institutions like the WTO.[6]

Given the preponderance of escape clauses in the sub-issue area of investment, it is useful to consider those in greater detail.[7] There are various forms of flexibility in BITs that fall under my conception of escape clauses. Recall that I use the term escape clause broadly to capture any provision that gives permission to a state to depart from full compliance under certain conditions. This broad definition thus captures the full range of permissible escape, from the most circumscribed and specific conditions to the most broad and vague. Departure from full compliance can be with respect to the entire agreement or with respect to a specific provision. The domestic circumstances that authorize a state to escape can also range from something as extraordinary as a civil war to some vague notion of "public interest."

BITs typically feature relatively broad and vague escape mechanisms motivated by "public interest" – although more recent BITs sometimes also include escape provisions that resemble those in some of the other sub-issue areas discussed earlier.[8] For example, Article 5 of the Agreement concerning the Promotion and Reciprocal Protection of Investments between Estonia and Denmark states,

---

[6] See also Sykes (1991), who focuses on the General Agreement on Tariffs and Trade (GATT).

[7] I thank Jeffrey Dunoff for pushing me to be more reflective about both the conceptualization and operationalization of this type of flexibility in investment treaties and reminding me that my definition of an escape clause is broader than that used by other scholars.

[8] See, e.g., Article 18 of the 2005 Treaty between the United States of America and the Oriental Republic of Uruguay Concerning the Encouragement and Reciprocal Protection of Investment, which provides that "[n]othing in this Treaty shall be construed ... to preclude a Party from applying measures that it considers necessary for ... the protection of its own essential security interests." Available at http://investmentpolicyhub.unctad.org/Download/TreatyFile/2380 [Last accessed July 23, 2015].

"Investments of investors of either Contracting Party shall not be nationalized, expropriated or subjected to measures having effect equivalent to nationalisation or expropriation (hereinafter referred to as 'expropriation') in the territory of the other Contracting Party except for a public purpose related to the internal needs of the expropriating Party . . . ."

Van Aaken (2014: 832–33), who studies the design of BITs using economic contracting theory, differentiates between two forms of flexibility: an implicit flexibility that comes through "indeterminate legal terms," which must be interpreted by a tribunal, and an explicit flexibility that "allows for state measures which may otherwise breach the treaty, such as non-precluded measure (NPM) clauses (necessity clauses) or *clauses explicitly allowing for certain measures to be taken in the public interest*, as e.g. the specification in Annex B of the US Model BIT 2012" (emphasis mine). Article 6 of the US Model BIT 2012, to which Annex B refers, uses similar language to the clause in the Estonia-Denmark example.[9] The typical BIT expropriation clause captures both dimensions of van Aaken's notion of flexibility: the term "public interest" is indeterminate, thus requiring interpretation, and the clause allows states under certain conditions to take actions that would otherwise not be permitted.

I know of no other class of agreements that stipulate anything akin to this kind of public interest contingency for one of the main substantive provisions. The NPT does not include a sub-provision, for example, that declares that nuclear weapons shall not be transferred to non-nuclear-weapons states except when that transfer is deemed to be in the public interest and compensation is paid; neither do agreements in more closely related sub-issue areas, like bilateral tax treaties. It is striking that BITs perhaps uniquely incorporate this flexibility with respect to the application of a major substantive provision.[10]

---

[9] Article 6 of the US Model BIT 2012 states: "Neither Party may expropriate or nationalize a covered investment either directly or indirectly through measures equivalent to expropriation or nationalization ('expropriation'), except: (a) for a public purpose; (b) in a non-discriminatory manner; (c) on payment of prompt, adequate, and effective compensation; and (d) in accordance with due process of law and Article 5 [Minimum Standard of Treatment] (1) through (3)." Available at www.state.gov/documents/organization/188371.pdf [Last accessed July 23, 2015].

[10] I say "perhaps" because although I do not know of any other international agreements that use such language, they may exist.

Because of this, some may argue that such provisions in BITs simply delimit the scope of the obligation not to expropriate. Nonetheless, they fall on the spectrum of escape clauses as defined here – albeit at one extreme end. In fact, the behaviors permitted under clauses generally are those that are forbidden under the circumstances that do not justify escape. Consider the context of driving laws. Drivers' violations of speeding laws can almost always be categorized as simple noncompliance, and a penalty usually follows. Occasionally, however, a driver violates the speeding law because of a domestic circumstance, like driving a pregnant woman to the hospital. That violation would (we hope) be waived as soon as the circumstances became clear to the arresting officer. There is an implicit escape clause in driving laws for such circumstances. Thus the same action may be a straightforward violation in one case and an excusable escape in another, depending on the circumstances. There is a parallel in human rights agreements: Particular rights are to be respected except in times of "public danger."[11]

Many fear that escape clauses encourage cheating and undermine the integrity of agreements. Proponents respond that without them states would be unwilling to pledge such things as major reductions in trade barriers in the first place. After all, states need to guard against unanticipated hardships with serious political ramifications. Rosendorff and Milner (2001) offer a sophisticated answer to this controversy, based on a formal model of escape clauses. If it is cheap to invoke the clause, they say, the clauses will imperil the overall agreement. If the costs are exorbitant, the clauses will be useless, and states may not sign the agreements. But if the costs are high but not prohibitive, escape clauses can actually sustain agreements by tempering the hardships caused by shocks. Nevertheless, as Pelc (2009: 352) states bluntly after scrutinizing the WTO: "Empirical observation does not match up with the implications of prevalent theory"[12] as states rarely provide compensation when invoking escape clauses, contrary to what we would expect if invoking them were costly. And

---

[11] See, for instance, the American Convention on Human Rights, Article 27.

[12] Pelc (2009) offers a first-rate and comprehensive study not only of how the escape clause in the WTO actually works; he also provides an account and sophisticated explanation for the evolution of the escape clause from GATT to the WTO.

even though they appear not to be costly, escape clauses are actually not used that frequently.

Pelc's observation about the WTO is true more broadly. According to the COIL data, only the sub-issue area of investment features costly escape clauses – that is, a state incurs some form of material penalty when escaping. In fact, only this sub-issue area features design provisions that correspond to economic models of efficient breach.[13] States that nationalize foreign investment often face legal claims by foreign investors. The state that is invoking the escape clause does so only if the expected benefits outweigh the expected costs. For example, Article 5 (1) in the Agreement for the Promotion and Protection of Investments between the United Kingdom and Yemen states that, if investments are expropriated (because of the public interest), compensation shall be paid immediately and is subject to judicial review.

In sum, while the requirements regarding what constitutes an allowable escape vary greatly, with the threshold set far lower in BITs than in the other areas for which escape is permissible (like quota-setting commodity agreements or standards-setting human rights agreements), the essence of the provision is similar. Despite the fact that escape is costly in the sub-issue area of investments as opposed to the human rights issue area, for example, in which there is no costly escape (that is, there are no material penalties or suspension of other rights that go along with escape), escape may happen more frequently in the context of BITs. Still, along the lines of Pelc and Urpelainen's (2015) excellent article, this consequence can be framed as part of BITs' rational institutional design.

Theory: Explaining the incidence of escape clauses

Under what conditions are escape clauses most valuable? As Chapter 2 identifies, when states are facing Uncertainty about the State of the World, that is, when their cooperative endeavors are likely to be characterized by shocks that could alter the distribution of gains from cooperation, flexibility can serve as an institutional solution. For example, if a particular shock affects an important domestic group,

---

[13] This finding is consistent with Pelc and Urpelainen (2015: 231): "Our model predicts that international trade agreements should spurn efficient breach, while investment agreements should favor it."

one could imagine the state in question wanting some time to protect this group while it either adjusts (if the shock is permanent) or waits it out (if the shock is temporary).

Furthermore, when the underlying cooperation resembles a prisoners' dilemma – that is, it is characterized by an Enforcement problem – escape clauses might be especially useful for protecting cooperation from unraveling. Specifically, when a state has to stop complying for domestic reasons, having "permission" for noncompliance without fear of retaliation and an unraveling of cooperation is very useful for both the state in question and its partners. Partners can thus have confidence that cooperation will resume once the shock has passed.

It is reasonable to assume that, absent a prisoners' dilemma-like structure, agreement shocks are likely to be handled through some other form of flexibility since no state fears the "sucker's payoff" (i.e., the result of cooperating while others defect) and *there is nothing to be gained by defecting temporarily while one's partner cooperates.* Many of the agreements characterized by underlying Uncertainty about the State of the World but not Enforcement problems tend to be those in which "apples are traded for oranges." For instance, the set of bilateral international agreements put in place to implement the United States' International Security Assistance and Arms Export Control Act of 1976 fits this pattern, in which the United States provides military aid to another state. While political shocks might affect the desirability to the United States of providing aid, the situation does not resemble a prisoners' dilemma. A similar dynamic operates in the bilateral agreements stemming from the United States' Agricultural Trade Development and Assistance Act.[14]

This reasoning suggests the following hypothesis:

(H5-1) Other things equal, agreements that are characterized by an underlying Enforcement problem *and* Uncertainty about the State of the World are more likely to include escape clauses than those not characterized by the interaction of these two cooperation problems.

Bringing the importance of domestic institutions into the picture, Baccini (2010) suggests an interesting extension of the COIL

[14] Certain exchange rate agreements are also characterized by Uncertainty about the State of the World but not by Enforcement problems.

theoretical framework. Baccini examines flexibility measures in EU trade agreements. Starting from the premise that uncertainty should lead to the incorporation of flexibility arrangements, Baccini acknowledges that flexibility measures may also present an opportunity to suspend obligations intentionally by exploiting information asymmetries: Claiming exceptional domestic circumstances, a government can try to obtain more favorable terms in an agreement by invoking escape clauses. Foreseeing this, governments will be reluctant to include flexibility arrangements in their agreements when it is difficult to gather information on the domestic politics of the other parties to an agreement. Hence according to Baccini's logic, domestic transparency would be an important determinant of the decision to include flexibility measures. Given that democracies are more transparent than non-democracies, Baccini's work suggests another variable affecting the inclusion of escape clauses, leading to an additional hypothesis:

(H5-2) Other things equal, agreements whose members are characterized on average by a high level of Democracy are more likely to include escape clauses than those whose members are characterized on average by a low level of democracy.

Empirical testing

The first column of Table 5.3 shows the results from a model that includes Uncertainty about the State of the World, Enforcement problems, and their interaction in addition to issue area indicator variables. In such a model with an interaction term, the coefficient estimates themselves cannot be interpreted as straightforwardly as in a model without an interaction. Effects can be calculated, however, and based on those calculations, the effect of Uncertainty about the State of the World is positive and statistically significant in the presence of Enforcement problems ($p = 0.022$), and similarly, the effect of Enforcement problems is positive and statistically significant in the presence of Uncertainty about the State of the World ($p = 0.000$). Thus H5-1 is strongly supported by the data. Enforcement problems have no significant effect in the absence of Uncertainty about the State of the World. More interesting, Uncertainty about the State of the World has a negative, significant effect in the absence of Enforcement problems. Thus agreements like those described earlier (i.e., bilateral

Table 5.3 *Presence of an escape clause*

	COIL model without Polity	COIL model with Polity
Enforcement problem	0.53	0.60
	(0.52)	(0.52)
Uncertainty State of the World	−0.90*	−0.87*
	(0.51)	(0.51)
Uncertainty State of the World	2.11***	2.04***
x Enforcement problem	(0.65)	(0.65)
Polity		0.02
		(0.03)
Economics	0.09	0.04
	(0.39)	(0.39)
Environment	−1.65***	−1.73***
	(0.54)	(0.55)
Security	−0.69	−0.74
	(0.49)	(0.47)
Constant	−1.22***	−1.33***
	(0.33)	(0.35)
N	234	234

Note: Probit results, robust standard errors in parentheses.
*** *significant at 1 percent;* ** *significant at 5 percent;* * *significant at 10 percent*
Uncertainty State of the World + Uncertainty State of the World × Enforcement problem = 1.21, p-value 0.02, Enforcement problem + Uncertainty State of the World × Enforcement problem = 2.64, p-value 0.00. I use the model in the first column to calculate the estimates.

agreements that trade apples for oranges) are employing other flexibility mechanisms, but not escape clauses. These results are quite consistent with the findings in Chapter 4 on duration and renegotiation provisions.

Figures 5.1 and 5.2 illustrate that the average marginal effects of Enforcement problems are small and statistically insignificant in the absence of Uncertainty about the State of the World, but substantively large and statistically significant in the presence of Uncertainty about the State of the World: In the presence of Uncertainty about the State of World, an agreement with an underlying Enforcement problem is about 54 percentage points more likely to have an escape clause

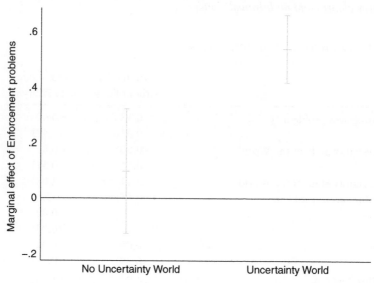

Figure 5.1 Average marginal effects of enforcement problem on the presence of an escape clause conditional on uncertainty about the state of the world

Note: Average marginal effects with 95 percent confidence intervals of Enforcement problem conditional on Uncertainty about the State of the World. Based on results in the first column of Table 5.3.

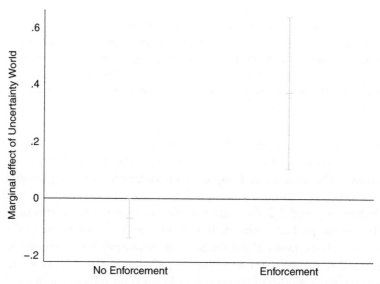

Figure 5.2 Average marginal effects of uncertainty about the state of the world on the presence of an escape clause conditional on enforcement problem

Note: Average marginal effects with 95 percent confidence intervals of Uncertainty about the State of the World conditional on Enforcement problem. Based on results in the first column of Table 5.3.

than an agreement without an underlying Enforcement problem (Figure 5.1). Likewise, in the presence of an Enforcement problem, an agreement characterized by underlying Uncertainty about the State of the World is about 37 percentage points more likely to have an escape clause than an agreement without underlying Uncertainty about the State of the World (Figure 5.2).

The model with Enforcement problems and Uncertainty about the State of the World added interactively has an extremely good fit: The area under the ROC curve is 0.902; a model without predictive power would yield a score of 0.5 and a perfect fit would yield a score of 1.[15]

The second column of Table 5.3 shows the results of a model that includes the average of the participants' level of Democracy, measured using Polity scores.[16] This measure of Democracy is not significantly correlated with escape clauses. The coefficient is small and not statistically significant at conventional levels.[17] Thus H5-2 is not supported.

Tables 5.3 also illustrates that economics and security agreements are not significantly different from the excluded category of human rights, once one controls for the relevant cooperation problem. Environmental agreements, on the other hand, are significantly less likely to include escape clauses than human rights agreements.

These results strongly suggest that, in addition to the commonly talked about Uncertainty about the State of the World as a driver of flexibility mechanisms, underlying Enforcement problems are almost a necessary condition for states to incorporate the specific flexibility mechanism of an escape clause.

The nuanced design of escape clauses

The statistics displayed in Table 5.3 do not imply that agreements have less bite in the presence of Enforcement problems. If flexibility were incorporated into agreements for which there are underlying incentives to defect without some form of safeguard against using such flexibility

---

[15] The ROC compares the fraction of agreements with escape clauses that are (correctly) predicted to have escape clauses with the fraction of agreements without escape clauses that are (incorrectly) predicted to have them.

[16] See Appendix 2, fn. 1.

[17] Likewise, when interacting Polity with Uncertainty about the State of the World and Enforcement problems, the effect of Polity is insignificant.

Table 5.4 *Escape requires approval*
         (number of agreements)

Escape requires approval	Enforcement problem		
	No	Yes	Total
No	6	9	15
Yes	1	28	29
Total	7	37	44

Table 5.5 *Escape requires proof of extraordinary circumstances*
         (number of agreements)

States required to prove extraordinary circumstances	Enforcement problem		
	No	Yes	Total
No	6	9	15
Yes	1	28	29
Total	7	37	44

opportunistically, we would indeed be in the world contemplated by Guzman (2008). Nonetheless, as Tables 5.4 and 5.5 reveal, although escape clauses are more frequent in the presence of Enforcement problems, their usage is also subject to more caveats and regulations.

Table 5.4 shows that, in the overwhelming majority of agreements with Enforcement problems, *escape requires approval* either *ex ante* or *ex post*. This approval often has to be granted by pre-existing bodies. By contrast, only one of the agreements without an underlying Enforcement problem requires approval for escape.

Table 5.5 shows a very similar pattern: Agreements with Enforcement problems typically require evidence or *proof of "extraordinary circumstances"* for escape to be approved.[18] Such detailed sub-provisions limit the ability of states to invoke escape clauses and opportunistically reap the benefits of others' cooperation, which in

---

[18] Although Tables 5.4 and 5.5 look identical, the set of agreements composing each group is slightly different.

turn makes states more comfortable about cooperating in the first place.

BITs feature escape clauses that require *ex post* "approval" and part of the argument in front of the tribunals which determine the appropriate compensation is whether the action meets the threshold for serving the "public interest." In fact, sometimes the compensation paid for breach is less than what it would have been in the absence of the "public interest" justification. For instance, in *James v. United Kingdom* (1986), in which the applicants claimed that the Leasehold Reform Act of 1967 deprived them of ownership of their properties,[19] the European Court of Human Rights stated that "Legitimate objectives of 'public interest,' such as pursued in measures of economic reform or measures designed to achieve greater social justice, may call for less than reimbursement of the full market value."[20]

Getting a sense of how often the "public interest" defense for expropriation (whether direct or indirect) is used and sanctioned is not at all straightforward.[21] One cannot simply count cases because litigants behave strategically as they do in all kinds of adjudication or arbitration. In addition to the usual selection into arbitration, investors might bring one kind of claim to a tribunal and settle for an alternative kind of claim. Notwithstanding those caveats, in terms of the cold statistics with respect to ICSID, states win over one-third of the cases, investors win less than one-third, and the rest are settled, retracted, or annulled.[22] How many of these cases involve either direct or indirect expropriation is not public knowledge at this point in time. Of course,

---

[19] This action was characterized as expropriation by the European Court of Human Rights.

[20] European Court of Human Rights, *James and Others v. The United Kingdom*, no. 8793/79, para. 54, February 21, 1986. This particular case has been referred to in *Tecnicas Medioambientales Tecmed S.A, v. The United Mexican States*, ICSID Award Case No. ARB (AF)/00/2, para. 122, May 29, 2003.

[21] Much of this paragraph is based on a conversation with Krzysztof Pelc, July 22, 2015.

[22] These statistics stand in contrast to the assertion made by Sheffer (2011: 484) who states: "The threat of a multi-million dollar adverse arbitration decision pressures States to placate MNCs [multinational corporations], and this limits a State's ability to regulate, even in important human rights-related policy areas. For example, MNCs have claimed millions of dollars in damages under BITs for State regulations addressing an emergency financial crisis, refusing to grant a license for a toxic waste facility, and enacting affirmative action legislation."

at least some of these cases do involve expropriation and hence, for present purposes, the important thing is that the statistics imply that not *all* expropriation meets the criterion of public interest and that the centralized body that needs to give approval *ex post* is not just a rubber stamp.

In sum, these analyses illustrate how flexibility devices like escape clauses are nuanced so as to provide states with a means to escape while at the same time protecting the rest of the member states from opportunistic behavior. When the underlying cooperation problem is one resembling a prisoners' dilemma, escape clauses tend to require both approval and proof of extraordinary circumstances. Given how easy it is for democracies to hide particular practices, the transparency that Baccini argues is necessary for escape clauses to be useful comes from the escape clause mechanism itself: States are required to provide information that is then judged by a third party. These results are compatible with Pelc's (2009) study of the WTO safeguard clause, which requires states to provide proof to a body.

The escape clause analyses also indicate that although certain arguments popular in the literature (such as costly escape clauses or the relationship between this type of flexibility and overall domestic transparency) might apply to particular cases, these arguments very likely do *not* hold in the general population of international agreements in force.

Withdrawal provisions

Definitions and descriptive statistics

Withdrawal clauses are provisions that allow a state to nullify its membership in an agreement without violating the agreement's institutional framework.[23] In some agreements, withdrawal is referred to as denunciation. Upon withdrawal, the agreement is no longer legally binding on the withdrawing party. Thus a withdrawal clause is permanent and comprehensive, covering all member obligations.

Withdrawal clauses are thus very different from other flexibility provisions because cooperative institutions cease to exist in a bilateral setting (by far, the majority of cases) or are characterized by changes in membership in the multilateral setting. The latter can be quite

[23] This section draws from Koremenos and Nau (2010).

consequential: When North Korea withdrew from the NPT, the agreement remained intact, yet the implications of the membership change were serious.

I do not offer a theory of the presence or absence of withdrawal provisions here because such clauses are generally incorporated as a protection from shocks that alter a state's basic interest in cooperation. Predicting such changes in preferences is outside the scope of rational choice theory. Given that COIL explains behavior at the institutional design stage of the cooperative endeavor, an assumption of fixed preferences is both realistic and useful. Other theories may be more relevant in explaining how these preferences might change over a longer timeframe.[24] For my purposes, it is enough to say that these shocks seem to be much less prevalent than those that motivate limited duration provisions or escape clauses, but the risk imposed by shocks that alter basic interests is great.[25]

Still, there are two interesting, and as I argue later, important dimensions on which withdrawal clauses vary, and it is here the COIL framework is relevant:

- The length of the notice period (if any) that states are required to give before exiting a treaty (*notice period*)
- The length of time that has to elapse between treaty ratification and a state being completely freed of its obligations, which includes the notice period where one exists (*wait period*).

While the notice period is self-explanatory and easily measured, the wait period is a bit more complex. Some agreements specify a certain amount of time that member states must remain bound by the agreement before they are even allowed to give notice to withdraw.

---

[24] Thus, while I incorporate Norm Exportation into the COIL framework, fundamental changes in a state's interests in cooperation (in this case, from viewing a cooperative endeavor as a positive sum game to viewing it as a losing proposition) are more revolutionary than are the relatively incremental changes in norms that are the goal of many human rights, environmental, and disarmament agreements.

[25] The relationship between "bedrock" preferences, which are fundamentally stable, and constraints, which arise from the fact that the state is a composite actor, also provides insight. Koremenos (2005) argues that withdrawal clauses are used in the event of "bedrock" changes (which are quite rare), whereas escape clauses are used in the event of unchanged bedrock preferences but different domestic constraints.

In addition, while members are usually freed from their commitments on withdrawal, some agreements extend a state's commitments *beyond* the point of its withdrawal. BITs, for example, usually extend protections for investments that were made before notice of termination an additional number of years. The withdrawal wait period can thus include up to three distinct periods: first, any period that does not allow withdrawal; second, the withdrawal notice period; and third, the length of time that states are bound to an agreement's provisions beyond withdrawal. An agreement may include any or all of these periods. The minimum total amount of time between the entry into force of the agreement and a full release of member obligation is the withdrawal wait period.

Consider the 1982 Agreement on the Mutual Protection of Investments between Sweden and China. Article 9 states:

(1) This Agreement shall enter into force immediately upon signature.
(2) This agreement shall remain in force for a period of fifteen years and shall continue in force thereafter unless, after the expiry of the initial period of fourteen years, either Contracting State notifies in writing the other Contracting State of its intention to terminate this Agreement. The notice of termination shall become effective one year after it has been received by the other Contracting State.
(3) In respect of investments made prior to the date when the notice of termination of this Agreement becomes effective, the provisions of articles 1 through 8 shall remain in force for a further period of fifteen years from that date.

The agreement, therefore, has a *thirty-year* withdrawal wait period: a minimum of fourteen years initial duration plus a one-year withdrawal notice period plus a fifteen-year period of coverage of any investments made before notice of termination is given.

Some agreements, such as the 1945 Franco-Belgian Agreement on Passenger Traffic, include contingent wait periods. Article 7 states: "This agreement shall remain in force at least until the cessation of hostilities in Europe and thereafter may only be denounced with one month's notice." Thus, the agreement has a notice period of only one month, but the withdrawal wait period was contingent upon the end of the war in Europe.

Tables 5.6 through 5.8 present a first glance at the incidence of the variables of interest. With a random sample of 234 agreements, some

Table 5.6 *Withdrawal clauses by issue area*
(percentage of each issue area)

	Withdrawal clause	
Issue area	Yes (%)	No (%)
Economic	61	39
Environmental	79	21
Human rights	90	10
Security	64	36
Total	70	30

N = 234

Table 5.7 *Withdrawal clauses by sub-issue area*
(percentage of each sub-issue area)

	Withdrawal clause	
Sub-issue area	Yes (%)	No (%)
Agricultural[26]	63	37
Finance	42	58
Investment	83	17
Monetary	18	82
Environmental	79	21
Human rights	90	10
Disarmament	89	11
Security	58	42
Total	70	30

N = 234

interesting findings emerge. Overall, 70 percent of the agreements contain a withdrawal clause. Table 5.6 shows that the incidence of a withdrawal clause varies by issue area: human rights agreements almost always include them, whereas only 61 percent of economic agreements do so.

The sub-issue area variation displayed in Table 5.7 is more interesting. Agreements in the sub-issues of monetary matters (which are

[26] The unrounded numbers for agricultural commodity agreements are 62.5 and 37.5 percent.

Table 5.8 *Length of notice period*

Length of time specified, in months	Number of agreements
0	7
1	6
2	1
3	18
4	1
6	51
7	1
9	2
10	1
12	75
24	1
N	164

essentially exchange rate agreements) and finance are more likely not to include withdrawal clauses than to include them; the opposite holds for agricultural commodity and investment agreements. Likewise, disarmament agreements almost always feature the formal exit option, whereas security agreements do so just over half the time. It is interesting to note that many of the agreements in monetary matters, finance, and security are of a finite and short duration, perhaps precluding the need for exit clauses. In fact, the two design provisions of a finite duration and a withdrawal clause are significantly and negatively correlated, suggesting that states may not fear fundamental changes in preferences in the short term.

Table 5.8 illustrates the variation in the length of notice periods of the 164 agreements in the random sample that have withdrawal clauses. Notice periods range from less than one month to twenty-four months, with a twelve-month period being the one most frequently chosen. It is important to note that, although twelve months is indeed the most common period, well over half of the agreements codify a different notice period, thereby supplanting the VCLT, Article 56 (2) default rule. For instance, notice period lengths of three months and six months are also chosen quite often.

Table 5.9 *Length of wait period*

Length of wait period, in fractional years	Number of agreements
Contingent	7
1 year or less	77
1–5 years	20
5–10 years	15
10–20 years	22
20–40 years	23
Mean	7.24
Std. dev.	9.31
N	164

Finally, Table 5.9 illustrates the substantial variation in the withdrawal wait periods for those agreements that include them. While the most common wait period is one year or less, the majority of agreements specify a period of time greater than this, with a non-trivial number of agreements specifying 10–40 years.

In the next section, I explain how the specific design of withdrawal clauses should be understood as a rational response to two underlying cooperation problems, Enforcement problems and Commitment problems. As suggested in Chapter 2, a "quick withdrawal" could offer a strategic advantage to the withdrawing state. In game theory, this is equivalent to the high payoff a defecting state receives in a prisoners' dilemma-type game when others cooperate. Even though withdrawing is lawful and not equivalent to defecting in that sense (Helfer 2005), strategically, withdrawing has the same effect as defecting: The state that is no longer abiding by the terms of the agreement gains while the states left cooperating lose. States can solve this strategic problem with a withdrawal provision that includes a notice period. Moreover, longer notice periods level the playing field for all states, reducing fears that cooperating states would be taken advantage of, thereby eliminating one of the advantages to withdrawing.

I also argue that when states face domestic Commitment or time-inconsistency problems, that is, when tying their hands is in their self-interest in the long run but often politically difficult in the short or medium run, they write agreements that include withdrawal provisions with wait periods and this wait period is likely to be long. Such provisions help the state with the Commitment problem rise above its predicament and assure its partner states that it is indeed a credible collaborator in the cooperative bargain.

Thus, if withdrawal clauses are designed optimally, we will see them being used only in the infrequent case of changes in the bedrock preferences for the cooperative endeavor. We will not see them employed for a quick strategic advantage over other states or for tempting short-term gains at the expense of long-run commitments.

A theory of withdrawal clause design

Withdrawal clauses in theoretical perspective

The process of negotiating treaty provisions is costly. If we assume that the signatory parties are rational actors, it follows that withdrawal clauses must be beneficial, or they would not appear in agreements. However, because states are sovereign actors, and given that there exists no overarching centralized mechanism for the enforcement of international agreements as there is in the domestic context, states retain the ability to unilaterally (and illegally) defect from agreements they conclude. This suggests two interesting puzzles: First, why would states codify practices that are already enabled by the anarchic nature of the international system? Second, what can account for the wide variations in the design of exit clauses?

In his 2005 *Virginia Law Review* article entitled, "Exiting Treaties," Laurence Helfer answers the first question and makes an important contribution by highlighting the very different consequences for a state party that ensue from a unilateral and unlawful breach of treaty obligations relative to a public and lawful exit. First, noncompliance[27] does not "necessarily result in termination of the defaulting state's membership" (2005: 1614). In contrast, not only do withdrawing states lose voice, but they can also be excluded from the benefits that accrue from membership.[28] Second, a state that denounces a treaty in a lawful and

---

[27] As Helfer points out, "breaches are highly varied. They may affect only a single treaty article, a handful of obligations, or the entire treaty." The argument put forth holds regardless of the extent of the breach (2005: 1614).

[28] The ability to exclude a withdrawing partner from the benefits of a treaty depends on the type of goods that are generated by it. In the case of private or

public manner cannot be exposed to intra-treaty sanctions. Other signatories cannot use the treaty's enforcement mechanism to punish or encourage certain types of behavior on the part of the withdrawing state. Finally, Helfer argues that "[t]he choice to denounce, together with any explanation the state offers to justify its decision, may signal an intent to 'play by the rules' of future treaties as well. As a result, harm to the withdrawing state's reputation as a law abiding nation may be minimal" (2005: 1621).[29]

In sum, Helfer shows that the breach of treaty obligations and the complete withdrawal of a state yield different payoffs; the presence of an exit clause in a treaty alters the incentive structure that states face when they weigh the costs and benefits of cooperation versus defection. From this vantage point, Helfer criticizes the extant IR literature by arguing that it has largely neglected the exit option by forcing the real world into 2 × 2 games like the prisoners' dilemma. According to Helfer, future research should thus expand the range of available strategies for the players.[30] Analysts should also consider the interaction of problem structure and exit clauses. I answer that call in what follows.

Theoretical argument

As mentioned, the theoretical and empirical work presented next focuses on two dimensions of withdrawal clause variation: the incidence and length of the period (if any) that states are required to give before exiting a treaty (notice period), and the incidence and length

---

club goods, exclusion is possible; in the case of public goods, which are non-rival and non-excludable, it is impossible to prevent a state that exits from free-riding on the contributions of the members that remain. On the collective action problem that arises when actors attempt to coordinate for the production of public goods, see generally Olson 1965. On the related problem of managing shared resources, see Ostrom 1990.

[29] In his article, Helfer offers a more nuanced version of this general argument by highlighting the importance of three variables on the reputational consequences of exit: "(1) the frequency of denunciation and withdrawal; (2) the relationship between entering and exiting treaties; (3) the risks of opportunism in light of the pervasive uncertainty of international affairs" (2005: 1622).

[30] Helfer considers the potential implications of extending the range of options to three games but does not offer a serious game-theoretic treatment of the question (2005: 1631–36).

of time that has to elapse between treaty ratification and a state being completely freed of its obligations (wait period).

Notice period

There is tremendous variation in the length of the notice period that states are required to give before exiting a treaty. What explains the inclusion and length of the notice period? Following Rational Design and COIL, we can ask, what strategic underlying problems might cause states to want a longer notice period? If states were required to modify domestic policies as a treaty enters into force, they would likely have to change domestic policies again to adapt to the change in circumstances caused by the withdrawal of another state from the treaty. Agreements based on reciprocal behavior would require a change in domestic policy for all parties if one state withdrew from the agreement.[31] A notice period would allow signatory states to adjust their own policies to allow for the change prior to the withdrawal of an individual state. This period to adjust policies is particularly important when states face an Enforcement problem because, even if a cooperative arrangement makes everyone better off, some or all actors may prefer not to adhere to it because they can do better individually by cheating.

As Chapters 7 and 8 illustrate, agreements whose goal it is to solve underlying Enforcement problems may include institutional design features like rewards and punishments or dispute resolution provisions to try to change the short-term incentives of states to defect. Still, there remains the possibility that a sudden withdrawal could offer a strategic advantage to the withdrawing state, in the same way that a suprise attack offers an advantage to a state at war. It can be assumed that the withdrawing state knows that it wants to withdraw

---

[31] Arms control agreements between superpowers are examples of agreements designed on the principle of reciprocal behavior. For instance, in the Anti-ballistic Missile Treaty (UNTS Reg. No. 13446), both the United States and the Soviet Union expected that the treaty's provisions would be upheld by each other. Without reciprocity, the foundation of the treaty would have been undermined. In the multilateral case, in some issue areas like disarmament, one withdrawal can change the game for all remaining members, especially if the reason for withdrawal is an intention to use the weapon in question. Even in less sensitive issue areas like commodity agreements, one state's withdrawal could essentially cause the collapse of the quota system for all other members, leading them to want to change policies.

before it announces it. If it could withdraw immediately, it could have a strategic advantage by surprising other states with the announcement since other states would not have had time to adapt. In a sense, including a notice period levels the playing field for all states, reducing the fear that the remaining states would be taken advantage of and eliminating the advantage to withdrawing.[32]

For these reasons, I propose the following hypothesis:

(H5-3) Other things equal, agreements that are characterized by an underlying Enforcement problem are more likely to include notice periods than those not characterized by an underlying enforcement problem.

Should states choose to include a withdrawal notice period in their agreements, the same reasoning applies to the length of the notice period. When states fear a bad payoff from another state's withdrawal because of the underlying strategic structure of the environment in which they are cooperating, they will want greater warning time to be able to adjust their policies.

For these reasons, I propose the following hypothesis:

(H5-4) Other things equal, if the parties conclude an agreement with a notice period, those agreements that are characterized by an underlying Enforcement problem are more likely to feature longer notice periods than those not characterized by an underlying enforcement problem.

Indeed, such reasoning is illustrated in the discussion regarding the withdrawal provision of the 2002 Treaty on Strategic Offensive Reduction (the Moscow Treaty) concluded between US President George W. Bush and Russian President Vladimir Putin. In the subsequent Hearing before the Senate Committee on Foreign Relations on July 9, 2002, Senator Feingold criticized the treaty's withdrawal provision:

This treaty, the Moscow Treaty, contains troubling language that would allow either party to withdraw in exercising its national sovereignty with only 3 months written notice. It does not require that either party cite extraordinary circumstances that jeopardize its supreme national interests.

---

[32] The discussion about the "breakout period" during the 2015 negotiation over Iran's nuclear weapons capability illustrates this idea: Under some circumstances, one state's cessation of cooperation could have dire consequences for states still cooperating. The design of the resulting agreement, the Joint Comprehensive Plan of Action, precludes this problem. See *infra* Chapter 8, fn. 25.

It does not require that any reason for the withdrawal be given at all. This treaty required only 3 months notice in writing. Most arms control treaties require at least 6 months written notice, as did the ABM treaty.[33]

In the Hearing on July 23, 2002, Christopher E. Paine, Co-Director of the Nuclear Warhead Elimination and Non-proliferation Project of the Natural Resources Defense Council, agreed with Feingold's criticism and pointed to the unusual wording of the Moscow Treaty's withdrawal provision in his prepared statement:

> .... The treaty has an exceedingly permissive withdrawal clause.
> In place of the usual six months advance notice of withdrawal, and an accompanying required statement to the parties of the extraordinary events that have jeopardized its supreme national interests, we find that each party to the Moscow Treaty may "exercise its national sovereignty" and withdraw from the treaty upon three months written notice.[34]

Paine then very directly points to the opportunistic behavior that such a short withdrawal notice period would encourage if it became a precedent for arms control agreements: "This is a formulation that would no doubt play well in Iraq and North Korea."[35]

Withdrawal wait period

Another very important design element of some withdrawal provisions is the *withdrawal wait period*. Recall that a withdrawal wait period is the designated period before a member that wants to withdraw from the agreement is fully freed from its commitments under the agreement.

What kind of strategic problem might call for a withdrawal wait period in the first place or a longer withdrawal wait period conditional on having one? Consider Commitment or time-inconsistency problems. Negotiating, ratifying, and complying with international

---

[33] US Congress. Senate. Committee on Foreign Relations. *Treaty on Strategic Offensive Reduction: The Moscow Treaty.* 2002. 107th Congress, 2nd Session, July 9, 17, 23 and September 12, p. 34.

[34] Ibid., 175.

[35] Ibid., 175. These quotes also make clear that it is the underlying Enforcement problem that is causing the consternation regarding the short notice period. Neither North Korea nor Iraq nor the Soviet Union are characterized by, for instance, a domestic Commitment problem at this point regarding this issue; nor is there great Uncertainty about (their) Preferences. Rather, Senator Feingold and Co-director Paine are worried about the opportunistic defection that is the hallmark of a prisoners' dilemma and the lack of adequate protection from such defection given the short notice period.

agreements often imposes some heavy initial costs before longer-term benefits can be enjoyed. Domestic political pressures may be such that certain leaders will want to withdraw because of these short-term costs before long-term benefits are realized.

This tradeoff between short-term costs and long-term gains is not only a problem for states vis-à-vis other states, but is also often an issue within a signatory state. A forward-looking leader may want to sign an agreement that is unpopular with the domestic audience because of costly technological adjustment or some other kind of initial heavy investment, but that will reap substantial social welfare enhancing benefits in the long run. Alternatively, a state with high levels of turn-over among political leadership may want to strengthen its credibility. The problem posed by short-term losses and long-term gains is very typical of a Commitment problem: an actor's best plan for some future period is inconsistent over time.

Also, because an early withdrawal by one state reduces the expected payoffs to the remaining states in the agreement, who then may have paid too high a price for the reduced expected payoffs, under certain conditions *ex ante* states would want to prevent themselves collectively from withdrawing prematurely to avoid a net loss. This might especially be the case when states must make asset-specific investments and worry whether cooperation will continue long enough to reap the benefits.[36]

I therefore hypothesize that agreements characterized by underlying Commitment problems are more likely to have wait periods than those not characterized by such problems. All states will find it in their interest to include such a provision, whether they are tying their own hands or those of their partner(s) in cooperation who have the Commitment problem.

---

[36] In the coding of the underlying Commitment problem, it was assumed that these problems feature less in states with a long history of respecting the rule of law. Imagine a cooperative endeavor that alters the future in terms of the development of a certain weapons system relative to what it would have been in the absence of cooperation. Consider the point of view of Canada. Such cooperation is less risky with the United States as Canada's partner in cooperation than it is with Nigeria. This is so not because Nigeria's benefits from defecting while Canada cooperates are any higher than the United States' benefits would be if it were the one defecting while Canada cooperates; rather, it is so because the unknown future leader of Nigeria cannot be trusted to respect the commitment to the extent that the unknown future leader of the United States can be trusted. A longer wait period alleviates this domestic Commitment problem.

For these reasons, I propose the following hypothesis, very much in the spirit of the conjecture presented in Chapter 2, grounded in the Legalization introduction, [37] that tying hands is a way to solve domestic Commitment problems:

(H5-5) Other things equal, agreements that are characterized by an underlying Commitment problem are more likely to include withdrawal wait periods than those not characterized by an underlying commitment problem.

Should states choose to include a withdrawal wait period in their agreements, the same reasoning applies to the length of the period. When states fear their own or another state's premature withdrawal because of an underlying strategic structure that poses short-term incentives to stop cooperating, they will want to tie their hands for a longer period. For these reasons, I propose the following hypothesis:

(H5-6) Other things equal, if the parties conclude an agreement with a wait period, those agreements that are characterized by an underlying Commitment problem are more likely to feature longer wait periods than those not characterized by an underlying commitment problem.

Empirical testing

To test hypotheses H5-3 and H5-4 as well as H5-5 and H5-6, I use both Probit and Ordinary Least Squares (OLS) regression models. Probit enables us to examine whether the particular cooperation problems of Enforcement and Commitment make it more likely that states will include notice periods and wait periods, respectively. OLS regression enables us to determine the effect that these particular strategic problems have on the length of the notice and wait periods for those agreements that incorporate them. I also include indicator variables for the human rights, economic, and environmental issue areas (security is the excluded category).

Hypotheses H5-3 and H5-4 predict that the greater the strategic advantage to be gained by a sudden withdrawal (i.e., the presence of an underlying Enforcement problem), the more likely there is to be

[37] Goldstein et al. (2000b).

Table 5.10 *Explaining notice periods*

	Probit		OLS
	Coefficients	Marginal	Coefficients
Enforcement problem	1.62***	0.44***	2.00***
	(0.27)	(0.05)	(0.59)
Economics	–0.46*	–0.12*	1.99**
	(0.25)	(0.07)	(0.94)
Environment	0.31	0.08	2.37**
	(0.33)	(0.09)	(0.98)
Human rights	1.06***	0.28***	1.89*
	(0.35)	(0.09)	(1.06)
Constant	0.06		5.87***
	(0.21)		(0.87)
R-squared			0.12
N	234	234	157

Note: Robust standard errors in parentheses.

*** *significant at 1 percent;* ** *significant at 5 percent;* * *significant at 10 percent*

a notice period as well as a longer notice period. Table 5.10 shows the results of the Probit analysis, the average marginal effects of the Probit analysis, and results from the OLS regression.

These analyses provide strong support for hypothesis H5-3 and H5-4. Having an underlying Enforcement problem is significant for explaining the notice periods of withdrawal clauses.[38] As the middle column of Table 5.10 illustrates, having an underlying Enforcement problem increases the probability of having a notice period by over 40 percentage points.[39] In the OLS regression results, having an underlying Enforcement problem increases the length of the notice period by two months, which, given the range of withdrawal notice periods described earlier, is quite large. Moreover, all of these results are highly statistically significant.

---

[38] The area under the ROC for the probit model is 0.820.

[39] The average marginal effect measures the average change in the predicted probability of an event (in this case, the inclusion of a notice period) given the values of the explanatory variable (in this case, the presence of an underlying Enforcement problem).

Table 5.11 *Explaining wait periods*

	Probit		OLS
	Coefficients	Marginal	Coefficients
Commitment problem	1.13***	0.35***	9.64***
	(0.29)	(0.07)	(1.70)
Economics	−0.59**	−0.18**	8.48***
	(0.25)	(0.07)	(1.73)
Environment	0.46	0.14	3.22***
	(0.29)	(0.09)	(0.90)
Human rights	0.64*	0.20*	−0.48
	(0.35)	(0.10)	(1.24)
Constant	0.34*		0.73
	(0.19)		(0.48)
R-squared			0.56
N	234	234	151

Note: Robust standard errors in parentheses.

*** *significant at 1 percent;* ** *significant at 5 percent;* * *significant at 10 percent*

Turning to withdrawal wait periods, I predict that agreements characterized by underlying Commitment problems are more likely to include a wait period than agreements that are not. Similarly, the short-term losses and long-term gains dynamic should increase the length of wait periods for those agreements that incorporate them. Table 5.11 illustrates the results of the Probit and OLS analyses.

These analyses provide strong support for hypothesis H5-5 and H5-6. As the first column in Table 5.11 illustrates, agreements that are characterized by an underlying Commitment problem are more likely to include a wait period.[40] In fact, the average marginal effects column indicates that an underlying Commitment problem increases the probability of having a wait period by 35 percentage points. Moreover, when looking at the length of wait periods, having a Commitment problem plays a very large substantive role in determining the length of the period. Having a Commitment problem increases the length of the wait period by almost ten years, all else held constant. All the effects are highly statistically significant as well.

[40] The area under the ROC for the probit model is 0.767.

Enforcement problems lead to a greater incidence of and longer notice periods, whereas Commitment problems lead to a greater incidence of and longer wait periods. Thus even the details of the final clauses are designed in ways to promote the incidence and robustness of cooperation.

Conclusion

Compared with finite duration or withdrawal provisions, escape clauses are incorporated far less often in international agreements. The data presented here stand in sharp contrast to the broad statements scholars focusing on the WTO tend to make. For instance, Pelc's otherwise excellent article begins with the statement, "Escape clauses are a regular feature of international agreements" (2009: 349). Still, the incidence of escape clauses is far from trivial, and their use in the WTO and in other agreements substantiates their importance. Perhaps more important, when they are incorporated, escape clauses are designed in ways that encourage states to join cooperative endeavors while at the same time ensuring states that they can escape when circumstances warrant it and that their partners will escape *only* when circumstances warrant it. Conversely, when incentives to act opportunistically are absent, provisions for approval and proof are far less likely to be incorporated.

Overall, these results square well with Kucik and Reinhardt's (2008) study of the WTO, which finds that flexibility provisions, like escape clauses, promote cooperation. Kucik and Reinhardt offer the most sophisticated evidence to date that escape-like clauses affect both the depth and the breadth of cooperation in the WTO in a positive direction. States are more willing to join the WTO and to make deeper concessions when they possess or establish domestic anti-dumping mechanisms – mechanisms that allow states to protect vulnerable domestic industries by escaping their WTO commitments and imposing anti-dumping duties on imports. While Koremenos' (2001) case study of the NPT suggests that, without the flexibility of the finite duration, critical states would not have joined that regime, Kucik and Reinhardt are able to leverage their research design to find scientific evidence of this dynamic across a large set of states in a particularly important institution. Although the mechanism they zero in on seems more like an institutionalized tit-for-tat reciprocity-enhancing device than a typical escape clause (especially given the WTO has a safeguard clause which is certainly an escape clause and is used often), they argue that the anti-dumping mechanism works as a flexibility device.

Even though withdrawal clauses are incorporated in the majority of agreements in the COIL sample, their use is far less frequent. It is tempting to draw immediate conclusions about the nonuse of provisions and argue that they have no effect in promoting international cooperation.

What the COIL framework calls attention to is the importance of the underlying model in predicting whether the design provision in question will be used *on or only off the equilibrium path* (see also Drezner 2003 and Thompson 2009). That is, the game-theoretic framework takes account of players' beliefs about what will happen in each potential stage of the game, even stages never reached in reality. These beliefs, in turn, affect states choices. The example from deterrence theory elaborated at the end of Chapter 2 is apt.

The same logic holds for many international law provisions. As stated in Chapter 2, if the design provision is a renegotiation provision, put in place at least in part to solve uncertainty about future bargaining power, we would indeed expect states to renegotiate the agreement – that is, to see the agreement provision employed. But if the design provision is a withdrawal clause, *its very incorporation into the agreement might make withdrawal less likely* since optimally designed withdrawal notice and wait periods preclude opportunistic withdrawal.

The data confirm that withdrawal notice periods are more likely to be incorporated into agreements with underlying Enforcement problems; the data also confirm that notice periods are longer in agreements with underlying Enforcement Problems relative to other agreements. States contemplating withdrawal, not because of foundational changes in their interests in the cooperative endeavor, but because they want the strategic advantage that comes from ceasing to cooperate while others continue cooperating, need only look down the game tree, so to speak, and see that their withdrawal will be matched by a complete unraveling of the cooperative endeavor as other states withdraw as well. They will thus be deterred from withdrawing.

This chapter highlights how two particular kinds of flexibility measures, escape clauses and withdrawal clauses, might enhance commitment. States are able to make commitments through international law in the face of uncertainty by building flexibility into their agreements, thereby making them politically palatable; at the same time, through sub-provisions like approval provisions or notice periods, states guard against the opportunistic use of these flexibility devices.

6 | *(Im)precision and reservations*

[T]he United States has attached to each of its ratifications a "package" of reservations, understandings and declarations (RUDs) ... As a result of those qualifications of its adherence, U.S. ratification has been described as specious, meretricious, [and] hypocritical [and confirmation] that United States adherence remains essentially empty.

(Henkin 1995b: 341, 346)

This popularity [of the ICCPR and CEDAW] ... has had a price: many of the ratifications have been accompanied by reservations that significantly reduce and in some cases effectively eliminate any obligations being assumed by the ratifying state.

(Schabas 1997: 110)

This chapter considers two additional forms of flexibility: *imprecision* in the language used to describe an agreement's substantive terms and *reservations* added to agreements that allow states to opt-out of certain provisions.[1] The COIL sample displays great variation on both of these dimensions.

In fact, the variation at first glance appears to be issue-area driven, with 32 percent of the human rights agreements having reservations attached to them at the time of entry into force as opposed to only 1 percent of the economics agreements. Moreover, only 2 percent of the economics sample can be characterized by very or somewhat vague language, whereas almost 40 percent of the human rights sample can. Do these descriptive statistics imply that human rights agreements are far less serious forms of international cooperation than are economics agreements, or even that human rights agreements are just scraps of

---

[1] Much of this chapter draws directly from Koremenos, Barbara and Mihwa Hong. 2013. "Explaining Away the Human Rights Dummy." Presented at New York University Law School, Hauser Colloquium, New York, New York, November 14, 2013.

paper or meaningless agreements, perhaps meant to placate an interest group, as some scholars like to argue?

In this chapter, I challenge the quotes that open this chapter, both of which engage the issue area of human rights, by providing a theoretical explanation for imprecision and reservations based on the underlying cooperation problems and the number of states involved in the cooperative endeavor. In doing so, not only can these two flexibility devices be understood as rational choices by states whose goal is indeed to cooperate, but the issue area of human rights loses much if not all of its explanatory power. Put differently, the design of human rights agreements can be explained within COIL's general theoretical framework.[2]

As in Chapter 5's analysis of escape clauses, interactions among the cooperation problems are also featured. Specifically, I refine the conditions under which flexibility can accommodate Distribution problems as the Rational Design conjecture *Flexibility increases with the severity of the Distribution problem* predicts. I find these particular kinds of flexibility mechanisms can help states solve their Distribution problems as long as these Distribution problems are *not* interacted with Coordination problems. Alternatively, one could say that Coordination problems require more rigidity and less flexibility, whether they interact with Distribution problems or not. I examine hypotheses about the rational design of agreements with particular combinations of these cooperation problems using the COIL data set. The empirical results support my expectations. I conclude the chapter by highlighting certain state behavior *after* the design stage. The behavior described is consistent with the underlying assumption that these kinds of flexibility mechanisms are used initially to help solve underlying Distribution problems.

Definition and descriptive statistics

In the COIL data set, the *precision* variable captures the degree of precision surrounding the main prescriptions, proscriptions, and/or authorizations embodied in an international agreement. The precision variable can take on four values, from very vague to very precise.

---

[2] Axelrod and Keohane (1985: 227) make a similar argument about economic and security cooperation being understood within the same framework.

An agreement's degree of *precision* or *ambiguity* refers to the exactness or vagueness of its prescribed, proscribed, and authorized behaviors. Precision is often reflected in clearly stated "shall/shall nots" as well as in the amount of detail accorded to each behavior. Ambiguity, in contrast, refers to how much doubt exists about the way in which the behaviors are to be executed. The main question coders are trained to answer when coding this variable is, "How easy or difficult would it be to tell if an actor is in compliance with the agreement?" The more precise the agreement, the easier it is to say, "Yes, that is compliance" or "No, that is not compliance." In other words, how clearly is the line drawn between acceptable and unacceptable behavior under the agreement? Coders are asked to decipher the degree of precision of the main prescriptions and proscriptions of an agreement on a case-by-case or individual level; coders then use that information when interpreting the overall precision of the agreement. The latter data on overall precision are used in the descriptive statistics and analyses later in the chapter.

Easily quantifiable behaviors, like those that dictate compliance with quotas, are usually very precise. For example, "Exporting Members shall not exceed the annual and quarterly export quotas allocated to them" (International Coffee Agreement of 1962, Article 36 [2]); the quotas are unambiguously set forth in an appendix. As another example, the 1964 Agreement for Financing Certain Educational Exchange Programs between the United States and Ecuador creates a bilateral commission to administer a joint educational exchange program, funded by Ecuadorian payments for surplus US agricultural commodities. The agreement describes (1) the administrative mechanisms for the management of the program; (2) the types of expenses that can be covered by the program, like transportation and tuition; and (3) the funding mechanisms to support the program. Article 8, which describes the funding mechanism, is more than a page, includes both specific amounts and the exchange rates to be used, and discusses the interaction between the US State Department and the US Treasury.

Agreements that cover a broader range of behavior, like forbidding actions of a military nature, are usually only somewhat precise. For example, Article 1 (1) of the Antarctic Treaty states: "There shall be prohibited, inter alia, any measures of a military nature, such as the establishment of military bases and fortifications, the carrying out of

military maneuvers, as well as the testing of any type of weapons." This
article is somewhat precise because it prohibits the testing of any
weapons and begins to define "military nature" as the establishment
of military bases and the testing of weapons; however, these terms do
not constitute an exhaustive list.

Generally stated behaviors, like those in many human rights
treaties, are vague. The African Charter for Human and Peoples'
Rights (UNTS Reg. No. 26363) contains articles that are both
somewhat and very vague. Article 9 (2), stating "Every individual
shall have the right to express and disseminate his opinions within
the law," is somewhat vague. Although the article specifies
a specific human right, the right to express and disseminate opinions, the boundaries of the term "opinion" are themselves quite
vague. Article 24, which declares, "All peoples shall have the right
to a general and satisfactory environment favorable to their
development," is very vague, as terms like "environment" and
"development" are never defined.

In coding such a variable for which no quantifiable guidelines have
been elaborated despite its prominence in both law and economics
and IR,[3] it is particularly important to use the same trained coders
who can identify the differences and similarities across a set of agreements based on their experience. The COIL project employed such
coders, and each agreement was carefully read and coded by two
independent coders. Still, as a check on the coding of precision
(which, unlike variables such as duration and withdrawal provisions,
requires a judgment call), a third coder examined the entire set of
agreements and focused only on precision, which permitted greater
sensitivity to any coding inconsistencies.[4]

Table 6.1 displays the descriptive statistics on the variable of precision across issue areas. In addition to the stark difference between

[3] See, for example, Ehrlich and Posner (1974) and the recent literature on
Legalization by Goldstein et al. (2000b).
[4] Based on the work of the third coder, 15 percent of the agreements were changed.
Only one agreement was changed by two categories/numbers with the rest
changed by one category/number. Moreover, an international environmental law
specialist checked the agreements with which he was familiar. His coding was
almost exactly the same as the final COIL coding; in one case, he coded "very
vague," while COIL recorded "somewhat vague." Finally, an international
human rights law specialist checked the agreements with which he was familiar;
he agreed completely with the final COIL coding.

Table 6.1 *Precision by issue area*
		(percentage of each issue area)

Issue area	Very vague/ambiguous (%)	Somewhat vague/ambiguous (%)	Somewhat precise (%)	Very precise (%)
Economics	0	2	62	36
Environment	2	28	49	21
Human rights	7	32	46	15
Security	2	17	45	36
Total	2	15	53	29

N = 234

economics and human rights agreements, there is some additional interesting variation. Security agreements tend to be on the precise side of the spectrum, with less than 20 percent in the vague or very vague category and over a third characterized as very precise (equivalent to the economics issue area). Almost a third of environmental agreements are characterized by vagueness, with the majority of that issue area being in one of the two middle categories.

A *reservation* is "a unilateral statement, however phrased or named, made by a State, when signing, ratifying, accepting, approving or acceding to a treaty, whereby it purports to exclude or to modify the legal effect of certain provisions of the treaty in their application to that State."[5] The reservation variable used in this chapter captures whether any state added a *substantive* reservation to an agreement at the time the agreement was initially opened for signature.[6]

Curiously, reservations are not frequently prohibited. Table 6.2 displays by issue area how often agreements in the sample prohibit reservations. Because the International Labour Organization (ILO)

[5] VCLT Article 2 (1)(d).
[6] I am interested here only in substantive reservations because COIL's definition of a Distribution problem pertains to substantive treaty obligations. The theory presented in this chapter does not address issues of territorial applicability for states like the United Kingdom or whether a state accepts the jurisdiction of the ICJ – a topic explored in Chapter 7. Thus, I modify the reservation variable accordingly, excluding reservations regarding territoriality or the ICJ.

Table 6.2 *Prohibition of reservations by issue area*
(percentage of each issue area)

Issue area	Prohibited (%)	Not prohibited (%)
Economics	2	98
Environment	5	95
Human rights	20	80
Security	9	91
Total	7	93

N = 234

Table 6.3 *Number of reservations by issue area*
(percentage of each issue area)

Issue area	No reservation (%)	1–5 reservations (%)	6 or more reservations (%)
Economics	99	1	0
Environment	98	2	0
Human rights	68	20	12
Security	87	9	4
Total	91	6	3

N = 234

does prohibit reservations to all conventions negotiated under its auspices, the human rights issue area, which features several ILO conventions, stands out a bit on this dimension.

Table 6.3 lists the number of reservations by issue area in place at the time the agreement entered into force. Despite the prohibition of reservations in ILO conventions, the proportion of human rights agreements that had reservations added is strikingly large at 32 percent, with 12 percent of the human rights sample having had more than 6 reservations added. Again, it is tempting to argue, as many do, that this disproportionate number of reservations illustrates that at least some states are not serious about their human rights obligations and try, therefore, to lessen their commitments through reservations. While no other issue area comes close to having proportionally as many reservations attached to its agreements as human rights, 13 percent of security agreements had reservations attached.[7]

Theory: Explaining imprecision and reservations

One possible explanation for the "uniqueness" of human rights agreements displayed in Table 6.1, consistent with the argument that such agreements are intentionally weak, is that the less precise an agreement, the more variability in potential outcomes. As Chayes and Chayes (1995: 12) so bluntly state: "[S]tates, like other legal actors, take advantage of the indeterminacy of legal language to justify indulging their preferred course of action." Likewise, Simmons (2010: 277) notes, "precision reduces the plausible deniability of violation by narrowing the range of reasonable interpretations." Therefore, it could be argued that imprecision, by allowing so much variability in outcomes, results in what is in reality noncompliance being justified as compliance. (A similar argument can be made about reservations.) Of course, as the law and economics literature argues, imprecision usually leads to more delegation, and that delegation reduces somewhat the variance of potential outcomes;

[7] The full COIL sample is used in this chapter because I follow Neumayer (2007: 406) who includes certain nominal "understandings" and "declarations" in his measure of reservations to the extent that these understandings and declarations are equivalent to reservations as defined in VCLT Article 2 (1)(a). Whether reservations can be added to bilateral agreements is an open question. Edwards (1989) argues that reservations can be made to bilateral treaties as a matter of international law. He notes that the term "multilateral" was dropped from the heading to the reservation section of the VCLT, including Articles 19–23. Edwards also refutes the President of the Vienna Conference's statement during the last consideration of the reservation articles in the Plenary Session on April 30, 1969 by saying that its authority itself is not clear because the Drafting Committee did not reach consensus regarding the applicability of Articles 19–23 to bilateral treaties. He then points to actual state practice regarding reservations and bilateral agreements, most of which involve the United States. As Lauterpacht (1953: 124) states: "The subject of reservations to multilateral treaties is one of unusual – in fact baffling – complexity and it would serve no useful purpose to simplify artificially an inherently complex problem." In any event, understandings and declarations are often added to bilateral agreements. (See United Nations. International Law Commission. "Report on the Law of Treaties by Mr. H. Lauterpacht, Special Rapporteur." A/CN.4/63, 24 March 1953. Available at http://legal.un.org/ilc/documentation/english/a_cn4_63.pdf [Last accessed June 11, 2015]).

hence it could be argued that compliance is still encouraged when a state knows it can be taken to court.[8]

Instead of being content simply to say, "well, human rights agreements are unique," I aim to unpack the black box of human rights in order to understand what it is that makes some human rights agreements less precise than other international agreements and much more likely to include reservations. I entertain the possibility that there may be another reason for the imprecision and reservations of some human rights agreements that is consistent with the argument that they are indeed meaningful. I exploit the COIL theoretical framework to understand if and why some human rights agreements are rationally designed to be imprecise and/or to incorporate reservations.

I focus on two cooperation problems in particular: Distribution problems and Coordination problems. I argue that, because human rights agreements are more likely than any other issue area to be characterized by Distribution problems *without* Coordination problems, large, heterogeneous groups of states with various cultures, ideologies, and institutional differences can solve their underlying Distribution problems over which norms should be articulated in human rights agreements through imprecise language and reservations. Imprecise language serves as a form of flexibility by allowing sufficient ambiguity in interpretation. Similarly, if a state has an objection to a particular human rights provision, it can add a reservation without completely undermining cooperation.

Underlying cooperation problems

Recall Table 3.3 from Chapter 3, presenting descriptive statistics regarding the cooperation problems underlying the agreements in the

---

[8] Koremenos (see fn. 1, Introduction to Part II) indeed finds a statistically significant inverse relationship between the precision of an agreement and whether it delegates dispute resolution authority to an international body. Also, Morrow (2007: 567) in his study of compliance with Laws of War agreements finds that "legal clarity matters when legal obligation does not exist, but it has no statistically discernible effect when both sides have ratified the relevant treaty. The difference in reciprocity across levels of legal clarity when at least one side has not ratified the relevant treaty is statistically significant at more than the .001 level, but it is insignificant and in the wrong direction when both sides have ratified the relevant treaty."

COIL random sample. Here I want to focus on two cooperation problems, Distribution and Coordination.

Human rights agreements are very likely to be characterized by Distribution problems because they regulate how a state treats its own citizens within its territory, which has long been the exclusive jurisdiction of the sovereign state. Distribution problems exist when there are multiple cooperative solutions possible and actors have different preferences among them. When sitting down at the table to negotiate human rights agreements, states can disagree about a number of things, chiefly, what rights should be included and how those rights should be defined. This Distribution problem may arise from ideological differences, from cultural differences, from domestic institutional differences, or from the gap between a state's current human rights practice and the proposed standard. (These are elaborated later.) Still, agreements in other issue areas are also characterized by Distribution problems.

Nevertheless, by examining the underlying cooperation problems that characterize human rights agreements, we discover a unique combination of cooperation problems, so to speak, that does distinguish many, but not all, human rights agreements from agreements in other issue areas. Unlike the classic issue areas for which there are Distribution problems, that is, territory or technical standards, the issue area of human rights does not pose a strict Coordination problem. Rather, in human rights agreements, we find the frequent occurrence of an underlying Distribution problem without an underlying Coordination problem. What does this look like in practice? In what follows, I elaborate the four possible combinations of Distribution and Coordination problems.

Interacting cooperation problems: distribution and coordination

Both distribution and coordination

In many issue areas where there is a Distribution problem, there is also a Coordination problem in which complete coordination is necessary, for example, one clear boundary or one clear technical standard. Consider the example of export quotas in a commodity agreement. When states wanted to cooperate to stabilize and raise the price of coffee, they needed to coordinate exactly on a supply of coffee to ensure that the price would be what it was intended to be. Oversupply by one state would cause the price to change, and defections in such strategic situations can cause the entire agreement to fail. This was the case for many attempts at coffee cooperation before the 1962 International Coffee Agreement (see Bates 1997; Koremenos 2002). Not only is complete coordination necessary or the parties will be worse off, but states also have to divide the coffee market – the epitome of a Distribution problem. Thus commodity agreements like the set of coffee agreements and the cooperation surrounding OPEC's production quotas exemplify the pairing of underlying Distribution and Coordination problems. Consider the famous Battle of the Sexes game. Coordinating on an exact movie (or ballet) is not mentioned as a necessary condition. But most would agree that, in such a situation, coordinating on different movies is worse than no cooperation at all!

Coordination but no distribution
Some issues are characterized by Coordination problems without Distribution problems. When the issue at stake is how to cooperate against frontier forest fires, states must completely coordinate their responses and have in place the directions and infrastructure to do so. One state would fight a raging fire very differently depending on whether it would be going it alone or coordinating with another state using some joint method known in advance. However, the Distribution problem in this issue is quite low – it is really not about who gets how much. Bilateral efforts to prevent double taxation also fit this category. States must coordinate their tax laws and information exchange in order to ensure the successful implementation of such agreements, which are aimed at both preventing tax evasion and limiting double taxation. Finally, bilateral efforts aimed at protecting classified information must first coordinate on what is considered classified and who exactly has access to such information.

Neither distribution nor coordination
Some cooperative endeavors have Neither Distribution nor Coordination problems underlying them, like those that encourage sharing of scientific information. For example, there is a set of agreements in the COIL sample for which Germany sends scientists to developing countries to help them with issues like plant protection.

Distribution but no coordination

Finally, some agreements have Distribution problems without Coordination problems. As I elaborate with spatial models later, in many human rights agreements, each state wants to see its preferred norm be the one that is codified or exported to other states. But if State B embodies a slightly different norm than the one promulgated by State A, State A can keep its norm and is not worse off than it would be without an agreement.

Descriptive statistics

Table 6.4 presents descriptive statistics on the four possible combinations across the four issue areas. Human rights agreements are most likely to be characterized by Distribution but No Coordination problems (51 percent). I describe how this combination manifests itself in human rights agreements in what follows. Interestingly, human rights agreements are hardly ever characterized by underlying Coordination problems.

Security agreements more than any other issue area are characterized by No Distribution but Coordination problems (40 percent), with the bilateral agreements regarding classified information mentioned earlier as the most common example of this combination. The next largest category for security agreements is No Distribution and No Coordination. The large number of bilateral security agreements between the United States and states like Luxembourg for which the United States

Table 6.4 *Combinations of distribution/coordination problems by issue area (percentage of each issue area)*

Issue area	Distribution, No Coordination (%)	No Distribution, Coordination (%)	Distribution, Coordination (%)	No Distribution, No Coordination (%)
Economics	0	12	18	70
Environment	14	9	5	72
Human rights	51	0	5	44
Security	21	40	4	34
Total	16	15	11	59

N = 234

provides military aid in the form of things like military equipment never meet the threshold for either Distribution or Coordination problems. These sort of agreements stand in sharp contrast to the very few security agreements, like the Treaty on Collective Security, which are characterized by both problems. The Distribution problem underlying this treaty stems from the initial lack of cohesion of the Commonwealth of Independent States with respect to issues like joint military command and distribution of forces, with some states not even sure they were in favor of a unified military force. This particular alliance thus serves as both a commitment-signaling device and a coordination device.

The issue area of the environment is the most likely to be characterized by neither Distribution nor Coordination. Agreements like those for plant protection or those for which a state like Germany or Denmark assists a less-developed state in protecting its environment make up this group.

Economics agreements are the most likely to address both Coordination and Distribution problems (18 percent), which is more than three times as much as any other issue area. However, for many readers, this statistic will seem rather low given the conventional wisdom that all economic agreements involve wrangling over scarce resources. The COIL data show otherwise. Recall from Chapter 3 that almost all of these cooperation problems underlie, at least in low levels, most of the agreements in the sample (or any effort at international cooperation for that matter). Still, the problem has to be judged to be high for it to be coded as characterizing the environment in which the agreement is being negotiated. Thus the bilateral agricultural commodity agreements in which the United States essentially gives foreign aid to another state by implementing the US Agricultural Trade Development and Assistance Act are not coded as having underlying Distribution problems. Neither is the 1994 International Coffee Agreement because, at that point in coffee cooperation, no attempt was made to establish quotas. Even BITs do not meet the threshold.[9]

---

[9] Such agreements are, however, characterized by underlying Commitment problems, Enforcement problems, and Uncertainty about the State of the World. These cooperation problems are present at sufficiently high levels to be considered major problems for states attempting cooperation in this sub-issue area.

A model of distribution but no coordination

I now elaborate what this combination of Distribution but No Coordination looks like in a typical human rights agreement negotiation. Consider the negotiation of a human rights agreement as a strategic interaction between two states, State 1 and State 2, which comprise the subcommittee drafting the agreement. These two states have asymmetric preferences over a particular substantive human rights norm yet they believe in the importance of human rights standards generally. This common interest sets them apart from certain other states that have no interest in setting and spreading human rights standards. It is assumed that each state prefers its own norm to be reflected in the final draft. It is also assumed that both desire to raise the bar of human rights above some threshold that might be held by third states. While States 1 and 2 are the drafters, they hope and expect other states to become members of the agreement, and they are assumed to hold so much of the power that the negotiation game is really between them alone.

Suppose the standard in question is women's rights and the scale of this norm ranges from 1 to 10. The norm equals 1 when women are considered not equal to men in any way and 10 when women are not only considered equal in every way, but also all national laws and pay rates reflect this standard. State 1 has norm 8, including non-discrimination against women in the workplace enforced by a state agency, while State 2 has a norm 6, including non-discrimination against women in the workplace. Three strategies are equally possible for each state: (1) proposing a standard based on its own norm, (2) proposing a standard based on the other's norm due to the process of persuasion, and (3) walking away from the negotiation. Consider the following scenario: If either state needs to change its standard, it prefers no agreement at all to an agreement with a standard different from its own. Specifically, State 2 would rather not be a part of any agreement at all than change (raise) its standard to norm 8; likewise, State 1 would prefer no agreement to changing (lowering) its standard to norm 6. Still, although both states strongly prefer to remain with their own specific norms, as long as they are not pressured to switch to the other's standard and thereby pay the implementation or other costs of such a change, they accept that the other party will remain regulated by its own norm. They do prefer an improved international human rights standard on women's rights to no agreement at all.

The outcome just described can be achieved through the design provision of vague language, a form of flexibility. The language of the treaty could read, "Women will not be discriminated against in the workplace, and this right shall be enforced by state agencies when possible given constitutional or other constraints," or "non-discrimination in the workplace enforced by state agencies, as long as the new policies do not run counter to national laws." Employing such language, human rights agreements accommodate states with asymmetric preferences over the specifics of substantive human rights standards but with a common desire to raise standards for third parties. Importantly to States 1 and 2 (represented by Group A in Figure 6.1), states whose behavior reflects norms that fall below that which can be interpreted through the vague language (represented by Group B in Figure 6.1), are forced to change at least somewhat if they want to be in compliance with the agreement.

The negotiation of the American Convention on Human Rights, one of the agreements in the sample, is indicative of this logic. This agreement, created by the OAS, contains a right to life provision, and this provision was the subject of great negotiation among the states, especially because 12 out of the 23 OAS member states permitted abortion in certain cases.[10] The Uruguayan draft article read, "Every person has the right to have his life respected. This right shall be protected by law, from the moment of conception. No one shall be arbitrarily deprived of his life."[11] The Chilean draft was similar in spirit.[12] As Forbes argues, "The members not only had heterogeneous interests on this issue, but these interests were institutionalized, making compromise much more difficult than before. If the right to life provision were adopted with this wording, these states would be obligated to change their domestic laws."[13] Because of the debate, the Inter-American Commission on Human Rights added the

---

[10] Organization of American States. *Annual Report of the Inter-American Commission on Human Rights 1980-1981*. Resolution 23/81, Case 2141 (United States). OAE/SER.L/V/II.54 (doc. 9 rev. 1) original: Spanish. 16 October 1981. Available at http://www.cidh.org/annualrep/80.81eng/US A2141.htm [Last accessed December 10, 2015].

[11] *Anuario Interamericano de Derechos Humanos 1968*. Washington DC: Gen. Secretariat of the OAS 1973: 298 [unofficial translation].

[12] Ibid., 280.

[13] Forbes, Amber. 2006. "Institutionalizing the Right to Life in the Americans' Unpublished student paper. University of Michigan: 4. This entire paragraph draws on the superb research of Amber Forbes.

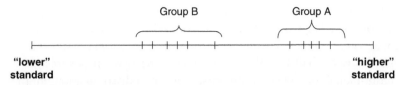

Figure 6.1 Vague language

phrase "in general" after the word "law" because it "sought to make this principle less strict."[14] Suffice it to say that in the end the wording "Every person has the right to have his life respected. This right shall be protected by law, in general, from the moment of conception. No one shall be arbitrarily deprived of his life" satisfied the abortion-permitting Brazil, Dominican Republic, and United States as well as the anti-abortion block that included Ecuador, Chile, and Uruguay. That less precise text became the final text of Article 4 (1).

Imagine instead that the issue being negotiated is resource exploitation or water rights, and the ideal points in Figure 6.1 pertain to various territorial boundary lines. Such issues combine underlying Coordination and Distribution problems. An agreement that somehow encompassed multiple ideal points through vague language like "The border will be somewhere between 82° 43' and 83° 44' W" would not make states feel comfortable in investing in resource exploitation given the absence of clarity with respect to property rights. Precision is necessary to solve Coordination problems with or without Distribution problems.

This logic, as illustrated in the spatial model, leads to the following hypothesis:

(H6-1) Other things equal, agreements that are characterized by an underlying Distribution but No Coordination problem are more likely to be imprecise than those characterized by Neither Distribution nor Coordination problems, whereas agreements characterized by underlying Coordination problems (with or without Distribution problems) are more likely to be precise than those not characterized by an underlying coordination problem.

In Ehrlich and Posner's (1974) analysis of the precision of law, a motivating factor is transaction costs minimization. Thus, one comparative static prediction emanating from their work is that, as the legislature grows in size, the transaction costs involved with

---

[14] See fn.11: 193.

Figure 6.2 Reservations

negotiating and formulating rules grow as well, and thus the law will be less precise. This reasoning leads to the following hypothesis:

(H6-2) Other things equal, as the Number of actors increases, the probability that the parties will choose precise agreements decreases.

While imprecision can solve the Distribution problem facing actors when their ideal points are at least relatively near each other, what happens when some states have preferences that are truly outliers, not necessarily on the overall agreement (if such were the case, they would generally not be at the negotiation table at all) but on particular provisions? Consider Figure 6.2, which illustrates a set of preferences on the proposed adoption provision in the CRC. Although some imprecision in language could probably resolve the Distribution problem regarding this provision for states in Group A, states in Group B have outlier ideal points. In situations with such a configuration of preferences, Group B states can add reservations to the agreement, specifically targeting the provision at issue. Reservations permit states to opt out of particular provisions while remaining as parties to the entire treaty. Indeed, this is what many states with entrenched alternatives to adoption did for this very convention.

In fact, the provision regarding adoption (Article 21) is the most reserved article in the entire CRC.[15] Canada entered a reservation to

---

[15] Nineteen states have lodged RUDs to Article 21: Argentina, Bangladesh, Brunei Darussalam, Canada, Egypt, Indonesia, Iran, Jordan, Kuwait, Maldives, Mauritania, Oman, the Republic of Korea, Saudi Arabia, Somalia, Spain, the Syrian Arab Republic, the United Arab Emirates, and Venezuela. (Over time, five of these states have withdrawn or partially withdrawn their RUDs.) For this illustrative example only, I count the number of RUDs added until January 10, 2016, not just those initially lodged when the treaty was open for signature. I include Iran, Mauritania, and Saudi Arabia, which lodged broad reservations regarding all articles contrary to Islamic law or moral conduct, given that Islamic law regarding adoption is quite clear and

this article in order to respect its indigenous groups' "alternative care" culture.[16] A large number of Islamic states also reserved Article 21 by referring to the incompatibility of adoption with Shari'a law. Cohen (1989) explains that it has long been argued in Islamic states that the inter-related extended family structure should be protected from the addition of an outsider. *Kafala*, which is like permanent foster care under which a child may legally and permanently live with a family but can neither use the family's name nor inherit from it, serves as an alternative instrument for taking care of abandoned or orphaned children in these states (Cohen 1989: 1451). Islamic states such as Oman and the United Arab Emirates could still commit to the CRC despite their different preferences regarding adoption by adding reservations to Article 21.[17] For example, the United Arab Emirates added a reservation to Article 21 that "since, given its commitment to the principles of Islamic law, the United Arab Emirates does not permit the system of adoption, it has reservations with respect to this article and does not deem it necesary [sic] to be bound by its provisions."[18] The US State Department notes that "there is a vast variance in the implications and observance of Shari'a law from country to country. Generally, however, Islamic family law does not allow for adoption, as that concept is understood in the United States."[19] This logic leads to the following hypothesis:

(H6-3) Other things equal, agreements that are characterized by an underlying Distribution but No Coordination problem are more likely to contain reservations than those not characterized by this combination of problems.

hence Article 21 is implicated. See http://treaties.un.org/Pages/ViewDetails .aspx?src=TREATY&mtdsg_no=IV-11&chapter=4&lang=en [Last accessed January 10, 2016].

[16] UNICEF. Innocenti Research Centre. 2007. "Law Reform and Implementation of the Convention of the Rights of the Child." Available at www.unicef-irc.org/pub lications/pdf/law_reform_crc_imp.pdf [Last accessed June 13, 2015], p. 10.

[17] Although Indonesia is not governed officially by Shari'a law, it is the most populous Muslim state in the world, and Shari'a law has great influence in certain regions like the Aceh province.

[18] See the following link to the OHCHR website for information about countries that made reservations to Article 21 of the CRC: http://indicators.ohchr.org [Last accessed July 11, 2015].

[19] US Department of State. Bureau of Consular Affairs. *FAQ: Adoption of Children from Countries in which Islamic Shari'a law is observed.* See https://travel.state.gov /content/adoptionsabroad/en/adoption-process/faqs/islamic-sharia%20law.html [Last accessed January 16, 2016].

Figure 6.3 Optional protocols

Finally, the design provision of optional protocols accommodates states whose norms exceed those which can be accommodated through vague language, often by allowing greater enforcement and monitoring of the standards incorporated in the substantive provisions and at times by adding additional standards. As Figure 6.3 demonstrates, Group A' states can be accommodated through this mechanism within the same international agreement. (Data limitations preclude testing any hypotheses about optional protocols.)

There are other scholars who argue that reservations are not detrimental to the legitimacy of human rights agreements. Their arguments are quite compelling, and many of them are captured in the spatial model of Figure 6.2. For instance, Neumayer (2007: 397) views reservations as a means to address diversity across states. By addressing this diversity, reservation provisions make broader participation possible. Put differently, by allowing a tailored exemption from a particular article to the extent that the exemption is not incompatible with the object and purpose of a treaty, states that would have otherwise stayed outside the treaty regime can participate (Goodman 2002; Harrison 2005; Helfer 2006; Miles and Posner;[20] Swaine 2006). Kearney and Powers (2011)[21] demonstrate that reservations allow states to accommodate domestic veto players (see Bradley and Goldsmith [2000] and Goodman [2002][22] for the US case). Furthermore, reservation

[20] Miles, Thomas J., and Eric A. Posner. 2008. "Which States Enter into Treaties, and Why?" *University of Chicago Law & Economics, Olin Working Paper* No. 420; *University of Chicago, Public Law Working Paper* No. 225. Available at SSRN: http://papers.ssrn.com/sol3/papers.cfm?abstract_id=1211177 [Last accessed June 24, 2015].

[21] Kearney, Patrick and Ryan M. Powers. 2011. "Veto Players and Conditional Commitment to U.N. Human Rights Agreements." Presented at the American Political Science Association 2011 Annual Meeting. Available at http://papers .ssrn.com/sol3/papers.cfm?abstract_id=1900266 [Last accessed June 23, 2015].

[22] Goodman (2002: 546) cites Kaufman (1990) to demonstrate that the US executive tends to "overcompensate in submitting its package of reservations to the Senate as a means of securing approval."

provisions also lead to deeper participation among states (Helfer 2006; Swaine 2006); states would draft much weaker treaties if reservations were harder to lodge.[23] Additionally, reservations are informative to non-reserving states aspiring to contract with reserving states (Swaine 2006). Reservations enable states to reveal their preferences and their domestic constraints, and thereby serve as a costly signal because they show a state's willingness "to subject its self-exemption to international scrutiny" (Swaine 2006: 338).

Some might be surprised by the kinds of states that take advantage of reservation provisions. Neumayer (2007) shows empirically that liberal democracies tend to add more reservations than any other regime type.[24] Relatively speaking, liberal democracies want to commit to only those treaty obligations with which they are able and willing to comply. On the other hand, non-democratic states that do not take international law seriously will not feel as compelled to add reservations (Goodman 2002: 551).[25] Drawing from Risse and Ropp (1999), Goodman (2002: 552) suggests that non-democratic states that do add reservations upon ratification signal that they begin to subscribe to "the prescriptive legitimacy of international rules" by "genuinely balancing competing goals."[26]

Reservations are reciprocal. That is, not only are obligations modified for the reserving state, the modifications apply to other state

---

[23] In *Reservations to Human Rights Treaties: Not an Absolute Evil ...*, Alain Pellet and Daniel Mueller reinforce Bruno Simma's argument in *From Bilateralism to Community Interest in International Law* (1994) that reservations to human rights treaties facilitate a wider acceptance of the core elements of the treaties and strengthen the global community interest. They acknowledge that opening up the rights of states to formulate reservations facilitates universal participation in treaties, though the freedom to formulate reservations needs to be limited.

[24] See, too, fn. 20.

[25] Miles and Posner also present a suggestive descriptive statistic in this regard. Based on their data set, "the average European country issues reservations in 44 percent of the multilateral treaties it joins, and the average Latin American country issues reservations in only 17 percent." See fn. 20: 11.

[26] Goodman (2002: 553) uses Chile's reservation to Article 2 of CAT as an example. According to Goodman, in response to the Committee against Torture's criticism of the validity of this reservation, the Chilean government explained that its reservation was formulated in order to reconcile domestic legislation with the obligations of CAT and that the next government could decide whether to abide by all the terms of CAT and thereby withdraw the reservation.

parties that the reservation is made "in regard to," that is, those which the reserving state's reduced obligations will affect. Thus, in situations characterized by underlying Enforcement problems (prisoners' dilemma-like incentives to defect), one member state's reservation, which would result in a reduced obligation for that state, affects the utility of other states such that they will want to reciprocate in reduced cooperation, thereby decreasing the benefits of cooperation for all. Put simply, in prisoners' dilemma-like contexts, reservations would likely result in lower levels of cooperation.

In many multilateral human rights endeavors, states do not face prisoners' dilemma-like incentives to defect. The strategy of conditional reciprocity so common in enforcing cooperation in situations with underlying Enforcement problems is thus not optimal or even useful in such human rights endeavors; such strategies hurt the "punishing state" and do not induce compliance in the defecting state. As Swaine (2006: 342) so expertly explains: "it is unlikely that a secular state would benefit from Sharia-related reservations, or that others would benefit from Belgium's (former) CEDAW reservation exempting Belgian law that required the sovereign and successors to the crown to be male." Thus reservations are more likely in situations *not* characterized by underlying Enforcement/prisoners' dilemma problems.

This reasoning leads to the final hypothesis:

(H6-4) Other things equal, agreements that are characterized by underlying Enforcement problems are less likely to contain reservations than those not characterized by enforcement problems.

Empirical testing

COIL variables

In the analyses, I invert the precision variable so that *very precise* = 4 while *very vague* = 1. Hence a greater number implies a more precise agreement, whereas a lower number implies a more vague agreement.

The reservation variable captures whether any state entered any substantive reservations to an agreement by the time the given agreement entered into force. As noted in footnote 7, I include understandings and declarations that play the same role as substantive reservations in the analyses that follow.[27] The reservations variable is coded as 1 if any reservations were lodged and 0 otherwise.

The main independent variables employed in the analysis of (im)precision are the Number of participants involved in the cooperative endeavor and the presence or absence of particular underlying cooperation problem(s) that states are trying to solve – specifically, the presence or absence of underlying Distribution problems and Coordination problems. The Number of participants is log transformed as discussed in Chapter 3. For the reservations analysis, in addition to the presence or absence of underlying Distribution and Coordination problems, I also include the presence or absence of an underlying Enforcement problem.

Given the general challenges of coding the underlying cooperation problems, I elaborate the coding of Distribution problems in the issue area of human rights because for some readers Distribution problems imply that material or security goods are at stake.

The nature and definition of a human right is very much determined by the political and cultural configuration of a state; thus, disagreement among states about the ideal cooperative solution is not surprising. Each state embraces a different understanding of human rights. Some understandings will be very disparate, some very close; the degree of the Distribution problem among states can thereby vary from high to low.

Naturally, a state will usually (but not always) strive to establish the same set of norms or values that are already present in its own culture or codified in its own domestic laws, thereby keeping the costs of joining a human rights agreement to a minimum. If an agreement establishes norms that differ greatly from or contradict the "core values" of an individual state, it will be very costly for this state to join and comply with the agreement. In addition to ideological or cultural barriers to cooperation, some states may be confronted by domestic institutional limitations (such as the need for both the president and the Senate to approve most human rights agreements in the United States) that are costly to overcome, thus making cooperation more difficult.

---

[27] To clarify, the coding instrument contains two separate sets of questions for reservations and declarations/understandings. For this chapter, a new coder identified the specific understandings/declarations that have the same force as reservations.

To ensure the most objective coding possible in this issue area, the COIL team identified three general sources of Distribution problems in human rights cooperation: ideological differences, cultural differences, and domestic institutional factors. Obviously, there are overlaps among these, as there are in many categories. Nonetheless, the human rights literature makes a compelling case for these three separate categories.

Ideology

The Cold War rivalry between the East and the West included sharp ideological divisions regarding human rights. While the West sought to promote civil and political rights such as freedom of speech and expression, the Soviet bloc instead focused on economic, social, and cultural rights such as the right to organize, the right to health care, and the right to housing (Cole 2005; Donnelly 1986; Glendon 2001). One result of this divide is the failure to negotiate one all-encompassing human rights convention during this period. Rather, two separate agreements, the ICCPR (and its Optional Protocols) and the International Covenant on Economic, Social and Cultural Rights[28] were established.

In addition to the Cold War rivalry, another ideological divide is that of labor versus capital, which can be captured partly as a rivalry between the United States and the Soviet Union, although the divide does not align neatly across superpower allies. In general, the United States favored less regulation with respect to workers' rights, whereas the Soviet Union along with many western European states desired increased protection for workers' rights. This particular divide manifested itself in the drafting of a number of ILO conventions during the Cold War, including the ILO Convention concerning the Application of the Principles of the Right to Organise and to Bargain Collectively (No. 98). In this case, the degree of the underlying Distribution problem is coded as high.

Culture

Distribution problems may also be rooted in differing cultures among states. Consider how the individual is viewed in relation to the group. While the West has a strong tradition of focusing on the individual,

---

[28] UNTS Reg. No. 14531.

Soviet and Asian states traditionally do the opposite, focusing on the group rather than on the individual (see, e.g., Cole 2005; Donnelly 2003; Glendon 2001).

During the drafting of the Universal Declaration of Human Rights, non-Western states (e.g., Asian states and Latin American states) supported by the Soviets were skeptical of Western individualistic concepts, as opposed to collectivist or socialist concepts of human beings (Cole 2005; Donnelly 2003; Glendon 2001). In particular, P.C. Chang, a Chinese delegate, elaborated the Asian understanding of a human being with its emphasis on an individual's duty to the community to which he or she belongs; the duty provides the foundation of the individual's existence per se (Glendon 2001). In the 1990s, "Asian Value" debates challenged the legitimacy of international human rights standards (Donnelly 2003: 107; Glendon 2001). For example, political leaders and intellectuals, such as Lee Kwan Yew in Singapore and Mahathir bin Mohamad in Malaysia, claimed that if a substantial deviation from a common international human rights standard is based on culture, it is legitimate (Donnelly 2003: 107). South American delegates to human rights negotiations have expressed similar views, requesting a balance between an individual's rights versus her duties (Glendon 2001). Finally, Cole (2005) points out that the 1990 Cairo Declaration of Human Rights is "quite explicit in declaring that divine law (Shari'a) pre-empts human rights as promulgated in international law" (473).

Domestic institutional factors
Depending on the size of the discrepancy between domestic human rights practices and international human rights standards, states face different costs to committing to human rights agreements (Hathaway 2003). The United States and the United Kingdom are very alike with respect to culture and ideology, but have institutional differences that might come into play for certain human rights agreements, like those involving the death penalty. The United States has many veto players when it comes to changing its laws regarding the death penalty and hence faces high costs to signing an agreement for which the death penalty is prohibited. As another example, underlying the Convention on the Non-applicability of Statutory Limitations to War Crimes and Crimes against Humanity are irreconcilable differences over the issue of non-retroactivity. For a number of states, the issue of

non-retroactivity is a key principle of criminal law, guaranteed in their constitutions. This principle protects individuals from being prosecuted for an action that was not considered a crime at the time the action took place.

It is worth noting that not all human rights agreements pass the threshold from low to high in the coding of underlying Distribution problems – 44 percent of the agreements in this issue area are coded as not having this problem. For example, the Agreement on Passenger Traffic between France and Belgium is not characterized by an underlying Distribution problem. Given the common history and close ties between France and Belgium, the terms and conditions of this agreement are not controversial. Furthermore, there existed neither ideological nor cultural divides nor institutional obstacles. Distribution problems are also coded as low in the set of bilateral human rights agreements that grant reciprocal voting rights in municipal elections.

Control variables: Polity and length of an agreement

To address Neumayer's (2007) claim regarding the association between liberal democracies and reservations, I include the average Democracy level of the initial participants to a given treaty for the reservations analysis. Specifically, I use polity scores from the Polity IV Project,[29] which range from –10 to 10. I also control for the length of an agreement: Longer agreements usually imply more substantive provisions for states potentially to reserve. I use the natural log of length because of the skewness of the variable's distribution.

Empirical analyses

The first column of Table 6.5 simply restates the descriptive statistics that begin the chapter: the human rights issue area is negatively correlated with the level of precision in treaty language when only issue area indicator variables are included in the model (note that the security issue area is the excluded category).[30] This result is statistically

---

[29] See Appendix 2, fn. 1.
[30] I use an ordinal logit model to make use of the full range of the precision variable.

Table 6.5 *Level of precision*

	Issue area only	COIL model
Human rights	−1.37***	−0.59
	(0.51)	(0.59)
Economics	0.41	0.52
	(0.37)	(0.38)
Environment	−0.85*	−0.54
	(0.50)	(0.52)
Distribution but No Coordination		−0.33
		(0.61)
Coordination with/without Distribution		1.51***
		(0.33)
Number (logged)		−0.19
		(0.20)
N	234	234

Note: Ordinal logit results, robust standard errors in parentheses. Cut points not reported here.

*** *significant at 1 percent;* ** *significant at 5 percent;* * *significant at 10 percent*

significant at the 1 percent level. When I introduce the logged Number of parties as well as the underlying cooperation problems through combinations of Distribution and Coordination problems, the effect of the human rights issue area on the level of precision practically disappears, both substantively and in terms of statistical significance.

More importantly for this book, the second column reveals that agreements with Distribution but No Coordination are less precise than those with neither Distribution nor Coordination, although this result is statistically insignificant, and agreements with underlying Coordination problems are significantly more precise than those with Neither Distribution nor Coordination, as H6-1 predicts. The combination of Neither Distribution nor Coordination is the excluded category.

Given the difficulty of interpreting the effects of explanatory variables in an ordinal logit model, the following example gives a sense of the substantive effects. The probability that an agreement is "very precise" is highest when it is characterized by an underlying Coordination problem with/without Distribution problems (52 percent), whereas the probability of an agreement being "very precise" when it is characterized by Neither Distribution nor Coordination and by Distribution but No Coordination is 21 percent and 16 percent, respectively. This is the order predicted in H6-1. All of the predicted probabilities are statistically significant at conventional levels; however, the difference in predicted probabilities is only statistically significant for the pair Coordination with/without Distribution and Neither Distribution nor Coordination.

Although the coefficient on Number is negative as expected, the variable fails to obtain statistical significance at any conventional levels (H6-2). Overall, the expected relationships between the underlying cooperation problems and the level of precision are supported. More broadly, this analysis lends support to COIL's premise that the design of human rights agreements can be explained within the same unifying framework that can explain agreements in economics, environment, and security.

Next, I use logit models to examine whether agreements characterized by underlying Distribution but No Coordination problems (H6-3) are more likely to include reservations than those not characterized by this combination and whether agreements characterized by underlying Enforcement problems are less likely to include reservations (H6-4). Again, the results corroborate my main claim that it is not the human rights issue area but the underlying cooperation problems that encourage states to lodge reservations.

Table 6.6 displays these results.[31] The first column essentially repeats the descriptive statistics presented earlier: The coefficient on the human rights issue area variable is positive and significant when only issue area indicator variables are included in the model. When I introduce the underlying cooperation problems and my control variables, average polity and agreement length, the effect of the human rights issue area becomes negative and loses its statistical significance (second column).

As expected, agreements characterized by Distribution but No Coordination problems are more likely to have reservations attached to them than the excluded category of Neither Distribution nor Coordination. This result is statistically significant at the 10 percent

---

[31] The area under the ROC curve for the models in the first and second columns are 0.838 and 0.936, respectively.

Table 6.6 *Presence of reservation(s)*

	Issue area only	COIL model
Human rights	1.15**	–0.10
	(0.55)	(0.81)
Economics	–2.70**	–3.01**
	(1.10)	(1.43)
Environment	–1.82	–1.45
	(1.10)	(1.16)
Distribution but No		1.95*
Coordination		(1.00)
Coordination with/without		0.16
Distribution		(0.99)
Enforcement problem		–1.13*
		(0.64)
Average Polity		–0.05
		(0.06)
Length (logged)		1.63***
		(0.48)
Constant	–1.92***	–4.81***
	(0.44)	(1.23)
N	234	223

Note: Logit results, robust standard errors in parentheses.
*** *significant at 1 percent;* ** *significant at 5 percent;* * *significant at 10 percent*

level (H6-3), although the sample size is relatively small given not much variation exists in my dependent variable. Additionally, agreements characterized by Distribution but No Coordination problems are significantly more likely to have reservations attached than agreements characterized by underlying Coordination Problems as indicated by a Wald test. Agreements with underlying Enforcement problems are significantly less likely to have reservations attached to them than are those without such problems, and this result is statistically significant at the 10 percent level (H6-4).

Table 6.7 displays the predicted probabilities and the associated average predicted effects. The combination of Distribution but No Coordination increases the probability of an agreement having at least one reservation attached by about 13 percentage points. Conversely,

Table 6.7 *Predicted probabilities and average predicted effects*

	Reservation
Neither Distribution nor Coordination	0.05
Distribution but No Coordination	0.18
Change predicted prob.	*0.13[†]*
No Enforcement problem	0.12
Enforcement problem	0.07
Change predicted prob.	*−0.05**

Note: All predicted probabilities in this table are significant at the conventional levels.
*** significant at 1 percent; ** significant at 5 percent; * significant at 10 percent; [†] p-value = 0.100*

when an agreement switches from having an underlying Enforcement problem to not having one, the probability of the agreement having at least one reservation attached almost doubles from 7 percent to 12 percent.

With respect to the control variables, the sign of the coefficient on the average polity score variable is negative and statistically indistinguishable from zero, which is contrary to the expectations in the literature (e.g., Neumayer 2007). On the other hand, longer agreements are more likely to have reservations attached to them than are shorter ones, as expected, and this result is statistically significant at the 1 percent level. Overall, H6-3 and H6-4 are supported by the data. Additionally, the human rights indicator variable loses its explanatory power when accounting for the underlying cooperation problems. Interestingly, the economics issue area remains negative and statistically significantly different from human rights and security but not from the environmental issue area.

Another way of framing these results (and the theoretical argument) is that Coordination problems require more rigid commitments. Precise language is one means, and the results presented here support that conclusion. It is worth mentioning that the absence of escape clauses is another way to establish more rigid commitments. Allowing a state to cease cooperation temporarily when the underlying structure contains elements of a Coordination problem would likely be detrimental to at least one if not both/all member states. Indeed, only 3 out of the 60 agreements with Coordination problems have escape clauses (5 percent), whereas among agreements without Coordination problems, almost 24 percent have escape clauses.

What happens over time?

I argue in this chapter that (im)precision and reservations are components of rationally designed agreements put in place to solve particular cooperation problems among states; the empirical results lend support to this argument.

Another research strategy to consider is what happens over time. Like constructivists, I believe one goal of human rights cooperation through international agreements is to export norms to places they do not exist and reinforce them in places where they may be tenuous. According to my argument, if imprecision and reservations are necessary to solve the underlying Distribution problem and thereby to allow cooperation to begin, as norms take hold or change in the direction contemplated by the agreement, we would predict two things: First, agreements dealing with similar sub-issues would become more precise over time; second, states that made reservations to solve the Distribution problem would begin to withdraw them.

With respect to the sub-issue of the death penalty, according to Simmons (2009), the language addressing the abolishment of the death penalty has become more precise over time across various human rights instruments. In the Universal Declaration of Human Rights, the death penalty is not explicitly banned. The ICCPR, adopted eighteen years later, prohibits the death penalty in a qualified manner. Seventeen years later, as Simmons (2009) notes, Optional Protocol No. 6 of the European Convention on Human Rights bans the death penalty but allows states to add reservations for the most serious crimes during war – although the narrower and more homogeneous membership in the European context diminishes the initial Distribution problem.[32] Likewise, the Second Optional Protocol to the ICCPR in 1989 bans the death penalty "in all situations, including war, unless a country specifies otherwise through reservation at the time of

---

[32] See Ehrlich and Posner (1974).

ratification" (Simmons 2009: 191).[33] These latter two occurrences also illustrate Figure 6.3 in practice, with states with the highest standards accepting optional obligations.

Human rights agreements can also become more precise over time through narrower treaty interpretation by courts (Helfer 2002). The European Court of Human Rights has done this slowly and cautiously and has succeeded by many accounts (Helfer 2008).

Regarding reservations, states who added reservations upon ratification or accession might withdraw all or some of them over time if either norms evolve on average toward those contemplated by the more passionate human rights champions or a change in domestic politics gives greater relative power to those who support additional human rights. For instance, with respect to CEDAW, 25 states have withdrawn reservations (Wotipka and Ramirez 2008), and half of the 16 Arab League states that added substantive reservations to CEDAW have either withdrawn their reservations or promised to do so.[34] This behavior is consistent with reservations serving as a form of flexibility to solve the initial Distribution problem: As this Distribution problem lessens, some flexibility is "withdrawn." If states were simply adding reservations to make noncompliance easier, why would they ever withdraw their reservations?

Whether reservations will be withdrawn is conditional on the type of Distribution problem being solved by the reservations in question. If the Distribution problem is ideological and enshrined in constitutions, this is not a matter of norms converging; thus *the flexibility needed to attain agreement will prevail.* Such is the case with the Convention on the Elimination of All Forms of Racial Discrimination (CERD) for which only one out of 37 reservations has been withdrawn. For instance, Article 4 of CERD contradicts the freedom of speech principle enshrined in many constitutions, including those of the United States and France, and was thus the most reserved

[33] The point about the norm taking hold (and the underlying Distribution problem being thereby lessened) is also valid if one looks at both the number of accessions over time as well as the number of withdrawals of reservations allowing the use of the death penalty during war. See http://treaties.un.org/Pages/ViewDetails .aspx?src=TREATY&mtdsg_no=IV-12&chapter=4&lang=en [Last accessed July 13, 2015].

[34] This example and the specific numbers are drawn from Hartig, Elizabeth. 2010. "The Withdrawing of Reservations to CEDAW: A Unique Type of Flexibility." Unpublished student paper. University of Michigan.

substantive provision with a total of 20 states lodging reservations to this article.[35]

Given this promising anecdotal evidence about states' reservations being used to solve the Distribution problem as opposed to making noncompliance easier, I also look at the withdrawal of reservations within the COIL random sample. For the twenty one agreements that had reservations added at the time of signature (one economics agreement, one environmental agreement, six security agreements, and thirteen human rights agreements), states have withdrawn reservations from the one economics agreement and from over half of the human rights agreements; in the latter case, multiple states withdrew their reservations across time.[36]

Concluding thoughts

Imprecision and reservations vary systematically across agreements, and they vary according to the particular underlying cooperation problems as predicted by the framework. The relative imprecision of certain agreements and the reservations added are rational responses to an underlying Distribution problem that is not complicated by an underlying Coordination problem. The original Rational Design conjecture *Flexibility increases with the Distribution problem* is thus refined when it comes to the particular flexibility devices of precision and reservations.

The analyses in this chapter also lend credence to the view that human rights agreements are meaningful components of international law and can be understood within the COIL framework. At the same time, the complementarity of various approaches to international cooperation is underscored. COIL explicitly incorporates an important

---

[35] Article 4 states: "States Parties condemn all propaganda and all organizations which are based on ideas or theories of superiority of one race or group of persons of one colour or ethnic origin, or which attempt to justify or promote racial hatred and discrimination in any form, and undertake to adopt immediate and positive measures designed to eradicate all incitement to, or acts of, such discrimination...."

[36] Late reservations are not contemplated by the VCLT so their validity is unsettled. If states can only withdraw reservations and not add reservations over time, this tilts the evidence in my favor. States for whom the Distribution problem worsened over time would have to find another option such as complete withdrawal from the agreement.

component of the constructivist research agenda – that of norm exportation – and shows how the withdrawal of substantive reservations
substantiates the claim that norms do take hold across states.
Finnemore and Sikkink (1998: 888) argue that there can exist a "life
cycle" of evolving norms, in which norm entrepreneurs attempt to
persuade certain important states to incorporate the new norm.
Norm "cascades" occur as "norm leaders" attempt to socialize potential "norm followers" by citing the potential for international legitimacy (1998: 895). Ultimately, the norm is internalized. They conclude
that these "internalized or cascading norms may eventually become the
prevailing standard of appropriateness" (1998: 895). I have shown that
this life cycle of norms may happen in the context of a treaty by initially
allowing more imprecise language and tailored exemption through
reservations, with treaties then evolving into more precise international
commitments and states withdrawing their initial reservations over
time.[37]

It is also useful to consider interactions among design variables
given the findings in this chapter. In recent work,[38] I take Erhlich and
Posner's (1974) theory to the international level. They argue the more
imprecise a domestic law is, the more authority is delegated to a court
to interpret things left incomplete. In the international context, however, there are no courts with automatic and authoritative jurisdiction
lurking in the background. Put differently, in the international context,
the precision of law and delegation to courts are *not* two sides of the
same coin. Drawing on this chapter and the theoretical argument of
Chapter 7, I hypothesize that the two variables, precision and third-
party delegation of dispute resolution, should be inversely related.
Empirical testing corroborates the hypothesis. Because internationally,
these are two separate choices, my data thereby allow a test of the law
and economics theory that is not possible in the domestic context.
The findings also imply that the noncompliance that some argue

---

[37] Here I differ from those who argue "Ideational arguments differ most
fundamentally from realist arguments in their reliance on a distinctive
conception of interstate interaction. They explicitly reject choice-theoretic
foundations and instead stress the transformative power of normative moral
discourse itself," which is Moravcsik's (2000: 223) summary of authors like
Finnemore and Sikkink 1998 and Donnelly 1986.
[38] See Introduction to Part II, fn. 1.

could be encouraged through imprecision is curtailed by the possibility of delegated dispute resolution.

Additionally, according to Hazen, the Optional Protocol to the CRC on the involvement of children in armed conflict (CRC Optional Protocol) illustrates how imprecision and RUDs can interact to solve an underlying Distribution problem, with the former providing flexibility and the latter more specificity.[39] Article 1 of the CRC Optional Protocol requires that "(those) who have not attained the age of 18 years do not take a direct part in hostilities." However, as Hazen argues, the CRC Optional Protocol and its *travaux préparatoires* do not clarify the distinction between direct and indirect participation in hostilities.[40] Upon ratification of the CRC Optional Protocol, however, the United States attached a number of understandings to clarify its interpretation of "direct" participation in hostilities. According to the United States, direct participation

  i) means immediate and actual action on the battlefield likely to cause harm to the enemy because there is a direct causal relationship between the activity engaged in and the harm done to the enemy; and
 (ii) does not mean indirect participation in hostilities, such as gathering and transmitting military information, transporting weapons, munitions, or other supplies, or forward deployment.[41]

As Hazen notes, the specificity given by the declaration, not surprisingly, lines up with US recruitment practices.[42]

The analyses in this chapter open up a few possible venues for future research on the effectiveness of international treaties, in particular, human rights agreements. This chapter also calls attention to the fact that, when scholars examine treaty compliance or effectiveness, they need to take into account inherent differences in treaty design in terms of flexibility mechanisms that allow different levels of treaty

---

[39] Hazen, Nicholas. 2014. "COIL Framework and the UNCRC Optional Protocol." Unpublished student paper. University of Michigan: 3.

[40] UNICEF 2003 "Guide to the Optional Protocol on the Involvement of Children in Armed Conflict." Available at www.unicef.org/publications/index_19025.html [Last accessed May 15, 2015]. Cited in Hazen 2014. See fn. 39: 3.

[41] United States. Understandings to the Optional Protocol to the Convention on the Rights of the Child on the Involvement of Children in Armed Conflict. Available at http://indicators.ohchr.org/ [Last accessed May 28, 2015].

[42] See fn. 39: 4.

obligations in the first place. Most of the extant studies on compliance/ effectiveness seem to assume that all members are subject to the same treaty standard of behavior, even though some states initially tailor treaty obligations to their needs, at least in the short run.

In this vein, the theory here engages Thompson and Verdier (2014) who also are interested in explaining institutional design and who reasonably assume that states are not homogeneous with respect to their incentives for compliance in any particular regime. Thompson and Verdier examine how, when designing regimes, states can customize obligations through their choice among multilateral agreements, bilateral agreements, or some combination.[43] In cases of Distribution but no Coordination problems, one state's less-than-full compliance does not impose externalities on other states. In this situation, I expect *differential commitment* through imprecision and reservations. Thompson and Verdier expect states to have *differential incentives* for the same commitment, *with varying degrees of compliance* with states at the design stage choosing the "cheap route" that involves multilateralism and no membership exclusion given the absence of externalities. An interesting way to differentiate these two arguments in human rights agreements is to examine whether states comply with differential commitments (COIL) or whether levels of compliance do not match commitments (Thompson and Verdier 2014).

Finally, scholars must also consider more medium and long-term data in studies of effectiveness since the mechanisms identified here are ones that have a dynamic element, as the preceding section highlighted. Flexibility devices that solve the underlying Distribution problems that are often coupled with Norm Exportation are necessary in the short and perhaps medium run for cooperation to begin, but these may be withdrawn over time as the norms take hold. Failure to address such factors and expecting immediate changes in behavior may result in the overestimation of noncompliance.

---

[43] Thompson and Verdier (2014) thus offer a rigorous analysis and refinement regarding the one Rational Design dependent variable not considered in this book: membership.

Centralization, scope, and control provisions in the design of international law

Introduction to Part III

The literature on international institutions historically has focused on information as the main problem of cooperation and information provision, usually through centralization, as the main solution. This historical emphasis on information provisions to help stabilize cooperation originated for a reason. Provisions calling for functions like monitoring are tremendously important if states are going to solve their joint problems through international law because information provisions reduce uncertainty, thereby reinforcing strategies of reciprocity that can be so critical to cooperation (Keohane 1984; Axelrod and Keohane 1985: 250).[1] Furthermore, the conventional wisdom suggests that, when such functions are centralized through international regimes, cooperation is more robust (Axelrod and Keohane 1985: 250). As Chapter 3 showcased, while the formidable Enforcement problems and Uncertainty about Behavior do not overwhelm the landscape of cooperation problems, they do underlie a non-trivial number of cooperative endeavors. As a result, provisions encouraging compliance in such environments are important to cooperation.

Part III of this book brings the focus to such provisions. It refines substantially earlier institutionalist arguments both theoretically and empirically. In particular, it reemphasizes a claim made earlier, as well as in Rational Design, regarding the absolute necessity of separating Enforcement problems from uncertainty problems and of differentiating among various kinds of uncertainties, something that the earlier emphasis on 2 × 2 games tended to obscure.

---

[1] Seminal, insightful works like these serve as springboards for further theoretical and empirical refinement in the field of international cooperation, playing a role similar to Schelling's seminal work in the field of international conflict.

Part III also differentiates the set of design provisions that have been traditionally labeled under the umbrella of "compliance provisions." So-called "compliance provisions" are the cornerstone of much IR scholarship, but they are often employed in the literature without carefully phrased definitional boundaries. Moreover, scholarship often equates such terms with "deep institutionalization," which itself is taken for granted as increasing the prospects for cooperation. In what follows, I separate the dispute resolution, punishment, and monitoring design dimensions and allow for the possibility that they may be performed in a decentralized and/or centralized manner. If delegation occurs, I further ask if it is external or internal. Finally, if it is internal, I consider the voting rules characterizing the delegated body.

Chapter 7 zeroes in on dispute resolution provisions and explains, first, when states are likely to incorporate such provisions into their agreements and, second, what kind of dispute resolution provision they will choose. I find, for instance, that Uncertainty about the State of the World, so much the focus of Part II, is not a relevant variable in explaining dispute resolution. Uncertainty about Behavior, in contrast, is important, but not for delegated dispute resolution. Enforcement and Commitment problems, on the other hand, drive states to choose such delegation. Thus the original Rational Design conjecture that *Centralization increases with Uncertainty about Behavior* is refined, whereas the conjecture that *Centralization increases with the severity of the Enforcement problem* is confirmed.

Chapter 8 provides a theory of punishment provisions, a form of scope increase. The descriptive statistics alone belie much of the conventional wisdom in realist scholarship about the absence of such provisions. Additionally, I show that most of the time when a punishment provision is needed to stabilize the cooperative equili-brium, the necessary provision is indeed formally incorporated into the agreement –that is, *Scope does increase in the presence of Enforcement problems*, as Rational Design argues.

Chapter 9 looks at monitoring provisions. Again, particular coop-eration problems drive states to include monitoring provisions, and interactions among cooperation problems explain the differences in the type of monitoring provision states choose. Uncertainty about Behavior alone is not enough for the centralization predicted in Rational Design to be incorporated in monitoring provisions; rather, Enforcement and Commitment problems combined with Uncertainty about Behavior drive states to incorporate centralized (delegated) monitoring.

Chapter 10 looks at the actual voting rules that characterize the centralized bodies discussed in parts of Chapters 7–9. The chapter also considers how power is generally reflected in the COIL sample, probing the Rational Design conjecture that *Asymmetric control increases with Asymmetric Power.*

Part III of this book also systematically explores the topic of informalism, in part by using the COIL theoretical framework as a baseline to predict the need for certain design provisions. Many scholars (in particular, Downs and Rocke [1990] and Lipson [1991]) have noted that some cooperation is optimally left informal. These earlier insights have not been systematically tested or refined in the past decades, perhaps because of the obstacles to quantifying what's informal. There are recent notable exceptions, including wonderfully rich case studies. Some of these also feature statistical analyses of particular institutions, especially the EU (see Kleine [2013] and Reh et al. [2010][2] on decision making within the EU and Stone's [2010] rigorous analysis of informal governance within three very formal institutions: the IMF, the WTO, and the EU.[3])

What the COIL data set allows me to do is to look at various forms of informality in a way that transcends the few popular (albeit important) institutions and provide a more systematic and general picture of the relationship between formal and informal design choices, a topic Stone so wisely calls attention to in his work. The COIL framework allows me to generate comparative static predictions on the need for certain design features, and the data set allows me to test these predictions, revealing what is incorporated formally by design and what might be consciously left informal.

As I elaborate in Chapters 7–10, I find Centralization and Control provisions to be particularly useful for examining various forms of informality in international law. The separate design dimensions analyzed in each chapter allow me to explore slightly different definitions

---

[2] Reh, Christine, Adrienne Heritier, Christel Koop, and Edoardo Bressanelli. 2010. "The Informal Politics of Legislation: Explaining Secluded Decision-Making in the European Union." Presented at the American Political Science Association 2010 Annual Meeting. Available at SSRN http://papers.ssrn.com/sol3/papers .cfm?abstract_id=1642265 [Last accessed June 25, 2015].

[3] I elaborate Stone's contribution in Chapter 8.

of informality within formal law and to utilize various methodologies. I exploit the COIL data set to test a deductive theory about informality in Chapter 8 and use the data inductively in Chapter 9 to generate some new theoretical puzzles. In Chapter 10, I suggest some avenues for future theoretical and empirical research by exploring a few of the COIL agreements through case study research.

Chapter 7, which focuses on dispute resolution provisions, showcases a rather straightforward kind of informality in international law: formal provisions that call for the resolution of disputes informally, that is, without third-party intervention. Descriptive statistics on how often informality is formally called for in the COIL sample are presented, including how often it occurs in the shadow of formal, third-party arbitration and/or adjudication provisions. This latter statistic is attention-grabbing: the great majority of agreements with formal procedures explicitly encourage informal settlement as well, and more than half of these impose time limits on the dispute resolution process. These statistics add credence to the "shadow of the law" argument and have enormous implications for how scholars should judge the effectiveness of formal dispute resolution.

Chapter 8 introduces a new research design that exploits the COIL sample to determine the set of agreements that are candidates for informal punishment provisions, that is, for punishment that is formally absent but understood to exist implicitly. I find that, with great Regime and Preference Heterogeneity and large differences in the economic Power of agreement members, informality provides states with the flexibility to tailor their responses to defection based on the realized specifics.

Chapter 9 showcases new research on informal NGO monitoring of the agreements in the COIL sample, much of which is layered on top of formal monitoring provisions. New puzzles are generated, such as why informal NGO monitoring does not take the place of missing state or IGO monitoring when the underlying cooperation problems necessitate it, but rather complements existing IGO monitoring.

Chapter 10 presents some descriptive statistics about how often the provisions of the agreements in the COIL sample reflect the underlying distribution of power. The case of the Australia, New Zealand, United States Security Treaty (ANZUS) suggests that voting rules were likely deliberately left unspecified so the disparity in state power could be informally exploited. An interesting question for future research is under what conditions do states use formal voting rules to reflect power asymmetries and when instead do they leave voting informal?

To foreshadow the chapters that follow in Part III, with respect to dispute resolution and punishment provisions, what is left informal is quite systematic and can be explained theoretically. None of the chapters provide evidence that what is informal trumps what is formal. Finally, what is informal often complements and/or substitutes for what is formal, but thus far there is no systematic evidence that the two conflict directly.

7 | *Dispute resolution provisions*

> [T]he student of law and the student of politics ... purport to be looking at the same world from the vantage point of important disciplines. It seems unfortunate, indeed destructive, that they should not, at the least, hear each other.
>
> *(Henkin 1979: 4)*

Only about one out of every two agreements in the COIL sample has any dispute resolution provision whatsoever.[1] This empirical observation begs for an explanation, and which half needs explaining depends on where one is sitting. The standard IR realist perspective tells us that the dispute resolution provisions in those agreements that have them are simply cheap talk – just like the entire agreements. As Mearsheimer (1994: 7) argues, institutions "have minimal influence on state behavior." A variant of this view is that international law does not change behavior because states enter into only those agreements that already align with their interests (Downs, Rocke, and Barsoom 1996). Consequently, it is irrelevant whether international agreements contain dispute resolution mechanisms. So the puzzle is why states bother putting such provisions in half of their agreements.

From many IL perspectives, the puzzle is why only half of the agreements have these provisions. Helfer and Slaughter (1997: 283), for instance, regard international tribunals as an integral part of "a global community of law." Brunnée and Toope (2011: 308), coming from a constructivist perspective, emphasize not only that a perception of legitimacy and legality must exist, but that "the obligatory effect of international law must be generated and maintained through practices that sustain legality over time." Based on the premise from the legalization literature that "courts and tribunals represent a key dimension

---

[1] Much of this chapter draws directly from Koremenos (2007) and Koremenos and Betz (2013), the latter of which corroborates and extends the findings of the former using the full COIL data set. I reproduce and expand on these findings in what follows.

of legalization" (Keohane, Moravcsik, and Slaughter 2000: 457), one could straightforwardly conclude that the existence and usage of dispute resolution mechanisms impart a more law-like character to international agreements, thereby enhancing their legitimacy and effectiveness. Thus, we would expect to see the inclusion of dispute resolution mechanisms in most, if not all, international agreements.

Indeed, Henkin's quote about the two very different vantage points of IR and IL is aptly illustrated by the disagreement over which half needs explaining: the half of the COIL sample that contains dispute resolution provisions or the half that does not.

International dispute resolution is now one of the most popular topics in studies of international cooperation. NAFTA and the institutions of the EU have been studied extensively (Garvey 1995; Stone Sweet and Brunell 1998; Stone Sweet 2010[2]). The transformation of a political negotiation style of dispute resolution under GATT to the formal legal process embodied in the WTO appears to have garnered the most attention (Busch 2000; Charnovitz 2001; Guzman and Simmons 2002; Jackson 1978; Pauwelyn 2001; Schloemann and Ohlhoff 1999; Schwartz and Sykes 2002; Steinberg 2002).

The literature on the WTO, in particular, greatly advanced our understanding of many facets of international dispute resolution mechanisms; however, this literature is also emblematic of two shortcomings of the field. First, single agreements, and often only one or two very specific details of an agreement, feature prominently. Although this approach sometimes provides a holistic picture of a single institution, the extent to which findings can be generalized is limited. Grando (2006), for instance, examines the allocation of the burden of proof in the WTO's dispute settlement system and derives policy prescriptions from her analysis. Of course, there is much to be gained from paying close attention to such details, especially when it is done in a theoretically informed manner.[3] Second, most authors examine the

[2] Stone Sweet, Alec. 2010. "The European Court of Justice and the Judicialization of EU Governance." *Living Reviews in European Governance* 5 (2). Available at www.livingreviews.org/lreg-2010–2 [Last accessed June 25, 2015].
[3] An exemplary piece in this regard is Brutger's (2011) analysis of how the participation of private parties affects the selection of complaints in the WTO and how this, in turn, helps explain the perceived dominance of resource-rich countries in the WTO's dispute settlement procedures. Thus, a rather minor design feature – the possibility of private contributions to litigation costs – has

implications of the WTO for its participants (Busch and Reinhardt 2003), make normative prescriptions (Barceló 2009), or remain largely descriptive (Charnovitz 2009). By contrast, few scholars attempt to explain systematically the design choices made by states.

Two recent books focus exclusively on international courts. Mitchell and Powell (2011) explain why states create and join certain types of international tribunals and not others. The authors divide states into three legal traditions: civil law, common law, and Islamic law. They argue that states create and join tribunals that most closely match their own legal tradition to increase the likelihood of a favorable experience before the tribunal and to signal their legal "type" and willingness to settle disputes amicably. They test their theory by examining the jurisdiction granted by states to the International Criminal Court and World Court (i.e., the Permanent Court of International Justice and its successor, the ICJ).

Alter (2014) argues that the explosion of international tribunals has brought on a legalized, "postrealist" era of international law, in which binding international judgments have increasingly led states to accede to international norms without force or the threat thereof. She further claims that these judgments do more than settle the particular dispute before the tribunal; they clarify the meaning of international laws, and the influence of such tribunals permeates domestic law and politics.

While a lot of attention has focused on NAFTA, the EU, the WTO, and certain prominent international courts,[4] in reality, institutionalized international cooperation is captured in the tens of thousands of agreements that are registered with the UN from which the COIL sample draws. Indeed, most cooperation is bilateral and has at its foundation an international agreement, not an international organization. What kind of picture regarding dispute resolution emerges if we consider this larger continent of international

---

far-reaching implications for the pattern of observed disputes. (Brutger, Ryan. 2011. "Private Parties: Hidden Actors of WTO Dispute Settlement." Working Paper. Princeton University, Department of Political Science.)

[4] For a notable exception, see Smith (2000), who studies differences in dispute resolution design across a large set of regional trade pacts (see also Chapter 3). And, for a refreshing study outside the trade issue area, see De Bruyne and Fischhendler (2013) for an analysis of the dispute resolution mechanisms of 182 transboundary water treaties.

cooperation, in which delegation to an international court is just one of the possible choices?[5]

I argue that the inclusion of dispute settlement procedures in international agreements is a deliberate choice by states, made to address specific cooperation problems. The implication is that international law is designed efficiently: dispute settlement procedures are likely to be incorporated into agreements if, but only if, they are necessary to solve specific cooperation problems. The half-and-half statistic is thus predicted by the COIL theoretical framework. Dispute resolution provisions are not incorporated according to some norm or idealized version of what international law is supposed to look like; nor are such provisions absent if they are necessary for states to realize the gains from cooperation. The data confirm this viewpoint.

I begin this chapter by defining my variables and presenting descriptive statistics. I then put forth a theory regarding when states are likely to incorporate dispute resolution provisions and what form such provisions will take and test this theory against the COIL data. In a nutshell, agreements addressing more challenging cooperation problems, that is, problems characterized by uncertainty about others' actions, prisoners' dilemma-like incentives to defect, and/or time inconsistency, are more likely to include such provisions. Importantly, however, these three cooperation problems do not lead to the same form of dispute resolution. Centralized (i.e., delegated) dispute resolution is necessary in the presence of underlying Enforcement and Commitment problems; decentralized (i.e., informal) dispute resolution helps solve Uncertainty about Behavior.

This chapter thus provides an enhanced theoretical and empirical picture of an important design dimension of international law, dispute resolution systems, by refining the original Rational Design

---

[5] Illustrative of the advantages of a broader approach is the article by Helfer and Slaughter (1997) on supranational adjudication. Through a process of induction, they distill a number of conditions that contribute to effective supranational adjudication and go on to explain other cases of adjudication as well. Helfer and Slaughter's work is an impressive improvement with respect to large parts of the IL and IR literatures. While the former typically welcomes international adjudication and strives to promote its reach and effectiveness (for a critical discussion, see the introduction in Posner and Yoo [2005]), most political scientists assume a more distanced position, assessing the effects and effectiveness of adjudication (e.g., Huth, Croco, and Appel 2011).

conjectures *Centralization increases with Uncertainty about Behavior* and *Centralization increases with Enforcement problems*: Centralized (i.e., delegated) dispute resolution increases only in the presence of cooperation problems for which incentives to defect are present.[6] Uncertainty about Behavior in the absence of incentives to defect that come from Enforcement and Commitment problems can be solved in a decentralized manner. In this way, this chapter begins Part III's consideration of "informality" in international law. Specifically, this chapter looks at how often and why the informal resolution of disputes is explicitly encouraged in the formal agreements of the COIL data set.

Additionally, data on reservations explicitly addressing the dispute resolution process are presented, challenging some of the IL and IR "intuitions" about such reservations. Finally, the idea of the "shadow of the law" is tackled, thereby illustrating the importance of carefully distinguishing between the use of dispute settlement mechanisms and their effects.

Definitions and descriptive statistics

Following some of my earlier work (2007), I identify four different types of dispute resolution mechanisms: informal mechanisms, mediation, arbitration, and adjudication. Informal mechanisms refer to diplomacy or friendly negotiations. Notably, informal mechanisms do not involve any actors other than the affected parties in the dispute. Moreover, even though states always have the option to settle informally, many agreements explicitly suggest that parties use diplomacy and friendly negotiations as a first means for resolving disputes. Mediation, the second form of dispute resolution, is more formal. Importantly, mediation involves a neutral third party, but it is non-binding – the mediator is supposed to assist the disputing parties in finding an agreeable solution but does not issue a formal ruling. This is different from arbitration, the third form of dispute resolution. In arbitration the disputants select a third party for the resolution of the dispute. This arbitrator may issue binding statements or simple recommendations, depending on the provisions in the agreement; however,

---

[6] Additionally, the Legalization conjecture regarding delegation and domestic time-inconsistency problems is incorporated and is confirmed.

Table 7.1 *Incidence of dispute resolution mechanisms by type and by*
          issue area
          (percentage of each issue area)

	Any dispute resolution (%)	Forms of dispute resolution			
Issue area		Informal (%)	Mediation (%)	Arbitration (%)	Adjudication (%)
Economics	52	50	17	41	23
Environment	30	23	14	19	21
Human rights	66	39	20	22	49
Security	38	38	11	2	4
Total	48	41	15	26	24

N = 234

the arbitrator is supposed to solve the dispute (unlike a mediator, who only helps the disputants reconcile their views). The fourth and final form is adjudication. Here, the agreement either establishes a court or delegates to a pre-existing one, and the specified court is authorized to issue a ruling, which may but need not be binding.[7]

Table 7.1 presents the incidence of various dispute resolution mechanisms, both for the entire sample and across issue areas. Almost half of the agreements in the sample, 48 percent, explicitly mention some form of dispute resolution, and 37 percent include a provision relating to one of the formal mechanisms (mediation, arbitration, and/or adjudication). At the same time, not every agreement is made more legalized through the inclusion of dispute settlement mechanisms. Finally, it is worth noting that many agreements provide for multiple forms of dispute settlement. In particular, 80 percent of the agreements with formal procedures explicitly encourage informal settlement as well.

Table 7.1 also reveals substantial variation across issue areas. Agreements concerned with economic issues, for example, are more than twice as likely to encourage explicitly the informal settlement

---

[7] The standard legal taxonomy of dispute resolution slices the world up slightly differently. See, for example, UN Charter, Article 33 (listing negotiation, enquiry, mediation, conciliation, arbitration, judicial settlement, resort to regional agencies, and other peaceful means of settlement).

Table 7.2 *Incidence of dispute resolution mechanisms by type and by sub-issue area*
(percentage of each sub-issue area)

Sub-issue area	Any dispute resolution (%)	Forms of dispute resolution			
		Informal (%)	Mediation (%)	Arbitration (%)	Adjudication (%)
Agricultural	17	17	4	8	0
Finance	42	38	8	4	8
Investment	93	90	33	93	52
Monetary	0	0	0	0	0
Environment	30	23	14	19	21
Human rights	66	39	20	22	49
Disarmament	67	67	33	11	22
Security	32	32	5	0	0
Total	48	41	15	26	24

N = 234

of disputes than are agreements addressing environmental issues. Human rights agreements rely much more often on adjudication than do agreements in any other issue area.

Table 7.2 looks at the incidence of the various dispute resolution mechanisms across sub-issue area. Table 7.2 makes it very clear that investment agreements are very different from agreements in the other economics sub-issue areas with respect to the more formal methods of arbitration and adjudication. In fact, almost every investment agreement contains a formal arbitration provision while very few agricultural commodity and finance agreements do and no monetary agreement does. Disarmament agreements are far more likely to include dispute resolution mechanisms than are security agreements; moreover, not a single security agreement calls for the arbitration or adjudication of disputes.

A second dimension of variation captured is whether the dispute resolution process is handled by internal or external delegation. Tables 7.3 and 7.4 present these statistics across issue area and sub-issue area, respectively. *Internal delegation* occurs when a body composed of representatives of the member states handles the arbitration or adjudication. For example, many agreements either call for the

Table 7.3 *Internal vs. external delegation by issue area*
(percentage of each issue area)

	Any dispute resolution (%)	Forms of dispute resolution	
Issue area		Internal (%)	External (%)
Economics	52	44	40
Environment	30	19	19
Human rights	66	27	51
Security	38	6	9
Total	48	29	32

N = 234

Table 7.4 *Internal vs. external delegation by sub-issue area*
(percentage of each sub-issue area)

	Any dispute resolution (%)	Forms of dispute resolution	
Sub-issue area		Internal (%)	External (%)
Agricultural	17	8	4
Finance	42	15	4
Investment	93	93	93
Monetary	0	0	0
Environment	30	19	19
Human rights	66	27	51
Disarmament	67	22	33
Security	32	3	3
Total	48	29	32

N = 234

creation of bodies composed of member states to which tasks such as dispute resolution are delegated or elaborate the rules for how such a body would be constituted in the event of a dispute. Regarding the latter, in most BITs, members involved in a dispute must each choose an arbitrator to be a part of an arbitration panel of three, with those two arbitrators together choosing the third member. In fact, this is a widely used design, accounting for almost all of the internal delegation in investment agreements showcased in Table 7.4.

On the other hand, *external delegation* occurs when a third party is without a doubt involved. This third party is usually an existing IGO, but I allow for the possibility that the third party is a state outside the agreement or an NGO. As the tables show, 19 percent of environmental agreements mention pre-existing third parties in their dispute resolution provisions.[8] For example, in the Convention on the Protection of the Marine Environment of the Baltic Sea, states seeking to solve a dispute first address their concerns through negotiation. Should their negotiation fail, however, they are to request mediation by a third party – specifically, "a third Contracting Party, a qualified international organization or a qualified person" (Article 26 [1]). If, after all of this, the parties fail to solve the dispute or cannot agree on these measures, the dispute "shall be, upon common agreement, submitted to an ad hoc arbitration tribunal, to a permanent arbitration tribunal, or to the International Court of Justice" (Article 26 [2]). The process is similar to that of the International Convention for the Prevention of Pollution of the Sea by Oil, where the ICJ is also explicitly named (Article 13). By contrast, the International Convention on Civil Liability for Oil Pollution Damage delegates to national courts.

Over half of the human rights agreements in the sample delegate this function to a third party. Many of the human rights agreements in the sample are ILO conventions, which fall under the auspices of the ILO Constitution. The ICJ is part of the dispute resolution process outlined in the ILO Constitution.[9]

The ICJ is a popular court for external delegation of dispute resolution but by no means the only IGO used, or necessarily the most effective. For example, Canada and the United States, when negotiating the 1991 Agreement on Air Quality, chose to delegate dispute resolution to the International Joint Commission (IJC), a bilateral institution established by the two states in the 1909 Boundary Waters Treaty. As one memorandum of intent indicated: "The IJC is a standing binational body which, over seventy years, has developed a reputation for

---

[8] Although the percentage of environmental agreements in the second and third columns of Table 7.3 is identical, the set of agreements in each group is not.

[9] ILO Constitution, Articles 26–34. Available at www.ilo.org/dyn/normlex/en/f?p= 1000:62:0::NO:62:P62_LIST_ENTRIE_ID:2453907:NO [Last accessed June 13, 2015].

thoroughness and impartiality."[10] The IJC is not included in studies of international courts (including Alter 2014) yet has proved successful. For instance, in their study of IGO mediation in interstate conflict, Hansen, Mitchell, and Nemeth (2008) include the IJC and find that it has an above average success rate in resolving conflict.[11] Another scholar, Hanson (2011: 324) states: "The boundary waters agreement of 1909, the migratory birds act, and the International Joint Commission are some of the most venerable and successful bilateral use and environmental protection arrangements in the world."

Theory: Explaining the variation

With respect to dispute resolution mechanisms, which are typically envisioned as a form of Centralization, four cooperation problems are especially relevant: Enforcement problems, Commitment problems, Uncertainty about the State of the World, and Uncertainty about Behavior.

Enforcement problems, which imply parties have incentives to defect from cooperation, can be ameliorated by dispute resolution provisions. By explicitly identifying violators (and violations), the provisions force noncompliant states to incur reputational costs. By authorizing punishments, sometimes collectively, dispute resolution provisions make punishments more credible and therefore more effective. Collective punishment in particular can be difficult to achieve, and Thompson (2009) aptly identifies a *sanctioners' dilemma*,[12] which can be alleviated through international institutions. This reasoning leads to the first hypothesis:

(H7-1) Other things equal, agreements that are characterized by an underlying Enforcement problem are more likely to include dispute resolution

---

[10] Canada/United States "Memorandum of Intent on Transboundary Air Pollution." Legal, Institutional and Drafting Work Group, July 31, 1981: 8–9.

[11] Based on author's calculation using data from Table 6 of Hansen, Mitchell, and Nemeth (2008: 317).

[12] Under Thompson's formulation, the sanctioners' dilemma occurs because, though all states would benefit from the imposition of sanctions, no state has an incentive to impose them because the costs outweigh the benefits for each individual state. As a result, no sanction is imposed, and all states are left worse off (Thompson 2009: 311).

provisions than those not characterized by an underlying enforcement problem.

Commitment problems arise if an actor's current optimal plan for the future will no longer be optimal once that future arrives and the actor has a chance to re-optimize. By rendering agreements more legalized, dispute resolution provisions offer a device to solve Commitment problems. As Goldstein et al. (2000b: 393) argue, by imposing constraints on domestic political behavior, international legalization can help governments tie the hands of their successors.[13] Dispute resolution mechanisms provide other actors recourse to punish a government for deviations from its announced plans, altering the incentive structure faced by governments. This reasoning leads to the following hypothesis:

(H7-2) Other things equal, agreements that are characterized by an underlying Commitment problem are more likely to include dispute resolution provisions than those not characterized by an underlying commitment problem.

Uncertainty about the State of the World implies that the future benefits (and costs) of cooperation are not easily predicted, and hence a dispute could easily break out, attributable to an unexpected shift in the distribution of benefits. While flexibility measures can facilitate cooperation under such circumstances (see Chapters 4–5; Helfer 2013; Kucik and Reinhardt 2008), dispute resolution provisions may prove valuable as well.

For these reasons, I propose the following hypothesis:

(H7-3) Other things equal, agreements that are characterized by underlying Uncertainty about the State of the World are more likely to include dispute resolution provisions than those not characterized by underlying uncertainty about the state of the world.

Additionally, Uncertainty about Behavior may trigger an unwarranted, and indeed unwanted, breakdown of cooperation – and, in turn, discourage cooperation in the first place. Dispute resolution may address such factual uncertainty in that it provides legalized ways to handle disputes, typically through a formalized procedure that collects and disseminates information. This resonates well with standard

---

[13] See, too, Abbott and Snidal (2000); Brewster (2006); and Guzman and Meyer (2010).

institutionalist arguments about the role of international agreements in providing information (Keohane 1984).

For this reason, I propose the following hypothesis:

(H7-4) Other things equal, agreements that are characterized by underlying Uncertainty about Behavior are more likely to include dispute resolution provisions than those not characterized by underlying uncertainty about behavior.

All four of these hypotheses are refinements of the broad Centralization conjectures presented in Chapter 2.

To summarize, states try to solve two categories of cooperation problems through dispute resolution mechanisms. First, they try to solve problems requiring punishment or enforcement power, which arise in the presence of Enforcement problems, Commitment problems, and Uncertainty about the State of the World. By providing enforcement power – both material and reputational – dispute resolution mechanisms alleviate these cooperation problems. The second category comprises informational problems, which arise in the presence of Uncertainty about Behavior. By providing information, dispute resolution mechanisms address this category of cooperation problems.

Regarding the two kinds of uncertainty, Uncertainty about the State of the World can bring about changes in bargaining power and/or the relative gains from cooperation, making a defection more attractive to one side. Being able to prevent defections is then particularly valuable and not solved by a simple exchange of information. In the context of Uncertainty about Behavior, states may misinterpret signals about their partners' compliance behavior and defect in response to what was actually cooperation by their partners. It is this informational problem that encourages defections, and it is more easily resolved through a simple exchange of information.[14]

If states include dispute settlement mechanisms to solve Enforcement problems, Commitment problems, and Uncertainty about the State of the World, we would expect the dispute resolution provisions to be

---

[14] Uncertainty about Behavior as an underlying cooperation problem is different from legal uncertainty, which refers to difficulties in the interpretation and application of rules. Naturally, dispute settlement mechanisms are relevant for legal uncertainty as well. See, for example, the scholarship of the managerial school of compliance (Chayes and Chayes 1993), according to which international institutions play a vital role in the interpretation of ambiguous rules.

such that punishment, material and/or reputational, could be brought to bear on the defecting state. The formalized mechanisms of arbitration and adjudication provide this power of enforcement.

For these reasons, I propose the following hypotheses:

(H7-5) Other things equal, agreements that are characterized by an underlying Enforcement problem are more likely to include *formal* (delegated) dispute resolution provisions than those not characterized by an underlying enforcement problem.

(H7-6) Other things equal, agreements that are characterized by an underlying Commitment problem are more likely to include *formal* (delegated) dispute resolution provisions than those not characterized by an underlying commitment problem.

(H7-7) Other things equal, agreements that are characterized by underlying Uncertainty about the State of the World are more likely to include *formal* (delegated) dispute resolution provisions than those not characterized by underlying uncertainty about the state of the world.

If states include dispute resolution mechanisms to solve informational problems, that is, noncompliance due to noisy signals about behavior, we would expect the dispute resolution provisions to feature consultations and deliberations rather than adjudication.

For these reasons, I propose the following hypothesis:

(H7-8) Other things equal, agreements that are characterized by underlying Uncertainty about Behavior are more likely to include *informal* dispute resolution provisions than those not characterized by this problem.

Finally, given that formal dispute resolution provisions are a form of centralization, one final hypothesis is relevant:

(H7-9) Other things equal, as the Number of states involved in the cooperative endeavor increases, agreements are more likely to include dispute resolution provisions, in particular, *formal* (centralized) measures.[15]

---

[15] Scott and Stephan (2011) in their work on the enforcement of international law adopt an approach that is very much in the same vein as this book's: They do not take formal enforcement through international tribunals as a given but rather try to explain why parties might choose this design choice. They, too, see the applicability of the contracting literature to international law. Rather than focusing on cooperation problems and actor characteristics to explain design choice, Scott and Stephan make the distinction so critical in contract theory

Empirical testing

In this section, I examine the hypotheses using the COIL sample. Parsing out the effects of punishment problems and informational problems allows me to draw some conclusions about the character of dispute resolution mechanisms. Of course, the two explanations need not be mutually exclusive.

Tables 7.5 and 7.6 provide the results from three probit regressions. The first column captures whether there is any kind of dispute resolution provision in the agreement, including provisions calling for solely informal settlements. The second counts only adjudication and arbitration, which are the two most legalized mechanisms. The third column captures an alternative dimension of variation in dispute settlement design: whether dispute settlement is delegated externally.

The set of explanatory variables is dictated by the hypotheses presented earlier and includes the variables that capture punishment problems (Enforcement problems, Commitment problems, Uncertainty about the State of the World) and informational problems (Uncertainty about Behavior). The cooperation problems are coded as 1 whenever they are found to be present to a high degree in an international agreement. The Number variable is log-transformed in order to capture the effects of percentage increases rather than absolute increases and to reduce skewness.

The regressions include a few control variables. A superpower binary variable is included, coded as 1 whenever the United States is a signatory to an agreement. A realist expectation is that such agreements are less likely to include dispute resolution provisions because the United States, which has the most to lose from international constraints, does not want to be bound by international law in unpredictable ways (Koh 1997: 2615–2617) (see also Brewster 2006, with an argument based in domestic politics). Additionally, issue-area variables are included.

between observable and verifiable conditions. According to Scott and Stephan, the latter is a necessary condition for formal enforcement to be the optimal choice. Scott and Stephan cover many more details regarding delegation to tribunals than I do here. The complementarities between Scott and Stephan's work and COIL's theoretical framework should be exploited in future research.

Table 7.5 *Incidence and form of dispute resolution provisions*

	Any dispute resolution	Arbitration/ adjudication	External
Enforcement	0.80**	1.20***	1.16***
problem	(0.37)	(0.23)	(0.26)
Commitment	1.85***	1.92**	1.70*
problem	(0.64)	(0.98)	(0.95)
Uncertainty State	−0.20	0.33	0.59
of the World	(0.57)	(0.43)	(0.37)
Uncertainty	0.32***	−0.39**	−0.72***
about Behavior	(0.11)	(0.18)	(0.24)
US	−0.43**	−0.22	−0.15
	(0.22)	(0.20)	(0.20)
Number (logged)	0.22***	0.54***	0.53***
	(0.07)	(0.06)	(0.09)
Economics	0.00	−0.27	−0.43***
	(0.12)	(0.20)	(0.16)
Environment	−0.46*	−0.28	−0.50
	(0.27)	(0.47)	(0.45)
Security	0.03	−1.82***	−1.43***
	(0.21)	(0.37)	(0.52)
Constant	−0.72***	−1.90***	−1.94***
	(0.19)	(0.29)	(0.38)
N	234	234	234

Note: Probit results, robust standard errors in parentheses, clustered on issue areas.
*** *significant at 1 percent;* ** *significant at 5 percent;* * *significant at 10 percent*

Table 7.5 presents coefficient estimates and standard errors for the probit regressions.[16] Since probit coefficients are hard to interpret directly, Table 7.6 reports predicted probabilities and the associated average predicted effects.

A few results stand out. First, Enforcement and Commitment problems always increase the probability that an agreement includes

[16] The area under the ROC curve for the models in the first, second, and third columns are 0.875, 0.944, and 0.926, respectively.

Table 7.6 *Predicted probabilities and average predicted effects*

	Any dispute resolution	Arbitration/ adjudication	External
No Enforcement problem	0.41	0.24	0.22
Enforcement problem	0.64	0.49	0.47
Change predicted prob.	*0.23***	*0.25***	*0.25***
No Commitment problem	0.36	0.21	0.20
Commitment problem	0.89	0.68	0.63
Change predicted prob.	*0.53****	*0.47***	*0.43**
No Uncertainty Behavior	0.45	0.36	0.35
Uncertainty Behavior	0.54	0.30	0.24
Change predicted prob.	*0.09***	*−0.06**	*−0.12***
Minimum Number (logged)	0.43	0.25	0.23
Mean Number (logged)	0.54	0.42	0.39
Change predicted prob.	*0.11***	*0.17****	*0.17****
No US	0.51	0.35	0.33
US	0.40	0.31	0.30
Change predicted prob.	*−0.11***	*−0.04*	*−0.03*

Note: For Number (logged), the predicted effect is for a change from an agreement with two participants to an agreement with eleven participants, roughly the sample average. All predicted probabilities in this table are significant at the 1 percent level.
*** significant at 1 percent; ** significant at 5 percent; * significant at 10 percent

a dispute resolution mechanism (H7-1 and H7-2). The probability that an agreement calls for either adjudication or arbitration doubles in the presence of Enforcement problems; it increases by a factor of 3 in the presence of Commitment problems. This is in line with theoretical expectations. Commitment and Enforcement problems are particularly severe problems and hence call for delegated and formal procedures (H7-5 and H7-6). By contrast, for the third variable in the category of punishment problems, Uncertainty about the State of the World, the results are not supportive of H7-3 and H7-7. The coefficients are relatively small, even negative for informal mechanisms, and never statistically significantly different from zero at any conventional level. One explanation for this result might be that Uncertainty about the State of the World is addressed more effectively by other design elements, as Chapters 4 and 5 demonstrate, which temper incentives to defect.

The results surrounding the variable Uncertainty about Behavior (H7-4 and H7-8) are also striking. Such a problem often can be resolved through the exchange of information, and hence formalized dispute procedures or court rulings are not required. Thus, it was expected that the effect should be weakest for the more formal, delegated mechanisms (H7-8). This expectation is consistent with the data – the coefficient is positive and statistically significant at the 1 percent level in the first column of Table 7.5, and, as indicated in the first column of Table 7.6, the probability that an agreement characterized by Uncertainty about Behavior includes a dispute resolution provision increases by 9 percentage points compared with an agreement without such an underlying cooperation problem. Unexpectedly, the signs of the coefficients turn negative and remain statistically significant once informal procedures are excluded from the dependent variable; looking at arbitration and adjudication only, the predicted effect is –6 percentage points and statistically significant at the 10 percent level. For external delegation, the coefficient is again negative and statistically significant at the 1 percent level.

The variable capturing Number of participants has the expected sign and is always statistically significant; the more participants an agreement has, the more likely is the inclusion of a dispute resolution mechanism. Moreover, the effect is stronger for more centralized provisions (H7-9).

From a perspective focused solely on power politics, it is surprising that US involvement has a statistically significant effect only when informal procedures are considered; the effect weakens substantially in size and significance as dispute resolution procedures become more formal.[17] Of course, the conventional wisdom is that the United States tends to attach a lot of reservations to its

---

[17] One could argue this result is even contrary to some realist expectations that US power could be marshaled more effectively in an informal rather than a formal setting to resolve disputes in the United States' favor.

agreements regarding dispute resolution and hence might be exempted from binding settlement mechanisms. But, as I show later in the chapter, such reservations are not the norm; additionally, the United States often voluntarily submits itself to externally delegated dispute resolution forums like the ICJ, even when it has an out.

On the most general level, the findings suggest that dispute resolution mechanisms assume very different tasks. These differential tasks are dictated by the underlying cooperation problems. Uncertainty about Behavior calls for informal resolution of disputes. As Chapter 9 shows, this cooperation problem is also usually solved through some kind of monitoring system, thereby lessening the need for centralized dispute resolution. Problems of Enforcement and Commitment, on the other hand, call for centralized (third-party) dispute resolution. And, finally, Uncertainty about the State of the World is unrelated to dispute resolution provisions and instead solved by the flexibility provisions analyzed in Chapters 4 and 5.

Loopholes in agreements. . .and in theories?

The previous section provided strong support for hypotheses based on the COIL framework. Still, two caveats need to be addressed. First, some dispute resolution provisions are non-binding, and others appear limited given that states often add reservations to their agreements to the effect that they must give permission before any instance of delegated dispute resolution occurs. Do such "loopholes" restrict the functioning of dispute settlement mechanisms and, in essence, render them meaningless design elements? Second, dispute resolution mechanisms may not be used very frequently in practice. Does this imply that dispute settlement mechanisms are useless or ineffective?

Restrictions and reservations

Formal dispute settlement mechanisms impose severe restrictions on state sovereignty (Abbott and Snidal 2000: 436). States may try to relax these constraints through two means. Formal dispute settlement mechanisms may allow for the lawful rejection of settlements (i.e., the

Table 7.7 *Possibility to reject settlements*
(percentage of each form of dispute resolution)

	Arbitration (%)	Adjudication (%)	External (%)
Yes	12	24	20
No	88	76	80
N	60	55	74

mechanisms are non-binding).[18] Alternatively, the parties to an agreement may attach reservations at the time of signature or ratification, thus gaining an exemption from the treaty provisions pertaining to the settlement of disputes.

Table 7.7 provides descriptive statistics on how often an agreement formally mentions the ability of states to reject settlements. The majority of agreements in the COIL sample do not provide for this possibility; the percentage is higher for adjudication and external delegation as opposed to arbitration but does not go above 25 percent for adjudication.

With respect to reservations, almost all agreements allow for some kind of reservation – that is, reservations are not explicitly prohibited in the majority of agreements (recall Table 6.2 in Chapter 6). More significant for this chapter, a closer look at the agreements in the COIL sample reveals that *only nine agreements (4 percent) actually have reservations that states to opt-out of dispute resolution*; eight of these agreements fall under the issue area of human rights, and one is concerned with the financing of terrorism.[19] Thus, there is little reason to be worried that states circumvent formally established dispute settlement procedures by exempting themselves *ex ante* through the use of reservations on a large scale.

Likewise, it is an empirical question whether states that attached reservations to their participation in dispute settlement procedures

---

[18] One could argue that no international ruling is ever binding so the term non-binding is hardly as meaningful in the international law setting as in the domestic setting. But see Alter (2013) for an argument as to why the distinction between international and national law may not be that important on this dimension.

[19] I consider here only reservations that were attached to an agreement at the time it entered into force.

indeed invoke these, or whether they decide to participate despite their reservations, which would further weaken the impact of reservations on the functioning of dispute settlement procedures. Anecdotal evidence suggests states use delegated dispute resolution mechanisms despite their reservations. For example, the United States withdrew its acceptance of the ICJ's compulsory jurisdiction in 1984 and since then has added reservations regarding the ICJ's jurisdiction to many of its treaties. Interestingly, the United States went before the ICJ an average of 0.34 times per year when it accepted its compulsory jurisdiction and an average of 0.32 times per year after withdrawing it, though some of those cases were pursuant to ICJ clauses in treaties that the United States joined before 1984.[20] This example is particularly illustrative given it implicates the behavior of the most powerful state in the system for whom many would argue informal dispute resolution might be beneficial.

Moreover, reservations need not be a state's final word. A number of states have withdrawn their respective reservations, mirroring a move towards greater acceptance of delegated dispute settlement mechanisms. The American Convention on Human Rights, one of the agreements in the COIL sample, provides an example, illustrating the power of soft, non-binding law, especially when viewed in its relationship to hard law, much in line with the argument made by Shaffer and Pollack (2010).

The American Convention delegates authority to both the Inter-American Commission on Human Rights and the Inter-American Court

---

[20] In principle, one could argue that the United States foresaw being taken to the ICJ at a much higher rate than before and hence was motivated to pre-emptively withdraw jurisdiction. Perhaps, for instance, the Nicaragua decision against the United States might have precipitated a cascade of small-state cases against alleged US uses of force. However, two factors might counterbalance this potential trend. First, the possible caseload of the ICJ is quite limited so dramatic increases in the rate at which any one state is before the ICJ are precluded. Second, while it is difficult to find any trends in ICJ caseload, a look at the case history of the ICJ reveals that there are spikes in cases at the beginning of the Cold War and then again in the 1990s. But there are no dramatic changes in individual appearances before the ICJ, except in the cases of France and the United Kingdom, who appear in front of the ICJ much less often after 1980. Thus, given the characteristics it has in common with these two very close allies, the United States probably would have predicted a decrease in its ICJ appearances or no change at all after 1980, but not an increase. (France withdrew compulsory jurisdiction in 1974, whereas the United Kingdom accepted it in 2004.) This is certainly an interesting question for future research.

of Human Rights.[21] The court is able to issue binding rulings on contentious cases and also has the authority to submit advisory opinions, that is, non-binding statements. In 1982, the commission urged Guatemala to suspend an extension of the death penalty to certain crimes despite a reservation Guatemala made allowing the practice. The commission then referred the matter to the court. While Guatemala did not recognize the jurisdiction of the convention's court in this matter, in response to the request by the commission, the court concluded that it was entitled to issue a parallel advisory opinion, which sided with the commission. As a result of this increased pressure, Guatemala's government eventually ceased the death penalty. In 1986 Guatemala withdrew its reservation, and in 1987 finally acknowledged the court's contentious jurisdiction. In essence, the non-binding, advisory opinion exerted pressure on the Guatemalan government that was arguably just as strong as that exerted by a binding ruling.[22] Therefore, even though Guatemala did not fall under the jurisdiction of the court, a less formal dispute settlement mechanism exerted sufficiently strong pressure on the government to change its behavior.

Effectiveness without usage

Although there is little evidence that reservations are frequently used by states to bypass dispute settlement procedures, it could be argued that formal mechanisms are not used with great regularity, outside some presumed exceptional cases like the WTO. This raises the question of whether "practice follows design" – are dispute settlement procedures used in practice and not simply theoretical constructs?

It would be a fallacy to infer from the nonuse of dispute settlement procedures that they are inconsequential, as some realist arguments would imply. Thus, while realists and I make similar predictions about the infrequent use of formal dispute settlement procedures, our explanations contrast starkly.[23] In particular, I contend that making the leap

[21] This discussion relies heavily on Beck, Katherine. 2011. "The Evolution of Dispute Resolution in the American Convention on Human Rights." Unpublished student paper. University of Michigan.

[22] Democratization might also explain such a change, but the process was not underway in a significant way at that time (Jonas 1988 and 2000).

[23] Moreover, even though the prediction with respect to usage is the same, the prediction with respect to design differs; the previous sections provide ample evidence in favor of forward-looking, rational design, not noisy variation.

from unused to ineffective settlement procedures overlooks the strategic interaction among and anticipative behavior of states. In fact, infrequent recourse to dispute settlement procedures may just as well indicate the effectiveness of this institutional design choice.

Two mechanisms explain such an inverse relationship between the use of dispute settlement procedures and their effectiveness. The first mechanism relies on the constraining power of treaties; the second relies on the influence of both conscious design and the shadow of the law in promoting informal settlement, thereby precluding the formal use of dispute settlement procedures.[24]

Constraining to solve underlying commitment and enforcement problems

The first mechanism explaining unused dispute settlement procedures is found in their constraining effects. As was argued previously, dispute resolution mechanisms provide an effective means to address both Commitment and Enforcement problems. However, states may still refrain from actually invoking formal settlement procedures.

If states anticipate the rulings of a dispute settlement mechanism and the associated punishment, they may refrain from a violation in the first place. This implies that the mere presence of a dispute settlement mechanism, particularly when fortified with punishment capabilities, will reduce the incidence of rule violations; of course, if there is no rule violation, recourse to the dispute settlement body is precluded as well.

As Chapter 3 demonstrates, about a quarter of agreements address Commitment problems, and such problems are especially prevalent in the issue areas of human rights and investment. Not coincidentally,

---

[24] Of course, it is quite possible that some dispute settlement mechanisms are never used because they are never established. In other words, even though they are envisioned on paper, they are never implemented in practice. On this point, see Haftel (2012) who examines not only the design of agreements creating Regional Economic Organizations (REOs) but the degree of the agreement's implementation. He finds when implementation follows design, effectiveness results. Haftel (2012: 106) states: "to the extent that REO members follow up on their signed agreements and implement them, they actually produce the pacifying effect." It is worth noting that most of the agreements in the COIL sample are not plagued by the problem of never being established since delegation to a pre-existing court or tribunal is a common design solution as is the creation of ad hoc tribunals on a case-by-case basis. In both cases, the shadow of the law could operate.

these are also the issue areas that are characterized by a high incidence of formal dispute resolution mechanisms. Thus delegated dispute resolution provisions are one design element helping states to solve Commitment problems, as Table 7.5 indicates. For instance, if a new leader comes to power with preferences that favor defection from an existing agreement, the potential costs that a court would impose could be enough to change the leader's payoffs into favoring cooperation. Thus, if delegated dispute resolution mechanisms function in this way, they are not used on the equilibrium path.

With respect to the Enforcement problem, when faced with incentives to defect, even states with stable preferences over time must incorporate the possibility of being punished through a court or other form of formal dispute resolution into their payoffs for defection. Again, if the threat is sufficiently high, defection may be deterred.

For instance, in the CWC intrusive inspections, harsh enforcement mechanisms (such as powerful sanctions and potential referral to the UNSC), and a highly legalized dispute settlement mechanism that allows for referral to the ICJ discourage noncompliance. Consequently, compliance with the treaty remains high.

It is worth noting that dispute resolution provisions might also serve a *screening function*: A credible dispute resolution mechanism separates out states not serious about complying. (Simmons [2009] provides an excellent discussion of this issue.) The underlying cooperation problem, Uncertainty about Preferences, has a positive, significant effect on the inclusion of delegated dispute resolution provisions; however, the effect disappears once one controls for the Number of participants to the agreement. These two variables are quite positively correlated;[25] therefore, the lack of significance on Uncertainty about Preferences in a multivariate regression may be attributable to this collinearity.[26]

---

[25] Uncertainty about Preferences is also highly correlated with the human rights issue area indicator variable.

[26] In the case of the CWC, one could argue that insincere ratifiers are screened out by design features like the one that is the focus of this chapter. However, the point remains that, whether the constraining or screening function is at play (or both given the heterogeneity characterizing the implicated states), there has been little need to invoke the dispute settlement mechanism; its incorporation either helps screen or constrain and thus it is not used often on the equilibrium path.

Table 7.8 *Explicit encouragement to settle disputes informally among agreements with formal dispute resolution provisions (percentage of each form of dispute resolution provision)*

	Arbitration (%)	Adjudication (%)	External (%)	Total (%)
Yes	95	75	82	80
No	5	25	18	20
N	60	55	74	81

Informalism and the influence of the shadow of the law

The second mechanism explaining unused dispute settlement proce-dures is the explicit design feature encouraging informal dispute resolution. These informal procedures often explicitly operate in the "shadow of the law." That is, these *provisions encouraging informal dispute resolution operate with formal dispute resolution provisions in the background.* Descriptive statistics on design elements encouraging informal dispute resolution are displayed in Table 7.8.

Of the agreements with formal dispute settlement mechanisms, the overwhelming majority also explicitly encourage the *in*formal settle-ment of disputes. Despite the fact that mechanisms stipulating adjudi-cation and external delegation allow for outside settlements less often, the pattern is impressive – very few agreements rule out the informal settlement of disputes in the shadow of formalized procedures. The question, of course, is how often and under what conditions states take advantage of this opportunity, an issue certainly warranting further research.

Moreover, if states do use informal procedures, why do they do so? It might be the legally binding (see Table 7.7), and therefore less calculable, character of formal dispute settlements that drives states into using informal procedures – but it may also be the reduced cost, confidentiality, and expedited procedure that informal settlements provide, especially compared with the highly legalized and lengthy procedures in adjudicated and externally delegated mechanisms. Again, detailed case studies would be necessary to obtain further insights into these questions.

It is also worth noting that more than half of the agreements that encourage informal settlements also impose time limits on the dispute resolution process. Hence, states may try to settle informally; but if they do not manage to resolve their disputes within a specified, finite period, the formal dispute settlement process kicks in. This implies that the formal procedures cast a rather strong shadow on informal settlements.

Concluding thoughts

The presence or absence of dispute resolution provisions is explained by the underlying cooperation problems states are facing when designing their agreements. Not only does the half-and-half statistic that began this chapter make sense when justified through COIL's theoretical lens; the choice between informal and formal venues also makes sense. The COIL data also illustrate that the formal venues to which states delegate are far broader than those select set of courts that are the focus of much of the literature.[27]

Although the chapter explains why the use of a dispute resolution mechanism is not directly related to its effectiveness, some may still reasonably ask of this analysis, what happens when a dispute arises and an agreement calls for delegation? Even though this is not the question of this book, it still is helpful to look very briefly into what happens in practice with a couple of agreements from the random sample from two different issue areas: economics and human rights.

In economics, a common type of agreement in the COIL sample is a BIT. It turns out that the record of compliance with international arbitration awards in investment disputes is markedly positive. Although statistical evidence is difficult to compile because many decisions remain private, Baldwin, Kantor, and Nolan (2006) note that the awards rendered by ICSID panels have largely been final and self-executing. From 1966 to 2006, only three cases appear to have been brought to national courts to challenge the enforcement and

---

[27] With respect to cooperation on air quality, COIL predicts that Canada and the United States would choose to delegate dispute resolution to some kind of third party, in this case the IJC, COIL does not offer any theory as to how this third party is chosen. Scholarly work on the choice of venue (e.g., Mitchell and Powell 2011) would complement COIL on this dimension.

execution of a panel's decision.[28] Moreover, just as BITs are on the rise, the rate at which disputes are submitted to ICSID also remains on the rise, and developing nations are increasingly using international investment arbitration.

As mentioned earlier, one of the human rights agreements from the random sample is the American Convention on Human Rights, which creates its own court, the Inter-American Court of Human Rights. Over the years, the Inter-American Court has seen numerous cases. As Tan (2005: 343) states, "Of those many rulings, only a few states have refused or been slow to comply with these Courts' orders." Indeed, citing international law scholar Douglass Cassel, Tan states, "the Court has only had one and a half full-blown, defiant responses" (2005: 321).[29]

These two examples from the investment and human rights areas also speak to the famous Downs, Rocke, and Barsoom (1996) argument that states self-select into those agreements that they deem to be in their interest anyway – as they put it, "most treaties require states to make only modest departures from what they would have done in the absence of an agreement" (1996: 380). Why would states ever need dispute resolution mechanisms if agreements are so shallow that no state needs to change its behavior to be a member and in compliance? The conflicts in the areas of investment and human rights just described would not have occurred if no party needed to change its behavior in any meaningful way. Moreover, given the number of agreements that delegate to the ICJ and the concern among scholars that reservations weaken the court, Llamzon's (2007: 852) finding that "the post-Nicaragua Court has indeed seen better compliance with its final judgments (albeit sometimes taking years before substantial compliance was achieved), regardless of the manner by which jurisdiction was acquired" is also suggestive.

There is every reason to think that dispute settlement provisions work at the international level at least to some degree. Given that domestic courts are not used in every dispute, that most of us do not

---

[28] If a defendant refuses to comply with the final decision of an ICSID panel, an investor can petition its home government to refer the case to the ICJ. For an overview and analysis of ICSID enforcement mechanisms, see Choi (1995).

[29] The article cited is Douglass Cassel, *Peru Withdraws from the Court: Will the Inter-American Human Rights System Meet the Challenge?* 20 *Human Rights Law Journal* 167, 167–68 (1999).

ever even go to court (at least in part because of the deterrence mechanism), and that rates of compliance are not perfect in the domestic context, the difference between the international and national settings on this dimension is a difficult empirical question that cannot be answered without evidence.

The evidence in this chapter does point to the rational design of dispute resolution mechanisms. The tremendous variation is fine-grained and systematic, and the choices states make are consistent with those that would stabilize cooperative outcomes. Any scholar asserting that dispute resolution provisions do not matter has to explain why states seem to exhibit such intentionality in the design of these provisions.

8 | *Punishment provisions*

[I]f the agreement is well-designed – sensible, comprehensible, and with a practical eye to probable patterns of conduct and interaction – compliance problems and enforcement issues are likely to be manageable, [and therefore strong enforcement mechanisms are unnecessary].

(Chayes and Chayes 1993: 183)

[Because] one player, by defecting, can reap rewards by placing the other player at an immediate and overwhelming disadvantage, ... there is little hope for stable, extensive cooperation [in security affairs]. [However], *[t]he dangers of swift, decisive defection do not apply in most international economic issues.*

(Lipson 1984: 14, 17)

These two quotes, the first by a pair of international law scholars, the second by a political scientist, are classic and important statements, representing two well-respected schools of thought. These quotes are also not quite consistent with one another. Additionally, we have the following descriptive statistics:

- Almost half of economics agreements contain a formal punishment provision.
- About one-sixth of security agreements contain such a provision.

How then do we reconcile these two statements not only with each other but also with the empirical reality? Specifically, first, why do so many economics agreements contain punishment provisions, a fairly strong form of enforcement provision, if "well-designed" agreements are unlikely to need them? Second, if security cooperation is so risky, why do so few security agreements contain formal punishment provisions?

In this chapter,[1] I provide a theory of punishment provisions that includes an articulation of when such provisions are themselves part of

---

[1] Most of this chapter draws directly from Koremenos (2013c).

a well-designed, "practical" agreement. I also use this design feature as a point of departure for an analysis of potentially informal provisions within formal international law, thereby addressing the unexpected absence of formal punishment provisions in particular cooperative endeavors. Of course, a key challenge in the study of informalism is identifying and quantifying what is indeed informal across more than a few, well-known cases. In this chapter, I offer a theory and method to analyze the role of informalism across the COIL random sample.

I first present a theory of punishment provisions and test the theory against the COIL data. I then turn to a consideration of informal punishment provisions. I briefly review a few important scholarly contributions on informalism as well as some important literature on compliance and the need for punishment provisions. I also propose a few ways to think about "missing provisions." I present hypotheses about whether punishments will be formalized or not and exploit a new research design developed in Koremenos (2013c) to test these hypotheses. Specifically, I exploit the model presented in the first half of the chapter to predict the presence of enforcement mechanisms in the COIL agreements. Next, I analyze those cases that are "misclassified" – cases in which the model predicts the presence of such mechanisms, but the agreements lack them. The two-stage approach is necessary because informal punishment provisions are generally unobservable. The misclassified agreements are thus candidates for informal enforcement. I show that misclassified agreements are systematically different from correctly predicted agreements in a manner that is consistent with my hypotheses. I also provide case study evidence that punishment does occur in cases in which the punishment provision was potentially left informal. Overall, the results on punishment provisions presented here provide further evidence that the details of international law are chosen systematically, including the details of what's left out!

This chapter thus provides an enhanced theoretical and empirical picture of an important design dimension of international law, punishment provisions, first by refining the original Rational Design conjecture, *Scope increases with the severity of the Enforcement problem* to consider when that increase in scope will occur formally and when it will be implicit or informal, second by engaging the Legalization volume and arguing that punishment provisions can help solve (domestic) Commitment problems, third, by testing and disconfirming the Rational Design conjecture that *Centralization increases with Uncertainty about Behavior*,[2] and fourth by drawing on the seminal work of Axelrod (1984) and Oye (1986) regarding Number and cooperation.[3]

Overall, the analyses show that in most cases when the underlying cooperation problems call for punishment provisions and the Number of actors is greater than two, punishment provisions are formally incorporated into international law. Still, in cases of great Preference Heterogeneity and economic Power Asymmetry among members, informality with respect to punishment provisions provides states with flexibility to tailor their responses to defection based on the realized specifics. As elaborated later, these results indicate that both efficiency concerns and power influence the design of international law, a finding that reinforces a central theme of this book.

Formal punishment provisions

Definitions and descriptive statistics

Agreements sometimes incorporate inducements to compliance, which are attempts to change the payoffs for cooperation and defection. In Rational Design (2001b), such inducements fall under the design dimension, scope. The inducements can take the form of rewards or punishments (including financial sanctions, non-financial sanctions, the curtailing of membership rights, or expulsion from the agreement).

As elaborated in Chapter 2, the 1962 Coffee Agreement includes a punishment provision that specifies that any exporter that exceeds its

---

[2] The finding that punishment provisions (over 90 percent of which entail some kind of centralization) are not correlated with underlying Uncertainty about Behavior is consistent with the findings in Chapters 7 and 9 that this cooperation problem is best solved with informal dispute resolution and with monitoring based on self-reports, respectively – neither of which demands centralization.

[3] Two Rational Design conjectures on issue scope are not engaged in this book: *Issue scope increases with greater Heterogeneity among larger Numbers of actors* and *Issue scope increases with the severity of the Distribution problem.* Both of these conjectures stem from bargaining theory (see, e.g., Sebenius 1983, Tollison and Willet 1979, and Raiffa 1982) and hence primarily address the *substantive* provisions of the agreement.

Table 8.1 *Inducements to compliance by issue area (percentage of each issue area)*

Issue area	Rewards (%)	Punishments (%)
Economics	0	46
Environment	0	9
Human rights	0	39
Security	2	17
Total	0	32

N = 234

quota will have the amount of the excess deducted from its next quota. If such noncompliance is repeated, double the amount can be deducted. If an exporter breaks the rules a third time, it can be expelled from the agreement.[4]

As revealed in Chapter 7, investment agreements generally prescribe arbitration as a method of dispute resolution. One of the third-parties to which multiple investment agreements in the COIL sample delegate is ICSID, which issues binding recommendations. Recall the finding by Baldwin, Kantor, and Nolan (2006) that the awards rendered by ICSID panels have largely been final and self-executing. These awards are a form of punishment for the party found to be in violation of the investment treaty.

Table 8.1 displays descriptive statistics on the dependent variable: whether an agreement has inducements to compliance. (An agreement may, of course, have more than one type of inducement to compliance.) Interestingly, only one agreement in the sample stipulates formal rewards for compliant behavior and this agreement, the Biological Weapons Convention (BWC), includes a punishment provision as well. In contrast, formal punishment provisions occur frequently in international agreements. In many cases, punishments are conducted by agreement members themselves or by intergovernmental bodies created by the agreement. However, punishments may also be delegated to already existing international institutions. In the context of punishment provisions, the most relevant institution is the UNSC. The UNSC is a source of punishments in multiple agreements in the

[4] See Article 36.

Table 8.2 *Inducements to compliance by sub-issue area*
(percentage of each sub-issue area)

Sub-issue area	Rewards (%)	Punishments (%)
Agricultural	0	33
Finance	0	0
Investment	0	93
Monetary	0	0
Environment	0	9
Human rights	0	39
Disarmament	11	44
Security	0	11
Total	0	32

N = 234

sample via states having the right to complain formally to the UNSC; consequently, these agreements, which include the 1975 BWC and the 1997 CWC, are coded as having formal punishment provisions.

Table 8.1 also reveals that the incidence of punishment provisions varies vastly across issue areas. Almost half of agreements in the issue areas of economics and human rights contain punishment provisions; the share is much lower for environmental and security agreements.

Table 8.2 displays these same descriptive statistics across the eight sub-issue areas featured in the COIL random sample. Finance and monetary agreements never feature inducements to compliance, whereas investment agreements almost always do. Disarmament agreements are much more likely to include formal inducements than are security agreements.

A theory of punishment provisions

In this section, I present a theory of punishment provisions. It is worth mentioning that the theory articulated here applies to inducements to compliance more broadly, that is, anything that changes the payoffs an actor receives from either cooperating or defecting. Thus, a reward is one kind of inducement in that it increases the payoff from cooperation; the flip side is a punishment that decreases the payoff from defection.

Because, as is indicated in Table 8.1, rewards are rarely *formally* incorporated into international agreements, I use the term punishment to capture either kind of inducement.[5] But as the case study on the NPT will show, rewards as well as punishments are employed in cases in which the inducements to compliance are left *informal*.

Questioning the importance of punishment provisions in treaties, Chayes, Chayes, and Mitchell (1995) point out that they are not aware of any environmental agreement that allows for military actions as punishment. It should be emphasized that punishment provisions need not involve military action. Nor do punishments have to involve economic sanctions, which are also rarely authorized in environmental agreements (Chayes, Chayes, and Mitchell 1995: 79). However, these authors do find that environmental agreements often authorize "membership sanctions," depriving violators of rights and privileges. The authors note that such membership sanctions are rarely used and thus dismiss them as ineffective. This is too quick a conclusion: The rare use of such sanctions may indicate their very effectiveness in detering violations and making actual punishment unnecessary.[6] Punishment provisions appear to be neither uncommon nor unnecessary for the functioning of international agreements.

The finding that punishment provisions such as membership sanctions are incorporated into international law poses another question, which is motivated by the realist literature: In response to a violation, states could revert to the status quo in place before the agreement was concluded; thus, why incorporate punishment provisions, whether formal or implicit, in the first place? That is, a lack of punishment provisions may indicate that the participating states already have an understanding of the potential response to rule violations: retaliation that ends cooperation.

Punishment provisions provide an important advantage over threats to revert to the status quo. Reversion to the status quo (realized via what game theory calls the "grim trigger strategy") is often "over-punishing" and results in the breakdown of cooperation entirely.

---

[5] Rewards should not necessarily be understood as irrelevant to agreement design just because we rarely see them incorporated formally. States sometimes negotiate stand-alone aid agreements that are closely associated with other agreements. How often and why they do so is worthy of future research.

[6] See more on this point later in the chapter.

Punishment provisions that do not end all cooperation avoid these pathologies and allow for more robust cooperation over time.

When would we expect to see punishment provisions incorporated into an international agreement? A prime condition calling for punishment provisions is the existence of an Enforcement problem: When the incentives to defect are large, states want to insure themselves against being the "sucker" by being able to punish the defector (see Chapter 2). One way to address Enforcement problems is to impose severe and credible sanctions on defectors. Lowering the noncooperation payoff of the original game, defections thus become less attractive for each party, and hence mutual defections are less likely to occur. Expecting the maintenance of cooperation, states are thus willing to sign onto agreements that would be infeasible in the absence of punishment provisions. Hence, a first hypothesis is as follows:

(H8-1): Other things equal, agreements that are characterized by an underlying Enforcement problem are more likely to include punishment provisions than those not characterized by an underlying enforcement problem.

Domestic Commitment problems constitute another factor that should, other things equal, result in the inclusion of punishment provisions in international agreements. In states that have not solved the credible commitment problem through domestic institutions, changes in the political support base of a government, for instance, may make it harder to comply with international commitments and thus trigger violations. Punishment provisions, whose negative consequences offset such political pressures, may deter violations. That states intentionally try to solve such Commitment problems through "tougher" agreements is also recognized in the Legalization literature (Goldstein et al. 2000b: 393), as Chapter 2 elaborates. This leads to a second hypothesis:

(H8-2): Other things equal, agreements that are characterized by an underlying Commitment problem are more likely to include punishment provisions than those not characterized by an underlying commitment problem.

Recall from Chapter 3 that overseeing complaints and punishments is one of the most popular tasks delegated to either a body created by an agreement or a pre-existing body. Over 90 percent of the agreements that incorporate punishment provisions centralize this task. Thus, a third cooperation problem potentially associated with the inclusion of punishment provisions is Uncertainty about Behavior, leading to the following hypothesis:

(H8-3): Other things equal, agreements that are characterized by an underlying Uncertainty about Behavior are more likely to include punishment provisions than those not characterized by underlying uncertainty about behavior.[7]

Punishment provisions also become more attractive in multilateral agreements. In bilateral agreements, no coordination is necessary to punish a defector – Axelrod's (1984) celebrated insights on tit-for-tat as a strategy in two-actor games underscore this point. As Oye (1986: 19) points out, as the Number of actors increases, the likelihood of including a state that is "too weak (domestically) to detect, react, or implement a strategy of reciprocity, that cannot distinguish reliably between cooperation and defection by other states, or that departs from even minimal standards of rationality" is increasing dramatically as well. Moreover, if punishments cannot be targeted to defectors, but apply to all participants of the agreement, strategies of reciprocity become impossible to implement if states do not want to risk the breakdown of cooperation. The fourth hypothesis, hence, is as follows:

(H8-4): Other things equal, Bilateral agreements are less likely to include punishment provisions than are multilateral agreements.

Empirical testing

Based on the hypotheses, we can build an empirical model of punishment provisions. Table 8.3 shows coefficient estimates and robust standard errors from a probit regression, with the presence of formal punishment provisions as the dependent variable; the regressors are based on the hypotheses regarding when a punishment provision is

---

[7] This is a variant of the Rational Design conjecture *Centralization increases with Uncertainty about Behavior* (Chapter 2; Koremenos, Lipson, Snidal 2001b: 787) since punishment is a task that can be, and almost always is in the COIL sample, centralized.

Table 8.3 *Presence of formal punishment provisions*

Enforcement problem	1.02***
	(0.23)
Commitment problem	1.40***
	(0.28)
Uncertainty about Behavior	0.30
	(0.35)
Bilateral agreement	−0.97***
	(0.30)
Economics	0.89**
	(0.39)
Environment	−1.04**
	(0.47)
Security	−0.02
	(0.42)
Constant	−1.04***
	(0.35)
N	234

Note: Probit results, robust standard errors in parentheses.
*** *significant at 1 percent;* ** *significant at 5 percent;* *
significant at 10 percent

needed, and all are coded as dichotomous variables. Issue area indicator variables address the stratified sampling in COIL.[8]

The hypotheses perform quite well. Except for the coefficient on Uncertainty about Behavior, all coefficients of interest are large in substantive terms and statistically significant at the 1 percent level. Table 8.4 displays predicted probabilities and associated average predicted effects. The predicted effects (first differences) tell us how much (in percentage points) the presence of some cooperation problem (i.e., moving from a coding of 0 to 1) increases the probability that an agreement contains a punishment provision. For instance, an agreement with an underlying Enforcement problem is on average 25 percentage points more likely to have a formal punishment provision than an agreement without an Enforcement problem.

The average predicted effects of Enforcement and Commitment problems as well as Bilateral agreement are large in substantive

[8] See Chapter 3.

Table 8.4 *Predicted probabilities and average predicted effects*

	Presence of formal punishment provisions
No Enforcement problem	0.23
Enforcement problem	0.48
Change predicted prob.	*0.25****
No Commitment problem	0.22
Commitment problem	0.60
Change predicted prob.	*0.39****
No Bilateral agreement	0.45
Bilateral agreement	0.24
Change predicted prob.	*−0.21****

Note: All predicted probabilities in this table are significant at the 1 percent level.
*** *significant at 1 percent;* ** *significant at 5 percent;* * *significant at 10 percent*

terms: On average, the presence of a Commitment problem, for instance, raises the probability that punishment provisions are included by 39 percentage points. Overall, judging from the significance and size of these predicted effects, the hypotheses regarding the need for punishment provisions perform extremely well.

Relying on the receiver operating characteristics (ROC), a heuristic used to evaluate fit of models with binary dependent variables (Greenhill, Ward, and Sacks 2011: 992), the model seems to perform well for predictive purposes. In short, the ROC compares the fraction of agreements with punishment provisions that are (correctly) predicted to have punishment provisions with the fraction of agreements without punishment provisions that are (incorrectly) predicted to have punishment provisions. The area under the ROC curve is 0.900, indicating an astonishingly good fit.[9] Consequently, agreements that were predicted to have but do not have punishment provisions can be viewed as outliers, that is, candidates for informal punishment provisions.

---

[9] Recall a model without predictive power would yield a score of 0.5 and a perfect fit a score of 1.

Informal punishment provisions

Informalism: Literature review

Both scholars and policymakers know that informalism is critical to international cooperation across many issue areas. Yet, scholars have struggled to articulate in any refined or testable way just when and how informalism is important and what role it plays either alone or in conjunction with formal cooperation. A key challenge in the study of informalism is identifying and quantifying what is indeed informal across more than a few, well-known cases.

Informalism has been defined in various ways in the IL literature. Schachter (1977) lists characteristics of legally non-binding agreements and considers such agreements as a whole informal (see also Aust 1986). Schachter mentions that imprecise, overly general wording in international agreements is often taken as indicative of non-binding intention and a low level of legal obligation. This account squares well with Abbott and Snidal's (2000) "soft law," characterized by weak legal obligations, vague wording, and weak or no delegation.

Coming from the IR side, Downs and Rocke (1990) highlight the role of tacit bargaining in fostering international cooperation, with tacit bargaining being more about action that signals intention than about formalized negotiation. They give many examples of tacit bargaining and importantly point out that most cooperation combines tacit and formalized communication. Lipson (1991) identifies a broad range of domestic factors that may motivate informal agreements. Compared to formally ratified treaties, informal agreements are easier for governments to negotiate, faster to implement, more flexible, and lack the public visibility of treaties. Lipson emphasizes the ability of informal agreements to address uncertain, changing environments since such agreements can be adjusted and renegotiated more easily than formal agreements.

More recently, the literature has shifted emphasis to the relationship between formal and informal agreements. Cogan (2009: 212), who examines informal agreements in the selection of international bureaucrats, provides a very clear rationale for why informal agreements enjoy such a prevalence in the international system: "informal agreements largely take account of, and reallocate authority to match, the differences in power and interests that pervade the international system when those differences cannot be acknowledged formally."

While these authors have noted that some cooperation is optimally left informal, none of their insights have been systematically tested or theoretically refined, perhaps because of the obstacles to quantifying what is informal. An exception is Stone's (2011) analysis of informal governance in three important formal international institutions: the IMF, the WTO, and the EU.[10] Stone explicitly considers the relationship between formal and informal governance and concludes that scholars "generally failed to connect the dots, because they have not appreciated that informal governance mechanisms exist primarily to serve the interests of powerful states, while formal rules are generally designed to protect the weak" (2011: 207). Unlike most extant studies, Stone explicitly acknowledges that informal elements co-exist with formal rules in many international agreements. Additionally, he argues that in many cases informal mechanisms modify and even overrule formal procedures. He contends that the balance between informal and formal elements within an institution is an equilibrium outcome, derived from the member states' power and interests.

My analysis connects well to Stone's work in that it examines the absence of inducements to compliance in international agreements as an example of informalism in formal international institutions. The agreement itself can still employ precise language and hence create strong legal obligations; nonetheless, at the time of negotiation, some subset of the agreement was left out to be regulated informally in the future. My analysis is also very much in the spirit of Lipson's (1991) with his emphasis on flexibility as a response to uncertainty.

Missing provisions?

What made states leave out a formal punishment provision in the NPT yet articulate very detailed formal punishment provisions in the series

---

[10] See also Kleine's particularly rich analysis of the EU presidency (Kleine, Mareike. 2010. "Making Cooperation Work: Informal Governance in the EU and Beyond." Presented at the 2010 American Political Science Association Annual Meeting. Available at http://papers.ssrn.com/sol3/papers.cfm?abstract_id=1641953 [Last accessed June 23, 2015]).

of International Coffee Agreements, which governed that commodity from 1962 to 1989? The NPT is important, has the support of major powers, and is arguably not just for show. In fact, the absence of a formal punishment provision in the NPT has not led to widespread noncooperation among members, despite the fact that incentives to defect do exist. Perhaps one could even jump to the conclusion that most states, most of the time, understand that defection will be noticed and potentially addressed – that is, punishment provisions exist but are left informal. In other words, within *formal* law, a consequential provision was left deliberately *informal*.

Before we can analyze the NPT, we must first ask the following general question: Why might specific design provisions be sometimes left out of international agreements? There are three potential explanations.

First, a specific provision might not serve any purpose because the situation does not call for it. For instance, consider dispute resolution procedures. As Chapter 7 shows, the inclusion of dispute resolution provisions is a deliberate choice in response to certain cooperation problems. When those particular cooperation problems are absent, dispute resolution provisions are rare. Put differently, the efficient design of international law implies that unnecessary design elements will be left out. When states face incentives to defect attributable to a prisoners' dilemma-like trade game, dispute resolution provisions make sense; when states find themselves in a simple coordination game to prevent frontier fires, dispute resolution mechanisms are unnecessary, and rational states should not pay the transaction and sovereignty costs of delegating such authority.

Second, other design features may fill the place of the "missing provision" so to speak; hence one design element is substituted for another. Extremely precise wording, for instance, may render dispute resolution mechanisms for agreement interpretation obsolete as I argue in the concluding section of Chapter 6. If precise wording allows parties to identify defection and hence predict with great certainty what would happen should dispute resolution be triggered, parties can save on delegation costs entirely. We rarely see speeding violations identified by radar challenged in court.

Third, despite being useful for the underlying problem structure, states may deliberately leave out parts of an agreement. In such cases, the potential for triggering the unwritten design mechanism is implicitly understood. As mentioned, the NPT is a striking example of this third category.

Of course, the literature provides alternative explanations as to why agreements like the NPT lack punishment provisions. Chayes and Chayes (1993), for instance, whose quote leads this chapter, strongly suggest that successfully negotiated agreements rarely need explicit punishment provisions. Yet, *punishment provisions could be one of the critical parts of such well-designed agreements.* The very existence of a punishment provision may tilt the calculus of states towards compliance, especially when states have incentives to defect.

A theory of informal punishment provisions

The design of punishment provisions: Formal or informal

What might explain why states leave out explicit punishment provisions in situations in which such provisions are deemed necessary? Informality is a form of flexibility, in that the particulars can be decided both at a later time depending on the circumstances and on a case-by-case, as opposed to uniform, basis. The definition of informality used in this analysis, the deliberate omission of a provision, is akin to an incomplete contract. Incomplete contracts arise because *ex ante* it is difficult to get a particular group to agree on specific provisions and because *ex post* parties may prefer discretion in how they react to particular events, like noncompliance.

In what follows, I first explain how Heterogeneity among the participating states is related to both the difficulty of getting things agreed upon *ex ante* as well as the usefulness of discretion *ex post* and how heterogeneity might therefore lead to informalism. I then explain how great differences in power might lead powerful states to prefer informal versus formal punishment as a way of exerting more control over outcomes.[11]

---

[11] Two other variables could influence the choice of formal versus informal punishment: renegotiation-proofness, that is, the delivery of the punishment is in the interest of all states other than the defector *ex post*, and the targetability of sanctions, that is, many agreements are best enforced through punishments in other issue areas, as in what Downs and Jones (2002: 107) call a "coercive linkage penalty." Future work should focus on developing consistent measures of these important concepts.

Heterogeneity among participants

Heterogeneity among parties to an agreement makes compromise harder to achieve. Decentralized (i.e., not formally and explicitly defined) punishment provisions thus become more attractive. Oates (1999) makes a similar point in the context of fiscal federalism: When preferences are diverse, rather than agreeing on a centralized, uniform mechanism, it becomes more attractive to delegate decision-making authority and fiscal autonomy to constituent units.[12] Ehrlich and Posner (1974) connect this mechanism to law-making: If compromise is hard to achieve, it becomes more attractive to leave out specifics. This argument is in line with one of the hypotheses in Chapter 6, which argues that a greater Number of participants makes it harder to agree on precise rules. Such rules could be substantive ones, as in Chapter 6, or they could be procedural, such as the punishment provisions examined here.[13]

The following quote from a US State Department briefing paper illustrates the difficulty of a uniform strategy and is from the period when CEDAW (coded below as having potentially informal punishment) was negotiated:

But what measures or combination of approaches will be most effective: pressure of public opinion, denial of trade or aid, or quiet diplomacy behind the scenes? Are there ways of providing incentives (as well as pressures) for improved human rights practices? ... And finally, what are the relative advantages and disadvantages of bilateral and/or multilateral approaches; how can they most effectively be used in combination?

Because of the complexities involved in the above factors, the Department has been unable to find any single formula for categorizing the human rights situations that require attention and action, and has tentatively concluded that decisions have to be made case by case from an analysis of all the circumstances involved.[14]

---

[12] Policies can then be tailored to the particularities of the subnational units.

[13] The argument here is that heterogeneity among participants affects the design of punishment provisions; in contrast, heterogeneity is assumed not to affect the likelihood that punishment provisions are required. Consider the example of the prisoners' dilemma: the actors are as alike as they can be in a game-theoretic sense; yet this homogeneity does not rule out the existence of an Enforcement problem and hence the usefulness of punishment provisions, especially in the multi-player case.

[14] US Department of State. Briefing Paper on Human Rights. National Archives, RG 59, L/HR Files: Lot 80 D 275, Human Rights S/P Study – Policy Planning

The following quote from the National Security Council about the lack of a punishment provision in the NPT makes the point even better:

In view of the difficulties of getting worldwide agreement on a system of sanctions to deter or punish violations of the treaty, the inclusion of provisions for sanctions is not recommended. It is expected, however, that *the tacit threat of sanctions by the major powers* will tend to deter smaller countries from violating this treaty.[15] (emphasis mine)

Thus, a first hypothesis is as follows:

(H8-5) Other things equal, agreements with informal as opposed to formal punishment provisions are characterized by greater Heterogeneity among participants.[16]

Power

Informal punishment provisions are also useful for accommodating power differences within international agreements. The declassified quote from the National Security Council regarding punishment in the NPT not only calls attention to the contracting problem; it very clearly exposes beliefs about the implications of power differentials. Tierney (2008: 284) argues powerful actors are very careful about preserving their freedom of action. This view squares well with Stone's (2011) insight that formal rules protect the weak and informal rules serve the powerful. Informal punishment provisions give powerful states more freedom with respect to the application of enforcement mechanisms and thus give strong states more options in how they can

Vol. II. Confidential. Available at http://history.state.gov/historicaldocuments/frus1969-76ve03/d264 [Last accessed October 11, 2012].

[15] US National Security Council. "Value and feasibility of a nuclear non-proliferation treaty." Confidential. Issue Date: December 10, 1964. Date Declassified: May 2, 1988. Sanitized. Complete. Page 19.

[16] Of course, an extremely high level of regime heterogeneity might lead to no agreement at all. Some scholars worry, and rightly so, about the conceptual and evidentiary consequences of focusing on the selected sample of realized agreements rather than on the latent population of all potential agreements. Appendix 3 addresses this topic, and Koremenos and Smith (2014) address it in greater detail (Koremenos, Barbara and Jeffrey Smith. 2014. "When to Select a Selection Model." Working Paper. Ann Arbor, University of Michigan). Notwithstanding, within the sample of actually realized agreements, the theoretical argument implies that the more heterogeneous the participants are, the more likely the agreement will have informal as opposed to formal enforcement provisions.

exercise their power. Stone (2011: 13) states: "[The formal rules] embody a broad consensus of the membership, while the informal rules allow exceptional access for powerful states." Cogan (2009), too, notes that informal law avoids explicitly acknowledging large differences in power and influence among participants to an agreement. Such logic is consistent with the Rational Design conjecture *Asymmetry of Control increases with Asymmetry Among Contributors* since the flexibility afforded by informality allows strong states to exercise more control over the institution (Chapter 2; Koremenos, Lipson, and Snidal 2001b: 791). For these reasons, the final hypothesis is as follows:

(H8-6) Other things equal, the larger the Power differentials among parties to an agreement, the more likely the agreement is to contain informal as opposed to formal punishment provisions.

Empirical testing

Using the coefficient estimates in Table 8.3, we can predict the probability that each agreement in the sample should, theoretically, include punishment provisions. The predicted probabilities range from 0 percent to 95 percent, with a mean of 32 percent and a standard deviation of 0.32. Using 0.5 as cut-off, about 85 percent of the agreements were predicted correctly – that is, were predicted to have punishment provisions and in fact had them formally incorporated, or were predicted to not have any punishment provisions and in fact did not have any. Table 8.5 shows the twelve agreements that were predicted to have punishment provisions with a probability of at least 50 percent, yet do not have any – that is, candidates for informal punishment provisions. This set of agreements, which I refer to as *misclassified agreements*, will be subjected to further inquiry in the following sections – in particular, whether the misclassified agreements do indeed have the characteristics they are predicted to have (greater Heterogeneity and greater Power differentials).

A number of robustness checks were performed with respect to methodological alternatives to identifying the set of misclassified agreements. The set of misclassified agreements using these alternative strategies is very similar to the one displayed in Table 8.5. Thus the main results of the paper hold under these alternative model specifications.

Table 8.5 *Misclassified agreements regarding punishment*

Agreement name	COIL ID	UNTS	Pred. prob.
International convention for the suppression of the financing of terrorism (with annex)	FN 2–17	38349	0.56
Exchange of letters constituting an agreement relating to investment guaranties	IN 16	6621	0.61
International convention on the protection of the rights of all migrant workers and members of their families	HR 2–5	39481	0.61
International convention on the suppression and punishment of the crime of apartheid	HR 22	14861	0.64
Convention on nature protection and wild life preservation in the Western Hemisphere	EN 48	485	0.74
Convention on the elimination of all forms of discrimination against women	HR 11	20378	0.75
International covenant on civil and political rights	HR 8	14668	0.75
Convention for the protection of human rights and fundamental freedoms	HR 10	2889	0.75
Convention on the rights of the child	HR 2–1	27531	0.75
Agreement with respect to quality wheat	AC 57	6389	0.81
United Nations convention on independent guarantees and stand-by letters of credit	FN 2–13	38030	0.89
Treaty on collective security	SE 2–18	32307	0.91

Agreements without punishment, yet predicted to include punishment with probability > 0.5.

Analyzing misclassified agreements: Formal versus informal punishment

The research design introduced in Koremenos (2013c) will now be exploited to shed light on the choice of formal versus informal punishment provisions by comparing the set of agreements that are correctly predicted to have punishment provisions and those that need punishment but lack formal provisions – the misclassified agreements. According to the theory, misclassified agreements should be characterized by informal punishment provisions. Still, within that set of agreements there could also be cases in which punishment is needed but not provided informally. The next section begins to address this conflation of categories given that research thus far indicates that well over a third are found to have some form of enforcement and only one thus far seems to be a clear case of failed cooperation. This research, therefore, is supportive of the following thesis: What's left out is often really there. The statistics are especially promising given that the inability to find examples of informal punishment could also be taken as a sign that implicit punishment is having a deterrent effect.

Heterogeneity among participants   I expect misclassified agreements to be comprised of more heterogeneous sets of states than agreements correctly classified to have punishment provisions.[17] To assess the relationship between heterogeneity and potentially informal punishment provisions, I examine both Regime-type Heterogeneity and Preference Heterogeneity. For the first type, two of the measures provided in the literature are considered: the Polity scores[18] and the Freedom House democracy rating.[19] For Preference Heterogeneity, I use the measure based on voting records from the UN General Assembly (UNGA), which is explained in Chapter 4.

Table 8.6 displays the results using the respective measures. To measure Regime-type Heterogeneity for bilateral agreements, the absolute difference in the respective democracy scores between the two participants is used. For multilateral agreements, first a data set with all

---

[17] If one compares the set of all misclassified agreements to the set of all other
      agreements, the results are slightly stronger than the results reported here.
[18] See Appendix 2, fn. 1.   [19] Ibid.

dyads in the multilateral agreement was created; the absolute difference in the democracy indices for the most dissimilar dyad then determines the heterogeneity measure for the agreement (the "weakest link" assumption). The rest of the heterogeneity measures are constructed in the same way. Two of the three measures of heterogeneity are substantively larger for misclassified agreements; using one-sided t-tests, the difference between misclassified agreements and correctly classified agreements is in the case of Freedom House statistically significant at the 10 percent level and in the case of UNGA statistically significant at the 1 percent level. The respective differences are 1.16 and 1.39. These results support H8-5, which states that informal punishment provisions are more likely in agreements composed of Heterogeneous states.

Interestingly, agreements with great homogeneity among participants are typically agreements composed of democracies; there are few homogeneous agreements in the COIL sample comprised largely of non-democratic states. Figure 8.1 plots average polity scores against the maximal difference in polity scores among the members to an agreement, the variable used in Table 8.6. The graph indicates a negative relationship between average polity scores and heterogeneity. Given that, in this context, heterogeneity implies agreements

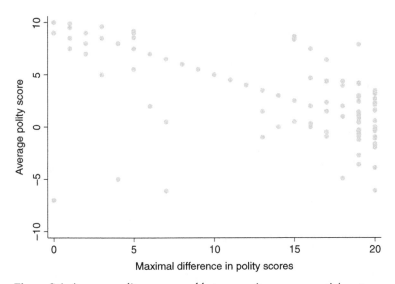

Figure 8.1 Average polity scores and heterogeneity among participants

Table 8.6 *Heterogeneity and misclassified agreements*

	Obs.	Mean	Std. Error
Freedom House			
Misclassified	4	4.25	0.52
All other	32	3.09	0.29
N	36	3.22	0.27
Difference		1.16*	0.85
Polity			
Misclassified	6	15.83	2.65
All other	44	12.36	1.09
N	50	12.78	1.02
Difference		3.47	3.13
UNGA ideal points			
Misclassified	6	3.43	0.59
All other	44	2.04	0.19
N	50	2.21	0.19
Difference		1.39***	0.56

Note: One-sided t-tests.

*** *significant at 1 percent;* * *significant at 10 percent*

that include non-democracies, attaining flexibility through informal provisions seems sensible.

Power I consider two kinds of Power: economic and military. Table 8.7 displays results from one-sided t-tests using the standard deviation in GDP among the participants and the standard deviation in military capabilities among the participants.[20] As before, the relevant comparison is between misclassified agreements and those agreements that are predicted to have punishment provisions and indeed have them. It should be noted that data availability severely limits the sample.[21]

The results suggest that differences in economic capabilities are substantively greater for informal punishment provisions (as captured by an agreement being misclassified); nonetheless, the same is not

[20] See Appendix 2, fn. 3 and fn. 4, respectively.

[21] For the models in Table 8.7, I include only those agreements with no more than 10 percent of the values missing for the GDP and military capabilities data (producing N = 44 and N = 61, respectively). Alternatively, as a robustness check,

Table 8.7 *Power differences and misclassified agreements*

	Obs.	Mean	Std. error
sd (GDP)			
Misclassified	4	958.49	515.57
All other	40	316.17	38.48
N	44	374.56	60.83
Difference		642.32***	189.77
sd (Military Capabilities)			
Misclassified	10	0.05	0.01
All other	51	0.03	0.01
N	61	0.03	0.01
Difference		0.02	0.02

Note: One-sided t-tests.
*** *significant at 1 percent*

true with respect to differences in military capabilities. The average disparity of GDP among member states in misclassified agreements is three times greater than that in correctly classified agreements. This difference is statistically significant at the 1% level. On the other hand, while the average disparity in military power among member states is greater in misclassified agreements than it is in correctly classified agreements, the difference fails to achieve statistical significance at any conventional level. Thus it appears that differences in economic power are positively associated with informalism, as both Stone (2011) and I predict, but the same is not true for military power as measured here.

Given that this is the first systematic treatment of informal provisions in formal law, formal and informal punishment provisions are treated as substitutes. In reality, informal efforts can supplement formal ones at any time. The complementarities might be like those

when I lower the cut-off to exclude agreements with any missing values for these two variables, the average disparity in both economic and military power is larger in misclassified agreements. The differences between misclassified agreements and the correctly predicted agreements are statistically significant at the 1 percent and 5 percent levels, respectively. However, this lower cut-off may restrict the sample too harshly (N = 38 for GDP and N = 49 for military capabilities), and we lose interesting multilateral agreements from the sample. These results thus may be driven by non-random selection.

analyzed by Verdier (2008) in the nuclear non-proliferation regime, where the United States supplements formal provisions with informal ones to target inducements to the particularities of the noncompliant state.

Does punishment ever occur in "misclassified" agreements?

The data point to Regime-type and Preference Heterogeneity and differences in Economic Power as promising explanations of when and why states leave punishment provisions informal. Still, an important issue must be addressed for the argument in this chapter to be compelling: What happens when a state defects and a punishment provision was left out? If nothing ever happens, one could argue punishment is not informal; rather, it is nonexistent.

Of course, it would be a fallacy to infer from the nonuse of punishment provisions, whether formal or informal, that they are inconsequential. Making the leap from unused to ineffective punishment provisions overlooks the anticipatory behavior of states. The logic follows the arguments made in Chapter 5 about withdrawal clauses and Chapter 7 about dispute resolution provisions. Infrequent recourse to actual punishment may indicate the effectiveness of this institutional design choice. If the threat of punishment, whether formalized or left informal, is credible, states that prefer defection do not even join the agreement, given that their preferred strategy is likely to be too costly to be beneficial once the threat of punishment is incorporated into their payoffs. For those that prefer long-term cooperation with their partner(s) to long-term defection but face incentives to defect, the threat of punishment may keep them from defecting. In other words, when the threat is credible, actual punishment is off the equilibrium path behavior.

Still, the potential for punishment does not perfectly deter noncompliance in the domestic context let alone the international one. Some states do indeed defect from international law. While there are examples of formal punishment occurring as, for example, in the case of BITs (and, of course, there exist examples of it failing to be employed as well),[22] there are also cases of informal punishment occurring.

---

[22] Importantly, detected noncompliance in the domestic law context does not always result in punishment. I have received only three speeding citations since I began driving but substantially more than three warnings. My spouse has a less fortunate ratio of warnings/citations, illustrating that heterogeneity in

Consider one of the misclassified agreements: The International Convention for the Suppression of the Financing of Terrorism. Given the underlying cooperation problems, one would predict the treaty would incorporate enforcement provisions. Yet, the treaty establishes no such mechanisms. As Rosand's (2003: 334) article on the convention puts it, "Some states still want their friends to be able to use terrorism to advance their favorite causes. The oft-repeated phrase 'one man's terrorist is another man's freedom fighter' unfortunately remains relevant." Rosand thus indirectly calls attention to regime heterogeneity as a possible explanation of the lack of formal punishment. There is good evidence this agreement is now being enforced, despite the lack of a formal enforcement provision. Specifically, when it was needed, a UNSC resolution was adopted that was based on the agreement and effectively enforces it – even though the UNSC is never mentioned in the agreement text (Szasz 2002). Thus it is not a large leap to say punishment was implicit despite being left out formally. This example also suggests the UNSC may play an even more important role for informal enforcement than what one would expect based on an evaluation of treaty texts. The following subsections reinforce this point about the role of the UNSC – an organization controlled by powerful states.

The Nuclear Non-proliferation Treaty

The NPT provides strong case study evidence in favor of the theoretical arguments presented here.[23] First, the UNSC has indeed acted to sanction states that are developing or threatening to develop nuclear weapons but who are not authorized by the NPT to do so. Furthermore, powerful states have acted alone to sanction violators, with varying degrees of punishment depending on the particulars of the noncompliant state. Second, and importantly, reactions to threats or instances of nuclear proliferation (real or presumed) are quite different depending on whether the state in question is a member of the NPT or not. In other words, the NPT itself seems to contain informal enforcement provisions, and the counterfactual that the UNSC or particular powerful states

"regime type" matters in this context as well, with police officers using discretion regarding how and how often to punish depending on the individual characteristics of the offender.

[23] The NPT is not in the COIL random sample and thus not on the list of misclassified agreements.

would have acted correspondingly without the independent effect of the NPT is not supported. I elaborate in what follows.

The NPT permits five states, the United States, France, Russia, the United Kingdom, and China, to possess nuclear weapons. However, over the course of history, other states have developed, or are believed to be developing, nuclear capabilities as well. Kazakhstan, Belarus, and Ukraine had nuclear weapons following the collapse of the Soviet Union, but promptly disavowed their weapons, signing the NPT and returning their nuclear weapons to Russia. Similarly, South Africa possessed nuclear weapons before signing the NPT but dismantled its weapons and signed the treaty. Four states – Iran, North Korea, Iraq, and Libya – are members that the IAEA believes (or once believed) to be in violation of the NPT.[24] Three other states possessing (or believed to possess) nuclear weapons – Israel, India, and Pakistan – are not parties to the NPT. These cases provide insight into when and how "informal" punishment occurs.

The case of Iran is, perhaps, the most straightforward example. The IAEA has reported its concerns regarding Iran's potential capability to develop nuclear weapons for quite some time. As a result, sanctions on Iran (primarily with regard to the sale of weapons or weapons materials) have been imposed through UNSC resolutions.[25] Furthermore, with House Resolution 1905 (112th): Iran Threat Reduction and Syria Human Rights Act of 2012,[26] the United States

---

[24] Some might argue that North Korea is no longer a member of the NPT, but its status is open to interpretation given its unconventional (and most likely unlawful) withdrawal. In 2003, North Korea withdrew with only a one-day notice, citing that it had already fulfilled the balance of the official three-month notice period when it gave notice of withdrawal in 1993, a withdrawal that it subsequently suspended. In any event, during the period in which the rewards and sanctions discussed here were part of the picture, North Korea was most certainly a member of the NPT. With respect to Libya, it dismantled its program to the satisfaction of the major powers prior to the collapse of the Gaddafi regime.

[25] At the time of publication of this book, these sanctions have been removed as part of the Joint Comprehensive Plan of Action of July 2015 concluded between China, France, Germany, the Russian Federation, the United Kingdom, the United States, the European Union, and the Islamic Republic of Iran. Specifically, the sanctions have been removed in response to Iran's implementation of certain measures with verification provided by the IAEA. Joint Comprehensive Plan of Action. 2015. Available at http://www.state.gov/e/eb/t fs/spi/iran/jcpoa/index.htm [Last accessed January 8, 2015].

[26] Available at www.govtrack.us/congress/bills/112/hr1905/text [Last accessed July 3, 2015].

went beyond the UN sanctions against Iran for noncompliance with nuclear safeguards. In other words, the United States has been enforcing the NPT in a broad sense, given Iran's history of not cooperating with the IAEA to the extent required by international law. And the United States is not alone; the European Union, Australia, and Japan, among other states, all have imposed sanctions against Iran.[27] Powerful states do at times punish what they consider breaches of international law.

The attempt to halt North Korea's program utilized carrots and sticks with a combination of threats, security guarantees, and aid packages, thereby illustrating the theoretical point that rewards and punishments are two sides of the same coin (Dorn and Fulton 1997). After the issuance of various (ineffective) threats, the United States (along with Japan and South Korea) offered North Korea two nuclear reactors, 500,000 tons of oil per year, and normalized political and economic relations.[28] The exchange ultimately failed, and North Korea was then threatened with further isolation and sanctions.

With respect to Iraq, in 1998 President Saddam Hussein expelled UN weapons inspectors. Subsequently, only two IAEA inspections occurred. In June 2001, the Nuclear Control Institute called attention to "troubling indications over the last two years that Saddam's nuclear-weapons program has not only survived, but been reinvigorated."[29] The United States and the United Kingdom invaded Iraq in 2003, and, although the invasion's prudence is hotly debated, many argued that Iraq's rejection of IAEA weapons inspection directly violated UNSC Resolution 687[30] and other UNSC resolutions and thus the invasion

---

[27] As elaborated in fn. 25, the nuclear-related sanctions have been removed. In the United States, sanctions related to terrorism and human rights abuses will not be removed as part of the Joint Comprehensive Plan of Action.

[28] For a more detailed discussion, see Chapter 11.

[29] Dolley, Steven, and Paul Leventhal. 2001. "Overview of the IAEA Nuclear Inspections in Iraq." *Nuclear Control Institute*, June 14, 2001. Available at www.nci.org/new/iraq-ib.htm [Last accessed October 11, 2012].

[30] UNSC Resolution 687 suspended the use of force in Iraq provided that Iraq continue to fulfill its UNSC obligations, including Iraq's requirements under the NPT (see paragraph 11). The resolution states: The UNSC became "*Concerned* by reports in the hands of Member-States that Iraq has attempted to acquire materials for a nuclear weapons programme contrary to its obligations under the Treaty on the Non-Proliferation of Nuclear Weapons of 1 July 1968." UNSC, Resolution 687, 8 April 1991. Available at www.un.org/Depts/unmovic/documents/687.pdf [Last accessed July 11, 2015].

was warranted. While perhaps not the most significant factor, the NPT was invoked by the United States as one justification of its "punishment."

These examples highlight how informal punishment can be more or less tailored to the specific regime in question. Both the UNSC and the United States have played roles in enforcing the NPT, despite the treaty's lack of formal provisions. Yet, not all violations of the NPT are dealt with by the UNSC or by other states. For example, although the IAEA has called attention to likely Syrian violations of the NPT,[31] no sanctions have been adopted by the UNSC. This is due to Russia's and China's continued support of Syria, even in the wake of current bloodshed. The Syrian example illustrates the discretion enjoyed by powerful states to withhold punishment if their interests dictate such a course of action.

The US response to a West German deal with Brazil is illustrative in this regard as well. In 1975, after West Germany had signed the NPT, its government signed a secret deal that would aid Brazil in the completion of eight nuclear power plants.[32] However, since Brazil was not party to the NPT, this deal violated an important part of the NPT, which gives preferential treatment to member states when it comes to gaining assistance with peaceful uses of nuclear technology. The United States and other powers, including the Soviet Union, disapproved of this deal.[33] Under President Ford, strong sanctions were considered, but "when it was suggested that U.S. troops stationed in Europe and joint initiatives with the Soviets be used to put pressure on the Germans, [US Secretary of State Henry] Kissinger felt obliged to argue that this was the wrong way to treat a close ally" (Kaiser 1978:89).

---

[31] The Guardian, "Syria Nuclear Weapons Site Revealed by UN Investigators," *The Guardian via Associated Press in Washington*, November 1, 2011. Available at www.guardian.co.uk/world/2011/nov/01/syria-nuclear-arms-site-revealed [Last accessed October 11, 2012].

[32] Flemes, Daniel. 2006. "Brazil's Nuclear Policy: From Technological Dependence to Civil Nuclear Power," Working Paper, *GIGA Research Program: Dynamics of Violence and Security Cooperation*. Hamburg, Germany: GIGA. Available at SSRN http://papers.ssrn.com/sol3/papers.cfm?abstract_id=909192 [Last accessed June 23, 2015].

[33] Nedal, Dani K. 2011. "The US and Brazil's Nuclear Program." Available at http://ri.fgv.br/en/node/2036 [Last accessed June 13, 2015].

The Syrian and (albeit less serious) German cases could be used as counter-arguments to the thesis that the NPT is enforced informally even when no formal punishment mechanism exists within the treaty's text. Yet, in both cases, sanctions were entertained. Additionally, when examining informal enforcement of international law, it is important to remember that no international – or for that matter domestic law – with formal punishment provisions is perfectly and consistently enforced either. Given that even under formal domestic law, violations are not always punished, consistent enforcement is a flawed benchmark for assessing whether or not failure to respond in these cases represents a deviation from the norm of informal punishment. And because Power Asymmetries characterize the NPT, we would expect powerful states to exploit their discretion from time to time. Finally, the Syrian case is far from closed.

It is instructive to compare cases of member violations with non-member "violations." If the treaty is key to the punishment of treaty violators, violators not party to the treaty should not be punished (or threatened with punishment) with the same frequency.

The facts do seem to support the hypothesis that violations of the norms of non-proliferation by nonmembers have, on average, received a weaker response from both the UNSC and the United States. Both Israel and India have become nuclear weapon states without ratifying the NPT and have received merely non-effectual condemnations. As Charnysh bluntly states: "The US government pursued a policy of silence towards the Israeli nuclear weapons program."[34] And ending a moratorium on nuclear trade with India, the 2008 US-India Civil Nuclear Agreement, which necessitated an official waiver from the Nuclear Suppliers Group, allows US companies to work in partnership with India on the development of nuclear reactors.[35] The agreement forces concessions on India, for example, India agreed to open itself to inspections by the IAEA; still, such concessions are not commensurate with the punishments directed toward member states in violation.

---

[34] Charnysh, Volha. 2010. "A Brief History of Nuclear Proliferation." *Nuclear Age Peace Foundation.* Available at www.wagingpeace.org/wp-content/uploads/2012/11/Proliferation_History.pdf [Last accessed June 12, 2015].

[35] Bajoria, Jayshree, and Esther Pan 2010. "The U.S.-India Nuclear Deal," *Council on Foreign Relations.* Available at www.cfr.org/india/us-india-nuclear-deal/p9663 [Last accessed October 11, 2012].

Brazil and Argentina provide another case in point. Both states had aggressive nuclear weapons development policies during the 1970s and 1980s, a time when both were nonsignatories to the NPT. Obviously, states like the United States did not support these policies. Still, little, if any, coercive pressure was used against these states by either the United States or the UNSC. The United States held back on transferring certain technologies (which is actually in the spirit of its NPT obligations) but did little else. In fact, the evidence indicates that harsher measures were considered against NPT member state, Germany, given its interaction with Brazil. It is not farfetched to argue that, had that United States wanted to coerce Brazil and Argentina into dismantling their programs, the United States would have had the economic and military power to do so. For example, "when Carter took office in 1977, he stepped up pressure on the Argentines to halt what his administration saw as gross human rights abuses. The United States cut back on military and economic aid and began collecting information on incidents of kidnapping, torture and killing."[36] Redick (1981), a specialist in Latin American nuclear energy programs, recounts the roots and manifestation of the rivalry between Brazil and Argentina and its evolution to today's situation in which both states have acceded to the NPT and the Treaty of Tlatelolco. He argues US pressure was quite low with respect to getting these states to change their policies.

Nonstate enforcement mechanisms

Human rights agreements often lack formal punishment provisions even though they are characterized by cooperation problems that call for such provisions. Hence such agreements dominate the set of misclassified agreements in Table 8.5. Simmons (2009) offers an explanation based on domestic political factors. She argues that human rights treaties become meaningful, and thereby exert compliance pressures, by empowering domestic (or transnational) individuals or groups. These empowered actors use human rights commitments to pressure governments into obeying higher standards. Moreover, international agreements may help local actors define their agendas more clearly, agree on a common set of priorities, and obtain additional

---

[36] Richter, Paul. "U.S. Feared a Nuclear Argentina", *Los Angeles Times*, 23 Aug. 2002. Available at www.latinamericanstudies.org/argentina/argentina-nuclear .htm [Last accessed October 9, 2012].

options for litigation, thereby gaining more effective bargaining positions vis-à-vis their governments. The presence of such mechanisms reduces the need for punishment provisions in some agreements and, as Simmons convincingly shows, especially in human rights treaties. Three of the misclassified agreements in Table 8.5 CEDAW, the CRC, and the ICCPR, are studied in depth in Simmons' book. It will be illuminating to study the remaining agreements in Table 8.5 from Simmons' perspective.

UNSC and US action in enforcing human rights agreements

One might ask whether the UNSC ever enforces issue areas that are beyond the traditional boundaries of security. In fact, many informal punishment mechanisms levied through UNSC Resolutions are aimed at human rights abuses. The UNSC has acted to impose punishments on Sudan (from shaming to travel ban and asset freeze)[37] and Sierra Leone (petrol sanctions, travel ban, and arms embargo),[38] to name just a few of the states targeted.

The case of Libya illustrates the references to international law quite well. UNSC Resolution 1970 from February 26, 2011 states, "*Considering* that the widespread and systematic attacks currently taking place in the Libyan Arab Jamahiriya against the civilian population may amount to crimes against humanity ... 2. Urges the Libyan authorities to: (a) Act with the utmost restraint, respect human rights and international humanitarian law, and allow immediate access for international human rights monitors."[39] These references to

---

[37] Resolution 1547 from June 11, 2004 "condemn[s] all actions of violence and violations of human rights and international humanitarian law," but introduces no punishments beyond the shaming inherent in condemnation. UNSC, Resolution 1547, 11 June 2004. Available at www .unhcr.org/refworld/docid/411356d24.html [Last accessed August 18, 2012]. Concrete punishments were introduced on March 29, 2005. UNSC, Resolution 1591, 29 March 2005. Available at www.unhcr.org/refworld/d ocid/42bc157e4.html [Last accessed August 18, 2012].

[38] UNSC, Resolution 1132, 8 October 1997. Available at www.unhcr.org/ref world/docid/3b00f16f78.html [Last accessed August 18, 2012].

[39] UNSC, Resolution 1970, 26 February 2011. Available at www.unhcr.org/ref world/docid/4d6ce9742.html [Last accessed August 18, 2012].

international humanitarian law suggest that the punishments contained in the resolution are directed at these violations of international law. The resolution itself contains the following punishments: an arms embargo, a travel ban, an asset freeze, and the possibility of sanctions against Libya; moreover, the situation is referred to the International Criminal Court.

A more recent resolution, UNSC Resolution 2009, adds additional references to international law to condemn "violence against civilians, or arbitrary arrests and detentions, in particular of African migrants," which violates the International Convention on the Protection of the Rights of All Migrant Workers and Members of their Families, as well as "sexual violence, particularly against women and girls,"[40] which violates CEDAW. Both agreements are listed as misclassified and hence candidates for informal punishment. Libya had acceded to both of these agreements at the time.[41]

The United States also acts alone with respect to the issue area of human rights. The Jackson-Vanik Amendment enacted by the US Congress (title IV of the Trade Act of 1974, P.L. 93–618) (the Amendment) denied nondiscriminatory (or most-favored-nation) treatment to products from any nonmarket economies (referring to communist or former communist states) without freedom of emigration. Such limitations on trade relations with various states were designed to address the Soviet Union's prohibitive East-to-West emigration policy and "to assure the continued dedication of the U.S. to fundamental Human Rights and welfare of its own citizens" (Sec. 409). The Amendment provided for a waiver that would allow nondiscriminatory treatment upon the president's approval. The granting of a waiver was conditional on assurances of emigration practices reform.

Although the passage of the Russia and Moldova Jackson-Vanik Repeal and Sergei Magnitsky Rule of Law Accountability Act of 2012 abolished the Amendment, prior to this, Congress gathered reports that highlight the United States' ability to utilize national legislation to advance international norms. Thus, even though

---

[40] UNSC, Resolution 2009, 16 September 2011. Available at www.un.org/News/Press/docs/2011/sc10389.doc.htm [Last accessed August 18, 2012].

[41] Future research should examine why the UNSC rarely, if ever, cites specific treaties and whether the permanent members have opinions on the topic based on their own ratification status.

the Amendment conditioned trade benefits solely on a state's freedom-of-emigration policy, broader human rights concerns were considered in waiver decisions. For instance, in the case of China, "violation of human rights in general (restriction of religious freedom and ethnic minority rights, forced labor) ... [and] proliferation of nuclear and other weapons"[42] constituted reasons for the disapproval of an annual extension of the Jackson-Vanik waiver authority. In the case of Vietnam, "Vietnam's unsatisfactory emigration policy, denial of human and religious rights, and lack of proper accounting for the POWs and MIAs"[43] were the basis of the opposition to the waiver extension.

The possibility of failed cooperation

Another reason why formal punishment provisions might be left out of agreements is that governments may have only weak preferences for cooperation. Thus the set of misclassified agreements, for instance, conflates two categories: agreements with implicitly informal punishment provisions and agreements without such informal punishments even though they are needed. Agreements in this second category might be considered "failed cooperation."

Such failed cooperation may arise because interest groups pressure governments into pursuing international agreements, especially in the issue areas of the environment and human rights. Instead of refusing to cooperate entirely, states may draw up an agreement that responds to interest group demands yet does not include any enforcement mechanism, explicit or implicit. Many human rights agreements and environmental agreements are subject to exactly this criticism: they state grand goals but fail to include any mechanisms to enforce those goals.

The Convention on Nature Protection and Wild Life Preservation in the Western Hemisphere, categorized as misclassified, arguably falls under this "umbrella." There is some evidence that participating states were reluctant to agree to the loss of sovereignty that would

---

[42] Pregelj, Vladimir N. 2005. "The Jackson-Vanik Amendment: A Survey" CRS Report for Congress. Available at www.fas.org/sgp/crs/row/98-545.pdf [Last accessed December 5, 2015].

[43] Ibid.

come with formal enforcement provisions; the Convention accordingly came under criticism (De Klemm and Shine 1993).

Yet, and from this perspective unexpectedly, even this agreement opened up opportunities for informal enforcement. In 1944, the United States considered pressuring Ecuador on the issue of preserving the Galapagos archipelago. It was only the prevalence of military considerations that led the United States to turn a blind eye. As Secretary of State Cordell Hull explained in a memorandum to President Roosevelt, the issue of the Galapagos archipelago was dropped "in order to avoid possible jeopardy to negotiations recently authorized relating to the use of [a military] base during the war," but would be put back on the table "at the earliest possible juncture."[44]

It should also be noted that "weak preferences" for cooperation are very different from the design of "weak enforcement" mechanisms. Weak enforcement, as considered by Downs and Rocke (1995), refers to the existence of punishments costless enough to allow defection from agreements from time to time (yet costly enough to prevent violations most of the time). Downs and Rocke point out that the GATT's weak enforcement norm allowed governments to suspend cooperation temporarily in response to pressures by domestic interest groups. The absence of strong enforcement mechanisms was a rational response to the prevalent uncertainty about interest group demands, which in turn arose from fluctuations in technology or the world market.

This discussion underscores that weak preferences and weak enforcement arise for opposite reasons. Weak preferences for cooperation arise when a government is not interested in cooperation and the outcome of an international agreement, but instead uses the agreement to placate interest groups. By contrast, weak enforcement arises when a government wants to form an international agreement, but fears that it will have to suspend cooperation temporarily to placate interest groups in the future (Downs and Rocke 1995: 88). In order to allow

---

[44] Memorandum by Secretary of State Cordell Hull to President Roosevelt, Washington, DC, March 30, 1944. Available at http://digicoll.library.wisc.edu/cgi-bin/FRUS/FRUS-idx?type=turn&entity=FRUS.FRUS1944v07.p1072&id=FRUS.FRUS1944v07&isize=M&q1=Convention%20on%20Nature%20Protection [Last accessed August 18, 2012].

such room to maneuver, the government prefers only limited enforcement mechanisms.[45]

The reader should also note that weak enforcement is not equivalent to informal enforcement. In fact, as explained earlier, informal punishments can be very specific, very targeted, and very severe. Weak enforcement, by contrast, is first and foremost characterized by being limited in size and scope. One may go even as far as saying that informal enforcement, by being in principle unlimited in size and scope, is located at the opposite end of the spectrum from weak enforcement.

Concluding thoughts

To this day, even scholars sympathetic to international law, like Guzman (2008), underestimate the potential power of formal punishment provisions, let alone informal ones. Adding to the extant theory and empirical analyses showing the rationality of the design of international law, I show here that even what's left out is rationally designed; furthermore, case study evidence suggests that what's left out can also be effective. My point offered in the introduction, that the absence of formal punishment provisions does not imply the absence of punishment, is valid.

I first present a theory of punishment provisions based on underlying cooperation problems and Number of actors, and the comparative static predictions flowing from this theory perform strikingly well when tested with the COIL data set. I then present theoretically motivated hypotheses based on *both power and efficiency* about whether any necessary punishment provision will be formal or informal. Informal punishment cannot be observed in the data set. Yet the research design I develop allows me to test whether the predicted systematic differences exist between agreements that incorporate formal punishment, on the one hand, and those that need it but do not incorporate it (and hence for which the punishment may be implicit), on the other hand. I am therefore able to test implications of my argument. Given that a different theory of formal-versus-informal punishment would not have the same implications, the overall

---

[45] See Chapter 5 on escape clauses, which demonstrates that "weak enforcement" is not always as weak as it sounds.

theoretical argument is buttressed. Finally, case study evidence suggests informal punishment indeed occurs.

This chapter thus shows not only the compatibility of power and efficiency considerations; the results indicate that most of the time when punishments are needed they are indeed formalized. Thus, even though informal law is systematic, it does not dominate formal law.

Two points are worth reemphasizing. First, not every misclassified treaty has been found to have informal enforcement (although future work relying on interviews and archives may uncover additional evidence), but there are treaties with formal enforcement mechanisms for which defection does not result in punishment. Second, and relatedly, when we do not see any informal punishment occurring in a misclassified treaty, we cannot jump to the conclusion that the informal punishment is not implicit any more than we can jump to the conclusion that treaties with unexploited formal enforcement are weak. The actual use of punishment provisions, formal or informal, may be off the equilibrium path.[46]

Given the findings in this Chapter, a research program is suggested. One potentially fruitful avenue would be to find the negotiating record of "misclassified" agreements. Was the need for punishment provisions mentioned? If so, how did actors arrive at the decision to leave them out formally? Did states have different bargaining positions on the issue? Additionally, future research should examine false positives, that is, those agreements that have punishment provisions but for which such provisions are deemed unnecessary. Three of the twenty false positives in this analysis are ILO conventions. While these three conventions address issues that do not warrant punishment provisions, they were negotiated under the auspices of the ILO, which automatically provides enforcement power. One testable implication then is that this enforcement power has never been used.

---

[46] See Chapters 2, 5 and 7 for a discussion of this issue in different contexts.

9 | *Monitoring provisions*

For the first time in 15 years, U.S. officials have lost their ability to inspect Russian long-range nuclear bases, where they had become accustomed to peering into missile silos, counting warheads and whipping out tape measures to size up rockets ...

"The problem of the breakdown of our verification, which lapsed December 5 [2009], is very serious and impacts our national security," Sen. Richard G. Lugar (R-Ind.), one of the chamber's top nuclear experts, said in a recent hearing ...

"It was the holy grail to get on-site inspections, boots on the ground in the Soviet Union," said Franklin Miller, who worked in arms control for more than two decades, ending up as special assistant to President George W. Bush.[1]

Monitoring systems are designed to inform states whether their partners in cooperation are complying with their obligations or not. Under many conditions, many of which are elaborated by game-theoretic models of cooperation such as the repeated prisoners' dilemma game (e.g., Axelrod 1984), information about compliance is crucial, and losing that information is indeed like losing the "holy grail." Thus it is not surprising that mechanisms identifying compliance were once thought to be the *raison d'être* of international institutions.

In reality, the incidence of monitoring provisions is neither trivial nor universal; nor, when provisions exist, do they exhibit the same form. Consider the following:

- 60 percent of the agreements in the COIL random sample call for the creation of monitoring arrangements; 40 percent do not.

---

[1] Each of these is a direct quote from a Washington Post article written on August 17, 2010. See Chapter 1, fn. 22.

- Not a single monetary agreement in the COIL samples calls for the creation of a system of compliance monitoring.
- An astonishingly high majority (89 percent) of disarmament agreements call for a system of monitoring.
- 63 percent of human rights agreements delegate monitoring to a pre-existing IGO, but only 10 percent of economics agreements do.

This chapter explains both the incidence and form of monitoring systems. In a nutshell, agreements are particularly likely to call for a system to collect and disseminate information when there is substantial Uncertainty about the Behavior of other states, thereby corroborating Keohane's classic argument about the role of international institutions in the provision and dissemination of information. Furthermore, by interacting Uncertainty about Behavior with incentives to defect, that is, underlying Enforcement problems, Commitment problems, Uncertainty about the State of the World, and/or Uncertainty about Preferences, the choice between delegated monitoring and self-reporting is explained. This chapter thus provides an enhanced theoretical and empirical picture of an important design dimension of international law, monitoring systems, by refining the original Rational Design conjecture *Centralization increases with Uncertainty about Behavior*: Centralized (i.e., delegated) monitoring increases under conditions of high Uncertainty about Behavior only in the presence of certain other cooperation problems.

The second part of the chapter continues the subtheme of Part III with an analysis of informal monitoring in international law. I focus primarily on monitoring that occurs by NGOs without being formally called for in the agreement. I do so because the conventional wisdom is that NGOs play a key monitoring role in international cooperation, especially in the issue area of human rights. Yet the COIL data provide no evidence of this conventional wisdom. As I elaborate later, only 1 percent of the COIL sample formally mentions NGOs in this regard. I thus look into the relationship between formal and informal monitoring. Finally, I briefly discuss the informal role of the United States in monitoring international law, thereby examining whether the interests of the most powerful state influence the overall monitoring regime.

Formal monitoring provisions

Definitions and descriptive statistics

COIL defines a monitoring system as a mechanism whereby other members or an internal or external body can distinguish whether or not a member is acting in accordance with the provisions of an agreement.[2] The system typically features collection of data or submission of reports and may include on-site investigations. The purpose of the system is to establish clearly whether or not a member is in compliance with the agreement's substantive prescriptions or proscriptions.

States have many options for designing monitoring provisions, in particular with respect to who conducts the monitoring. An example of an agreement in which monitoring is conducted by member states is the 1963 Agreement Concerning Co-operation in the Matter of Plant Protection between Austria and Hungary. The goal of the agreement is to prevent the spread and introduction of plant diseases and pests. The agreement obligates both states to report annually "on the appearance and spread of such diseases and pests during the year in question, specifying, in so far as possible, the infected or infested areas (towns, communes) and the control measures taken" (Article 5).

An agreement between Denmark and Sweden on the Protection of the Sound Oresund from Pollution provides an example of monitoring conducted by an internal body. The agreement establishes a commission, composed of three members from each state, which is tasked with reporting on the pollution situation in the Sound and also with "actively follow[ing] the [fulfillment] by each country of the requirements connected with this Agreement" (Article 7), thereby monitoring the behavior of member states.

The International Convention on the Suppression and Punishment of the Crime of Apartheid is an example of an agreement with monitoring involving a pre-existing IGO, in this case the UN. Article VII obliges parties to the convention to submit periodic reports, which are transmitted through the secretary-general of the UN to a special committee

---

[2] This section draws from Koremenos, Barbara and Kal Raustiala. "Information and International Agreements." Presented at New York University Law School, Hauser Colloquium, New York, New York, October 20, 2010. This section also overlaps with Betz and Koremenos (2016).

Table 9.1 *Compliance monitoring by issue area*
(percentage of each issue area)

Issue area	No compliance monitoring (%)	Compliance monitoring (%)
Economics	43	57
Environment	49	51
Human rights	41	59
Security	23	77
Total	40	60

N = 234

Table 9.2 *Compliance monitoring by sub-issue area*
(percentage of each sub-issue area)

Sub-issue area	No compliance monitoring (%)	Compliance monitoring (%)
Agricultural	17	83
Finance	62	38
Investment	31	69
Monetary	100	0
Environment	49	51
Human rights	41	59
Disarmament	11	89
Security	26	74
Total	40	60

N = 234

on apartheid. Article X goes further in terms of the monitoring mandate and specifies that reports prepared by organs of the UN may be used to compile "a list of individuals, organizations, institutions and representatives of States which are alleged to be responsible for the crimes enumerated in ... the Convention." Thus, data assembled by UN organs are employed in the monitoring process.

Tables 9.1 and 9.2 report the number of agreements that create a system of compliance monitoring, breaking down the numbers according to the four broad issue areas and the eight sub-issue areas featured in the COIL random sample. More than one-half of the agreements contain monitoring provisions. While there is not as much variation across issues, the variation across sub-issue areas is tremendous – the vast majority of agricultural commodities and disarmament agreements contain monitoring provisions, whereas far fewer finance and none of the monetary agreements do. Even closely related sub-issue areas differ substantially: Over two-thirds of investment agreements call for monitoring, but, as mentioned, no monetary agreement does.

If a monitoring system does exist, a set of questions ascertains who does the monitoring: member states in a self-reporting fashion, other member states (who act as monitors of each other), an internal body that is created by the agreement,[3] an IGO, an NGO, or some other entity. These "other" entities might be individuals or firms or third-party states outside the agreement.[4]

Within the 141 agreements that call for a compliance monitoring system, the actors formally involved in the monitoring procedures are revealed in Table 9.3. Monitoring functions can be delegated to more than one entity within a single agreement.

As Table 9.3 illustrates, whenever monitoring tasks are specified, member states assume the primary role regardless of the issue area, although they are almost matched by "other" actors in the economics issue area. These other actors are usually individuals and firms acting in an independent capacity in the context of BITs.

NGOs are, perhaps surprisingly, given little formal role in monitoring agreements regardless of the issue area; only three human rights agreements (out of 41 human rights agreements in the sample) explicitly give this role to NGOs. Pre-existing IGOs, on the other hand, are formally involved in the monitoring process in 28 percent of the

---

[3] Following scholars of Congress in American Politics, monitoring conducted by bodies composed of a subset of members is considered a form of delegation/centralization. See also Koremenos (2007).

[4] For an alternative dimension, the distinction between monitoring on a regular basis ("police patrols") and monitoring in response to allegations of non-compliance ("fire alarms"), see Barbara Koremenos and Timm Betz. "Information and International Agreements." Presented at the Annual Conference of the International Studies Association, San Diego, California, April 2012.

Table 9.3 *Given a system of compliance monitoring, who monitors*
          behavior?
          (percentage of each issue area)

Issue area	Member states (%)	Internal body (%)	IGO (%)	NGO (%)	Other (%)
Economics	51	5	10	0	47
Environment	82	50	36	0	5
Human rights	88	54	63	13	0
Security	92	31	31	0	3
Total	72	27	28	2	21

N = 141

Note: Given each agreement can be monitored by more than one type of entity, the percentages do not add up to 100.

agreements that have monitoring systems, and particularly often in human rights agreements.

An interesting finding showcased in Table 9.3 is the dense monitoring of human rights agreements and, to a lesser extent, environmental and disarmament agreements. Almost 60 percent of human rights agreements contain some form of monitoring provision (see Table 9.1); Table 9.3 shows that, among those human rights agreements that create monitoring systems, 88 percent involve member states in the process. In addition, internal bodies and pre-existing IGOs each monitor more than half of those human rights agreements that have any monitoring provision, and, as mentioned, three human rights agreements involve NGOs. In fact, a monitored human rights agreement involves more than two monitoring entities on average, perhaps reflecting the difficulties of monitoring such agreements.

Table 9.4 looks at sub-issues, again conditional on the presence of a monitoring provision. The data reflect the tremendous variation within economics and security, in particular. With respect to disarmament agreements, 75 percent involve member states in the monitoring process, and 63 percent involve IGOs. This pattern contrasts markedly with other security agreements, less than a quarter of which rely on IGOs.

Similarly, 95 percent of the agricultural commodities agreements with monitoring are monitored by member states but never by

Table 9.4 *Given a system of compliance monitoring, who monitors behavior?*
(percentage of each sub-issue area)

Sub-issue area	Member states (%)	Internal body (%)	IGO (%)	NGO (%)	Other (%)
Agricultural	95	10	15	0	0
Finance	80	0	20	0	0
Investment	10	3	3	0	97
Monetary	0	0	0	0	0
Environment	82	50	36	0	5
Human rights	88	54	63	13	0
Disarmament	75	38	63	0	0
Security	96	29	21	0	4
Total	72	27	28	2	21

N = 141

Note: Given each agreement can be monitored by more than one type of entity, the percentages do not add up to 100.

"other" entities, whereas all but one investment agreement rely on "other" entities to monitor compliance.[5]

Monitoring in the international relations/law literature

Formal models of cooperation in repeated games call attention to the importance of monitoring mechanisms. Fudenberg, Levine, and Maskin (1994) show that imperfectly observed but public signals about the actions of others are not much of a problem for cooperation. By contrast, if players possess private information, not only is cooperation much more brittle; it may depend on very complex strategy profiles, and the set of possible equilibrium payoffs can be restricted substantially. If international agreements produce and disseminate information, one possible interpretation is that they turn private signals into public signals. Consequently, monitoring enables

---

[5] As stated earlier, these other entities are typically private actors in BITs. The one investment agreement without involvement of "other" actors is the 1970 Exchange of Letters Constituting an Agreement Concerning the Guarantee of Investment Securities between New Zealand and Western Samoa. The agreement also calls only on the government of Western Samoa to submit self-reports; New Zealand is exempted from similar obligations.

deeper and more stable patterns of cooperation by overcoming the problems arising from private or asymmetric information – what is labeled in the COIL framework as Uncertainty about Behavior.

Yet how exactly this monitoring function works has not received extensive attention. IL and IR scholars have closely and helpfully examined several treaty monitoring systems, but much of this work is based on single case studies and unconnected to larger theories.[6] Victor, Raustiala, and Skolnikoff (1998), for instance, examine how international environmental agreements incorporate "systems of implementation review" or SIRs. SIRs are defined as sub-institutions through which the parties share information, compare activities, review performance, handle noncompliance, and adjust commitments. These studies illustrate that there is substantial variation in how SIRs are structured formally and that there are, in practice, a multiplicity of modes within a given regime by which treaty-relevant information is gathered, distributed, and assessed. While important in documenting this variation across environmental agreements, the approach is largely descriptive.

Hence although scholars frequently acknowledge the importance of information, they have rarely hypothesized about how information is provided in different international agreements or engaged in comparative empirical analyses of how this is achieved. Thus, we know little about the empirical variation across agreements.

Mitchell (1998) and Dai (2002) provide two exceptions. Mitchell looks at what he terms as "information systems." His study focuses broadly on the issue of transparency in international regimes. Regime transparency depends, he argues, upon both the demand for information and the supply of information, and he identifies several factors that affect supply and demand: the capabilities and incentives of relevant actors, the structure of the underlying problem, the nature of the rules in question (e.g., is the rule a ban, which is easy to monitor, or a more complex regulatory scheme?), and the nature of the regulated behavior (ocean dumping that is easily concealed or obvious ballistic missile tests?). Thus, Mitchell offers a theory to explain the design of information systems in international agreements, and he illustrates his argument with many examples from specific international agreements.

---

[6] Exceptions include Abbott (1993); Szasz (1999); and Alston and Crawford (2000).

His article is quite consistent with COIL's focus on underlying cooperation problems.

Dai (2002) similarly focuses on how specific international institutions structure the provision of information. She stresses two explanatory factors: a convergence of interests between the victims of noncompliance and states, on the one hand, and the presence of victims as low-cost monitors, on the other. When states are good agents of victims, interests are aligned, and states create effective information systems. Victims are low-cost monitors when noncompliance with an agreement is apparent (rather than latent) and the source of noncompliance is easily identified. The presence of low cost monitors, Dai argues, results in less centralized information systems. Dai selects several prominent institutions in different areas – trade, human rights, money – to explore this approach. She finds, consistent with her framework, that the IMF has a strong, centralized information system. Creditor states have a strong incentive to create monitoring arrangements because they are the victims of noncompliance. Yet they are not well-placed to detect violations. "Centralized monitoring thus emerges," Dai argues, "as an efficient and feasible solution" (2002: 422). By contrast, the WTO relies on both a centralized information-gathering arrangement – the Trade Policy Review Mechanism – and decentralized action through the judicial process known as the Dispute Settlement Understanding. This arrangement "is consistent with a strategic environment that is characterized by the ability of private producers to detect noncompliance" (2002: 424).

The theory discussed next builds on Mitchell by emphasizing the underlying cooperation problems to explain the design of monitoring provisions in international agreements.[7]

A theory of the incidence and design of monitoring provisions

In this section, theoretical conjectures about the existence of monitoring provisions and the choice of whether or not to involve other actors in the monitoring mechanism are presented.

---

[7] The work referenced in fn. 4 builds on Dai's argument and is consistent with her findings.

Monitoring provisions are a response to informational problems in international cooperation, in particular, Uncertainty about Behavior. On the most intuitive level, if states don't know what other states are doing with respect to their agreement obligations, they would like to obtain additional information – and monitoring provisions are an institutionalized solution to provide such information. Absent such additional information, cooperation is fragile as states may stop cooperating in response to doubts about the other side's behavior or they may apply unwarranted punishment strategies. As pointed out by Morrow (1994: 387), "applying the proper sanctioning strategy is difficult when compliance is difficult to monitor." Moreover, if the behavior of other states is not perfectly observable, what is actually observed is often easily misinterpreted – the most prominent and dramatic examples are when flocks of geese and meteor showers supposedly triggered nuclear alerts during the Cold War. Not coincidentally, Abbott (1993) refers to some monitoring provisions as "assurance provisions." Thus, the first hypothesis is as follows:

(H9-1) Other things equal, agreements that are characterized by underlying Uncertainty about Behavior are more likely to include monitoring provisions than those not characterized by underlying uncertainty about behavior.

When it comes to designing monitoring provisions, one important choice is whether monitoring is delegated to other actors or whether states rely on self-reporting. As just discussed, Uncertainty about Behavior can be considered a prerequisite for the existence of monitoring provisions because, if there is no such uncertainty, there is little need to gather information on compliance. However, the effect of Uncertainty about Behavior on the design of monitoring provisions is influenced by the strategic incentives of states.

Specifically, self-reporting is not problematic if there are no incentives to defect and therefore no incentives to misreport information. Why would states misreport their own behavior in settings where the underlying problem is one of relative harmony, for instance? In such situations, states might still find it very useful to gain information on each other's behavior, especially if they need to condition their actions on this information as in certain scientific endeavors. But given that each state can be expected to reveal this information truthfully, self-reporting is an efficient mechanism; at the same time, states give up little sovereignty since they are not inviting other actors to monitor their behavior.

However, as Abbott (1993: 26–27) notes, the utility of self-reporting is limited by fears that states will fail to report their behavior accurately. These fears are particularly pressing when states are facing incentives to defect from an agreement. In such a situation, self-reporting is hardly useful to resolve Uncertainty about Behavior. In fact, if behavior is not easily observed and states have incentives to defect, it is tempting for states to behave one way and claim to have behaved another way. For instance, in some environmental agreements, states have good reason to claim publicly that they are enforcing standards that are costly to their domestic industries while in fact turning a blind eye to the enforcement of these standards. In this case, states, fearful of being cheated on, will craft agreements that involve other actors (either a body created by the agreement itself and/or some third-party actor[s]) in the monitoring process.

COIL identifies several cooperation problems that generate incentives to defect from a cooperative agreement. These are Enforcement Problems, Uncertainty about Preferences, Uncertainty about the State of the World, and Commitment Problems. Under these conditions, states could either find it in their own interest to defect, worry that their partner(s) will, or both. These cooperation problems are aggregated under the label "incentives to defect," leading to the following hypothesis:

(H9-2) Other things equal, agreements that are characterized by underlying Uncertainty about Behavior are more likely to incorporate self-reporting only if there are few incentives to defect. Agreements will feature delegated monitoring only if Uncertainty about Behavior is aggravated by incentives to defect.

This two-part conjecture contends that states are more likely to delegate monitoring functions in response to high Uncertainty about Behavior only if they face incentives to defect at the same time. Absent incentives to defect, states have little reason to give up sovereignty by inviting other actors to monitor their behavior and instead can rely on self-reporting.

Finally, given that monitoring is often a form of centralization, one final hypothesis is relevant:

(H9-3) Other things equal, as the Number of states involved in the cooperative endeavor increases, agreements are more likely to include monitoring
provisions, in particular, formal delegated measures.

Empirical testing

The dependent (design) variables have already been described.
The coding of Uncertainty about Behavior and the Number of actors
is described in Appendix 2. Hypothesis 9-1 contends that if states are
facing Uncertainty about Behavior, they are more likely to include
monitoring provisions in their agreements. To evaluate this claim,
a simple probit model is used, where the dependent variable is the
presence of any monitoring provision in the agreement text. Aside
from the variable on the presence of Uncertainty about Behavior,
indicator variables for three of the four issue areas in the sample are
included. The estimation results are displayed in Table 9.5.[8]

As expected, the coefficient on Uncertainty about Behavior is positive and statistically significant at the 1 percent level. In substantive
terms, the effect is tremendous. Figure 9.1, which shows the average
predicted probabilities and 95 percent confidence intervals, illustrates

Table 9.5 *Presence of system of compliance monitoring*

Uncertainty about Behavior	1.11***
	(0.25)
Environment	−0.62**
	(0.26)
Human rights	−0.41
	(0.25)
Security	0.17
	(0.26)
Constant	0.17
	(0.12)
N	234

Note: Probit results, robust standard errors in parentheses.
*** *significant at 1 percent;* ** *significant at 5 percent;* * *significant
at 10 percent*

---

[8] The area under the ROC curve is 0.701.

Figure 9.1 Presence of system of compliance monitoring
Note: Average predicted probabilities with 95 percent confidence intervals.
Based on results in Table 9.5.

the results: When states are facing Uncertainty about Behavior, the probability that an agreement includes a formal system of compliance monitoring increases from 51 percent to 86 percent. This result provides strong support for H9-1. While this might seem an almost obvious result, it is important nevertheless. The result supports the notion that the variation showcased in the descriptive statistics is not just random, but a purposeful response to a distinct cooperation problem: Uncertainty about Behavior. Just as important, when such uncertainty is absent, states are less likely to incorporate formal monitoring provisions in their agreements.

To test H9-2, two probit models are employed. In the first model, the dependent variable is coded "1" whenever member states self-report information and the agreement does not stipulate who verifies this information.[9] In the second model, the dependent variable is coded "1" whenever states delegate the monitoring process to other actors. The conditional nature of H9-2 is captured by including two variables

---

[9] The results are similar when the dependent variable is coded "1" whenever only member states monitor compliance.

in each model in addition to Uncertainty about Behavior: the variable "incentives to defect" and an interaction term between this variable and Uncertainty about Behavior. The conjecture predicts that, in the first model, Uncertainty about Behavior has a positive effect only in the absence of incentives to defect. Thus, the coefficient on Uncertainty about Behavior should be positive, but the coefficient on the interaction term should be negative such that the overall effect of Uncertainty about Behavior is negated. In the second model, the effect of Uncertainty about Behavior should be significant only in the presence of incentives to defect. Thus, the overall marginal effect of Uncertainty about Behavior should have a positive sign in the presence of incentives to defect; in the absence of incentives to defect, we expect a small and insignificant effect of Uncertainty about Behavior. I also include the logged Number of participants, given H9-3 which argues centralization (here, delegated monitoring) increases with Number, and three issue-area indicator variables.

The estimation results, reported in Table 9.6, provide strong support for the COIL theoretical framework. The first column displays the results where the dependent variable is self-monitoring.[10] Figure 9.2 visualizes the average marginal effects and 95 percent confidence intervals for the relevant scenarios. In the absence of incentives to defect, Uncertainty about Behavior has a strong and statistically significant effect on the probability that an agreement calls exclusively for self-monitoring, which practically triples from about 26 percent to almost 72 percent. By contrast, if states have incentives to defect, Uncertainty about Behavior has virtually no effect (the probability that an agreement calls for self-monitoring increases by only 4 percentage points); with a p-value of 0.69, the effect is also statistically indistinguishable from zero. In other words, in the presence of incentives to defect, the 95 percent confidence interval for the average marginal effect of Uncertainty about Behavior includes zero in Figure 9.2, whereas it is clearly above zero in the absence of incentives to defect. This result supports H9-2 that states rely on self-reporting in the presence of Uncertainty about Behavior only if there are few concerns that other states will defect from the agreement.

---

[10] The area under the ROC curve is 0.798.

Table 9.6 *Self-monitoring and delegated monitoring*

	Self-monitoring	Delegated monitoring
Uncertainty about Behavior	1.47***	−0.34
	(0.46)	(0.51)
Incentives to defect	−0.53**	0.84***
	(0.26)	(0.26)
Uncertainty about Behavior × incentives to defect	−1.29**	1.06*
	(0.62)	(0.61)
Number (logged)	−0.38**	0.34***
	(0.19)	(0.10)
Environment	−0.30	−0.53*
	(0.33)	(0.28)
Human rights	−1.02**	−0.16
	(0.42)	(0.29)
Security	−0.13	0.20
	(0.32)	(0.28)
Constant	−0.01	−1.42***
	(0.32)	(0.27)
N	234	234

Note: Probit results, robust standard errors in parentheses.

*** *significant at 1 percent;* ** *significant at 5 percent;* * *significant at 10 percent*
Uncertainty about Behavior + Uncertainty about Behavior × incentives to defect =
0.18, p-value 0.69, based on the results in the first column: Self-monitoring.
Uncertainty about Behavior + Uncertainty about Behavior × incentives to defect =
0.72, p-value 0.03, based on the results in the second column: Delegated monitoring.

The second column in Table 9.6 shows similarly strong support for the second part of H9-2: Not only are states cautious about relying on self-reporting when faced with a combination of Uncertainty about Behavior and incentives to defect, they also turn to alternative means of information gathering by involving other actors in the monitoring process.[11] In fact, and as expected, the results shown in Figure 9.3 are the mirror image of Figure 9.2: Uncertainty about Behavior alone has no significant effect on the probability that states delegate monitoring tasks; the effect is

[11] The area under the ROC curve is 0.773.

Figure 9.2 Self-reporting by member states

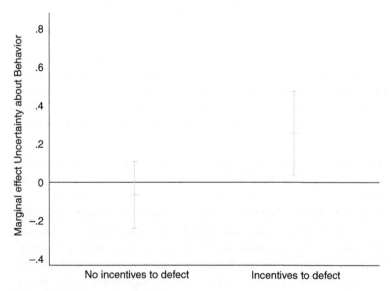

Figure 9.3 Delegated monitoring
Note: Average marginal effects with 95 percent confidence intervals of
Uncertainty about Behavior conditional on incentives to defect. Figure 9.2 is
based on the results in the first column of Table 9.6, and Figure 9.3 is based on
the results in the second column of Table 9.6.

negative, but small in size (a change of less than 7 percentage points) and statistically insignificant. However, when states face incentives to defect, Uncertainty about Behavior has a large, positive, and statistically significant effect on the probability that monitoring tasks are delegated. This probability increases from 42 percent to 68 percent, and the effect is statistically significant with a p-value of 0.03. Thus, Uncertainty about Behavior alone is not sufficient for states to delegate monitoring tasks; only in combination with incentives to defect are states willing to give up control over the monitoring process. The conjecture about Number, H9-3, is also strongly supported. Centralizing monitoring saves on transaction costs with larger Numbers of actors.

Similar in spirit to the reservations discussed in Chapter 7 by which some states disengage themselves from centralized dispute resolution, a few of the human rights agreements in the sample require that states opt in to delegated monitoring. Only one agreement in the sample, the International Convention on the Protection of the Rights of All Migrant Workers and Members of their Families (ICRMW), both has such a clause and lacks the requisite number of ten states declaring that they recognize the competence of the Committee on Migrant Workers to help monitor the behavior mandated by the agreement (Articles 76 and 77). In the few other human rights agreements that feature noncompulsory delegated monitoring, enough states have opted in to the delegated monitoring to make it operational for those states. The results in Table 9.6 are robust to the exclusion of the ICRMW from the category of delegated monitoring. The results in Table 9.6 are also robust to including only monitoring that is delegated to some kind of IGO and excluding any monitoring delegated solely to private or other nonstate actors or third parties.

Overall, then, Uncertainty about Behavior leads states to rely on self-reporting only if there are few incentives to defect; by contrast, delegated monitoring occurs when states face Uncertainty about Behavior and incentives to defect. By looking at the interactions of some of the COIL cooperation problems, another important dimension of the design of monitoring provisions is explained, one that engages one of the more controversial design elements (at least in the IR literature) – delegation to a third party.

The following statements made during the Senate Foreign Relations Committee Nuclear Nonproliferation Treaty Hearings regarding monitoring for the NPT are suggestive with respect to how states choose the appropriate monitoring design.[12] As Secretary of State Dean Rusk recalled: "From the outset the Soviets opposed the idea of accepting Euratom safeguards as a complete substitute for IAEA safeguards under the treaty, on the ground that Euratom safeguards amounted to self-inspection of Euratom members."[13] Later in the hearing, the following exchange occurred:

Senator SPARKMAN. As I recall from one of your statements Russia objected to using the Euratom formula, but was willing to use the International Atomic Energy Agency system.
Secretary RUSK. The objection raised by the Soviet Union was, if you relied solely upon the Euratom arrangements, this would be tantamount to having allies inspecting themselves.[14]

Thus, in this context, even though Euratom is a pre-existing IGO, it was not considered as "objective" as the IAEA, at least in the eyes of the Soviets, and their view prevailed. In fact, given the underlying Enforcement problems surrounding the issue of nuclear nonproliferation coupled with the Uncertainty about Behavior inherent in that subject area, delegated monitoring as opposed to monitoring that relies on self-reports is what the COIL theoretical framework predicts. What is interesting in this case is that the Soviets considered the delegated third-party monitoring of Euratom a form of self-monitoring in actuality, which the Soviets could not rely upon given the underlying incentives to defect.

Additionally, in the long negotiations leading to the Limited Test Ban Treaty, "[t]he Western powers were determined to ensure that no agreement would be vulnerable to clandestine violation. In test-ban negotiations, as well as in other arms control efforts, they considered that it would be dangerous to their security to accept simple pledges without the means of knowing that they would be observed."[15]

---

[12] To my knowledge, creating a new body within the context of the NPT was never seriously entertained as a design option.
[13] See Chapter 3, fn. 31: 6.   [14] Ibid., 14.
[15] US Department of State. Bureau of Arms Control, Verification, and Compliance. Treaty Banning Nuclear Weapon Tests in the Atmosphere, in Outer Space and Under Water. Available at www.state.gov/t/isn/4797.htm [Last accessed May 16, 2015]. I thank David Adgate for pointing me to this quote.

The causal mechanism outlined in the COIL theoretical framework is certainly not foreign to actual negotiators.

Informal monitoring provisions

I now turn to informal monitoring provisions in international agreements. I proceed in a much more inductive fashion compared with the analysis of informal punishment provisions in Chapter 8, mainly because of the absence of strong theory guiding any expectations regarding formal versus informal monitoring. Nevertheless, this analysis brings nonstate actors into the study front and center. Specifically, I examine the role of NGOs in monitoring formal international law.

I begin with the same methodology I developed for the analysis of informal punishment provisions in Chapter 8. I generate a list of international agreements that are candidates for informal monitoring. I then examine actual NGO monitoring in the entire COIL sample. The results generate some new puzzles for scholars to explain. For instance, what explains the layering of monitoring provisions? Why do NGOs continue to have an *informal* as opposed to formal role in monitoring formal agreements, despite their pervasiveness in monitoring across many issue areas? I conclude the section on informal monitoring with a brief discussion regarding the role of the United States in monitoring outside the treaty framework.

Predicting formal delegated monitoring provisions

Recall H9-2: *States rely on delegated monitoring only if Uncertainty about Behavior is aggravated by incentives to defect.* Remember also the empirical support it garnered, as reported in Table 9.6.[16] Following Chapter 8, agreements without delegated monitoring provisions that are predicted to have them are candidates for informal monitoring.

---

[16] It is important to note that the marginal effects of the cooperation problems are largely the same across issue areas, which implies that no particular issue area is a greater candidate for informal monitoring than any other issue area. The table illustrating these results is available on the COIL website. See Chapter 3, fn. 14.

Specifically, based on the coefficient estimates, we can predict the probability that each agreement in the sample should theoretically include delegated monitoring provisions. The predicted probabilities range from about 2 percent to 98 percent, with a mean of 39 percent and a standard deviation of 0.24. Using 0.5 as cut-off, 69 percent of the agreements were predicted correctly. That is, they were predicted to have centralized monitoring provisions and did in fact have them, or they were predicted *not* to have centralized monitoring provisions and in fact had none. Table 9.7 shows those agreements that were predicted to have delegated monitoring provisions with a probability of at least 50 percent yet do not have any. These agreements are candidates for informal monitoring and, following the research design introduced in Chapter 8, what I label as "misclassified."

Table 9.7 *Misclassified agreements regarding delegated monitoring*

Agreement name	COIL ID	UNTS	Pred. Prob.
Protocol relating to refugee seamen	HR 18	13928	0.50
Agreement with respect to quality wheat	AC 57	6389	0.53
European agreement on the restriction of the use of certain detergents in washing and cleaning products	EN 24	11210	0.56
Memorandum of understanding between the Ministry of Interior of the Republic of Turkey and the Ministry of Internal Affairs of the Republic of Belarus on cooperation in the field of combating trafficking in human beings and illegal migration	HR 2–7	44197	0.58
Charter of the Collective Security Treaty Organization	SE 2–3	39775	0.59
Treaty on cooperation in protection of the borders of States participating in the Commonwealth of Independent States with countries not forming part of the Commonwealth	SE 2–17	33648	0.61

Table 9.7 (*cont.*)

Agreement name	COIL ID	UNTS	Pred. Prob.
Constitution of the International Refugee Organization and Agreement on interim measures to be taken in respect of refugees and displaced persons	HR 33	283	0.63
Convention on the prevention and punishment of crimes against internationally protected persons, including diplomatic agents	HR 15	15410	0.66
Convention on the prevention and punishment of the crime of genocide	HR –2	1021	0.70
Exchange of notes constituting an agreement relating to military assistance: Eligibility requirements pursuant to the International Security Assistance and Arms Export Control Act of 1976	SE 17	16034	0.72
United States and Kuwait: Technical security arrangement concerning special security measures	SE 40	16314	0.72
Agreement between the Department of Defense of the United States of America and the Ministry of Defense of the Kingdom of Thailand concerning the measures to be taken for the transfer, security, and safeguarding of technical information, software and equipment to the Ministry of Defense to enable industry to operate, maintain, and expand Royal Thai Air Force air combat maneuvering instrumentation range facilities	SE 2–11	40309	0.72

Table 9.7 (*cont.*)

Agreement name	COIL ID	UNTS	Pred. Prob.
India and Zambia: Mutual agreement to combat illicit trafficking in narcotic drugs and psychotropic substances and money laundering (with annexes)	SE 2–21	31241	0.72
International Convention on Civil Liability for Oil Pollution Damage	EN 49	14097	0.73
Convention on long-range transboundary air pollution	EN 55	21623	0.79
Convention on fishing and conservation of the living resources of the high seas	EN 25	8164	0.80
Treaty on the prohibition of the emplacement of nuclear weapons and other weapons of mass destruction on the sea-bed and the ocean floor and in the subsoil thereof	DS 5	13678	0.83
Convention on prohibitions or restrictions on the use of certain conventional weapons which may be deemed to be excessively injurious or to have indiscriminate effects	DS 3	22495	0.84

Agreements without delegated monitoring provisions, yet predicted to include delegated monitoring provisions with probability > 0.5.

Analyzing misclassified agreements

What might lead states to leave out delegated monitoring when the underlying cooperation problems call for it? In the majority of cases, monitoring is not as intrusive as punishment and not as costly either. Punishing another state for a human rights violation, for example, might require military action; monitoring compliance most likely would not. The differential treatment that is often desirable when it comes to punishment is arguably thus not as valuable in the case of monitoring. Therefore, unlike the case of punishment provisions, no theory guides the researcher as to under what conditions informal as opposed to formal monitoring might be chosen.

Looking more closely at both the correctly predicted agreements and the misclassified agreements seems like a reasonable next step. One surprising finding presented at the beginning of this chapter is the very small formal role NGOs play in monitoring international commitments. This finding is certainly counter to the conventional wisdom in IR and IL that NGOs play an important role in monitoring agreements in the issue areas of human rights and the environment. Given this disjuncture, in what follows, I present the results of extensive research on NGO monitoring of the agreements in the COIL sample as a first step in investigating the relationship between formal and informal monitoring.

NGO monitoring in the COIL sample

Three categories of potential NGO monitoring are considered.[17] First, when is NGO monitoring officially sanctioned by the agreement? Is the NGO the sole monitor or do states or an IGO also monitor compliance? Is there evidence that NGOs actually monitor? Second, how often do NGOs monitor agreements that do not call for NGO monitoring but that are predicted to need monitoring and that stipulate other delegated monitoring mechanisms? This is the category of correctly predicted agreements. Third, how often does NGO monitoring take place in "misclassified" agreements – that is, agreements that, given the underlying cooperation problems, should have delegated monitoring but do not?

Both the second and third categories of NGO monitoring can be considered informal monitoring by NGOs: NGOs are not mentioned in that capacity formally but they do still monitor. Importantly, comparing the incidence of monitoring in these latter two categories also sheds light on an important question regarding informal provisions in general: To what extent do informal provisions complement or substitute for formal provisions? (The case of antagonists does not make sense in the context of informal monitoring: When behavior is

---

[17] This section on NGO monitoring relies on the excellent research of Julia Gysel.

already transparent and hence no formal monitoring system is called for, not only is informal monitoring unnecessary; there is also nothing controversial about it since nothing is hidden.)

Formal NGO monitoring   Regarding the first category, three agreements call on NGOs to perform some kind of monitoring function, and all three are in the issue area of human rights: the Convention for the Protection of Human Rights and Fundamental Freedoms (which allows NGOs to be victims and thus act as fire alarms), the 1950 Geneva Convention Relative to the Treatment of Prisoners of War, and the American Convention on Human Rights. The latter two invite NGOs to give reports concerning compliance. These three agreements have other forms of monitoring as well resulting in multiple monitoring systems. Here, then, NGOs *formally complement* other monitoring systems.

In practice, NGO monitoring does occur in these agreements. With respect to the Convention for the Protection of Human Rights and Fundamental Freedoms, NGOs are certainly monitoring the rights stipulated in that agreement, but they do not mention the agreement itself, somewhat like the UNSC resolutions described in Chapter 8 that mention human rights but not the treaties that establish them. While the monitoring role of the International Committee of the Red Cross (ICRC)[18] is well known, its functions go well beyond monitoring in armed conflicts, and most of its public reporting focuses on its role in promoting adherence to international humanitarian law in general.[19] The other NGOs that monitor issues related to the 1950 Geneva Convention do not name the convention itself. Well-known NGOs, like Human Rights Watch and Amnesty International, monitor the American Convention on Human Rights.

Informal NGO monitoring on top of formal delegated monitoring   Regarding the second category, which refers to informal NGO monitoring layered on top of formal delegated monitoring, the results are astounding. *In the set of agreements that need and have formal*

---

[18]   The ICRC is the only NGO mentioned by name in the entire COIL sample.
[19]   Reports resulting from the ICRC's monitoring of the Geneva Conventions are kept confidential.

delegated monitoring provisions, over 70 percent are also informally monitored by NGOs.[20]

Consider first the issue area of human rights. In the set of agreements that need and have formal delegated monitoring provisions, almost 80 percent are also informally monitored by NGOs. Moreover, no evidence of NGO monitoring does not mean it is not occurring. Small, local NGOs may not have the means to publicize their results, for instance. Thus all data reported in this section on NGOs are either accurate or understated. About 80 percent of the human rights agreements that have informal NGO monitoring specifically refer to the agreement itself, whereas 20 percent monitor in the specific subject area without mentioning the agreement.

The Convention against Torture (CAT) is an example. Because NGOs are not mentioned in CAT, they play a technically informal role in their relationship with CAT and the Committee against Torture. However, the committee has long respected the opinions of NGOs and, through tradition, has established a process in which they receive input from NGOs. The committee obtains information about member states at "different stages of the reporting process and also meets with them during the session examining the report for which they have submitted information."[21] These meetings take place before the formal examination of a State's self-report by the committee. The ways in which NGOs and National Human Rights Institutions (NHRIs) interact with the Committee against Torture include: "Written information for the LOIs [list of issues] and LOIPR [list of issues prior to reporting]; Written information for the examination of the State party's report; NGOs in-session briefings as well as NHRIs and NPMs [National Preventive Mechanisms] briefings; Written information for the follow-up to the Committee's concluding observations recommendations."[22]

Another example is the CRC. The NGO Group for the Convention on the Rights of the Child is a coalition of over 50 international NGOs.

---

[20] As I elaborate later, NGO monitoring of the specific subject area of the agreement is counted as NGO monitoring, even if the agreement itself is not named. If a stricter requirement is employed (i.e., the agreement itself must be named), the percentage drops from 74 to 63, which is still quite high.

[21] Committee against Torture. "Information for Civil Society Organisations and National Human Rights Institutions (NHRIs)." Available at www.ohchr.org/EN/HRBodies/CAT/Pages/NGOsNHRIs.aspx [Last accessed July 3, 2015].

[22] Ibid.

There are even more (almost countless) NGOs working in the field of children's rights. Often, they do refer to the CRC, but they usually do not in every single report. One such NGO is the American Children's Rights Organization, which does not refer to the CRC perhaps because the United States has not ratified the convention.

CEDAW is an example of an international agreement whose formal text does not mention NGOs but which has evolved to include them. The Committee on the Elimination of Discrimination against Women monitors implementation of CEDAW. This committee was established by the member states and invites NGOs to submit reports. Many NGOs are indeed involved in the committee's work, with the most prominent ones being Amnesty International and Human Rights Watch. For example, with respect to Indonesia's compliance with CEDAW, Amnesty International filed a report to the committee in 2012 in which it highlighted "five areas of concern."[23] In Egypt, there exists a collection of NGOs dedicated to monitoring CEDAW called the Egyptian CEDAW Coalition.[24]

As one final example in the issue area of human rights, the ICCPR has formal delegated monitoring by the Human Rights Committee, an IGO created by the treaty. Many NGOs around the world submit reports to the Human Rights Committee, including the ICCPR Task Force in the United States as well as Amnesty International and Human Rights Watch.

Outside of human rights, the sub-issue area of disarmament is by far the most striking, with statistics that surpass the human rights issue area in some regards. All five of the disarmament agreements that delegate monitoring are also informally monitored by NGOs that very specifically mention the agreement by name. These agreements are the BWC, the CWC, the Mine Ban Treaty,[25] the Convention on the Prohibition of Military or any Other Hostile Use of Environmental Modification Techniques, and the Treaty for the Prohibition of Nuclear Weapons in Latin America and the Caribbean (Treaty of Tlatelolco).

[23] Amnesty International. "Indonesia. Briefing to the UN Committee on the Elimination of Discrimination against Women." Available at www2.ohchr.org/english/bodies/cedaw/docs/ngos/AmnestyInternationalForTheSession_Indonesia_CEDAW52.pdf [Last accessed July 3, 2015].
[24] I thank Leah List for alerting me to this network.   [25] See Chapter 3, fn. 33.

For example, the "Landmine and Cluster Munition Monitor" (Landmine Monitor) is a coalition of NGOs that monitors the Mine Ban Treaty as well as the Convention on Cluster Munitions. Landmine Monitor is now the de facto monitoring regime of the Mine Ban Treaty.[26] Landmine Monitor cooperates closely with governments and receives a large part of its funding from agreement members.[27] It tracks systematically and comprehensively compliance with all treaty obligations by all treaty parties in the form of a very detailed yearly report.[28]

Consider also the BioWeapons Prevention Project (BWPP), which is a broad network of over 50 NGOs that monitors compliance with the BWC by means of the annual publication, BioWeapons Monitor. The BWPP uses its network of civil society actors around the world to compile information about activities of states (and other actors) relevant to the BWC and tries to relate the data systematically to the treaty provisions.[29] The authors of the report use open-source data as well as information that they request from governments, research institutions, and industry.

In the issue area of the environment, eight out of the ten agreements with formal delegated monitoring are also informally monitored by NGOs. Almost all of these agreements (seven out of eight) are named by the NGOs that monitor their subject area.

The only two sub-issue areas for which formal, delegated monitoring is not complemented by informal NGO monitoring are

---

[26] Landmine and Cluster Munition Monitor. Available at www.the-monitor.org/ [Last accessed July 3, 2015]; and Bruneau, Richard. 2006. "Unofficial Monitoring of Compliance With Arms Control Treaties: A Survey." *Canadian Centre for Treaty Compliance, Compliance Chronicles*, no. 2. Available at http://carleton.ca/npsia/wp-content/uploads/CC2.pdf [Last accessed June 13, 2015].

[27] Meier, Oliver, and Clare Tenner. 2001. "Non-governmental Monitoring of International Agreements." In *Verification Yearbook 2001, VERTIC*, eds. Trevor Findlay and Oliver Meier. Available at www.vertic.org/media/Archived_ Publications/Yearbooks/2001/VY01_Meier_Tenner.pdf [Last accessed June 24, 2015].

[28] For more information, see The Landmine Monitor Report 2014. Available at http://the-monitor.org/index.php/LM/Our-Research-Products/LMM14 [Last accessed July 3, 2015].

[29] See Bruneau 2006, fn. 26.

agricultural commodities (AC) and investment (IN). (There is one AC agreement that could potentially be monitored by an NGO and one IN agreement.)

These results show overwhelmingly that *informal monitoring provisions often complement formal ones.* This finding generates a number of new puzzles for scholars to explain. For instance, why do IGOs allow and even encourage NGO monitoring when the IGOs have a formal monopoly on monitoring (or share formal authority with the member states)? Drawing on the seminal work by Selznick (1949) on cooptation, Mattli and Seddon (2015) discuss informal cooptation, in which an organization over time reallocates authority to another organization (the coopted organization) as a means to survive. One avenue for future research is to delve into whether IGOs are limited in their tactics for monitoring and thus informally coopt NGOs, who, by remaining outside of the treaty framework, are able to monitor in less constrained, even "illegal" means, and thereby contribute to the survival of the treaty regime. This cooptation could potentially even expand the treaty regime given that NGOs often monitor states not party to the regime and draw attention to such states' behavior. This attention could catapult other actors to pressure these nonmember states into joining the regime.

A study by Vabulas (2013) is consistent with this thesis. Vabulas argues that IGOs tasked with monitoring are more likely to grant consultative status to NGOs because these NGOs can name and shame dissident states in ways IGO bureaucrats or member states cannot. Her argument is supported by an analysis of an original data set of NGO consultative status across approximately 300 IGOs. Additionally, her study of state-level decisions about NGO accreditation in the UN Economic and Social Council over the last 30 years shows that states select NGOs that can act as allies in monitoring and enforcing international agreements. She concludes that states wishing to solve Enforcement problems form strategic relationships with NGOs to preserve rather than inhibit their autonomy.[30]

---

[30] The work of Tallberg et al. (2013) should also prove informative for future research on this topic, in particular on the topic of intentionality: Do negotiators know in advance that NGOs will help states monitor? If so, does this knowledge affect the design of the initial monitoring system? Many NGOs gain access to IGOs over time and with different degrees of formality. Thus COIL with its coding of initial agreement design should be informed by work like Tallberg et al., which looks at the evolution of NGO-IGO connections.

Informal NGO monitoring when formal delegated monitoring is missing What is striking is that the category of informal NGO monitoring when formal monitoring is missing has less informal NGO monitoring than the preceding one. In fact, in this category, only 33 percent of the agreements for which NGO monitoring could substitute for the "missing" delegated monitoring have been found to have NGO monitoring; two-thirds of the agreements in the category show no evidence of NGO monitoring.[31]

Like in the earlier category, the issue areas of human rights and disarmament are characterized by informal NGO monitoring, but the statistics are very different. Only 40 percent of the "misclassified" human rights agreements and 50 percent of the "misclassified" disarmament agreements are informally monitored by NGOs, whereas in the previous category, in which NGO monitoring complements formal monitoring, the numbers for the human rights and the disarmament issue areas are 79 percent and 100 percent, respectively. There are four misclassified environmental agreements of which three are in specific subject areas monitored by NGOs, although the environmental agreements themselves are never named. This percentage is slightly smaller than that in the earlier category, where 80 percent of the environmental agreements are monitored by NGOs. The sub-issue areas of agricultural commodities and security show no evidence of informal NGO monitoring of their misclassified agreements.

As one example of informal monitoring in this category of substitutes, the Convention on the Prevention and Punishment of the Crime of Genocide does not have the theoretically predicted centralized monitoring, but there are over 50 NGOs and research institutes active in the field that try to monitor relevant activities. Two such NGOs are the Genocide Prevention Advisory Network and Genocide Watch. On the whole, though, NGO informal monitoring works strikingly more as a *complement to* than a substitute for formal monitoring.

It is worth emphasizing one of the surprising discoveries of this research: the extent to which agreements in the sub-issue area of disarmament are monitored by NGOs. It is also noteworthy that, while the monitoring of human rights or environmental agreements is

---

[31] If the stricter definition is applied (see fn. 20), the percentage drops to 16.

often carried out by NGOs with a focus on advocacy and campaigning, the NGOs that unofficially monitor disarmament agreements are, in most cases, independent research institutes, such as the Verification Research, Training and Information Centre and the Harvard Sussex Program.

US domestic law as a monitoring mechanism

I considered how NGOs might substitute or complement international bodies in monitoring international law. I now ask whether the most powerful state in the system, the United States, uses its domestic institutions to complement or substitute for international law provisions regarding monitoring.

Likely no one is surprised by the assertion that domestic law can work as an enforcement mechanism for international law. Simmons' (2009) seminal book on the enforcement of human rights agreements calls attention to the role of domestic courts. Following the ratification of human rights agreements, domestic courts can be used to hold state leaders accountable for the human rights practices to which they had agreed. In Simmons' account, NGOs often are the catalyst for such enforcement. Here I ask how power might enter into the explanatory picture – that is, if the most powerful state's interests are aligned with certain pieces of international law, does even more monitoring occur through the state's domestic institutions?

Indeed, the United States through its formal law plays an informal role in monitoring compliance with a host of international agreements. Consider first the security issue area, in particular, non-proliferation. The US Congress has enacted several bills that require reports on non-proliferation developments around the world. These include House Resolution 4310 (112th): National Defense Authorization Act for Fiscal Year 2013,[32] with Title X Subtitle E requiring reports on nuclear weapons not only in the United States, but also in China[33] and the Western Pacific region,[34] and Subtitle G mandating reports on military and security development involving North Korea and Syria. These reporting requirements make clear that the United States monitors

---

[32] Available at www.govtrack.us/congress/bills/112/hr4310/text [Last accessed July 3, 2015].
[33] Title X, Subtitle E, Sec. 1045.   [34] Title X, Subtitle E, Sec. 1046.

security developments in various states that concern the international community as a whole. Thus, in addition to IAEA monitoring of the NPT, the United States monitors and investigates as well.

The US Congress has also exercised its power to monitor and advance human rights practices, many of which are codified in human rights agreements. Table 9.8 displays various reports prepared by either the US State Department or the US Department of Labor and the Congressional legislation requiring submission of such reports.[35] Given that the United States initiated compilation of these reports through national legislation, one could argue that these reports show monitoring efforts that go beyond the obligations found in the relevant human rights agreements.

Of course, this short section is simply suggestive and opens the door to more systematic and comparative research on the topic. For instance, the anecdotal evidence does not tell us whether power is a necessary or sufficient condition for monitoring through domestic means. Other potential explanatory variables, like regime type, are also worthy of future research.

Table 9.8 *Statutorily required US administrative reports on global human rights practices*

Report	Legislation
Country Reports on Human Rights Practices[36]	Foreign Assistance Act of 1961
International Religious Freedom Reports	International Religious Freedom Act of 1998
Trafficking in Persons Report	Victims of Trafficking and Violence Prevention Act of 2000
Findings on the Worst Forms of Child Labor	Trade and Development Act of 2000
Advancing Freedom and Democracy	Advance Democratic Values, Address Nondemocratic Countries, and Enhance Democracy Act of 2007

---

[35] Further information available at www.humanrights.gov/reports/ [Last accessed July 3, 2015].

[36] Available at www.state.gov/j/drl/rls/hrrpt/humanrightsreport/index.htm#wrapper [Last accessed July 3, 2015].

Concluding thoughts

This chapter provides strong support for Keohane (1984): International institutions assume an important function for international cooperation by collecting and disseminating information. At the same time, Keohane's theory is elaborated in two respects. First, by disaggregating the dependent variable of an "international institution," the differences concerning *when* and *how* international agreements structure the collection of information is given priority. Second, by moving away from 2 × 2 games and separating Enforcement problems from Uncertainty about Behavior, the choice between delegated monitoring and self-reporting can be explained.

The research on NGO monitoring of the agreements in the COIL sample reveals how often monitoring outside the treaty framework complements formal monitoring systems. Nonetheless, formal agreements and their details remain important. The example of START, mentioned in the introduction to the book, not only shows that even the most powerful states subject themselves to intrusive inspections; it also demonstrates the importance of monitoring provisions for this agreement to work, and in particular the importance of the formal provisions within this formal agreement. One could even argue that the confidence building that resulted from the on-site monitoring in such bilateral arms control agreements contributed more to conflict resolution between the two superpowers than the actual substantive arms reduction. Once START expired, the United States had to interrupt its inspections immediately, despite being the most powerful state in the world. Moreover, while the enforcement of START can rely on reciprocity, reciprocity requires information about the behavior of other states. Put differently, in many contexts, monitoring provisions are what enable Axelrod's (1984) celebrated tit-for-tat to take place. Absent monitoring provisions, simple strategies like tit-for-tat cannot function properly, even for the most powerful actors in the system.

10 *Asymmetric design rules, voting, and power*

[The realists] believed instead in the polarity of law and power, opposing one to the other as the respective emblems of the domestic versus the international realm, normative aspiration versus positive description, cooperation versus conflict ...

(Slaughter Burley 1993: 207)

[T]he international legal system also seems to distance itself from predominant power: based on sovereign equality, it is disinclined to grant formal recognition to structures of superiority and leaves them to the political realm.

(Krisch 2005: 370)[1]

Extreme positions are not succeeded by moderate ones but by extreme positions of the opposite kind.

(Nietzsche [1887] 1967: 35)

Do formal voting rules and other aspects of agreement design reflect or ignore the realities of power? In this chapter, I examine whether the conjecture *Asymmetry of Power is reflected in Asymmetry of Control* is supported by the COIL data.[2] If power is at least somewhat reflected in the provisions of international law, Krisch's depiction of the relationship between law and power seems questionable. At the same time, if the provisions of international law correspond always and exactly to the configuration of power, one cannot plausibly argue that law has any kind of constraining effect on powerful states. Of course, at least

---

[1] To be fair, this quote does not necessarily reflect Krisch's position; he summarizes some classic views of power and international law as does Slaughter Burley.
[2] This chapter focuses on the relationship between power and control. See Chapter 3, in particular, fn. 36, regarding the Rational Design conjectures *Control decreases with Number* and *Control increases with Uncertainty about the State of the World*.

one other possibility remains: As mentioned in Chapter 8, Stone (2011) and Cogan (2009) argue that the Power Asymmetries inherent in many cooperative endeavors most likely manifest informally, while formal law represents a consensus among all state parties. Thus looking at the degree to which the hypothesis about Asymmetry of Power is or is not supported by the data might also give us a sense of whether and how often formal and informal provisions might conflict.

In what follows, I begin by presenting the (moderate) view of this book: Agreement design neither completely reflects nor completely ignores the realities of power. I then present some descriptive statistics about how often the provisions of the agreements in the COIL sample reflect the underlying distribution of power. I probe the conjecture regarding power and institutional design with the data to see how well it is supported. I then present three case studies (using agreements from the sample) that illustrate some of the themes of this chapter and generate some interesting questions for future research.

Overall, the findings are mixed with respect to how often power is reflected in institutional design. With respect to asymmetric monitoring and punishment, there are significant differences in design depending on whether powerful states are involved in the endeavor. Nonetheless, power-based decision-making rules like weighted voting are less frequent than one might expect. Many of the findings point to important future research questions, especially given the number of times voting rules are left unspecified.

The delicate balance of law and power

The extreme positions quite popular in the IR debates among various paradigms are usually quite unhelpful if the goal is to explain most state behavior most of the time. Like most institutionalists, I take a moderate position when it comes to power: Power Asymmetries are very real phenomena, but they do not imply that cooperation or law is trivial. Most of us in this school of thought would agree that power is reflected in cooperative endeavors but that states will also impose constraints on their power in order to realize other goods. Put differently, *the pursuit and maintenance of power is not a lexicographic preference for rational states*. (In a world of lexicographic preferences, states would unconditionally prefer an agreement that gives them the most power regardless of the amount of other goods they might be giving up with such a choice – including solving a prisoners' dilemma-like public goods problem by delegating some authority to a third party; they would never trade off even a bit of power to realize other goals.)

What does this moderate position imply for how powerful states will design their agreements? Simply put, most of the time powerful states want their asymmetric power reflected in the terms of the agreement, but this desire is not synonymous with having complete control over the cooperative endeavor and its evolution. Rather, elements of agreement design like weighted voting or the discretion to punish differentially or not all (discussed in Chapter 8) might suffice to make powerful states comfortable about submitting themselves to the constraints imposed by international law.

Furthermore, before starting any design analysis, it is important to note that we should not always expect Power Asymmetries to be reflected in the design dimensions of law. This is so because often the substantive terms themselves reflect what powerful states desire.[3] This is nowhere clearer than in the NPT, where certain powerful states are allowed to keep their nuclear weapons while no other state is allowed to obtain them. In this case, the powerful states are also protected by the rule for amendments, which stipulates that amendments must be approved not just by a majority of states but by all the nuclear weapon states as well. However, all of the other design provisions, including the IAEA monitoring and duration provisions, are symmetric. At the same time, the negotiation record of the NPT reveals that the United States and the Soviet Union compromised on a number of provisions. Their combined power did not result in these two superpowers pushing through their desired treaty draft unaltered. In fact, as Chapter 4 illustrates, the superpowers were forced to compromise their initial position on duration after six years of negotiation.[4]

Consider, too, Article 1 (1) of the Convention on the Prohibition of Military or Any Other Hostile Use of Environmental Modification Techniques (ENMOD), one of the security agreements in the COIL

---

[3] This point is worthy of future exploration perhaps in a sub-sample of the COIL agreements, in particular, if the preparatory and other negotiating documents are available. If a powerful state wins on substance, is veto power less important? If, on the other hand, it compromises on substance, does centralization of certain functions become less desirable?

[4] See Koremenos (2015) for other examples of superpower compromises made during the NPT negotiations to get the non-nuclear weapon states on board, including mandatory review conferences every five years.

random sample, which states: "Each State Party to this Convention undertakes not to engage in military or any other hostile use of environmental modification techniques having widespread, longlasting or severe effects as the means of destruction, damage or injury to any other State Party." According to Juda (1978: 980), when this provision was discussed in the UN General Assembly, several representatives argued that the inclusion of words like "widespread" and "severe" might end up legitimizing the use of ENMOD techniques that were not so widespread and severe. The United States, which drafted the treaty along with the Soviet Union, argued against any change in the language, and the draft article was not revised.[5] (Later, I describe how the two superpowers' design preferences were also accommodated for the most part.)

However, even the desire to have power reflected in the substantive terms will be conditioned by the underlying cooperation problems. This is a point that was made well by the 2 × 2 game framework: It is useful to exert power during the negotiation stage of a "Battle of the Sexes" but not so in, what is traditionally called, a "pure Coordination game" (see, e.g., Krasner 1991).[6]

Definitions and descriptive statistics

In this section, I examine two means by which power might be exerted through the design of international agreements. The first looks at any kind of asymmetry present in the agreement; the second looks at the decision-making rules of any body created by the agreement.

COIL asks whether the agreement in question is symmetric, mildly asymmetric (i.e., *procedurally* asymmetric, as in one-sided monitoring or punishment or weighted voting), or profoundly asymmetric (clearly favoring one state or set of states in terms of *substantive* rights, as does the NPT). This book focuses on the procedural aspects of international law so the focus of this chapter is procedural or mild asymmetry, not substantive asymmetry. Still, it is worth noting that COIL does not

---

[5] Juda, Lawrence, 1978. "Negotiating a Treaty on Environmental Modification Warfare: The Convention on Environmental Warfare and Its Impact on Arms Control Negotiations." *International Organization* 32 (4): 975–91. Cited in Elizabeth Watchowski. 2013. Untitled. Unpublished student paper. University of Michigan: 5.

[6] I address this issue in the concluding section of this chapter.

Table 10.1 *Incidence of procedural symmetry/
asymmetry by issue area
(percentage of each issue area)*

Issue area	Symmetric (%)	Asymmetric (%)
Economics	83	17
Environment	88	12
Human rights	100	0
Security	51	49
Total	80	20

N = 234

code as substantively asymmetric agreements that trade "apples for oranges" because there is no way to compare across issue or subject areas in that way. Thus an agreement that trades aid for the ability to station military bases is coded as symmetric given the inability of coders to determine from the agreement text or even background research whether such an agreement is substantively asymmetric.

Table 10.1 presents descriptive statistics regarding the question of procedural asymmetry in the COIL sample. The security issue area stands out in this regard, with almost half of the agreements characterized by some form of design asymmetry.

Besides weighted decision making (elaborated later), what other forms of procedural asymmetries exist in international agreements? An agreement is coded as mildly asymmetric if the agreement delegates a task such as punishment to the UNSC and the membership of the agreement comprises at least one UNSC P5 state and one non-P5 state. ENMOD provides a good illustration. States were divided over how potential violations should be addressed. The superpowers' draft stipulated that complaints should be submitted to the UNSC. Not surprisingly, smaller states desired a system independent of the UNSC, given that the permanent members of the UNSC would always be able to use their veto to protect themselves and their allies from punishment. Eventually, the Netherlands proposed a compromise, which was eventually accepted: the UNSC would still address complaints and punishments, but an ad-hoc committee of experts, under the guidance of the Secretary General, would be assigned a fact-finding role. This agreement meets the threshold of mildly asymmetric, given the punishment design does rely on the UNSC; indeed, the compromise between the powerful and not so powerful member states was "mild."

One-sided monitoring is also quite prevalent. In a mutual security agreement[7] between the United States and Malaysia, which came into force in 1977, Malaysia provides the following assurance: "it will permit continuous observation and review by, and furnish necessary information to, representatives of the United States Government with regard to the use of such services or training."

Sometimes the agreements in the sample do not explicitly mention monitoring, but they refer to the Foreign Assistance Act of 1948 (also known as the Economic Cooperation Act).[8] For example, the Exchange of Notes Constituting an Agreement Between the United States of America and Turkey Relating to Mutual Security from 1952 states the following: "The Government of Turkey has expressed its adherence to the purposes and policies of the Economic Cooperation Act of 1948 as heretofore amended . . . ." The 1948 act requires that states receiving assistance conclude an agreement with the United States that stipulates the regular transmission of compliance-related data:

In addition to continued mutual cooperation of the participating countries in such a program, each such country shall conclude an agreement with the United States in order for such country to be eligible to receive assistance under this title. Such agreement shall provide for the adherence of such country to the purposes of this title and shall, where applicable, make appropriate provision, among others, for . . .

(7) publishing in such country and transmitting to the United States, not less frequently than every calendar quarter after the date of the agreement, full statements of operations under the agreement, including a report of the use of funds, commodities, and services received under this title;

(8) furnishing promptly, upon request of the United States, any relevant information which would be of assistance to the United States in determining the nature and scope of operations and the use of assistance provided under this title.[9]

---

[7] The official title of the agreement is the Exchange of Notes Constituting an Agreement Relating to Military Assistance: Eligibility Requirements Pursuant to the International Security Assistance and Arms Export Control Act of 1976.

[8] US Congress. "Foreign Assistance Act of 1948." 80th Congress, 2nd Session, Chapter 169, April 3.

[9] Ibid., 151-152.

Because, as noted in Chapter 3, such references to domestic acts were taken into account in the coding of the design provisions, these agreements are considered to have formal (and in this case, one-sided) monitoring.

As an additional example, many of the bilateral agricultural commodity agreements in the sample that implement the United States' Agricultural Trade Development and Assistance Act are coded as mildly asymmetric. One such example is the Agreement for Sales of Agricultural Commodities between the Dominican Republic and the United States. The United States monitors the Dominican Republic and is allowed to terminate the agreement, *not vice versa*.

It is noteworthy that human rights agreements are never characterized by asymmetries of any kind. The few substantively asymmetric agreements are in the issue area of economics.[10]

Weighted decision-making rules, perhaps surprisingly, are not as common as other forms of procedural asymmetry. In what follows, I look closely at some of the rules governing any intergovernmental body created by an agreement.[11]

Whenever a body is created by an agreement in the sample, a number of questions are asked about its characteristics, including its decision-making procedures. There are multiple ways decision making in a body can favor certain states over others. First, representation in the body, instead of reflecting some sort of equality among member states, may be proportional to some form of power – like population, financial contribution, nuclear status, or market share. The CWC stipulates that when electing the 41 members of the Executive Council, attention be "specially paid to . . . the importance of chemical industry, as well as to political and security interests."[12] Later the agreement clarifies what is

---

[10] The infrequency of profoundly asymmetric observations most likely reflects either the point made earlier that an agreement's main substantive provisions will often be those that correspond to what the most powerful state or set of states wanted or the difficulty of making such a judgment when different parties obtain different things from the cooperative agreement. Still, regarding the latter, without a doubt agreements like the Biological Weapons Convention or the Genocide Convention do not favor any state substantively.

[11] Recall from Chapter 3 that 44 percent of the agreements in the sample call for the creation of an intergovernmental body composed of some subset of member states. Recall also that COIL's definition of an IGO is not as restrictive as COW's definition, for example, no permanent headquarters or secretariat is required for a body to meet COIL's criteria.

[12] Article VIII (C) (23)

meant by "importance of chemical industry" with the following language: "most significant national chemical industry in the region as determined by internationally reported and published data."[13] Second, the allocation of votes within the body, instead of reflecting some sort of equality among member states, may too be proportional to some form of power – like population, financial contribution, nuclear status, or market share. For instance, in the International Sugar Council established by the 1973 International Sugar Agreement, collectively the sugar exporting states and importing states each hold 1,000 votes; however, these votes are distributed among the two groups of state parties according to a rather complex formula, based entirely on economic factors like export or import market share and, in the case of exporters, production (Articles 9[4] and 9[5]).

COIL asks both questions for each body created by an agreement. Asymmetry can therefore be present in representation, vote allocation, or both. Tables 10.2 and 10.3 showcase the descriptive statistics regarding representation and vote allocation of the bodies created by the agreements in the COIL sample. The tables feature the 102 agreements, or the relevant subset that create a total of 159 bodies. In the 26 agreements that create multiple bodies, the body deemed to be tasked with the most substantively important obligations (e.g., setting quotas as opposed to setting the time/location for a meeting) is the one that is used for both the descriptive statistics and the analyses that follow.[14]

The descriptive statistics alone are surprising, especially in light of the findings on procedural asymmetry more generally, which indicate that power is reflected in institutional design overall about one-fifth of the time. Only 7 percent of the agreements that create bodies use some form of power-based decision-making rules.[15]

---

[13] Article VIII (C) (23) (a)-(e)
[14] The breakdown is as follow: 76 agreements create 1 body, 12 agreements create 2 bodies, 7 agreements create 3 bodies, 2 agreements create 4 bodies, 1 agreement creates 5 bodies, 3 agreements create 6 bodies, and 1 agreement creates 7 bodies.
[15] As I note in the text earlier, only one body per agreement is chosen for these statistics, a coding judgment having been made in agreements with multiple bodies regarding which body handles the most important, substantive tasks. If different judgment calls were made, the percentage could increase from 7 to 10. Still, this implies that at most only 4 percent of the total sample (which includes agreements that do not create bodies) has some kind of power-based decision-making rules. Thus, the one-sided monitoring and punishment account for most of the procedural asymmetry displayed in Table 10.1.

Table 10.2 *Representation on bodies*
          (number of agreements)

Issue area	Equal	Based on power	Non-power consideration	Not specified
Economics	43	1	5	3
Environment	20	0	2	1
Human rights	4	0	13	0
Security	8	2	0	0
N	75	3	20	4

N = 102

Table 10.3 *Vote allocation on bodies*
          (number of agreements)

Issue area	Equal	Based on power	Non-power consideration	Not specified
Economics	35	4	0	7
Environment	7	1	0	8
Human rights	4	0	6	7
Security	5	1	0	3
N	51	6	6	25

N = 88

Note: The sample size is 88 because agreements whose bodies feature unanimity decision making are excluded.

The specific breakdown is as follows. In agreements that create bodies and when using just one body per agreement, in 2 percent of the agreements power is reflected both in how representation is determined and in how votes are allocated. The United States is a member of both agreements. The 1956 Agreement for Financing Certain Educational Exchange Programs between the United States and Ecuador creates a Board of Directors composed of three US citizens, three Ecuadorian citizens, and one other American, who will serve as the Honorary Chairman of the Board and "shall cast the deciding vote in the event of a tie" (Article 4). The CWC, discussed earlier, is the other agreement.

Five agreements have one or the other power-based decision-making rules. The Treaty on Collective Security, which includes Russia, is the only agreement for which the main body uses power-based representation.[16] Out of the four agreements for which vote allocation is based on power, three are multilateral agricultural commodity agreements, and the fourth is the African Migratory Locust Convention of 1952, for which all contracting parties are equally represented, but the vote allocation is proportional to the parties' financial contribution (Articles II [5] and VI [2]).

Finally, there are also agreement bodies that do not reflect Power Asymmetry, but for which some other characteristic, such as expertise, is reflected in the design. CEDAW stipulates that the Committee established under Article 17 (1) shall consist of "experts of high moral standing and competence . . . and shall serve in their personal capacity, consideration being given to equitable geographical distribution and to the representation of the different forms of civilization as well as the principal legal systems."

There are quite a few bilateral agreements in the sample that create bodies, most prominently, BITs. The typical BIT arbitral body is composed in the following way: each member chooses one arbiter, and those two together choose a third. If they cannot agree (usually within a certain time period), arbitration is delegated externally. Thus even though in the example of Ecuador and the United States regarding educational exchange, power asymmetry was incorporated into the voting rules, bilateral agreements are not usually prone to such design.

With respect to how a body makes decisions, COIL allows a number of possible voting rules: unanimity, majority, super-majority, and special majority. Additionally, some agreements specify that voting rules for the body in question vary depending on the issue being decided. Finally, sometimes bodies are created, but their decision-making procedures are left unspecified.

Table 10.4 displays the descriptive statistics regarding voting rules. As in Tables 10.2 and 10.3, the most important body is chosen for agreements that create multiple bodies.

---

[16] The International Convention for the Conservation of Atlantic Tunas (with Final Act and Resolution adopted by the Conference of Plenipotentiaries) creates multiple bodies. One of those, but not the one considered most significant, stipulates that "[i]n elections to the Council the Commission shall give due consideration to the geographic, tuna fishing and tuna processing interests of the Contracting Parties" (Article V [1]). That is, representation in the Council may reflect market shares; how votes are allocated is not specified.

Table 10.4 *Decision rules by issue area*
(number of agreements)

Issue area	Unanimity	Simple majority	Special majority	Super-majority	Varies	Unspecified	N
Economics	2	36	0	0	3	7	48
Environment	7	2	2	2	2	8	23
Human rights	0	6	1	1	1	8	17
Security	1	1	0	0	3	5	10
N	10	45	3	3	9	28	98

Note: The sample size is 98 because one-person arbitral bodies were excluded.

Interestingly, except in the issue area of economics, the modal category is "not specified." In economics, the modal category is simple majority rule, despite the prevalence of bilateralism in this sub-issue area; recall, for instance, the internal arbitration bodies in most BITs, described earlier, which tend to feature simple majority rule. Finally, power can be exerted informally when voting rules are "not specified," as is vividly illustrated in the case study of ANZUS discussed later.[17]

Theory: How and when is power reflected in formal law?

Recall Table 10.1, in which the second column listing asymmetric agreements contains a zero only for human rights agreements, whereas in the issue area of security, almost half of the agreements are characterized by procedural asymmetry. Can power account for the variation in asymmetry displayed in Table 10.1? This leads me to the first hypothesis:

(H10-1) Other things equal, agreements that are characterized by a high Asymmetry of Power among the participants are more likely to incorporate some kind of design or procedural asymmetry than those not characterized by a high asymmetry of power.

Tables 10.2 and 10.3 look specifically at power-based decision-making rules for any body created by an agreement. Obviously, power is already reflected in the small set of agreements in the second columns of these tables. Still, it is important to ask whether *raw* economic or military power accounts for the pattern. This leads me to the second hypothesis:

(H10-2) Other things equal, for agreements that create an IGO, those that are characterized by a high Asymmetry of Power among the participants are more likely to incorporate some form of power-based decision-making rules than those not characterized by a high asymmetry of power.

---

[17] Tackling the "what actually happens when voting rules are left unspecified?" is part of a new multi-year research program sponsored by the Swiss Network for International Studies entitled, "The Politics of Informal Governance" (Oliver Westerwinter, University of St. Gallen, Principal Investigator). A team of assistants and I will investigate the COIL sample with respect to the implementation stage of cooperation with one of the goals being the identification of informal procedures if they exist (i.e., how does punishment, monitoring, decision making, etc. occur in the absence or even presence of formal provisions?) and, if so, coding whether the behavior complements, substitutes for, or contradicts what is in place formally.

Additionally, according to Stone (2011), and consistent with the results in Chapter 8, powerful states might exert their power informally. Thus if the details regarding how representation on an agreement body is determined are left unspecified, there is room for power to exert itself. The same is true when nothing is specified about vote allocation or decision-making rules. This leads me to a third hypothesis:

(H10-3) Other things equal, for agreements that create an IGO, those that are characterized by a high Asymmetry of Power among the participants are more likely to incorporate unspecified decision-making rules than those not characterized by a high asymmetry of power.

The voting rules within the bodies created by agreements (see Table 10.4) also provide a means for controlling the institution. Specifically, unanimity-voting rules provide all states, including powerful ones, with a veto for any decision making. This leads me to a fourth hypothesis:

(H10-4) Other things equal, for agreements that create an IGO, those that are characterized by a high Asymmetry of Power among the participants are more likely to incorporate some form of veto power than those not characterized by a high asymmetry of power.

Empirical testing

Table 10.5 shows the results from a model that includes three measures of Power Asymmetry: a US indicator variable (US power, however defined, was paramount throughout the entire period of the COIL sample) and, as in Chapter 8, two measures that capture the military and economic Power Asymmetry among the member states.[18]

Both US membership and Asymmetry of Power as measured by differences in military capabilities (I use the standard deviation in military capabilities among the participants) are statistically significant predictors of procedural asymmetry.[19] With respect to the substantive

---

[18] See Appendix 2, including fn. 3 and fn. 4. The kind of power relevant for the various sub-issue areas is likely to vary. Future research on what power means in each context and how to measure it would be very welcome.

[19] The areas under the ROC curve for the models in the first, second, and third columns are 0.849, 0.824, and 0.726, respectively.

Table 10.5 *Procedural asymmetry*

	US	Military	Economic
US	1.24***		
	(0.23)		
sd (Military Capabilities)		8.42***	
		(1.77)	
sd (GDP)			−0.05
			(0.09)
Economics	5.04***	4.30***	4.55***
	(0.22)	(0.17)	(0.16)
Environment	4.70***	4.29***	4.34***
	(0.30)	(0.27)	(0.27)
Security	5.69***	5.22***	5.45***
	(0.22)	(0.20)	(0.22)
Constant	−6.42***	−5.77***	−5.35***
	(0.24)	(0.11)	(0.04)
N	234	231	185

Note: Probit results, robust standard errors in parentheses.

*** *significant at 1 percent;* ** *significant at 5 percent;* * *significant at 10 percent*

effects, Table 10.6 illustrates the predicted probabilities of the two explanatory variables that attain statistical significance in Table 10.5. The probability that an agreement calls for procedural asymmetry increases by almost 30 percentage points when the United States becomes a participant. The probability that an agreement has procedural asymmetry increases by almost 9 percentage points when the standard deviation in military capabilities among participants shifts from the 25th percentile to the 75th percentile. The three issue areas displayed in Table 10.5 actually call attention to the human rights issue area. They are all significantly more likely to incorporate procedural asymmetry than the excluded issue area of human rights, which as Table 10.1 illustrates, is never characterized by procedural asymmetry. Overall, H10-1 is supported by the data.

With respect to H10-2, the findings are very different. Neither US involvement nor the two measures of raw economic and military power are significant in explaining power-based decision-making rules. This is an interesting finding. The power that matters is even more

Table 10.6 *Predicted probabilities and average predicted effects*

	Procedural asymmetry
No US	0.09
US	0.39
Change predicted prob.	*0.30****
25 percentile of sd (Military Capabilities)	0.11
75 percentile of sd (Military Capabilities)	0.20
Change predicted prob.	*0.09****

Note: All predicted probabilities in this table are significant at the 1 percent level.
*** significant at 1 percent; ** significant at 5 percent; * significant at 10 percent

refined than sub-issue area specific power: it is narrow subject area specific power. Thus, Brazil's, Colombia's, and the Ivory Coast's power in the coffee industry is reflected in agreements governing that commodity in the 1960s; likewise, for sugar cooperation, Cuba holds overwhelming power in the late 1960s. In some of these agreements, the United States also holds power because, for instance, the United States is the largest coffee importer. But the P5 generally do not control decision making in the coffee or sugar agreements.

Of course, one could argue that much will depend on the underlying cooperation problem(s) being solved. That is, in cooperative endeavors with minimal underlying Enforcement problems, for instance, powerful states may not require some kind of weighted voting. Perhaps surprisingly, interacting all three measures of power with an underlying Enforcement problem yields statistically insignificant results. (Recall from Chapters 5, 6, 7, 8, and 9 that other design provisions are used systematically to confront underlying Enforcement problems.) Raw military and/or economic power cannot explain weighted decision making with or without an underlying Enforcement problem. Thus H10-2 is not supported.

Nor is H10-3 supported. Notwithstanding the case study of ANZUS discussed later, agreements for which some aspect of decision making is left unspecified or informal are not significantly different from those that specify rules for every aspect of decision making with respect to any measure of power used in this book. Of course, many of the agreements for which some aspect of decision making is left unspecified dictate that the rules will be decided at one of the first meetings of the body.[20] Future research along the lines of Tallberg et al. (2013) regarding how IGOs evolve would complement the findings and remaining puzzles of this chapter.[21]

Finally, with respect to H10-4, again, there is no evidence that raw economic or military Power Asymmetry or US involvement lead to more unanimity requirements.[22] In fact, agreements with US membership are significantly *less* likely to incorporate unanimity voting. This finding has implications for another important topic in the international cooperation literature: institutional change. That is, agreements can change without the approval or buy-in from the powerful.[23] This finding engages Morse and Keohane's (2014) concept of "Contested Multilateralism," in which a group of actors dissatisfied with the governance of an issue within a multilateral regime attempt to either shift governance to another institution or create a new institution. When unanimity characterizes the original institution, contested multilateralism is more likely to ensue given the difficulty of change. But if unanimity does not characterize the original institution, as it seems to be the case in most institutions, change may occur from within leaving the institution intact. However, given that some members may not agree with the change, they may shift to a different institution or create one from scratch.[24] Future research

[20] Of course, if at least some aspects of decision making are not specified, how the rest will be decided is unclear!
[21] See, too, fn. 17.
[22] In contrast, among agreements with amendment provisions, 52 percent of agreements with US membership have non-binding amendments, while among those without US membership, only 17 percent have non-binding amendments. Thus, the United States can simply not accept an amendment it has not voted for in the majority of cases.
[23] See also Blake and Payton (2014) on the responsiveness of different voting rules in IGOs.
[24] The 1946 International Convention for the Regulation of Whaling (UNTS Reg. No. 2124), which calls for the formation of the International Whaling Commission (ICW), is an interesting case. A change in the preferences of the most powerful member, the United States, from a whaling to a non-whaling state allowed it to lead the way in changing the organization in a fundamental way: In the early 1980s, a moratorium on commercial whaling was enacted with a *three-quarters majority* vote. Thus, the organization changed in a way that accommodated its most powerful member. At the same time, Norway and Iceland, whose pro-whaling preferences did not change, created a contested IGO, the North Atlantic Marine Mammal Commission (NAMMCO), but did not withdraw from the ICW. Pro-whaling Japan, on the other hand, objected to the moratorium but did not join NAMMCO. Instead, Japan started

on voting rules, the presence or absence of powerful member states, and contested multilateralism could push forward the literature on institutional change.

Additionally, it is also possible for powerful states to use threats or promises to ensure that the policy changes they desire come to fruition. Alternatively, flexibility provisions, like finite duration provisions that force renegotiations at particular intervals, allow agreement change. One testable implication derived from both the COIL framework and Morse and Keohane's contested multilateralism is that treaties that have the optimal flexibility might be less contested because they change from within. In fact, as Chapter 4 notes, agreements that include superpowers among their members are just as likely to have finite duration provisions and thus be renegotiable as are agreements without superpowers. Similar findings appear in other chapters. Indeed, future theoretical and empirical research on when powerful states contest institutions, when they bribe or coerce smaller states to get the changes they want, and how both are affected by the flexibility incorporated into the agreement design would be useful.

Overall, the empirical results presented in this section reveal that sometimes power is reflected in the design of international law, sometimes the law is silent (as in unspecified voting rules), and sometimes law is quite symmetric. I return to these issues in the conclusion of this chapter.

Case studies

In what follows, I look at a few agreements from the random sample to get a more in-depth look at formal voting rules. In particular, I ask whether these rules are perceived to govern state behavior or whether states simply anticipate circumventing them informally.

The first case, the Moon Treaty, is not designed according to the conjecture *Asymmetry of Power leads to Asymmetry of Control*. This case thus gives us the opportunity to see how states responded to this "mistaken" formal design. The second case, the set of International

---

a "scientific" whaling program soon after the beginning of the moratorium. Japan continued whaling under the pretense of scientific purposes until Australia claimed that Japan's whaling program was not scientific; the ICJ agreed and ruled against Japan in 2014. See Mitchell and Keilbach (2001) for a terrific discussion of the IWC framed in the language of Rational Design.

Coffee Agreements,[25] does stipulate voting rules that reflect relative power. What is interesting in this case is that states made the voting weights renegotiable so that the formal rules were kept in line with power changes. Finally, the ANZUS Treaty leaves voting rules unspecified. Power is indeed exerted informally, but by being left unspecified, the formal rules are not contradicted by this informal decision-making structure but rather filled in.

The Moon Treaty

There is an agreement in the COIL sample that could be considered a "failed" agreement and for which the design of the treaty does not coincide at all with the underlying cooperation problems: The 1979 Moon Treaty.[26]

The Moon Treaty is in force only for about 15 states, none of which has any interest in and/or capacity for reaching the moon in the near future. (This is a far different statistic than that for the Outer Space Treaty,[27] which does not violate any COIL design principles and is in force for 98 states including the United States, China, and Russia.)[28] The Moon Treaty is not written according to COIL principles – it completely ignores the realities of international politics. The hypothesis that *Asymmetry in Power should lead to Asymmetric Control* is without a doubt implicated in this case given the potential resources on the moon and the almost prohibitive expense of exploiting them.

Article 4 of the Moon Treaty states: "The exploration and use of the moon ... shall be carried out for the benefit and in the interests of all countries, irrespective of their degree of economic or scientific development." Furthermore, the Moon Treaty calls for the creation of an international regime in the future that would govern the exploitation of the moon's resources when such exploitation becomes

---

[25] Only one coffee agreement appears in the sample, but I use it as an opportunity to study the set of them.

[26] The official name is Agreement Governing the Activities of States on the Moon and Other Celestial Bodies.

[27] The official name is Treaty on Principles Governing the Activities of States in the Exploration and Use of Outer Space, including the Moon and Other Celestial Bodies. UNTS Reg. No. 8843.

[28] Signatory list: www.state.gov/t/isn/5181.htm#signatory [Last accessed August 6, 2015].

feasible (Article 11 [5]). The voting rules for this future regime are not stipulated. Article 15 (3) further states, "If difficulties arise in connexion with the opening of consultations or if consultations do not lead to a mutually acceptable settlement, any State Party may seek the assistance of the Secretary-General [of the UN]." Thus the treaty mentions the Secretary-General but *not* the Security Council, which, of course, is composed of the only states currently able to reach the moon.

The Moon Treaty also provides that the moon and its natural resources are the "common heritage of mankind" (Article 11 [1]). The principle contained in the Outer Space Treaty is the "province of all mankind" (Article 1 [1]). The province of all mankind and common heritage principles are two very different principles. The "province of all mankind" principle in this issue area implies that all states have the nonexclusive right to use space. It does not imply any legal status regarding assets and/or property rights. The "common heritage" principle contained in the Moon Treaty refers to the legal status of property rights.[29] In the Moon Treaty, therefore, there is no incentive for the rich and powerful states to contribute to exploiting the moon's resources since all states will benefit equally and, presumably, will have equal say.

In an issue area like the exploitation of the moon, which involves major financial investment and the exercise of great technological capability, states are unwilling to cede control to an undefined international regime. The discussions before the US Senate Subcommittee on Science, Technology, and Space suggest that these provisions were at least partially responsible for the United States' failure to ratify the treaty. Art Morrissey, Senior Policy Analyst in the Office of Science and Technology Policy, admitted in his statement that these provisions of the treaty gave rise to the concern that it "will have the undesirable effect of discouraging American industry from undertaking the long-term planning and investment necessary to engage in exploitation of

---

[29] The superpowers and the developing states disagreed on this point. The developing states won the negotiation game (an interesting outcome worthy of future research). The treaty was drafted during the 1970s, when many developing states promoted the New International Economic Order. Some developing states explicitly referred to these principles in the *travaux préparatoires* (Danilenko 1989: 224-226; Reynolds 1995: 115).

the natural resources of celestial bodies."[30] Similarly, Robert B. Owens, State Department Legal Adviser, described one of the "principal concerns" of the Moon Treaty's opponents:

[B]ecause no one can now tell what sort of legal regime for the Moon will be developed at the future conference 15 or 30 years from now, it is not to be expected that in that 15- to 30-year interval American companies will be willing to invest the capital necessary to achieve private American exploitation of the Moon's resources. The uncertainties and the risks are too high, it is said, and in that sense the present situation is thought to create a de facto moratorium precluding American exploitation.[31]

The option of overriding the future formal rules informally evidently either was not considered or posed too risky a solution for any powerful state on which to gamble.

The involvement of the secretary general but not the UNSC, the latter of which would give powerful states indirect control, put another nail in the coffin. The Outer Space Treaty, too, is symmetric in terms of its substance and procedures but, substantively, does not ask large states to transfer their resources or share their power with small states.

COIL cannot explain why the Moon Treaty was designed this way. A declassified report from 1974 suggests that the treaty was not seen to be that important or urgent to either superpower, perhaps because the Outer Space Treaty was in place and resource exploitation was certainly not around the corner.[32] The COIL framework does, however, shed light on the Moon Treaty's paltry ratification record and its status as a "failed" agreement. In this case, the formal voting rules were taken seriously enough to precipitate the failure of this treaty.

International coffee agreements

The 1962 ICA and the rest of the series of quota-setting agreements that followed are clear examples of agreements whose voting rules reflect

---

[30] US Congress. Senate. Subcommittee on Science, Technology, and Space. Committee on Commerce, Science, and Transportation. 1980. *The Moon Treaty*. 96th Congress, 2nd Session, July 29 and 31, p. 30.

[31] Ibid., 5.

[32] United States. Paper prepared by the Department of State, Washington, D.C., May 3, 1974. Foreign Relations of the United States 1969–1976 Volume E–3, Documents on Global Issues, 1973–1976, Document 94: https://history.state .gov/historicaldocuments/frus1969-76ve03/d94 [Last accessed April 12, 2014].

relative power but do not completely mirror it. The 1962 ICA establishes multiple bodies. The International Coffee Organization (ICO), for instance, administers the ICA from its headquarters in London. The Council of the ICO, which is composed of a representative of each member state, is the body charged with making decisions that are consequential for member states (i.e., that have potentially material consequences). Voting power on the Council is distributed according to the volume of imports (for consumer states) and exports (for producer states), with some adjustments at the top end to prevent the United States (on the consuming side) and Brazil (on the producing side) from having excessive influence. That is, the voting rules *mostly* reflect underlying bargaining power as reflected in relatives shares of exports and imports, but *lack the one-to-one correspondence* that would essentially give the largest exporter (Brazil) and the largest importer (the United States) veto power.[33] Under the agreement, most important decisions require a distributed 2/3 majority, that is, a 2/3 majority of the votes cast within the importers group and a 2/3 majority of the votes cast within the exporters group. This voting structure ensures that neither the consumer states nor the producer states can dominate the proceedings. Not surprisingly, the member states of the ICO carefully circumscribe the powers of the Council of the ICO through limitations on the matters it may consider and through the imposition of stringent supermajority voting requirements.

The battle over the exporters' quota shares, which would determine voting weights, was fierce. South American states, like Brazil and Colombia, wanted to lock in their dominance at the time, whereas many African states, who were witnessing rapid growth in their production capabilities as well as increased demand for their coffee, wanted a flexible approach. In the end, the limited duration and renegotiation provision of the 1962 agreement provided the solution: The 1962 International Coffee Agreement could be sustained as an equilibrium institution because it was in the interest of all the states involved to adhere to it for its limited duration. Once it came to an end, cooperation in coffee could continue as an equilibrium outcome because a new agreement could be negotiated that reflected the new political realities. Quota shares and thus relative voting weights would

---

[33] Likewise, the IMF's weighted voting rules reflect but do not mirror Power Asymmetries. See Stone 2011, chapter 4.

change to reflect the new configuration of power. Indeed, the relative quota shares of the African states did increase in the 1968 agreement. Congruently, between the 1962 and 1983 agreements, Brazil's share of the total export quota fell from 39.2 percent to 30.8 percent, and its voting weights decreased accordingly.

It is interesting to note that a similar solution was chosen for the international cocoa agreements. In the 1960s, Ghana was one of the leading cocoa producers, accounting for more than one third of world production. Not surprisingly, Ghana's relative power was reflected in the first International Cocoa Agreement of 1972, in which its basic quotas were 38 percent of the total.[34] Between 1972 and 1976, Ghana's real GDP per capita declined by 8 percent.[35] Ghana's relative quota also changed in the 1975 agreement to 33 percent – a 13 percent decline.[36]

What is interesting about these cases is that states demanded that the *formal voting rules be responsive to changes in bargaining power*. Obviously, states did not want to rely on informal voting rules to trump what was on paper. They also did not rely on unspecified voting rules. A question for future research is why? For instance, did the *large Number* of participants involved in these commodity agreements (compared to the case of ANZUS, discussed next) drive the need for formal rules as opposed to unspecified rules?

The case of coffee also illustrates the constraining power of international law, even for the most powerful state in the system. The United States initially supported a coffee "cartel" (against its free-market ideology) because it feared that the economies of its Latin American neighbors were in danger of collapse given dramatic instability in the price of coffee. As one US State Department official stated in a 1965 hearing before the House Committee on Ways and Means:

The freely competitive interplay of economic forces in the United States is one of the basic elements of our past and present national strength. A free market economy in coffee should perhaps be an ultimate goal. But the reality is that many of the developing countries of the world which depend so much on coffee cannot now cope with the severe economic dislocations which are

[34] International Cocoa Agreement (with annexes). October 21, 1972. Annex A. UNTS Reg. No. 12652.
[35] See Appendix 2, fn. 3.
[36] International Cocoa Agreement (with annexes), October 20, 1975, Annex F, UNTS Reg. No. 15033.

caused by wide swings in the price of their principal revenue and foreign exchange earner .... The coffee agreement ... serves our foreign policy objectives of building strength and freedom in developing areas of the world while protecting the American consumer .... [T]he key question is whether it is in the U.S. interest to allow these countries, a large number of them, to go through the wringer, as it were, at a time when populations are doubling every 18 to 20 years and take a chance that they would stay on our side of the curtain which divides the free and the Communist world ...[37]

Thus the United States' motives were geopolitical.[38] The 1983 agreement was extended multiple times while the states tried to negotiate a replacement. When the Cold War ended, the member states were in one of these extension intervals. The United States did not immediately give notice that it would withdraw (which would have been lawful); instead, the United States stayed with the agreement until the next extension and simply did not approve it. It stayed in the agreement longer than was in its interest; it stayed until it faced the same choice every other state faced: to continue or not. Only at that point did it cease its participation.

Australia, New Zealand, United States Security Treaty

One of the most interesting findings in the COIL data set is the frequency with which actual voting rules are left unspecified. For example, the Australia, New Zealand, United States Security Treaty (ANZUS) creates a Council composed of the foreign ministers (or their deputies) to help implement the treaty, but the voting rules for the Council are not specified. Such design in a sense leaves the voting rules informal. Looking into this case further reveals that the most powerful state, the United States, did and does seem to call the shots when it comes to the operation of the treaty.

ANZUS has endured various challenges originating from the Power Asymmetry and the consequent tension among the member states. Yet,

---

[37] US Congress. House of Representatives. Committee on Ways and Means. 1965. *International Coffee Agreement*, 89th Congress, 1st Session, April 13 and 14: 5, 9.

[38] Krasner (1973: 512) argues that the US government was able to garner coffee-industry support for the agreement by "taking advantage of the noneconomic aims of corporate managers." By involving industry leaders in the policy process, the government helped convince them to support the agreement out of a sense of public duty.

the continuing operation of the treaty is indeed based upon effective control by the United States. In particular, reactions to Australian criticism of the treaty alliance and the nuclear policy dispute with New Zealand, both elaborated later in this sub-section, highlight how the United States dominates treaty implementation through these unspecified voting rules, also known as, informal mechanisms. In a nutshell, even with the Australian and New Zealand forces fighting in the United States' wars, the United States has blocked attempts to weaken its authority by imposing sanctions and refusing to recognize other member states' rights in the treaty.

Consider first Australia. According to Tow and Albinski (2002: 154), the lack of clarity in the Unites States' commitment to the future defense of Australia, the Australian Defence Force's heavy reliance on the US military, and Australian policymakers' reluctance to deviate from US policy all show that the United States continues to exercise its dominance. As Tow and Albinski argue, even though ANZUS was originally expected to protect Australia against regional threats, the actual implementation looks somewhat different. In fact, Australia supported US military operations in Vietnam. Even today, there is usually an Australian contingent deployed with the US military, as there was most recently in Iraq and Afghanistan.

With respect to New Zealand, Lamare (1987) states that, following the new Labour Government's 1984 decision to ban a US nuclear ship from visiting (citing the party's antinuclear policy), the United States claimed that the ban would violate the ANZUS treaty. The Reagan administration resorted to measures such as a reduction in the flow of military intelligence information to New Zealand, the exclusion of New Zealand in previously scheduled military exercises, the discontinuation of spare parts sales to New Zealand's military, and threats to impose economic sanctions.

The case of ANZUS thus suggests that voting rules were likely deliberately left unspecified so the disparity in state power could be informally exploited. Following the analysis of punishment provisions in Chapter 8, an interesting question for future research is under what conditions states leave voting informal. Does the answer have to do with Number as suggested by the case studies of coffee and ANZUS? The COIL data enable the testing of such future hypotheses.

It is also worth mentioning that even in cases in which the decision-making rules reflect power, as in the example of the CWC discussed earlier, institutional design may not completely reflect power, leaving room for informal influence. In fact, this lack of one-to-one correspondence between power and influence over decision making was a point of contention during the US Senate hearings regarding the CWC. Dr. Jeane J. Kirkpatrick, Ronald Reagan's former advisor and ambassador to the UN, testified against the convention, arguing that "the United States would frequently fail to gain a voice in the decisions of the Executive Council" because the United States would have to compete with the European Union over seat allocation.[39] But as Caspar Weinberger, Secretary of Defense under President Reagan, argued (although he also opposed the convention), the United States would be funding 25 percent of the convention's costs and thus "we are certainly going to be listened to" because "anybody who was President ... would make it quite clear that we require for our contribution a very genuine decisionmaking role."[40]

Conclusion

Not a single one of the human rights agreements that the US Senate has approved gives extra rights, special privileges, or greater control to the United States. The US Senate finds lots of things to nitpick, but this symmetry in human rights agreements does not bother Senate members at all. Why? Because the underlying cooperation problems are such that, through reservations and imprecise language, US interests are served and symmetric voting is not controversial (Chapter 6).

On the other hand, during the Bretton Woods negotiations, the US executive used its negotiating power to limit the maximum contribution to the IMF to what Congress would be willing to authorize, thereby ensuring that no other state would have greater control, given

---

[39] US Congress. Senate. Committee on Foreign Relations. Chemical Weapons Convention. 1997. 105th Congress, 1st Session, April 8, 9, 15 and 17, p. 98 (Cited in Walko, David. 2014. "Voting Rules and Power in the Chemical Weapons Convention." Unpublished student paper. University of Michigan: 11).

[40] Ibid., 46–47.

weighted voting.[41] Why? Because the underlying cooperation problems are such that Congress would give scarce economic resources to an IGO only if it could exert at least partial control over it, somewhat akin to the Moon Treaty.[42]

Before we can jump to extreme conclusions about the finding that not all treaties reflect the underlying configuration of power or the equally true finding that many treaties do reflect the underlying configuration of power and even evolve to maintain that correspondence after bargaining power changes, we must refine our theories and our data. For instance, not only do the particular flexibility measures contained in the human rights treaties just mentioned solve the cooperation problems sufficiently for the United States; the United States is also close to the median voter in most human rights cooperative endeavors (with the Scandinavian states at one extreme and states such as Thailand at the other). Thus the configuration of *interests* regarding the substantive provisions matters, too, since the United States is no more likely to mobilize for change in a typical human rights agreement than the median voter is in domestic politics. In human rights, symmetric voting satisfies the *interests* of the United States, regardless of its overwhelming relative power. In the terminology of "is it better to be powerful or lucky?" (Barry 1980), the United States is lucky enough to be in the majority, and so it need not expend its power. Theories about how power is reflected in international law must take account of states' interests as well.

In Koremenos (2015), I apply the COIL framework to shed light on the negotiation stage of international cooperation, in particular, whether powerful states will control the agenda or not by putting forth the first draft of an international agreement and remaining in control of subsequent drafts. The article focuses on the two combinations of cooperation problems that are the focus of Chapter 6: Distribution and Coordination, and Distribution but No Coordination. When the former

---

[41] Wheelbarger, Katie. 1999. "The Bretton Woods Institutions: How and Why States Cooperated to Organize the International Monetary Agreement." Bachelor's Thesis. University of California, Los Angeles.

[42] As economist Harry G. Johnson (1972: 284) put it, the IMF proposals treated states "according to the principle of Orwell's *Animal Farm*, that 'All animals are equal, but some are more equal than others.'" Cited in Noble, Victoria. 2015. "From Informality to Legalism, and Back Again: The Role of Informal Agreement in Balance of Payments Adjustment between the United Kingdom and the United States." Unpublished student paper. University of Michigan.

characterizes the issue area, I argue the substantive terms of the agreement will most likely reflect powerful states' interests; this is not the case with the latter combination.

Work in this vein should be developed and would complement this chapter given the challenge (both theoretical and empirical) of understanding the interplay between power, substance, and design. For instance, an obvious next step is looking at the negotiating history of issues that are characterized by the presence of underlying Enforcement problems.

That said, while it is important to separate "power" from "luck," especially for states like the United States who are both powerful and perhaps the foremost participants in the world of international treaty law, systematic testing like that presented in this book is not possible with such research given that deriving the configuration of preferences regarding substantive provisions in some kind of random, scientific sample is not possible. That obstacle does not imply that careful case study work and/or smaller (sub)issue-specific studies should not be undertaken. Without such work, we cannot make progress theoretically, which is critical regardless of the large-n obstacles to testing.

11 | *Conclusion*

I began this book with some simple, yet stunning, numbers about the body of international treaty law now in existence. What can we conclude about this (overall increasing) body of international law? All of the analyses confirm that even though international law is widely varying, it is not wildly varying – that is, it is neither random nor uniform but instead follows identifiable regularities.

When we examine the continent of international law through the game-theoretic lens of the underlying cooperation problems states are trying to resolve, we expect *systematic* differences across international agreements and institutions. The empirical results confirm that states are shaping agreements in ways that solve their specific problems. As Stein (2008: 212) states: "While it may be difficult analytically to assess the impact of institutions, it remains striking that states use institutions to arrive at the outcomes they want." Not only do states use institutions; the fact that international agreements obey statistically meaningful regularities in their design indicates that serious efforts are made for them to be able to regulate interactions in lasting and successful ways. So because agreements matter, they are designed in rational ways, and the fact that people make efforts to design them in such ways corroborates their significance.

To elaborate, this book first showcases and explains the *non-random, systematic variation in the provisions of international law*, including their final clauses, which are not simply copied from one treaty to another as Chapter 5's analyses of withdrawal provisions demonstrate. If these provisions do not matter, why are they not just noisy variation or extremely similar but instead astoundingly systematic in their variation?

Second, the case studies in this book, while they do not constitute the empirical focus, demonstrate that *states spend time and energy negotiating the details of international law*, suggesting that the details and the law itself are far from marginal in the landscape of international politics. For instance, states were still negotiating the duration provision of the NPT six years after negotiations began. States vehemently debated the right to life provision in the American Convention on Human Rights, which, contrary to Goldsmith and Posner's (2005) argument, is consistent with states taking modern human rights treaties seriously.

Third, and on a related note, case studies provide evidence of the causal mechanisms articulated in the hypotheses. The colorful quote from the Italian representative to the NPT negotiations that opens Chapter 4 and the more straightforward quote from the Swiss representative to the said negotiations are evidence that, while the limited duration makes the NPT an equilibrium institution, it is the cooperation problem of Uncertainty about the State of the World that *caused* the limited duration. Similarly, the OAS negotiation over the right to life provision in the American Convention on Human Rights shows that disagreement between states like Brazil that prohibit abortion under most if not all circumstances and states that permit abortion under most circumstances shaped the debate. The debate over the wording was not driven by states arguing random positions; rather the debate reflected contestation among states with deep convictions and the resulting Distribution problem over whose norms would be codified in the final draft.

Finally, this book illustrates that even though international law reflects the interest of powerful states, *the correspondence between power and law is not one-to-one, and powerful states are constrained by international law*. The United States and the Soviet Union compromised their position on the NPT duration and ultimately agreed to limit it to an initial period of 25 years. The United States did not use its greater relative power to continue monitoring the Russian nuclear arsenal when START expired. Even though the United States won the Cold War, it gave up the "holy grail to get on-site inspections"[1] because international law mandated such behavior. Powerful states like the United States and the United Kingdom add many reservations to agreements, an act paradoxical to the thesis that such states can simply not comply whenever it suits their interests regardless of what the written law mandates.

[1] See Chapter 1, fn. 22.

Pushing forward the theoretical and empirical research frontiers

The research program presented in this book pushes the theoretical and empirical frontiers of scholarship on international law and international relations in productive directions. It does so through theoretical refinements of both the Rational Design and Legalization frameworks and through empirical testing of these refinements with a scientific data set. When the more general institutionalist research program tackled issues of international institutional design, it started out rather broadly because beginning with broad and even vague concepts is a useful way to identify important phenomena (i.e., the vast range of formal ways that international cooperation is organized). Premature efforts to impose narrower definitions to variables like "centralization" or "flexibility" would only have made it harder to see the greater generality of these design choices and would have led to definitional debates. As the phenomena are better understood, however, broad concepts are less useful for more focused research and should be replaced by more detailed concepts. Just as Rational Design and Legalization shifted the focus from broad overarching concepts like regime (or institution) to more detailed and precise concepts like control, flexibility, and centralization, COIL, in turn, refines these concepts further. In doing so, however, it neither introduces new jargon nor departs conceptually from its institutionalist foundations; rather, COIL's innovations are simply directing that literature to a place where rigor in both theory and testing can be exploited.

Similarly, Rational Design's consideration of cooperation problems in isolation from each other was an important first step for a rational choice theory of international institutional design. Given the advances made in the study of institutional design, an obvious next step is the study of interactions. Interactions among cooperation problems are indeed considered in this book and help explain more nuanced design choices, such as imprecision in language as opposed to the broad choice of flexibility (Chapter 6). Thus, Uncertainty about Behavior can explain monitoring provisions quite well; but by interacting Uncertainty about Behavior with Enforcement problems, the choice between self-reporting and delegated monitoring is explained (Chapter 9). At each stage, theoretical predictions are corroborated with the random sample, giving us confidence that further refinements build on solid foundations.

With respect to the overall conventional wisdom regarding institutional design, the findings summarized here confirm certain elements of it but challenge others. Both Enforcement problems and Commitment problems lead to centralized dispute resolution, monitoring, and punishment provisions. But Enforcement and Commitment problems are also ameliorated by the sub-provisions of withdrawal clauses – withdrawal notice and wait periods, respectively. At the same time, not every design provision is used to solve an Enforcement problem. For example, there is no theoretical or empirical connection between precision and Enforcement problems or between duration and Enforcement problems.

Uncertainty about Behavior in the absence of Enforcement problems does *not* lead to centralized monitoring or dispute resolution or any form of punishment provision. This is not only a "correction" of the original Rational Design conjecture; it clarifies decades of institutionalist work on the role of institutions in information provision. Instead, Uncertainty about Behavior in the absence of incentives to defect is best solved with informal dispute resolution and with monitoring based on self-reports – neither of which demand centralization.

Uncertainty about the State of the World is indeed solved by some forms of flexibility, like finite duration provisions and escape clauses, but in the latter case, it is the interaction of Uncertainty about the State of the World and Enforcement problems that necessitates escape clauses. Distribution problems can be solved through the flexibility devices of imprecision and reservations only in the absence of Coordination problems. The other side of the coin is that Coordination problems demand the rigidity that comes from precision and not allowing escape, regardless of the presence of a Distribution problem.

Large Numbers always lead to centralization. Asymmetries of Power lead to procedural asymmetry like one-sided monitoring or punishment; nonetheless, weighted voting is rare and, when it exists, is not explained by raw military or economic power.

Part II on flexibility mechanisms also shows compellingly that what other scholars imply are "softening" provisions (see, e.g., Guzman 2006) actually strengthen agreements. The NPT has both finite duration and exit provisions but is hardly softened by their inclusion; rather, certain flexibility mechanisms allow states to make deeper, not shallower, commitments to each other. Goldsmith and Posner assert that "Many treaties are mistakes or are quickly rendered irrelevant by rapidly changing international relations" (2005: 103) without marshaling any evidence for their statement at all. On this point, COIL demonstrates how changing circumstances can be accommodated in international agreements and offers empirical evidence that in fact the necessary flexibility mechanisms are indeed incorporated into such agreements when they are necessary. Again, design is consistent with the goal of effectiveness.

Moreover, Chapters 4–6 showcase and explain not only the great variation in flexibility mechanisms across real international law; taken together, these chapters also make clear that various flexibility provisions are responses to unique problems. Specifically, just as Koremenos (2005) tests whether other forms of flexibility (escape clauses and withdrawal provisions) can substitute for duration and finds most of the independent variables predicting duration provisions do a very poor job of predicting escape and withdrawal clauses, Chapter 5 *explains* this result by demonstrating that escape and withdrawal clauses follow their own sophisticated logic. While flexibility provisions are extremely common, they are not substitutes for each other; they are not simply chosen as a set; and particular pairs are not inevitable. The problems these provisions uniquely solve occur in different combinations depending on the underlying cooperation problems. The result is that the landscape of flexibility in international agreements is far from crude.

A fruitful next step is the consideration of design interactions, that is, when are the various design dimensions of international law substitutes, complements, or even conflicting design principles? Can states substitute one dimension for another to achieve a similar result, making the combinations somewhat like examples of multiple equilibria? If so, is there any basis on which to compare these combinations to see whether, under any conditions, one is superior to the other(s)? The analyses in Parts II and III of this book can be built upon in the next stage of research. For example, Koremenos (2013a) develops conjectures about the relationship between the overall *incompleteness* of an international contract and *delegation* of dispute resolution provisions, thereby implicating the tradeoff between the broader design choices of flexibility and centralization.

It is important to emphasize that the COIL theoretical framework, with its set of cooperation problems, captures both what scholars have identified as the crucial problems of international cooperation and what truly underlies real international law. COIL also unites the separate issue areas of international law. Thus if a scholar has a hunch about a design pattern that stems from an interesting case study he or she knows well, the COIL theoretical framework can be used as the lens to see if the hunch is consistent with COIL's logic, and the COIL data set can be exploited to see if the hunch holds more generally and is not just an exceptional case.

An important sub-theme of Part III is the *interaction between formal and informal design elements*. In Chapter 7 I look at provisions that stipulate the informal resolution of disputes and how often such provisions are paired with formal, delegated dispute resolution provisions. I explore this potential interaction between formal and informal design elements in Chapters 8 and 9 by, first, presenting a theory of when certain design dimensions are necessary for states to solve their cooperation problems; second, testing these predictions about design against the COIL data set of formal provisions within formal agreements; and, third, using the results as the baseline to consider what might be left informal. In Chapter 10, I present some descriptive statistics and case studies to probe whether power is reflected formally or informally through voting rules and other design provisions.

With respect to dispute resolution and punishment provisions, what is left informal is quite systematic and can be explained theoretically. None of the chapters provide evidence that the informal trumps the formal. Finally, what is informal often complements and/or substitutes for what is formal, but thus far there is no systematic evidence that the two conflict directly.

Perhaps more important, one needs a separate theory of what is optimally left informal for each design provision in question. Just as Chapters 4 and 5 demonstrate that certain features of withdrawal clauses cannot be explained with the same variables that explain finite duration provisions, informal punishment provisions and informal monitoring provisions are not explained by the same logic. Informality is not a single thing; rather states' decisions to adopt formal or informal rules depend on the type of rules in question.

It is worth emphasizing that much of Part III showcases theoretical and empirical refinements of the original institutionalist variables as articulated by Keohane (1984) and Axelrod and Keohane (1985).

Additionally, the book begins to fill one of the gaps of institutionalism more generally expressed by the authors of the introduction to the Legalization volume. Goldstein et al. (2000b: 392) argue that "Institutionalist theory ... which stress[es] the role of institutions in reducing uncertainty and transaction costs, ha[s] seldom dealt directly with the distinction between legalized and nonlegalized agreements" with the exception of Lipson (1991). They continue by stating that "[i]nstitutionalist theory has explained how cooperation endures without legalization, but it has not explained legalization" (Goldstein et al. 2000b: 392).

Recall my explication in Chapter 3 that almost all of the cooperation problems featured in this book underlie attempts at cooperation but they are coded as meeting the threshold of high only if they are relatively severe. The findings in Parts II and III reveal that when these problems are at relatively *mild* levels and hence coded as 0, very little "extra-legalization" via detailed institutional design provisions is needed. In other words, cooperation based on reciprocity and minimal institutionalization, if any, suffices. Of course all the agreements analyzed in this book are legalized in the sense that they are codified, registered with the UN, and hence considered legally binding.[2] But with respect to other kinds of legalization, for example, whether any form of delegation is mandated, there is indeed variation.

The framework employed here not only explains the variation in monitoring or dispute resolution provisions; it also explains the absence of such provisions – that is, it explains when states simply codify their cooperation without much delegation or precision or any other form of legalization. Therefore, while fifteen years ago the following statement was accurate, "On the basis of institutionalist theory one should expect frequent informal agreements, some formal rules, and loopholes that provide flexibility in response to political exigencies" (Goldstein et al. 2000b: 392), progress on that front has been made. Institutionalism, slowly but surely, is explaining more of the intricacies of international cooperation, including when we should expect more of

---

[2] Articulating and then testing a theory of which cooperative endeavors become codified is an important next step in the institutionalist research program, although the measurement problems with respect to enumerating the entire population of cooperative endeavors (formal and informal) are, practically speaking, insurmountable. See Appendix 3 for a discussion of related issues.

certain aspects of legalization and when decentralized cooperation should prevail.

The introduction of a research design to study systematically what is potentially informal sets the stage for a next iteration of research on the relationship between formal and informal design elements. Chapter 9 on monitoring by itself generates a number of potential research questions, both theoretical and empirical, that build on the foundations of this book. For instance, theoretical work can focus on the alignment (or not) of interests between states and NGOs and if and when allowing access to NGOs increases or decreases states' power (or if some states win, while others lose). Empirical work can examine the timing of NGO involvement in monitoring treaty regimes and the conditions under which NGOs have privileged information on state behavior.

Design over time

There is evidence that the design of international law is becoming more rational over time. Figures 11.1 and 11.2 show that over time states become more, not less, likely to incorporate the monitoring and

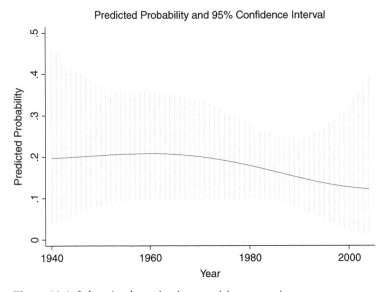

Figure 11.1 Suboptimal monitoring provisions over time

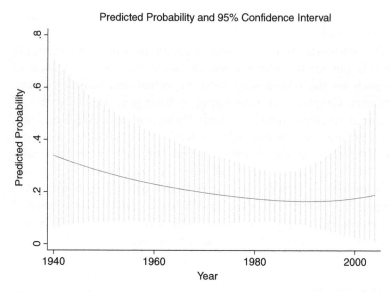

Figure 11.2 Suboptimal punishment provisions over time

punishment provisions that are necessary to solve their underlying cooperation problems.

Exploiting the methodology introduced in Chapters 8 and 9, Figure 11.1 illustrates how agreements that should include delegated monitoring, given the underlying cooperation problems, but do not, are becoming less likely over time. These suboptimal centralized monitoring provisions are identified by first estimating a model of centralized monitoring provisions in international agreements. The results from this model are then used to identify agreements that, although they are expected to include such monitoring provisions, do not incorporate them. A variable is then constructed that is coded 1 for all such suboptimal agreements and 0 for all agreements that actually include formal monitoring provisions, the relevant reference category.

Figure 11.1 shows the predicted probabilities and 95 percent confidence intervals, obtained from regressing the variable identifying suboptimal monitoring on variables for year and year squared.[3]

---

[3] The graph excludes the oldest agreement in the sample, an ILO Convention adopted in 1925, because it is an outlier in terms of its age; the next agreement follows only fifteen years later. There is no other similarly large gap in the distribution of agreements over time.

The graph displays a slight downward trend, suggesting that suboptimal monitoring provisions have become less likely over time: they begin at 20 percent in 1940, reach their highest in 1960 at 21 percent, and then the probability drops to its lowest of 12 percent in the mid-2000s. Put differently, while in the 1950s almost one-fifth of all agreements are suboptimal in this regard, this is true for only one in eight agreements in the 2000s. The theory of agreement design outlined in this book, and specifically its application to formal monitoring provisions, appears to have more bite as time progresses.

Figure 11.2 shows the equivalent for punishment provisions. The probability of agreements with "suboptimal" punishment provisions is also decreasing over time. The probability starts out highest in 1940 at 34 percent and reaches its lowest point in 1991 at 17 percent; after 1991, the probability increases slightly to 19 percent at the end of the sample period. The confidence intervals are wide in both figures, which might be due in large part to the small sample size in the case of misclassified agreements. (Recall, too, that in the case of punishment, informal provisions often are substitutes for formal ones; hence the term "suboptimal" is less accurate in this context.)

The increasing democratization of states since 1940 may explain these trends. As Chapter 8 illustrates, agreements with more homogeneous membership (a.k.a., more democracies) are more likely to incorporate formal punishment provisions. This finding may apply to other design dimensions. For instance, democratic states might be more comfortable with the transparency that goes along with delegated monitoring provisions.

In any event, these trends present a puzzle for more pessimistic scholars. What is the point of learning over time and making it more likely that the agreements will solve the underlying cooperation problems if the law itself is trivial?

Politics and law matter

This book builds an explicit bridge between international law and international politics, but it also builds a bridge between international law and domestic law, given that the same logic explains domestic contracts and law and international agreements. In the end, I argue that law matters, as do the realities of politics. Both the kind of international law that emerges and its influence on cooperation are heavily

circumscribed by international politics.[4] Agreement design helps make
international law an equilibrium institution within the (oftentimes
harsh) international political environment. One cannot possibly entertain a positive theory of international law without considering international politics – in particular, how power and self-interest matter for
both the design and enforcement of international law. This statement
contrasts sharply with the view of some international law scholars, like
Brunnée and Toope (2010) who, as Abbott and Snidal (2013: 39–40)
argue, "aim to insulate legal analysis from politics – and (to a lesser
extent) from economics, history, and even sociology. In no small part,
their agenda is to make international law as a discipline safe from
external intrusions."

Yet, at the same time, powerful states are constrained. The idea that
the "pursuit of power marginalizes *all* other objectives," which is
Donnelly's characterization of realism (2008: 150), is not even
a stylized fact, let alone an empirical truth, in regards to the body of
international law governing much if not most international cooperation. The United States' behavior in the Coffee Agreement after the fall
of the Berlin Wall and its continued presence before the ICJ despite
receiving multiple unfavorable judgments are two facts that belie such
a statement.

The time spent designing human rights agreements and the care that
great powers like the United States and the United Kingdom invest in
adding reservations to their treaties (some of which are added by the
US Senate Foreign Relations Committee) also show that self-interested
preferences cannot be defined narrowly as they are in many realist
accounts. States can and do have altruistic preferences, like caring
about human rights standards outside of their own territories.
The data on the withdrawal of reservations featured in Chapter 6
also show that norm exportation does at times take hold; otherwise,
why would a state ever withdraw reservations (especially given that

---

[4] Some may argue that whether international law emerges at all is at least in part
governed by powerful states like the United States. Whether we consider the set
of missing bilateral agreements between the United States and Cuba, the
nonratification of SALT II and the CTBT, or potential agreements to replace the
Kyoto Protocol, the United States is keeping international law from entering into
the "observed" population. One problem with this argument, however, is that
we have no way of enumerating the set of failed agreements "caused" by
non-powerful states. See Appendix 3 for an elaboration of some of these issues.

reciprocity is not a useful mechanism in most human rights agreements with reservations)?[5]

Further, the evidence suggests that states act just as rationally in the design of human rights agreements as they do in the realm of security. As Chapter 6 in particular makes clear, once one controls for the underlying cooperation problems and the number of states, the design of human rights agreements on the dimension of precision is no different from the design of economic, environmental, or security agreements. The same is true for other design dimensions.[6] While states might cooperate more often in the realm of economics than human rights, the quality of cooperation as reflected in the choice of design provisions does not differ across the issue areas. Assertions that certain issue areas are governed by different "logics" than other issue areas find absolutely no support in this book. In all four of these issue areas, the evidence is consistent with the thesis that states, including powerful ones, use international law to advance their interests.

It is thus not far-fetched to argue that states have a long-term interest in international law, including adhering to the constraints imposed by it, even during the times in which those constraints are not in their immediate self-interest. Yet, coming from a realist tradition, Goldsmith and Posner (2005) downplay the power and significance of international law by claiming that states comply with international law if and when acting out of self-interest aligns with such compliance. Additionally, they state: "Although the terms are common, the victim of a violation almost always has to enforce the terms itself through the threat of retaliation.... The lack of third-party enforcement, except in unusual instances, is strong evidence against the view that multilateral collective goods are created, as the game theoretic models all require" (2005: 88). However, Goldsmith and Posner lack systematic evidence for their view.

Chapter 7 demonstrates that, when facing Enforcement problems, states are likely to delegate dispute resolution authority to a third party.

---

[5] On this matter COIL is easily complemented by other theories, especially arguments about how norms actually take hold.

[6] Some issue area indicator variables have significance in some analyses, but there is not one issue area that is consistently or systematically different from another issue area across the various analyses presented in Parts II and III.

In almost every instance of such third party delegation, the dispute resolution can result in punishment. Goldsmith and Posner assert that such punishment will rarely if ever be carried out. Their case studies are limited, however, and they acknowledge that it is possible for other scholars to discover areas of treaty law that reflect multilateral cooperation. As mentioned in Chapter 7, one of the human rights agreements in the COIL sample is the American Convention on Human Rights, and the court it creates has issued many rulings with which member states have complied. According to Tan (2005), compliance is the rule not the exception. The domain of BITs also belies the view that dispute resolution with material consequences is just a game-theoretic creation without any grounding in reality, although to be fair, scholars like Goldsmith and Posner selectively limit their consideration to only a few multilateral treaties.

Additionally, as Chapter 8 illustrates, "retaliation" does occur, even when the punishment provisions are left informal, refuting Guzman's (2008) assertion that reputation is the only reliable mechanism at work in the enforcement of treaties and not a very consistent one at that. For Guzman, the reputation of a state helps states make more credible, hence deeper, commitments, but it does not depend much on the institution in question. In fact, Guzman argues that reputation may carry over from other institutions and even other issue areas, which, in turn, opens up questions that go well beyond the COIL framework, such as the scope for states to acquire and strategically manipulate their reputational capital. COIL, on the other hand, which links institutional design to the specific strategic problems faced by states, *expects and explains the vast variation in the design of enforcement provisions present in real international law, including what is left informal.* If reputational mechanisms that transcend agreements are where the real action is, why does agreement design vary with respect to enforcement provisions? Additionally, as Thompson (2009: 308) states, Guzman's "bottom line is in fact fairly pessimistic in the end – echoing Realist themes as much as Neoliberal ones." Even Guzman himself states that reputation as a compliance mechanism operates only at the margin (2008: 117).

In reality, there are no systematic data on how often third-party enforcement occurs but rather only (spotty) case study evidence; and some of that evidence indicates that third-party enforcement is far from "unusual" or unreliable in real international law.[7] What can be said definitively is that the *design of enforcement mechanisms* in international law is consistent with the goal of effectiveness.

Thus, as a juxtaposition of the titles themselves reveals, Goldsmith and Posner's *The Limits of International Law* is much more pessimistic than *The Continent of International Law*. COIL's conclusions, importantly, are drawn from both formal underpinnings and a scientific data set. Goldsmith and Posner's conclusions are not. As Raustiala (2006: 424) so bluntly states about *The Limits of International Law*, "the book is unjustifiably skeptical about the ability of international law to influence state behavior." Guzman (2006: 534), too, states, "the authors have assumed this result – ruling out the possibility that they can be said to have demonstrated it." Guzman (2006: 535) continues: "the theory does not lead to the pessimistic view of international law they advance." In fact, Raustiala's and Guzman's views are perhaps why some accuse Goldsmith and Posner of advancing a normative agenda, despite their claims otherwise.[8]

The theoretically predicted, fine-grained systematic variation in duration provisions, escape clauses, withdrawal provisions, the precision of substantive terms, reservations, dispute resolution provisions, punishment provisions, monitoring provisions, and procedural asymmetry showcased in this book is consistent with the following thesis: International law helps all states, including powerful ones, increase the prospects and robustness of mutually beneficial cooperation.

Implications for policy, effectiveness, and legitimacy

Policy implications

While COIL has been used to *explain* the tremendous variation in the design of international law and reveal how systematic that variation is, the framework can also be used *prescriptively*. Thus, while the typical agreement in the COIL sample follows "rational design" principles, the framework also identifies outliers and can sometimes even explain their

[7] For instance, Goldsmith and Posner (2005: 100) claim the "legalization" camp does not provide a good explanation of compliance in either trade or human rights law, but they do not systematically test either their or the "legalization" camp's theories.

[8] See, for example, Berman (2006) and Rajagopal (2005).

ineffectiveness through their failure to adhere to these principles. The COIL research program to some extent thus answers the call for pragmatism articulated quite nicely in Katzenstein and Sil (2008), although many of the authors they cite firmly reject the notion that scholarship based on rational choice theory can be pragmatic.

As elaborated in Chapter 10, the COIL framework can explain the Moon Treaty's paltry ratification record and its status as a "failed" agreement. If powerful states decide they want a regime to govern exploitation of the moon, the COIL framework gives us insight into how that regime will need to be designed if it is to have relevance. As another example, the long-lasting peace in Antarctica, which began with a flexible treaty that ingeniously did not try to solve every problem immediately, can be a model for peace treaties more generally.

COIL can even shed light on some of the most difficult security issues of our time and bring attention to aspects of the underlying strategic situations that might not be the usual focus of policy-makers. Consider, for instance, the problem of designing international law for the Korean Peninsula – in particular, a regime to replace the 1994 Agreed Framework between North Korea and the United States.[9]

While the traditional focus is on the problems between North Korea and the rest of the world, there exists a unique combination of cooperation problems nested within the broader framework of any such agreement between North Korea and the world. The set of actors relevant to this "nested" agreement consists of South Korea, Japan, and the United States – the founders of the Korean Peninsula Energy Development Organization (KEDO), put in place in 1995 to help implement the 1994 Agreed Framework.[10] Put bluntly, these states need to bribe North Korea to accomplish their goals. Given that reality, the KEDO group faces three particularly challenging cooperation problems that were not adequately solved in the original KEDO framework: The interaction of a Distribution problem with a Coordination

---

[9] Agreed Framework between the United States of America and the Democratic People's Republic of Korea, Geneva, October 21, 1994. Available at https://www.iaea.org/sites/default/files/publications/documents/infcircs/1994/infcirc457.pdf [Last accessed December 10, 2015].

[10] Agreement on the Establishment of the Korean Peninsula Energy Development Organization. UNTS Reg. No. 32002.

problem, which necessitates a precise agreement as described in Chapter 6, and a domestic Commitment problem, which calls for delegation of dispute resolution, as described in Chapter 7.

Consider the Distribution/Coordination problem. The bribe is both very costly and controversial. As Ambassador Stephen Bosworth stated: "They are three countries dealing with a question in which they have a common stake, but over which they have severe differences on how to deal with the DPRK" (quoted in Wit 1999: 64). Thus the various ways to change the incentives of North Korea, and the various ways of splitting the costs of doing so, are at the heart of the Distribution problem. Moreover, given the characteristics of the recipient, coordinating on the exact nature and specifics of the bribe is paramount. Otherwise, North Korea could renege, under the pretense that the bribe was not as promised.

Put differently, if we were to consider various ways to split the cost of the reward to North Korea, choosing *one completely coordinated solution* is essential, for example, either "30% 30% 40%" or "40% 40% 20%" or "State A is responsible for one reactor regardless of whether it can entice other actors to contribute, or not" Suppose KEDO employed vague language like, "The United States will pay a substantial amount toward the cost of the heavy fuel oil." One can imagine the endeavor being seriously undermined because the phrase "a substantial amount toward" could be interpreted in almost endless ways, depending on the political preferences of those with the purse strings. Frankly, with imprecise language, any attempted solution to the Coordination problem will fail.

Nonetheless, KEDO's cooperation was anything but precise, as one of Snyder's (2000: 20) paper headings so aptly captures: "KEDO's internal co-ordination challenge: Who pays for what?" While the inability to estimate the exact costs of the project is understandable, the members still need to define either the shares that each will pay once the costs become clear or exactly which state will be responsible for which component regardless of the ultimate costs. Instead, the three states agreed that, with respect to the reactors, South Korea would "assume 70 percent of the cost, Japan would make a significant contribution ..., and the United States would seek a significantly smaller 'symbolic contribution' from the Congress. On heavy fuel oil, the United States would take the lead in making a financial contribution and in raising funds from other countries. Japan would contribute some funds to this project" (Wit 1999: 66). As Wit so rightly concludes, "these understandings are insufficient" (1999: 66).

With respect to the Commitment problem, even though democracies like those that make up KEDO are usually not coded as having domestic time-inconsistency problems, for this narrow subject area, such problems do indeed underlie the cooperative endeavor. Any hint at noncompliance by North Korea affects public opinion in the United States, Japan, and South Korea, which in turn affects legislative bodies' willingness to continue supporting the project. For example, with respect to the heavy fuel oil, Japan contributed $19 million in early 1996, only later to withdraw and refuse to pay any additional funds (Wit 1999: 67). As Snyder (2000: 15) explains, "the Agreed Framework implicitly depends on the idea that the LWR [Light Water Reactor] project itself cannot go forward to full completion unless North Korea also improves its relationships with KEDO members; however, the flip side ... is that KEDO is vulnerable to political tensions." In the United States, it seems President Bush had very different preferences than those of President Clinton. Changes in Congress also undermined the ability of the United States to follow through on its commitment.[11] Similar dynamics were present in Japan, as the following quote from 1998 reveals:

Japan's decision to resume over Korean Peninsula Energy Development Organization (KEDO) cooperation has sparked an acrimonious fight between the government and the ruling Liberal Democratic Party (LDP), as well as tension among government agencies over how to disburse the contribution to KEDO. In view of such internal disarray, getting an already skeptical Diet's approval for KEDO funding is likely to be extremely difficult.[12]

Finally, South Korea also is subject to such pressures: "In Korea, support for the LWR project has reflected the ups-and-downs of inter-Korean relations ...."[13]

---

[11] The fact that the Framework Agreement was not legally binding exacerbates these issues.

[12] US Department of State. *Japan: Spat over KEDO Issues*. Washington, D.C.: US Department of State, Bureau of Intelligence and Research, October 29, 1998. PDF.

[13] US Department of State. *Asia: Impact of the Financial Crisis on KEDO Funding*. Washington, D.C.: US Department of State, Bureau of Intelligence and Research, December 11, 1997. PDF.

In the presence of domestic Commitment problems, the COIL framework prescribes some kind of centralized body that can interpret and/or adjudicate any dispute or issues of noncompliance. Nonetheless, the 1995 KEDO founding agreement lacks any such provisions.[14] Delegation to a third party, like an arbitration tribunal, would give each KEDO member more credibility – that is, there would be an additional hurdle to a new president or a changed Congress undermining or weakening the United States' commitments under the agreement or a new Diet doing a similar thing in Japan. The tribunal could be set up along the lines of those found in many economic agreements – each disputing party chooses one of the arbitrators and the two then agree on a third. Or a mechanism could be set up within the broader KEDO group. Importantly, this body to which a dispute or disagreement over interpretation would be delegated would have to be set up precisely in advance, just as it is in so many well-designed agreements with underlying Commitment problems (see Chapter 7).

Thus, while the 1994 Agreed Framework and the creation of KEDO certainly went part of the way toward solving important problems, the next set of negotiated agreements would benefit from many more substantive and procedural provisions that make the commitments more precise and verifiable. Delegation to solve disagreements within KEDO would also greatly help sustain the cooperative endeavor. COIL makes it clear what the necessary procedural provisions are in such contexts.

In sum, the theories of the 1980s (and 1990s) provided abstract suggestions to policymakers (like "increase the shadow of the future"). COIL, on the other hand, focuses on the details of international law and speaks to the design of monitoring mechanisms, withdrawal notice periods, and time limits to agreements. The overall move of COIL from less parsimony to greater accuracy, while still being disciplined by its game-theoretic foundations, pushes the institutionalist research agenda towards an increasingly applied and policy-relevant research program. There is a role for academics to inform the policymaking process and to streamline the learning process that might be taking place over time, as illustrated in Figures 11.1 and 11.2.

[14] See fn. 10.

Effectiveness

Although the focus of this book is the systematic design of the detailed provisions of international law, the book also has implications for our understanding of the determinants of effectiveness and hence speaks to that literature. Effectiveness is a difficult concept to measure in any general way, as I make clear in the concluding section of this chapter. Still, there are various indirect and enlightening means by which to shed light on the topic, many of which zero in on a sub-issue area of international law. For example, ratification is related to effectiveness, and studies that focus on explaining ratification behavior across states add to our knowledge of the overall effectiveness of international law.

Consider Tokhi and Lockwood Payton who address the question of state commitment to international agreements.[15] Their central claim is that states have strong incentives to ratify international security treaties when these agreements can mitigate mutual uncertainty and the fear of cheating – the central cooperation problems in international security. These are akin to COIL's Uncertainty about Behavior and Enforcement problems. Their original data set features the ratification behavior of all 193 UN member states vis-à-vis 24 global and regional disarmament, non-proliferation, and arms control treaties. Chapter 9 argues that the interaction of these two cooperation problems necessitates delegated monitoring, and Chapter 8 argues that an underlying Enforcement problem leads states to incorporate punishment provisions. Likewise, Tokhi and Lockwood Payton find that centralized verification and enforcement procedures (i.e., carried out by IGOs) provide the strongest incentives for states to commit to arms control and disarmament treaties.[16] In sum, the more a given disarmament agreement provides states with grounds to believe that the central cooperation problems in international security will be alleviated and that the commitments made will be implemented, the more likely states will be to recognize and bind themselves to this institutional authority. Put differently, the right agreement design matters for ratification.

---

[15] Tokhi, Alexandros and Autumn Lockwood Payton. 2014. "Arms Control
      Commitments and International Authority." Presented at the Annual
      Convention of the International Studies Association, Toronto, March 26–29,
      2014.
[16] Ibid.

Such complementary research agendas can inform each other; they will most certainly pave the way for the next round of refinement of this important research program on international cooperation through law.

Legitimacy

In recent decades, IL and IR theorists have confronted various questions of international institutional legitimacy: what it means to be legitimate; what features cause institutions to be perceived as legitimate; and to what extent institutional legitimacy exerts a pull toward compliance (Hurd 1999). What can this book's findings contribute to this conversation?

Some of the institutional features that scholars have suggested bestow objective legitimacy on an institution are the same ones that exist in predictable, logical patterns in the COIL data set. It is undisputed that international agreements arise out of state consent, which was "the traditional basis of international legitimacy," as "institutions could trace their legitimacy back to the treaties that created them" (Bodansky 2013: 330). But increasingly, scholars have argued that consent is not enough (Bodansky 1999; Buchanan and Keohane 2006: 412–414). Institutional attributes like fair third-party dispute resolution processes, opportunity to choose not to be bound indefinitely, equal-weighted voting procedures, and transparency through reporting and monitoring are now often recognized as key aspects of legitimate institutions (though not necessarily entirely sufficient ones), according to many (see, e.g., Bodansky 2013: 330-331).[17]

Of course, these design features are not ubiquitous. In general, they appear only where they make sense given the underlying challenges to cooperation; not every agreement has third-party delegation and monitoring that enhances transparency, for example. I assume that states comply with agreements that include provisions like third-party delegation not because these provisions increase the pull toward compliance, but because such features more effectively solve the

---

[17] "Input-based legitimacy derives from the process by which decisions are made, including factors such as transparency, participation, and representation" (Bodansky 2013: 330).

problems states are facing in those particular cooperative endeavors (in other words, out of self-interest).

Although I do not believe that states do (or should) choose design provisions on the basis of legitimacy, assuming, as I do, that rationally designed procedural provisions promote more effective institutions, these features are likely to promote descriptive/sociological (or output) legitimacy.[18] That is, by helping agreements to serve better the interests of states (and their citizens), rationally designed procedural provisions should bolster actual international support for these institutions. And as Hurd (1999: 387–389) and others note, the widespread belief that an institution is legitimate, all else equal, may improve compliance with institutional rules.[19] If this reasoning holds, rational design facilitates better outcomes, not just through better-designed institutions, but also through states' increased willingness to join and cooperate within those institutions. That is, rational design enhances output legitimacy.

Concluding thoughts

To this day, introductory textbooks of modern international law begin with some form of the question, "Is international law a reality?" In *International Law Frameworks*, Bederman (2010: 6-12) begins by briefly laying out, and then dispelling with anecdotal evidence, five "myths about international law." These myths – "international law is its own distinct legal system," "international law is all theory and no practice," "international law is not real law," "no one obeys international law," and "international law is what the United States says it is" – will seem oversimplified to most readers. Yet, more subtle versions of these statements still animate much debate in the IR-IL scholarship. Bederman (2010: 6) accurately reflects the discipline when he states: "Why then – if international law is so historically legitimate and ethically relevant, so doctrinally robust and functionally

---

[18] An institution possesses descriptive or sociological legitimacy when "actors subjectively believe that an institution has a right to rule." It therefore turns on "the attitudes of the ruled," not the "qualities of the ruler" (Bodansky 2013: 327).

[19] "[C]ompliance with a rule may be motivated by a belief in the normative legitimacy of the rule (or in the legitimacy of the body that generated the rule)" (Hurd 1999: 387).

necessary – do so many people (including lawyers and policymakers) believe it does not exist? Why does it seem to be the step-child of legal studies, a discipline in search of its own reality?"

The empirically tested COIL framework has something to say on this topic. While anarchy may make international law *quantitatively* different from domestic law (less enforcement, less monitoring), the same theoretical framework explains institutional design in both arenas. Scientific testing confirms the appropriate design in the international case. Therefore, we cannot say that international law and domestic law are entirely *qualitatively* different. If the two endpoints are anarchy and domestic law, international law is closer to the latter. The incomplete contracting framework on which the conjectures are based, which was developed to apply in a domestic context, has resounding success when applied to the international context.

The numbers that opened this book tell us unequivocally that cooperation through law is anything but trivial. Year after year, states codify their cooperative understandings into legally binding international agreements and thereby neither fail to cooperate, nor rely solely on CIL, general principles, or informal understandings. Furthermore, they do not simply codify their understandings: they debate and/or fine-tune the provisions of these agreements, substantive and procedural, from the right to life provision in a human rights agreement down to the withdrawal notice period of a disarmament agreement. This behavior is consistent with the conclusions of those who study institutions at all levels: Institutions matter because they can reassure, change incentives, allow for adjustment to shocks, and make commitments more credible, among other things.

But at the international level in particular, institutions will matter only when they are designed to take both interests and power into account. They will not matter simply because they are "law." Nor will they *not* matter simply because they are *considered* law. In fact, the false dichotomy between "motivation by self-interest" and "motivation by law" (as Norman and Trachtman [2005: 541] so aptly describe Goldsmith and Posner's [2005] assumption that drives so many of their assertions) is superficial.[20] In reality, there is no such rigid "dichotomy."

---

[20] As one example, Goldsmith and Posner (2005: 225) state that the reason for states' compliance with international law is "not that states have internalized international law, or have a habit of complying with it, or are drawn by its moral pull, but simply that states act out of self-interest."

Behavior, whether individual, firm, or state, is best understood as a strategy in a game played with other players and, as such, determined by the goals or interests of each player, the choices of the other players, and the institutions that regulate the interaction. Changing institutions such as law modifies the (self-interested) strategies of the players. Consequently, there is no logical basis for the dichotomy; it only creates confusion.

This book provides a clear and logical alternative that shows how institutions are designed so that they are in equilibrium, which in the international environment implies they are self-enforcing given the configuration of interests and power of the actors that create them. I identify the factors (the nature of the underlying cooperation problems and characteristics of the participants) that shape the institutional outcome. As a result, most of the time, the detailed agreement provisions are "incentive compatible" such that actors create, change, and adhere to international law because it is in their interest. And I expect (and in some cases demonstrate) that when these outcomes are not shaped the way I predict, one of three things will happen: a formal or informal modification of the institutional structure will ensue, the institution will fail to be formed altogether, or it will fall short of the membership needed to make the institution consequential (as in the Moon Treaty).

This approach differs not only from the artificial distinction of Goldsmith and Posner (2005), but also from many of the other approaches in international law and international relations discussed in Chapter 1. Instead, this approach follows both centuries of research on institutions and the actual design of institutions. For example, the founding fathers of the American constitution designed it so that power would be cancelled by power and that decisions against the interest of the ordinary citizen would be difficult to make. Montesquieu was also addressing questions of institutional design when he advocated bicameral parliaments so that the interests of the aristocracy would not always be trumped by the interests of common people, just as Livy's *History of Rome* and Aristotle's *Politics* pay close attention to institutional design.

Of course, in all these cases of domestic institutions, the government or the state has the monopoly of power; therefore, any legal system is enforceable because of this concentration of power. Nevertheless, what I have shown in this book is that international agreements – multilateral and bilateral, finance and disarmament – create a set of similar constraints in this somewhat different context.

Still, some may argue that, while international law may be rationally designed and may often incorporate provisions that constrain future actions, it is only effective at solving certain kinds of problems (Goldsmith and Posner 2005), or it often does not cause behavior different from what states would have done in its absence (Downs, Rocke, and Barsoom 1996). The problem with any conclusion about effectiveness is that, for any study that shows the ineffectiveness of a particular international agreement, another study shows the opposite is true for another international agreement or even the same international agreement.[21] Furthermore, many of these studies focus on a few provisions of the agreement in question. Any generalization from these kinds of studies can only be suggestive. These studies are still useful, and some are carried out in an excellent and scientific fashion, as when large-n evidence and case studies are brought to bear on particular questions (see Simmons [2009] for a state-of-the-art example).[22] But we cannot say anything definitive about whether international law as a whole is effective based on these individual analyses of effectiveness.[23]

---

[21] See, for example, Hill (2010) and Fariss (2014), who come to opposite conclusions regarding the effectiveness of CAT. Additionally, such studies are plagued by the usually insurmountable problem of establishing the counterfactual – what behavior would have been in the absence of the law (see, too, Martin [2013]). Finally, given the theoretical argument of Chapter 6 regarding imprecision and reservations, when IR scholars examine treaty compliance or effectiveness, they need to take into account inherent differences in treaty design in terms of flexibility mechanisms that allow differential treaty obligations in the first place. Most of the extant studies on compliance/ effectiveness use crude data that imply all members are subject to the same treaty standard of behavior. At the research design stage, studies of compliance *must* take into account the rational design of treaties if we are to learn anything about true compliance or effectiveness.

[22] See von Stein (2013) for a cutting-edge review of the literature on compliance.

[23] For instance, Goldsmith and Posner (2005) rely primarily on case studies to support their theories about the "limits of international law." Though case studies have several benefits, they also have significant limitations. As Guzman argues, the lessons from Goldsmith and Posner's case studies are not generalizable to international law as a whole. Rather, "[t]he most [the case studies] can do is provide an account suggesting that a treaty has failed to solve the problem in a particular instance," or, with CIL, "that a particular rule of CIL failed to influence the behavior of a particular state in a particular context at a particular time" (Guzman 2006: 539).

In reality, the effectiveness of domestic law overall is subject to this same problem of inference. The efficacy of policies regarding speed limits, school vouchers, incarceration, and gun control (to name just a few) are vehemently debated and will most likely continue to be well into the future. Would anyone argue that domestic law fails to constrain as a whole?

In fact, I am not even arguing that the *design* provisions of international law are always followed, even when following them is equilibrium path behavior according to the underlying logic. However, that the design provisions of international law are not always followed does not mean international law does not influence behavior and is unworthy of systematic study. Indeed, the design provisions of domestic law are not always followed, and no one would dare claim that domestic law is therefore not influencing behavior and not worthy of systematic study. As Representative Jim Cooper (D-Tenn) argues, "'The trouble with sunset clauses is usually they're not enforced, because Congress is either too busy – or, more accurately – too neglectful' .... A 'sunset clause is a very appropriate remedy. But it's got to be enforced to mean anything.'"[24] Thus, according to case study evidence, limited duration provisions (sunset provisions) are sometimes followed domestically and internationally and sometimes ignored domestically and internationally. Until someone brings large-n scientific evidence to bear on the topic, it is mere speculation to argue how different these two arenas are in this regard.

In sum, centuries of work on institutions, more generally, shows that, although they are created with interests and power in mind, this does not preclude them from constraining the future actions of the very actors that created them. Indeed, that's their point. From the brilliance of the founding fathers who created the US Constitution to the hundreds of negotiators whose work results in the agreements studied here, the same logic is corroborated.

This book explains how international law can be structured to make international cooperation most successful. Instead of random variations among agreements or replication of the same agreement

---

[24] David A. Fahrenthold, "In Congress, Sunset Clauses Are Commonly Passed But Rarely Followed Through." *Washington Post*, December 15, 2012. Available at https://www.washingtonpost.com/politics/in-congress-sunset-clauses-are-commonly-passed-but-rarely-followed-through/2012/12/15/9d8e3ee0-43b5-11 e2-8e70-e1993528222d_story.html [Last accessed December 9, 2015].

provisions over and over, we observe that the detailed provisions of international law are chosen in ways that increase the prospects and robustness of international cooperation. This continent of international law is nuanced and sophisticated, and it can speak to scholars in any discipline where institutions and thus institutional design matter.

For those who still want to assert that international law does not matter, this book makes clear that there is no scientific basis for this belief. This belief is in direct conflict not only with the beliefs of the negotiators; it is in conflict with their actions and the resulting outcomes with respect to design. At this point, it is the "disbelievers" that need to justify their argument that international law does not matter because such proclamations are inconsistent (out of equilibrium) with the tremendously systematic design of agreements across issue areas, across regions, and across regime types. Moreover, there is no evidence that only certain types of "easy" problems are confronted by rationally designed international law; rather, as Parts II and III illustrate, law is designed to solve Enforcement, Commitment, Distribution, and Coordination problems as well as Uncertainty about Behavior and Uncertainty about the State of the World.

International institutions, as exhibited in the international agreements studied here, follow the same logic as do other institutions. The institutions typically studied by institutionalists are created against a backdrop of an enforceable legal system. In stark contrast, international institutions develop and operate in the midst of anarchy. In spite of that, a whole continent of international law that prescribes or proscribes behavior has developed, and this continent grows significantly every year. That the logic developed in the former case explains the design outcomes in the latter, much harder "test" case has implications beyond how we understand international politics and the true consequences of anarchy. It confirms the relevance of institutionalism as an overarching paradigm that can transcend not only local and country-level differences, but a much more profound difference: that between hierarchy and anarchy.

Appendix 1 List of agreements in COIL sample

Economics

	Agreement name	Signatories	Signature year	UNTS
1.	Reciprocal Trade Agreement between the United States of America and Mexico	(US – Mexico)	1942	81
2.	Monetary Agreement between the Netherlands and the United Kingdom of Great Britain and Northern Ireland	(Netherlands – UK)	1945	24
3.	Agreement relating to the purchase by Poland of surplus property prior to January 1, 1948	(US – Poland)	1946	5851
4.	Monetary Agreement between the Government of Belgium and the Government of the United Kingdom of Great Britain and Northern Ireland	(Belgium – UK)	1947	367
5.	Exchange of notes constituting an agreement relating to guarantees authorized by Section 111 (b) (3) of the Economic Cooperation Act of 1948, as amended	(China – US)	1952	1837
6.	Agreement concerning the disposition of certain accounts in Thailand under Article 16 of the Treaty of Peace with Japan of September 8, 1951	(Multilateral)	1953	2913
7.	Convention between Her Britannic Majesty in respect of the United Kingdom of Great Britain and Northern Ireland and His Majesty the King of the Belgians for the avoidance of double taxation and the prevention of fiscal evasion with respect to taxes on income	(Belgium – UK)	1953	2526
8.	Exchange of notes constituting an interim agreement relating to the purchase of surplus agricultural commodities	(Japan – US)	1954	3239

(*cont.*)

	Agreement name	Signatories	Signature year	UNTS
9.	Agreement between Thailand and Japan concerning settlement of "Special Yen Problem"	(Japan – Thailand)	1955	3172
10.	Agreement for financing certain educational exchange programs	(US – Ecuador)	1956	4114
11.	Agricultural Commodities Agreement under Title I of the Agricultural Trade Development and Assistance Act (with agreed minute and memorandum of understanding)	(Israel – US)	1957	4365
12.	Exchange of notes constituting an agreement relating to the guaranty of private investments	(US – Nicaragua)	1959	4922
13.	Agricultural Commodities Agreement under Title I of the Agricultural Trade Development and Assistance Act, as amended (with exchange of notes)	(Republic of China – US)	1960	5579
14.	Exchange of notes constituting an agreement relating to the guaranty of private investments	(US – Liberia)	1960	5596
15.	Agreement with respect to quality wheat	(Multilateral)	1962	6389
16.	Exchange of letters constituting an agreement relating to investment guaranties	(US – Colombia)	1962	6621
17.	Convention concerning the encouragement of capital investment and the protection of property	(Netherlands – Tunisia)	1963	7558
18.	Exchange of notes (with annex) constituting an agreement regarding the changes which the Government of the United Kingdom propose to introduce in their production and trade policies relating to cereals	(Argentina – UK)	1964	7450

No.	Agreement	Parties	Year	No.
19.	Agreement concerning the collection of bills, drafts, etc.	(Multilateral)	1964	8851
20.	Exchange of notes constituting an agreement relating to investment guaranties	(US – Zambia)	1966	8901
21.	Exchange of notes constituting an agreement concerning trade in cotton textiles (with annex)	(Mexico – US)	1967	9770
22.	Exchange of notes constituting an agreement relating to investment guaranties	(US – Cameroon)	1967	9855
23.	Agreement for sales of agricultural commodities	(Dominican Republic – US)	1968	10249
24.	Supplementary agreement for sales of agricultural commodities	(Republic of Vietnam – US)	1968	10135
25.	Convention for the avoidance of double taxation and the prevention of fiscal evasion with respect to taxes on income	(Japan – United Arab Rep.)	1968	10576
26.	Exchange of notes constituting an agreement regarding the guarantee by the Government of the United Kingdom and the maintenance of the minimum sterling proportion by Ireland	(Ireland – UK)	1968	9374
27.	Exchange of letters constituting an agreement concerning the Guarantee by the Government of the United Kingdom and the maintenance of the Minimum of Sterling Proportion by the Government of Sierra Leone	(Sierra Leone – UK)	1968	9806
28.	Exchange of notes constituting an agreement concerning the Guarantee by the Government of the United Kingdom and the maintenance of the Minimum Sterling Proportion by the Government of Libya	(Libya – UK)	1968	9815
29.	Exchange of notes constituting an agreement concerning the Guarantee by the Government of the United Kingdom and the maintenance of the Minimum Sterling Proportion by the Government of Iceland	(Iceland – UK)	1969	9800

(*cont.*)

	Agreement name	Signatories	Signature year	UNTS
30.	Agreement for sales of agricultural commodities	(Paraguay – US)	1970	11046
31.	Agreement for the avoidance of double taxation and the prevention of fiscal evasion with respect to taxes on income and capital gains	(UK – Barbados)	1970	10955
32.	Exchange of letters constituting an agreement concerning the guarantees of investment securities	(New Zealand – Western Samoa)	1970	11642
33.	Agreement concerning the compensation of Netherlands interests	(Netherlands – Egypt)	1971	11868
34.	Agreement for sales of agricultural commodities	(Republic of Vietnam – US)	1972	12254
35.	International Sugar Agreement, 1973 (with annexes)	(Multilateral)	1973	12951
36.	Agreement for sales of agricultural commodities (with annex and memorandum of understanding)	(Bangladesh – US)	1973	13092
37.	Convention on the protection of investments	(France – Mauritius)	1973	13396
38.	Agreement for sales of agricultural commodities	(Egypt – US)	1974	13629
39.	Agreement concerning financial assistance	(Federal Rep. Germany – Tanzania)	1974	14366
40.	Exchange of notes constituting an agreement concerning grain to be supplied by the Government of the United Kingdom of Great Britain to the Government of Mali within the framework of the Cereals Food Aid Programme of the European Economic Community	(Mali – UK)	1975	14430
41.	Exchange of notes constituting an agreement concerning the delivery of a linear accelerator to the Cancer Institute	(Denmark – India)	1975	14491
42.	Agreement for the promotion and protection of investments	(UK – Egypt)	1975	15181

No.	Agreement	Parties	Year	No.
43.	Agreement for sales of agricultural commodities (with agreed minutes regarding the Public Law 480 Title I Agreement for fiscal year 1976)	(India – US)	1976	15915
44.	Agreement relating to the transfer of agricultural commodities	(Mozambique – US)	1977	17753
45.	Convention concerning the mutual promotion and protection of investments	(France – Syrian Arab Rep.)	1977	19570
46.	Agreement for the sale of agricultural commodities (with minutes of negotiations of March 20, 1978)	(Lebanon – US)	1978	18143
47.	Agreement concerning financial co-operation	(Federal Rep. Germany – Niger)	1978	20214
48.	Treaty concerning the promotion and reciprocal protection of capital investment (with protocol, exchange of letters of 29 June 1978 and exchange of notes of 5 August and 10 October 1983)	(Federal Rep. Germany – Benin)	1978	24681
49.	Exchange of notes constituting an agreement relating to Canadian investments in Western Samoa insured by the Government of Canada through its agent, the Export Development Corporation	(Canada – Western Samoa)	1978	17730
50.	Agreement concerning economic, scientific and technical co-operation in the field of sugar production and sugar by-products (with additional note)	(Cuba – Mexico)	1979	20684
51.	Convention for the avoidance of double taxation and the prevention of fiscal evasion with respect to taxes on income and on capital (with protocol)	(Czechoslovakia – Norway)	1979	18930
52.	The Second ACP-EEC Convention (with protocols, final act and minutes of the Convention)	(Multilateral)	1979	21071
53.	Foreign Investment Insurance Agreement	(Canada – Senegal)	1979	24875

(*cont.*)

	Agreement name	Signatories	Signature year	UNTS
54.	Agreement concerning financial co-operation on the Lake Volta Transport System	(Federal Rep. Germany – Ghana)	1980	21671
55.	Agreement for the promotion and protection of investments	(UK – Bangladesh)	1980	19536
56.	Agreement on the mutual promotion and guarantee of investments	(Denmark – Romania)	1980	20625
57.	Agreement concerning financial co-operation	(Federal Rep. Germany – Nepal)	1980	21731
58.	Agreement concerning financial co-operation	(Federal Rep. Germany – Thailand)	1981	21732
59.	Convention for the avoidance of double taxation and the prevention of fiscal evasion with respect to taxes on income	(Australia – Italy)	1982	25393
60.	Agreement concerning financial co-operation	(Federal Rep. Germany – Indonesia)	1982	22444
61.	Agreement for the promotion and protection of investments	(UK – Yemen)	1982	22810
62.	Agreement on the mutual protection of investments (with exchange of notes)	(Sweden – China)	1982	22733
63.	Agreement on reciprocal promotion and protection of investments	(France – Equatorial Guinea)	1982	24657
64.	Agreement on processing and protection of investments (with exchanges of letters)	(France – Panama)	1982	24235
65.	Agreement concerning financial co-operation	(Federal Rep. Germany – Congo)	1983	22976
66.	Exchange of notes constituting an agreement relating to Canadian investments in the Kingdom of Thailand (with related letters)	(Canada – Thailand)	1983	24956

No.	Agreement	Parties	Year	No.
67.	Agreement for the promotion and protection of investments	(UK – Panama)	1983	24700
68.	Agreement concerning financial co-operation	(Federal Rep. Germany – Somalia)	1983	22962
69.	Agreement concerning financial co-operation	(Federal Rep. Germany – Cent. Afr. Rep.)	1984	24332
70.	Agreement on the mutual promotion and protection of investments (with exchange of letters)	(France – Haiti)	1984	24323
71.	Agreement concerning the encouragement and reciprocal protection of investments	(Denmark – Sri Lanka)	1985	23607
72.	Agreement concerning financial co-operation	(Federal Rep. Germany – Bangladesh)	1986	25472
73.	Agreement concerning financial co-operation – Loan to the Development Finance Company of Kenya	(Federal Rep. Germany – Kenya)	1987	26480
74.	Agreement for the Promotion and Reciprocal Protection of Investments	(UK – Hungary)	1987	27032
75.	Agreement for the Promotion and Protection of Investments	(Jamaica – UK)	1987	25985
76.	Agreement for the promotion and reciprocal protection of investments (with exchange of letters).	(Sweden – Hungary)	1987	27077
77.	Agreement on the promotion and protection of investments (with exchange of notes)	(New Zealand – China)	1988	31058
78.	Belgium, Luxembourg, and Union of Soviet Socialist Republics: Agreement on the mutual promotion and protection of investments (with protocol)	(Multilateral)	1989	33361
79.	Agreement on the supply of agricultural and mineral commodities from Australia to the Union of Soviet Socialist Republics (with attachment)	(Australia – USSR)	1990	27471

(*cont.*)

	Agreement name	Signatories	Signature year	UNTS
80.	Exchange of notes constituting an agreement regarding the use of British capital untransferable accounts in Egypt (with exchange of notes of February 13, and April 7, 1992)	(UK – Egypt)	1990	29460
81.	Agreement regarding trade of agricultural products	(Austria – Turkey)	1991	30409
82.	Agreement concerning the promotion and reciprocal protection of investments	(Estonia – Denmark)	1991	30890
83.	International Sugar Agreement	(Multilateral)	1992	29467
84.	Agreement on the reciprocal promotion and protection of investments	(Spain – Uruguay)	1992	31039
85.	Agreement on reciprocal obligations concerning the introduction of Litas as the Monetary Unit of the Republic of Lithuania	(Lithuania – Russian Federation)	1992	31335
86.	Exchange of letters constituting an agreement concerning agricultural products (with annexes)	(Austria – Hungary)	1993	30629
87.	Exchange of letters constituting an agreement concerning agricultural products (with annexes)	(Austria – Bulgaria)	1993	30630
88.	Treaty between the Federal Republic of Germany and the Republic of Uzbekistan for the promotion and reciprocal protection of investments	(Germany – Uzbekistan)	1993	35902
89.	Agreement concerning the promotion and reciprocal protection of investments	(Denmark – Bulgaria)	1993	33613
90.	Agreement on the reciprocal promotion and protection of investments	(Estonia – Poland)	1993	30492

91.	International Coffee Agreement, 1994	(Multilateral)	1994	31252
92.	Agreement on the reciprocal promotion and protection of investments	(Ecuador – France)	1994	33847
93.	Agreement between the Government of Canada and the Government of Ukraine for the promotion and protection of investments	(Canada – Ukraine)	1994	34948
94.	Agreement between the Republic of Finland and the Kingdom of the Netherlands for the avoidance of double taxation and the prevention of fiscal evasion with respect to taxes on income and on capital (with protocol)	(Finland – Netherlands)	1995	37104
95.	United Nations Convention on Independent Guarantees and Stand-by Letters of Credit	(Multilateral)	1995	38030
96.	Agreement on economic and financial cooperation between the Kingdom of Spain and the Republic of Argentina	(Argentina – Spain)	1995	34755
97.	Agreement on the reciprocal promotion and protection of investments	(Spain – Dominican Republic)	1995	33395
98.	Agreement between the Kingdom of the Netherlands and the Republic of India for the promotion and protection of investments	(India – Netherlands)	1995	39911
99.	Agreement between the Government of the United Kingdom of Great Britain and Northern Ireland and the Government of the Sultanate of Oman for the avoidance of double taxation and the prevention of fiscal evasion with respect to taxes on income and capital gains	(UK – Oman)	1998	35805

(cont.)

	Agreement name	Signatories	Signature year	UNTS
100.	Agreement for the promotion and reciprocal protection of investments between Spain and Ukraine	(Spain – Ukraine)	1998	36612
101.	Agreement between Denmark, Finland, Iceland, Norway, and Sweden on the establishment of the Nordic Environmental Finance Corporation (NEFCO)	(Multilateral)	1998	36248
102.	International Convention for the Suppression of the Financing of Terrorism (with annex)	(Multilateral)	1999	38349
103.	Agreement on the promotion and reciprocal protection of investments between Spain and Jamaica	(Jamaica – Spain)	2002	39125

Environment

	Agreement name	Signatories	Signature year	UNTS
104.	Convention on Nature Protection and Wild Life Preservation in the Western Hemisphere	(Multilateral)	1940	485
105.	African Migratory Locust Convention	(Multilateral)	1952	10476
106.	International Convention (with annexes) for the Prevention of Pollution of the Sea by Oil	(Multilateral)	1954	4714
107.	Convention on Fishing and Conservation of the Living Resources of the High Seas	(Multilateral)	1958	8164
108.	Agreement concerning the protection of frontier forests against fire	(Argentina – Chile)	1961	9075
109.	Agreement concerning co-operation in the matter of plant protection	(Austria – Hungary)	1963	6989
110.	Agreement on plant protection and phytosanitary quarantine	(Bulgaria – United Arab Republic)	1966	9963
111.	International Convention for the Conservation of Atlantic Tunas (with Final Act and Resolution adopted by the Conference of Plenipotentiaries)	(Multilateral)	1966	9587
112.	European Agreement on the restriction of the use of certain detergents in washing and cleaning products	(Multilateral)	1968	11210
113.	Exchange of letters constituting an agreement concerning the free passage of salmon in Vanern Lake	(Norway – Sweden)	1969	14017

(*cont.*)

	Agreement name	Signatories	Signature year	UNTS
114.	International Convention on Civil Liability for Oil Pollution Damage	(Multilateral)	1969	14097
115.	Convention on fishing and conservation of the living resources in the Baltic Sea and the Belts	(Multilateral)	1973	16710
116.	Agreement for the protection of migratory birds and birds in danger of extinction and their environment	(Australia – Japan)	1974	20181
117.	Agreement on co-operation in the field of environmental protection	(UK – USSR)	1974	13920
118.	Agreement concerning the protection of the Sound Oresund from pollution	(Denmark – Sweden)	1974	13823
119.	Agreement on co-operation in the field of environmental protection (with agreed minutes)	(Japan – US)	1975	15109
120.	Agreement on co-operation in the field of environmental protection	(German Democratic Republic – Sweden)	1976	20644
121.	Agreement for plant protection – Sudan quelea bird research project	(Sudan – US)	1977	17308
122.	Memorandum of understanding on cooperation in earth sciences and environmental studies	(UK – US)	1979	19699
123.	Exchange of notes constituting an agreement concerning land use and soil conservation in the eastern Amazon region	(Brazil – Federal Rep. Germany)	1979	17973
124.	Convention on long-range transboundary air pollution	(Multilateral)	1979	21623
125.	Agreement concerning financial co-operation – Refuse Disposal in the Freetown Metropolitan Area	(Federal Rep. Germany – Sierra Leone)	1980	21678

No.	Title	Parties	Year	Ref.
126.	Community-Cost Concentration Agreement on a concerted action project in the field of analysis of organic micro- pollutants in water	(Multilateral)	1980	20754
127.	Agreement for cooperation relating to the marine environment	(Canada – Denmark)	1983	22693
128.	Exchange of notes constituting an agreement on the project "Soil management and conservation in East Amazonia"	(Brazil – Federal Rep. Germany)	1984	23031
129.	Agreement between the Government of the United States of America and the Government of Canada on the conservation of the Porcupine Caribou Herd	(Canada – US)	1987	38202
130.	Montreal Protocol on Substances that Deplete the Ozone Layer	(Multilateral)	1987	26369
131.	Exchange of notes constituting an agreement on a project concerning environmental impact of large dams	(Brazil – Germany)	1987	24819
132.	Agreement on Danish support for the establishment of a desalination plant in Male in the Republic of Maldives	(Denmark – Maldives)	1989	27580
133.	Central American Convention for the Protection of the Environment	(Multilateral)	1989	40570
134.	International Convention on oil pollution preparedness, response and cooperation (with annex)	(Multilateral)	1990	32194
135.	Agreement on co-operation in the field of protection and enhancement of the environment	(Australia – USSR)	1990	27468
136.	Memorandum of understanding between the Environmental Protection Agency of the United States of America and the Secretariat of the Environment of the Presidency of the Federal Republic of Brazil with the Brazilian Institute of Environment and renewable natural resources	(Brazil – US)	1990	39083

(*cont.*)

	Agreement name	Signatories	Signature year	UNTS
137.	Agreement on air quality (with annexes)	(Canada – US)	1991	31532
138.	Convention on the protection of the marine environment of the Baltic Sea (with annexes)	(Multilateral)	1992	36495
139.	Agreement on cooperation in the field of environment	(Estonia – Sweden)	1992	30486
140.	Agreement concerning co-operation in the field of environmental protection	(Finland – Russian Federation)	1992	29998
141.	Agreement on the conservation of small cetaceans of the Baltic and North Seas (with annex)	(Multilateral)	1992	30865
142.	Agreement concerning environmental cooperation	(Canada – Russian Federation)	1993	32671
143.	Agreement for environmental co-operation	(Denmark – Oman)	1993	31060
144.	Agreement on co-operation in the field of environmental protection	(Republic of Korea – Japan)	1993	30595
145.	Convention (176) concerning safety and health in mines	(Multilateral)	1995	35009
146.	Agreement on the conservation of cetaceans of the Black Sea, Mediterranean Sea and contiguous Atlantic area (with annexes)	(Multilateral)	1996	38466

Human rights

	Agreement name	Signatories	Signature year	UNTS
147.	Convention (No. 19) concerning equality of treatment for national and foreign workers as regards workmen's compensation for accidents	(Multilateral)	1925	602
148.	Agreement on passenger traffic	(Belgium – France)	1945	132
149.	Constitution of the International Refugee Organization and Agreement on interim measures to be taken in respect of refugees and displaced persons	(Multilateral)	1946	283
150.	Convention on the prevention and punishment of the crime of genocide	(Multilateral)	1948	1021
151.	Geneva Convention relative to the Treatment of Prisoners of War (135)	(Multilateral)	1949	972
152.	Convention (No. 98) concerning the application of the principles of the right to organise and to bargain collectively	(Multilateral)	1949	1341
153.	Convention for the Protection of Human Rights and Fundamental Freedoms	(Multilateral)	1950	2889
154.	Convention (with final protocol) concerning the reciprocal grant of assistance to distressed persons	(Multilateral)	1951	2647
155.	Convention (No. 105) concerning the abolition of forced labor	(Multilateral)	1957	4648
156.	Convention (No. 111) concerning discrimination in respect of employment and occupation	(Multilateral)	1958	5181

(*cont.*)

	Agreement name	Signatories	Signature year	UNTS
157.	Convention (No. 118) concerning equality of treatment of nationals and non-nationals in social security	(Multilateral)	1962	7238
158.	International Covenant on Civil and Political Rights	(Multilateral)	1966	14668
159.	Convention on the non-applicability of statutory limitations to war crimes and crimes against humanity	(Multilateral)	1968	10823
160.	American Convention on Human Rights: "Pact of San José, Costa Rica"	(Multilateral)	1969	17955
161.	OAU Convention governing the specific aspects of refugee problems in Africa	(Multilateral)	1969	14691
162.	Convention on the prevention and punishment of crimes against internationally protected persons, including diplomatic agents	(Multilateral)	1973	15410
163.	Protocol relating to refugee seamen	(Multilateral)	1973	13928
164.	International Convention on the Suppression and Punishment of the Crime of Apartheid	(Multilateral)	1973	14861
165.	Agreement on the fundamental rights of nationals	(Congo – France)	1974	21833
166.	European Convention on the Non-Applicability of Statutory Limitation to Crimes against Humanity and War Crimes	(Multilateral)	1974	39987
167.	Convention (No. 143) concerning migrations in abusive conditions and the promotion of equality of opportunity and treatment of migrant workers	(Multilateral)	1975	17426

168.	Convention of establishment	(France – Mali)	1977	20762
169.	Convention on the Elimination of All Forms of Discrimination against Women	(Multilateral)	1979	20378
170.	Convention (No. 155) concerning occupational safety and health and the working environment	(Multilateral)	1981	22345
171.	Convention against Torture and Other Cruel, Inhuman or Degrading Treatment or Punishment	(Multilateral)	1984	24841
172.	International Convention against Apartheid in Sports	(Multilateral)	1985	25822
173.	European Convention for the prevention of torture and inhuman or degrading treatment or punishment	(Multilateral)	1987	27161
174.	Convention on the Rights of the Child	(Multilateral)	1989	27531
175.	Exchange of letters constituting an agreement recognizing the right of Dutch nationals in Spain and Spanish nationals in the Netherlands to vote in municipal elections	(Netherlands – Spain)	1989	27588
176.	Exchange of notes constituting an agreement recognizing the right of Danish nationals in Spain and Spanish nationals in Denmark to vote in municipal elections	(Denmark – Spain)	1989	27957
177.	Exchange of notes constituting an agreement recognizing the right of Norwegian nationals in Spain and Spanish nationals in Norway to vote in municipal elections	(Norway – Spain)	1990	28246
178.	Exchange of notes constituting an agreement recognizing the right of Swedish nationals in Spain and Spanish nationals in Sweden to vote in municipal elections	(Sweden – Spain)	1990	28247

(*cont.*)

	Agreement name	Signatories	Signature year	UNTS
179.	Agreement on human contacts and humanitarian cooperation	(Australia – USSR)	1990	27469
180.	International Convention on the Protection of the Rights of All Migrant Workers and Members of their Families	(Multilateral)	1990	39481
181.	Agreement establishing the Fund for the Development of the Indigenous Peoples of Latin America and the Caribbean	(Multilateral)	1992	30177
182.	Agreement between the Government of the Republic of Latvia and the Government of the Russian Federation on regulation of the resettlement process and protection of the rights of resettlers	(Latvia – Russian Federation)	1993	40921
183.	European Agreement relating to persons participating in proceedings of the European Court of Human Rights	(Multilateral)	1996	37247
184.	Convention for the protection of human rights and dignity of the human being with regard to the application of biology and medicine: convention on human rights and biomedicine	(Multilateral)	1997	37266
185.	Agreement on readmission of persons	(Latvia – Sweden)	1997	34250
186.	United Nations Convention against Transnational Organized Crime	(Multilateral)	2000	39574
187.	Memorandum of understanding between the Ministry of Interior of the Republic of Turkey and the Ministry of Internal Affairs of the Republic of Belarus on cooperation in the field of combating trafficking in human beings and illegal migration	(Belarus – Turkey)	2004	44197

Security

	Agreement name	Signatories	Signature year	UNTS
188.	Inter-American Treaty of Reciprocal Assistance and Final Act of the Inter-American Conference for the Maintenance of Continental Peace and Security	(Multilateral)	1947	324
189.	Security Treaty between the United States of America and Japan	(Japan – US)	1951	1835
190.	Security Treaty between Australia, New Zealand and the United States of America	(Multilateral)	1951	1736
191.	Exchange of notes constituting an agreement relating to mutual security	(Greece – US)	1951	2382
192.	Exchange of notes constituting an agreement relating to mutual security	(Luxembourg – US)	1952	2384
193.	Exchange of notes constituting an agreement relating to mutual security	(Italy – US)	1952	2365
194.	Exchange of notes constituting an agreement relating to assurances under the Mutual Security Act of 1951	(Portugal – US)	1952	2799
195.	Exchange of notes constituting an agreement relating to mutual security	(Turkey – US)	1952	2361
196.	Exchange of notes constituting an agreement relating to mutual security	(Korea – US)	1952	2359
197.	Exchange of notes constituting an agreement relating to mutual security	(Belgium – US)	1952	2356

(cont.)

	Agreement name	Signatories	Signature year	UNTS
198.	Treaty for the Prohibition of Nuclear Weapons in Latin America (with annexed Additional Protocols I and II)	(Multilateral)	1967	9068
199.	Treaty on the prohibition of the emplacement of nuclear weapons and other weapons of mass destruction on the sea-bed and the ocean floor and in the subsoil thereof	(Multilateral)	1971	13678
200.	Convention on the prohibition of the development, production and stockpiling of bacteriological (biological) and toxin weapons and on their destruction	(Multilateral)	1972	14860
201.	Interim Agreement on certain measures with respect to the limitation of strategic offensive arms	(USSR – US)	1972	13445
202.	Security Agreement concerning certain exchanges of secret information	(France – Sweden)	1973	14951
203.	Convention on the prohibition of military or any other hostile use of environmental modification techniques	(Multilateral)	1976	17119
204.	Exchange of notes constituting an agreement relating to military assistance: Eligibility requirements pursuant to the Foreign Assistance Act of 1973 and the International Security Assistance and Arms Export Control Act of 1976	(Greece – US)	1976	16035
205.	Exchange of notes constituting an agreement relating to military assistance: Eligibility requirements pursuant to the International Security Assistance and Arms Export Control Act of 1976	(Indonesia – US)	1976	16034

No.	Title	Parties	Year	Number
206.	Technical Security Arrangement concerning special security measures	(Kuwait – US)	1976	16314
207.	Agreement on the prevention of accidental nuclear war	(UK – USSR)	1977	17086
208.	Exchange of letters constituting an agreement on a defense security arrangement	(Australia – Netherlands)	1977	21950
209.	Exchange of notes constituting an agreement relating to military assistance: eligibility requirements pursuant to the International Security Assistance and Arms Export Control Act of 1976	(Malaysia – US)	1977	17310
210.	Agreement governing the activities of states on the moon and other celestial bodies	(Multilateral)	1979	23002
211.	Convention on prohibitions or restrictions on the use of certain conventional weapons which may be deemed to be excessively injurious or to have indiscriminate effects	(Multilateral)	1980	22495
212.	Co-operation Agreement on civil defense and security	(France – Morocco)	1981	20783
213.	Agreement between the United States of America and Japan relating to a program for the development by Japan of the XSH-40 J weapon system	(Japan – US)	1987	39954
214.	Treaty on Collective Security	(Multilateral)	1992	32307
215.	Convention on the Prohibition of the Development, Production, Stockpiling and Use of Chemical Weapons and on their Destruction	(Multilateral)	1993	33757
216.	Agreement between the Department of Defense of the United States of America and the Ministry of Defense of the Kingdom of Thailand concerning the measures to be taken for the transfer, security, and safeguarding of technical information, software and equipment to Ministry of Defense to enable industry to operate, maintain, and expand Royal Thai Air Force air combat maneuvering instrumentation range facilities	(Thailand – US)	1993	40309

	Agreement name	Signatories	Signature year	UNTS
217.	Memorandum of understanding pertaining to the provision of communications security equipment and services	(Republic of Korea – US)	1993	30579
218.	Mutual Agreement to combat illicit trafficking in narcotic drugs and psychotropic substances and money laundering (with annexes)	(India – Zambia)	1993	31241
219.	Agreement between the Government of the Republic of Hungary and the Government of the United States of America concerning security measures for the protection of classified military information	(Hungary – US)	1995	35344
220.	Agreement between the Government of the Republic of Hungary and the Government of the Kingdom of Sweden concerning security measures for the protection of classified military data	(Hungary – Sweden)	1995	35341
221.	Western European Union (WEU) Security Agreement	(Multilateral)	1995	37024
222.	Treaty on cooperation in protection of the borders of States participating in the Commonwealth of Independent States with countries not forming part of the Commonwealth	(Multilateral)	1995	33648
223.	Agreement on confidence- and security-building measures complementing the OSCE Vienna document of 1994 and on the development of military relations between the Government of the Republic of Hungary and the Government of Romania	(Hungary – Romania)	1996	35339
224.	Convention on the Prohibition of the Use, Stockpiling, Production and Transfer of Anti-Personnel Mines and on their Destruction	(Multilateral)	1997	35597

225.	Memorandum of understanding between the Government of the Federative Republic of Brazil and the Government of the Argentine Republic for the establishment of a bilateral commission on border security	(Argentina – Brazil)	1997	34795
226.	Agreement between the Government of the French Republic and the Government of the Czech Republic on cooperation in the fields of police, civil security and public administration	(Czech Republic – France)	1997	36142
227.	General Agreement on security between the Government of the French Republic and the Government of the Slovak Republic (with annex)	(France – Slovakia)	1997	35581
228.	Agreement between the Government of the Federal Republic of Germany and the Cabinet of Ministers of the Ukraine on the mutual protection of classified information	(Germany – Ukraine)	1998	36200
229.	Agreement between the Government of the Hellenic Republic and the Government of the Federal Republic of Germany on the reciprocal protection of sensitive information	(Germany – Greece)	1999	36542
230.	Agreement between the Government of the Republic of Estonia and the Government of the United States of America concerning security measures for the protection of classified military information	(Estonia – US)	2000	36675
231.	Framework Agreement between Denmark, Finland, Norway And Sweden Concerning Cooperation in the Field of Defence Matériel	(Multilateral)	2000	37734

(cont.)

	Agreement name	Signatories	Signature year	UNTS
232.	Agreement between the Government of the Republic of Latvia and the Government of the Kingdom of Sweden concerning the protection of classified information	(Latvia – Sweden)	2002	38896
233.	Charter of the Collective Security Treaty Organization	(Multilateral)	2002	39775
234.	Agreement between the Government of Australia and the Government of the United States of America concerning security measures for the protection of classified information	(Australia – US)	2002	39242

Appendix 2 Coding rules

Below I briefly describe the coding of high or low for the seven cooperation problems not discussed in detail in the text. Recall a coding of low does not imply the cooperation problem is not present; rather, a coding of low simply implies the cooperation problem is not severe enough to meet the threshold for high. I also explain how the actor characteristics were measured. Identification of the various design provisions is detailed in the chapters devoted to them in Parts II and III.

Enforcement problems: For this problem to be coded as high, coders had to establish that free-riding on another's cooperation, that is, choosing to defect while another cooperated, would make at least some subset of states better off than mutual cooperation. Another way of looking at this is asking whether, if one state defects, the other state wants to defect as well or whether it could be just as well off continuing to cooperate. Arms control is typically characterized by an underlying Enforcement problem for at least some subset of states. Coders could easily make the case that limiting some kind of weapon while one's partner cheated was not in a state's interest. This argument is not compelling for women and children's rights. If one's partner starts to defect by eliminating the right to vote for women, it is easy to make the case that the best response for the state left cooperating is to continue to cooperate – that is, to continue to give women the right to vote. In other words, that issue area is not well described by the prisoners' dilemma game structure. Additionally, a prominent theme in liberal approaches to international law is the idea of the two-level game (Putnam 1988), which highlights the presence of differentiated "state" actors on the international and domestic scenes, and in particular that governments may have incomplete control over domestic agents. For instance, firms affected by environmental agreements or labor standards will have incentives different from those of the government. COIL acknowledges the existence of such two-level problems in its coding of underlying Enforcement problems because sub-state actors whose behavior is governed may have incentives to defect even if the national government does not.

Distribution problems: For this problem to be coded as high, coders had to demonstrate that the subject area at stake was almost zero-sum in nature, lacked focal points that could facilitate a bargaining solution, and/or engaged subject areas for which high domestic distributional conflict exists or which are close to the basic identity of a state and hence for which compromise would be difficult. Many human rights are enshrined in constitutions and have become part of the basic identity of particular states (e.g., freedom of speech in the United States and France) but not of every state. Human rights negotiations that engage such issues thus met the threshold for high; in contrast, the bilateral reciprocal voting rights agreements between Spain and states like Norway did not meet the threshold. Voting is only for municipal elections, and a focal point exists in this context – namely, symmetric rights are exchanged. With respect to domestic distributional conflict, trade agreements that involve trade protection met the threshold of high, whereas bilateral agricultural commodity aid agreements did not. Similarly, for disarmament agreements, certain all-out prohibitions like those for chemical weapons (even though disagreements existed regarding what chemicals to include) are not nearly as divisive as nuclear weapons negotiations among the superpowers, especially given the divergent relative advantages of each state with respect to particular offensive and defensive weapons. Thus the former would be coded as low, while the latter would be coded as high. Finally, agreements involving some kind of territorial boundary or property rights issues would be coded as high given their zero-sum nature.

Commitment problems: For this problem to be coded as high, coders looked for evidence of domestic regime instability in at least one of the member states in the decade before signature. Stable western democracies, like the United Kingdom, were never coded as having an underlying Commitment problem regardless of the issue area. Yet, the 1982 BIT between the United Kingdom and Yemen is coded as high because of Yemen's instability in this respect. Informed by Moravcsik (2000), who argues that newly democratic states often use international human rights agreements to tie their own hands, a number of the multilateral human rights agreements in the sample are coded as high for Commitment problems if at least one member fits this profile. For instance, the American Convention on Human Rights features a number of Latin American states whose regime stability and respect for the rule of law (Simmons 2009) were less than stable during the period before they signed onto the agreement.

Coordination problems: Traditionally (e.g., Stein 1982; Snidal 1985) a Coordination problem exists if states are better off matching policies – coordinating on either a movie or a ballet, for example. Because the overall purpose of codifying law is to coordinate at least loosely, COIL has a higher threshold for a Coordination problem: The policy matching has to be almost exact if states are to be better off cooperating. To pass the threshold for a Coordination problem, coders thus were asked to explain how not changing policies at all (i.e., not cooperating) would make a state better than only loosely matching policies with its partner. For example, under extremely loose rules regarding where property rights begin and end, it is better to not cooperate and thereby not invest in exploiting a scarce resource than to cooperate. The everyday examples employed as models for the coders were the following: "it is better to not fly at all if one is not sure which flight paths are earmarked for one's use at any point in time" (Coordination problem) versus "it is better to clean up the park with friends even if one is not sure if others are cleaning up as efficiently as you are" (no Coordination problem).

Uncertainty about Behavior: For this problem to be coded as high, coders asked rather straightforwardly, how easily is compliance observed in the absence of any institutional design tools that allow intrusive monitoring? For instance, if the agreement addresses exchange rate policies, compliance (or noncompliance) is transparent. If the agreement addresses biological weapons, noncompliance is easily hidden. Thus only the latter meets the threshold for high. Given the decades of work in the international cooperation literature on information problems and the straightforwardness of its interpretation, this variable was rarely difficult to code.

Uncertainty about Preferences: For this problem to meet the threshold of high, a coder had to establish that great uncertainty existed regarding at least one member's true motives with respect to participating in the agreement. In the economics issue area, this threshold was never met, regardless of the states involved. That is, no coder could make the case that preferences were sufficiently unclear with respect to any of the economic agreements in the sample. In the issue area of human rights, on the other hand, about one third of the agreements met the threshold for high because the motives of at least one of the members were ambiguous. Simmons' (2009) argument that the true preferences of certain states with respect to this issue area are unclear – the states she labels as the "insincere ratifiers" – informed the coding. Several multilateral disarmament agreements, for which the intentions of states like Iran, for instance, could not be fully known or trusted, also met the threshold for high.

Uncertainty about the State of the World: For this problem to meet the threshold of high, coders had to argue that the environment was one in which changes or shocks could cause the distribution of gains from the agreement to vary substantially over time or in which great uncertainty existed about how the agreement would work in practice. The coding for this variable is elaborated sub-issue-by-sub-issue area in Koremenos (2005). Here I give a few examples. Economic agreements subject to supply-and-demand shocks like those governing coffee or sugar quotas met the threshold for high; double-taxation agreements did not. Environmental agreements addressing plant or bird protection were coded as low, whereas for agreements concerning pollution abatement or fishing, coders made the case for high: Pollution control as well as sea resources implicate competitive industries; shocks affecting availability or dependence on the resource (fish) or technology (in pollution control, expected positive developments may not be forthcoming) can alter the distribution of gains. Even some human rights agreements like those governing refugees met the threshold for high, as coders made the case that political shocks may dramatically change the flow of refugees and thereby change the distribution of gains.

Number: The Number variable corresponds to the number of participants initially involved in some way in the negotiation. Often the official UNTS version of an agreement lists the participants and their signature date. The UNTS, unfortunately, has changed the way it reports this information over time. Additionally, the UNTS now varies in how it reports this information across agreements. That said, the Number variable was coded to represent as accurately as possible the number of states initially involved in the treaty negotiation by not counting, for instance, a state which did not exist at the time of negotiation but acceded much later. A number of robustness checks have been conducted with slightly different versions of this variable.

Domestic Regime-type Heterogeneity: Two measures for regime type heterogeneity among member states in an agreement are employed: Polity (level of democracy) scores and the Freedom House index.[1] To measure heterogeneity for bilateral agreements, the absolute difference in the respective democracy scores between the two participants was used. For multilateral agreements, first a data set with all dyads in the multilateral agreement was created; then, following the "weakest link" assumption (Dixon 1994; Oneal and Russett 1997), the absolute difference in the democracy indices for the most dissimilar dyad was used as the heterogeneity measure for the agreement.

Preference Heterogeneity: Ideal point estimates from Bailey, Strezhnev, and Voeten (2015)[2] were calculated based on states' voting positions in the UN General Assembly. To measure states' Preference Heterogeneity, the standard deviation of ideal points among participants of an agreement was calculated. An alternative preference heterogeneity measure using the maximal difference was also used. For bilateral agreements, the absolute difference in ideal points between the two participants was used. For the multilateral agreements, first a dyad was created for each pair of participants. Hence, if there were three members, there were three dyads; if there were four members, there were six dyads, and so on. For each multilateral agreement, the "weakest link assumption," was used, taking the absolute difference in respective ideal points of the dyad with the least similar interests. The further apart the member states' ideal points, the greater the Preference Heterogeneity was in an agreement.

Power Asymmetry: For economic Power Asymmetry, the standard deviation in GDP among participants of an agreement was calculated using data from the Penn World Table (PWT 7.1).[3] For

---

[1] For the Polity scores, see Marshall, Monty G., Ted Robert Gurr, and Keith Jaggers. 2014. Polity IV Project: Political Regime Characteristics and Transitions, 1800–2013, Dataset Users' Manual and Dataset. Version p4v2014. Center for Systemic Peace. Available at http://www.systemicpeace.org/inscrdata .html [Last accessed May 20, 2015]. For the Freedom House data, see Norris, Pippa. 2009. Democracy Time-series Dataset: Variable Labels. Version 3.0. Available at https://sites.google.com/site/pippanorris3/research/data [Last accessed May 20, 2015].

[2] See also Strezhnev, Anton and Erik Voeten. "United Nations General Assembly Voting Data." Harvard Dataverse. Available at http://hdl.handle.net/1902.1/ 12379 [Last accessed May 20, 2015].

[3] Heston Alan, Robert Summers, and Bettina Aten. 2012. Penn World Table Version 7.1. Center for International Comparisons of Production, Income and Prices at the University of Pennsylvania. Available at http://pwt.econ.upenn.edu/ [Last accessed May 20, 2015].

military Power Asymmetry, the standard deviation in military
capabilities among participants of an agreement was calculated
using the Correlates of War Composite Index of National
Capability scores found in EUGene (version 3.204) (Bennett and
Stam 2000).[4]

---

[4] See also Bennett, D. Scott, and Allan Stam. 2010. EUGene Version 3.204
[Computer Software]. Available at www.eugenesoftware.org [Last
accessed May 20, 2015].

Appendix 3 Selection issues in international cooperation data sets

In this appendix, I outline and discuss selection issues that potentially affect the COIL data set and other data sets used in the international cooperation literature, more generally. Indeed, one potential criticism of the analyses presented in Parts II and III of this book centers precisely on the assumed correspondence between the population of interest, that is, the population of international agreements implicated by the theories of agreement design, and the COIL sample used in the analyses below for testing these theories.

In cases for which researchers rely on samples from available populations, and those populations represent non-random subsets of the population of interest, the conclusions drawn may suffer from what the broader literature terms "selection bias," which is to say bias that results from using a sample selected not at random from the population of interest. Thus, COIL draws from the UNTS, but are the agreements registered with the UNTS the relevant population of interest?

Koremenos and Smith's "When to Select a Selection Model" (2014) lays out an algorithm for researchers to follow as they consider the potential for selection bias problems in particular substantive contexts.[1] Koremenos and Smith argue that researchers and critics sometimes overstate the importance of selection as a result of misunderstanding the population of interest in particular studies. In some cases, the population of theoretical and empirical interest corresponds exactly to that from which the available data are sampled, and no further concerns about selection arise once the researcher makes this case. In other cases, the populations differ, but a compelling case can be made that the observed population represents a random subset of the population of interest from the point of view of the relationship under study, in which

[1] See Chapter 8, fn. 16.

case empirical conclusions from a (random) sample drawn from the observed population generalize to the population of interest.[2]

This appendix summarizes a few of the main points from Koremenos and Smith's rather technical manuscript and zeros in on examples most relevant to this book: the design of international agreements. Readers are directed to Koremenos and Smith (2014) for a fuller treatment of these issues and for examples broader than those considered here.

One of the main goals of this appendix is to help scholars understand under what conditions they need to use a selection model and the thoughtful steps that must go into the justification of using one or not. The next section introduces some statistical notation to clarify what is meant by a selection problem in technical terms. Even those who do not perform statistical analyses themselves will benefit from the discussions in the sections following the subsequent one so that they can better understand the strengths and weaknesses of the conclusions drawn from large-n analyses in the fields of IR and IL.

Basic setup and notation

To make things concrete in terms of notation, assume the following relationship holds in the population of interest:

$$Y = \beta_0 + \beta_1 X_1 + \ldots + \beta_k X_k + \varepsilon. \tag{1}$$

In this notation, Y indicates the dependent variable (in the COIL context, most likely a design provision), $X_1, \ldots, X_k$ denote independent variables with X_1 the variable whose coefficient is of primary interest (in the COIL context, most likely the type of cooperation problem), and ε is the unobserved random component of the outcome (a.k.a., the error term). One can think about the error term as containing all of the unobserved (but not necessarily unobservable) variables that affect Y other than $X_1, \ldots, X_k$. I refer to (1) as the "outcome equation."

The sub-population of international agreements that we can observe (for instance, all international agreements that are written down and registered with the UN) is called the "observed" population; the remainder of the population of interest is called the "latent" population. The selection problem results from the concern

---

[2] Technically speaking, and as explained below, the error terms in the selection equation and the outcome equation have a zero correlation.

that estimating (1) on the observed population, or on data from a random sample of the observed population as in the case of COIL, may lead to biased coefficients and misleading inferences about the parameter of interest defined for the population of interest.

More formally, the factors that determine whether an agreement is in the observed population or the latent population are represented by the simple linear index function:

$$D^* = \delta_0 + \delta_1 Z_1 + \eta. \tag{2}$$

In this equation (the "observation equation" or the "selection equation"), D^* is the index that indicates the likelihood that an agreement resides in the observed population, $Z_1, \ldots, Z_i$ are independent variables that affect whether or not an agreement resides in the observed population, and η is the unobserved random component of the likelihood of observation (a.k.a., the error term). As with ε, η is conceptualized as including all of the variables other than $Z_1, \ldots, Z_i$ that influence whether or not an agreement resides in the observed population. Without loss of generality, assume that agreements are observed rather than latent when $D^* \geq 0$, and define the indicator variable $D = 1$ if $D^* \geq 0$ and $D = 0$ otherwise. More prosaically, D is an indicator (i.e., dummy) variable that equals 1 for agreements in the observed population and 0 for agreements in the latent population.

It is useful to define the outcome equation for the observed population. So, within the observed population, i.e. the population with $D = 1$, we have the following relationship between Y and the independent variables:

$$Y = \gamma_0 + \gamma_1 X_1 + \ldots + \gamma_k X_k + v. \tag{3}$$

This is the same equation as (1), but with gammas replacing the betas and a different error term.

The betas and the gammas will differ only if ε has a non-zero correlation with η. A non-zero correlation between the two error terms means that some unobserved factors affect both whether the agreement resides in the observed population and the dependent variable (the design provision) Y conditional on $X_1, \ldots, X_k$.

In contrast, this correlation equals zero in two cases, and hence in those cases, there is no "selection problem." First, and most obviously, when the observed population is the population of interest, (1) and (3) coincide so that $\beta_j = \gamma_j$ for $j = 0, \ldots, k$. Second, when the observed population and the population of interest differ, but ε and η do not have any (unobserved) variables in common, the observed population is a random subset of the population of interest and so has exactly the same properties. In this second case, once again, the gammas equal the betas.

Choosing the population (and parameter) of interest

Proper definition of the population of interest underlies any serious empirical study but becomes particularly necessary when concerns about selection arise. To help make things concrete, first consider this question in the context of this book: international law. In that context, consider two possible populations of interest. (There might be others, but these two suffice to make the point.) One would be the population of agreements defined by the UNTS. These comprise international agreements in force that have been registered with the UN as required under international law. An alternative population of interest consists of the union of the UNTS population with the latent population of "near-misses," defined as agreements that reach some stage of serious contemplation or negotiation but never make it all the way to entry into force. This latent population includes some notables, of course, such as the Comprehensive Test Ban Treaty. What sort of arguments could a researcher make in this context to justify a focus on one population of interest or the other?

One way to justify a focus solely on the observed population of UNTS agreements builds on general ideas about the sorts of populations in which it makes sense to test particular theories. For example, one might argue that theories of agreement design have meaning only when the political will to negotiate an agreement exists. In a broad sense, there are an infinite number of potential agreements that do not enter into force (I say more about this in what follows) in any given issue area. Do theories of agreements that no one has the political will to see through to entry into force really add much to our knowledge? We can imagine interesting theories regarding the characteristics of agreements that do and do not reach entry into force from particular points in the process such as having meetings, producing a draft, signing the agreement, putting it up for ratification, and so on.[3]

---

[3] Haftel and Thompson (2013) undertake a smart and insightful analysis on the time between signature and ratification in the world of BITs, which includes the

Yet, in this book, the theories really are about patterns of provisions in agreements that pass a cost-benefit test as signaled by entry into force. If the total gain from an agreement is small and the costs of setting up an agreement – that is, negotiation costs and institutional set-up costs – are large, states will rationally choose not to establish an agreement. Cooperation is not always worth it. *Theories of agreement design make sense at the stage at which cooperation is thought to be worth it.* As Keohane states: "Rationalistic research on international institutions ... begins with the premise that if there were no potential gains from agreements to be captured in world politics ... there would be no need for specific international institutions" (1988: 386).

One can also make a practical argument in favor of declaring the UNTS population the population of interest, and that concerns the difficulty of defining (and implementing) a precise and theoretically compelling notion of near-misses. Should the latent population include agreements that get negotiated and signed but fail to come into force? Should it include negotiations where physical trips are made but no agreement is concluded? Should it include thoughts leaders have about the possibility of cooperation but which they decide not to act upon? Or should the latent population consist of all possible agreements addressing some particular issue or set of issues? In general, theoretical rather than practical concerns should trump when defining the population of interest, but practical concerns will nonetheless play a role.

A positive argument for including the latent population of near-misses in the population of interest when studying the relationship between agreement design and cooperation problems could go in a couple of directions. First, it seems like theories about agreement design ought to apply to near-misses, at least those that come reasonably close to entry into force, particularly since ratification by certain key states, which might be mandatory for entry into force, might often fail for reasons unrelated to agreement design. A finding that theories like those advanced elsewhere in this book did not hold for near-misses but did hold for agreements in force might give cause

possibility that the BIT will never enter into force and thus would be considered "failed" by some measures. Importantly such failed BITs do not stimulate investment as do BITs in force. Haftel and Thompson's research design is exemplary, including their choice of BITs as a vehicle to study this important issue. Future work should build on this article.

for concern. Or, alternatively, it would provide some evidence that agreement design matters greatly.[4]

Consider the case where the UNTS population differs from the population of all agreements in force due to the failure of certain states to register some or all of their agreements. This scenario seems much more compelling in terms of a divergence between the observed population, in this case agreements registered with the UNTS, and a population of interest, consisting of all international agreements in force. What is more, it is easy to imagine factors such as the quality of a state's diplomatic corps that would affect both whether agreements get registered and decisions about agreement design. This potential divergence suggests a future research agenda for area specialists: one could collect data in Namibia and Angola, which are two of the states that ratify the fewest agreements in the COIL sample. One question is whether these states simply do not enter into very many international agreements or the agreements in which they do enter are often not registered with the UNTS. If the latter is true, one could subject those agreements to the sorts of analyses in this book to see whether the COIL conjectures explain design or not.[5]

As a final example, consider the study of American exceptionalism as it manifests itself in the realm of international agreements. A natural question in that context concerns whether the characteristics of international agreements that the United States ratifies differ from the characteristics of agreements that other states (or perhaps some subset of other states, such as other democracies) ratify? Such a study necessarily has as its population of interest the population of all agreements in force and registered with the UNTS (since this is the route such states use). Using a sample from that population, a researcher might also investigate other questions of interest, such as the following: Does the United States participate in fewer international agreements than other states? Is the nature of these agreements unique? If so, at the level of issue area? At the level of commitments? If the United States helps create an international institution, does it make sure

---

[4] See the discussion of the Moon Treaty in Chapter 10, which is in force but which has not been ratified by very many states because of its poor design.

[5] If one state acting alone can register an agreement, any such effect would seem to be tempered. That is, only those agreements between or among states for which both or all have "less-developed" diplomatic corps would be less likely to be registered.

it has veto power for major decisions? Does the United States delegate less to international institutions? Does the United States add more reservations to agreements? The relevant population in this context is indeed the set of agreements in force.

Of course, one could also imagine questions that would imply different populations of interest. For example, conditional on consideration of a potential international agreement, does the United States bring more potential agreements to the serious negotiation stage than other states? The example of American exceptionalism illustrates that in some substantive contexts, it may not be a question of just one population always being the population of interest. Instead, there may be multiple populations of interest.

A crucial component of any empirical study consists of defining and defending a choice for the population of interest. This question closely intertwines with the choice of a parameter of interest; in my notational framework, this means a choice between estimation of β_1 and estimation of γ_1. In some substantive contexts, the population of interest may coincide with the observed population, even if the observed population represents a non-random subset of some broader population. *Just because there is selection does not mean there is a selection problem.* It all depends on the question of interest, and that depends on the theory being tested or the policy question being addressed. It does not follow directly from the data.

Are the error terms correlated?

I now proceed to the case where the researcher has decided that the population of interest differs from the observed population, that is, the researcher has decided that β_1 represents the parameter of research interest. That decision leads immediately to an important substantive question: are ε and η correlated? To see what this means in substantive terms, recall that one should think about the error terms as containing all of the unobserved factors that affect the outcome of interest (in the case of ε) or the probability of observation (in the case of η). Unobserved factors that appear in both error terms generate a correlation between them.

As noted in the preceding section, researchers might worry about typically unobserved variables, such as the skill of the diplomatic corps and/or the determination of political leaders to conclude an agreement.

These might generate a correlation between the errors in the outcome equation of interest and the observation equation.

I consider three separate examples wherein the correlation plausibly does equal zero. I devote more time to this case because many readers will find it generically implausible. And, indeed, it may be empirically infrequent. However, such a case of zero correlation is possible, and even in cases where it is *a priori* implausible the research enterprise may benefit from explicit consideration of just why it seems implausible in particular substantive contexts.

As a first example of a plausibly zero correlation, suppose we are trying to estimate if and when the United States' massive power asymmetry is incorporated into the design of its bilateral agreements with much smaller but strategically important states, like its Caribbean neighbors. In this substantive context, do missing agreements between the United States and Cuba pose a problem? We would like to make statements about the population consisting of the United States and all its small but strategically important neighbors, but we do not observe (many) agreements with Cuba, given the history of antagonism between the two states since the Cuban revolution. Thus, the observed population excludes Cuba, but the population of interest includes it.

In this particular example, it is actually possible to estimate the number of *missing agreements* between the United States and Cuba. First, there is an identifiable timeframe: from 1960, when the United States officially breaks diplomatic ties with Cuba, until 2015, at which point diplomatic ties were restored. Second, it is possible to find a state that resembles Cuba in many ways, in particular, in terms of its geography, proximity to the United States, and GDP: the Dominican Republic.[6]

Between 1960 and 2015, there have been only five bilateral agreements registered with the UN between the United States and Cuba. In contrast, over the same time period there have been 56 bilateral agreements between the United States and the Dominican Republic. Among the subjects of those bilateral agreements are military assistance, sale of agricultural commodities, the Cooperative Meteorological Program, postal issues, loans, tax agreements, and missile-testing sites. We can plausibly conjecture that, had the United

---

[6] The Dominican Republic is slightly smaller in population but quite comparable in terms of GDP.

States not broken diplomatic ties with Cuba, there would have been another 51 or so US-Cuban agreements in the UNTS data. The important question at this stage is, had there not been the political shock with Fidel Castro, is there any reason to think that the ensuing US-Cuban agreements would have been designed any differently than the extant ones between the United States and the Dominican Republic? I think probably not. For instance, the same issue areas would certainly be the relevant ones given the similarities between the two states.

Given the research question of whether power asymmetries are reflected in provisions like those governing disputes or monitoring, there is no reason to think the factors that caused Castro to come into power overlap with those governing the relationship between power asymmetries and agreement design. In other words, the reasons the United States broke off ties with Cuba, a decision which ultimately resulted in a set of agreements missing from the observed population, are unrelated to how power asymmetry is reflected in agreement design. Thus there is no reason to think that the error terms in the selection equation and the outcome equation, ε and η, respectively, would have a non-zero correlation in this case. Thus there is no selection problem.

The Cuba example illustrates an important general point. Arguing that the correlation between the two error terms equals zero does not imply a "theory of frivolous commitment-making" to use the colorful phrasing in Simmons and Hopkins (2005). Selection into the observed population from the population of interest may be decidedly non-random, as indeed it is in the Cuba case, and yet still be unrelated to the relationship under study.

Of course, the more that is known about the observation rule, the easier it is to sort out what set of assumptions is most plausible in a given substantive context. *This calls attention to the need for theory and evidence regarding the observation rule itself.*

As an example of a potential observation rule that is theoretically informed, consider Bueno de Mesquita and Smith's (2007) application of selectorate theory, in which they argue that certain pairs of states are more likely to engage in aid-for-policy deals than other states. Selectorate theory, as developed and presented by Bueno de Mesquita et al. (2003), assumes that political leaders are concerned with gaining and then holding on to power and hence need the support of a group of people, who constitute the winning coalition. The size of this winning coalition is a distinct institutional feature of societies and typically (but not necessarily) embodied in constitutions and electoral laws. The members of this winning coalition are drawn from the selectorate, which comprises all citizens who can express an effective preference over the choice of the leader. To stay in power, the political leader needs to gain and maintain the support of the winning coalition. To do so, the leader provides a mix of public and private goods; private goods are handed out to members of the winning coalition exclusively, while public goods benefit everyone. Since private goods are relatively more costly to provide in large numbers, the provision of public goods becomes more attractive to the leader the larger the size of the winning coalition. Hence a key theoretical insight of selectorate theory is that societies with larger winning coalitions provide more public goods, like economic growth, investment in education and the rule of law, and/or an independent judiciary.

Bueno de Mesquita and Smith's (2007) application of this principle rests on a complementarity of interests among states. It is assumed that the citizens in the aid-giving state benefit from a policy concession by the state that is a recipient of the aid. Put differently, the policy concession constitutes a public good for the citizens of the aid-giving state. From selectorate theory, it follows that leaders with large winning coalitions are most likely to seek such aid-for-policy deals. For the recipient state, sacrificing the public good in return for aid is most attractive if its winning coalition is small (relative to the selectorate) since then the policy concession is relatively less expensive and the additional financial resources more valuable. This asymmetry in the winning coalitions of these leaders, in turn, makes the aid-for-policy deal incentive compatible for the pair.

To recap, selection into the observed population for aid-for-policy deals is governed completely by domestic factors like asymmetries in the size of the leaders' winning coalitions. Suppose we are interested in testing a theory about how the presence or absence of an Enforcement problem influences the incorporation of delegated dispute resolution provisions into these deals. We can imagine a situation for which the subject matter of the deal addresses the use of land for military bases in exchange for aid. If the pair of states is the United States and Turkey, both states have low incentives to defect from such a deal given their joint membership in NATO. In other words, the degree of the Enforcement problem is arguably low. There will be no need to delegate dispute resolution to any third party regardless of the size of domestic winning coalitions. More generally, in this example, selection into the observed population will arguably depend on factors largely unrelated to the relationship under study. Hence the correlation between ε and η equals zero.

On the other hand, if we are interested in testing a theory about whether escape clauses are incorporated into aid-for-policy deals, the error terms might indeed be correlated. Escape clauses are incorporated into international agreements in anticipation of unpredictable domestic political shocks that might require temporary suspension of the cooperative endeavor while the domestic house is put back in order. The potential for such shocks and the need for the government to be able to respond to them by invoking an escape clause is determined in part by some of the same, unobserved factors that determine the size of the winning coalitions and whether the typical goods provided by the government are public or not. In this example, then, it is likely that the error terms, ε and η, are correlated, and thus there exists a selection problem because the observed population is not a random subset of the population of interest.

One final example of an argument in favor of a zero correlation builds on the notion that the difference between the observed population and the population of interest may result from differences in the speed with which learning about how to structure the agreement occurs in different contexts. The following quote from renowned international law scholar Richard Bilder, who spent years in the US State Department negotiating real international agreements, provides insight in this regard. Bilder (1963: 335) is speaking to the history leading up to the series of successful (for the governments, not so much for coffee drinkers) international coffee agreements that are described in Chapters 4 and 10 and that governed this international commodity from 1962 until 1989.

The growth of international cooperation with respect to coffee is fairly typical of such developments in other areas in the international economic field. At first, each country attempts to deal with the problem on its own. However, since no one country is ordinarily in a position either to control the international market or to effectively insulate itself from it, these unilateral measures have only an indifferent degree of success, and there is a slowly growing realization that the problem cannot be successfully dealt with in this way. A considerable period may follow in which the countries concerned

slowly grope towards bilateral and then multilateral solutions. The problem
is discussed in various international meetings, study groups are formed, and
tentative and often unsuccessful first experiments at international
agreements are made. During this incubation period, problems are
gradually defined, possibilities grasped, experience accumulated, and
policies crystalized. Also, the principal government and industry officials
concerned get to know their counterparts in other countries and to
understand each other's views. Finally, the climate of international opinion
in the field may at last be prepared for substantial innovation, and the stage
set for an attempt at effective agreement.

This quote is important more generally because it illustrates two vital
points: first, there has to be a realization/learning that cooperation is
Pareto-improving and therefore that an agreement is useful; second,
cooperation problems, like Uncertainty about Preferences, must be
below a certain threshold for cooperation to be undertaken. Thus, one
could view all the years of not seeing a coffee agreement as part of the
"near-misses" population or (and more consistent with Bilder, who is
a real-life negotiator), these same years could be characterized as ones
during which states are learning enough to bring a cooperative endeavor
into the Pareto-improving category. For theories of agreement design,
the latter makes more sense. Once a cooperative endeavor is recognized
to be at least potentially Pareto-improving, it must be designed optimally
to make that a reality. Theories of international agreement design are
then conditional on states being aware that cooperative endeavors will,
at least in expectation, make them better off.[7] So long as this temporal
process of learning and realization is unrelated to the relationship under
study, differences between the population of interest and the observed
population that arise because of it do not imply a non-zero correlation
and so do not imply a selection problem.

Two final points round out this section. First, the plausibility of
arguments that the correlation between the outcome and selection
equation error terms equals zero depends critically on the set of
available explanatory variables $X_2, \ldots, X_k$ and $Z_1, \ldots, Z_i$. These
variables implicitly define the error terms; put differently,
explanatory variables included among the covariates necessarily are
not included in the errors. Another way of thinking about this is that

---

[7] This statement is consistent with the Keohaen's (1988) quotation earlier in this
appendix.

the higher the explanatory power of a theory (as reflected in measures like the Receiving Operator Characteristic [ROC curve] first discussed in Chapter 3), the more convincing a scholar's argument for zero correlation between the error terms is likely to be.[8] Second, the correlation need not equal zero exactly for it to make sense to impose a zero correlation, or at least to take seriously the zero correlation case when doing an empirical study. Sartori (2003) makes this clear by delving into cases for which the correlation differs from zero but only modestly so.

Measuring the population of interest

In cases where the population of interest does not coincide with the observed population and where the error terms in the outcome and selection equations have a non-zero correlation, a further implementation issue may arise in some substantive contexts: Can the researcher enumerate the members of the population of interest? The standard methods for dealing with the selection problem require that the researcher enumerate the population of interest (or at least somehow define a random sample from that population). Enumeration is required so that the researcher can estimate a version of the selection equation (2). In the context of international law, such estimation requires data on both observed agreements and latent agreements. Obtaining sufficient data on the latent agreements to estimate equation (2) implies the ability to enumerate those agreements; put more formally, *enumerability is a necessary but not sufficient condition for the application of standard selection correction methods.*

A few examples should help to make the point. First, consider a study of the existence (or not) of alliances. For each pair of states, we can think of the presence of an alliance relationship as a binary outcome equal to 1 in the presence of an alliance and 0 otherwise. As the number of states is small and finite, it is easy to enumerate all possible dyads and thus all possible patterns of alliances. In such a study, equation (2) becomes an additional object of direct scholarly interest, rather than just a way station to obtaining consistent estimates

---

[8] I use the word "likely" because it is not necessarily the case that greater explanatory power implies less of a selection problem. Put differently, the claim does not hold in any formal way but rather as an informal rule of thumb.

of equation (1) for a population other than the population of observed alliances.

Indeed, some researchers have already enumerated the full set of possible alliances. The three most important studies are Lai and Reiter (2000), Leeds et al. (2002), and Gibler and Sarkees (2004). These studies differ in terms of the data set used – Lai and Reiter (2000) and Gibler and Sarkees (2004) use Correlates of War (COW) data, while Leeds et al. (2002) use their Alliance Treaty Obligations and Provisions (ATOP) data. These studies also differ in terms of the time periods considered – Lai and Reiter consider 1816–1991, Leeds et al. consider 1815–1944, and Gibler and Sarkees examine 1816–2000. All three studies estimate equation (2) using a probit model where the dependent variable is coded 1 if a dyad has any kind of alliance (defensive, offensive, or neutrality pact) in a given year and coded 0 otherwise. The key point here is that, if we know the set of alliances that did not form and the characteristics of the states that did not form them, we can generate the data required to estimate equation (2).

Suppose now a researcher wants to study the effects of Uncertainty about the State of the World on agreement duration. Suppose further that the researcher wants to study this relationship for the population consisting of observed and near-miss environmental agreements. Enumerating the observed agreements poses no problems when using, for example, the UNTS or Mitchell's International Environmental Agreements (IEA) database to define the population. In contrast, counting near-misses requires more work in two senses. First, just what constitutes a near-miss (as opposed to a more distant miss) requires careful thought and definition. Second, the researcher must scour the Internet and other sources to find all of the near-misses, however she defines them. Depending on the expansiveness of the definition, and the degree of secrecy surrounding the particular issue area, this may or may not yield the relevant population with reasonable certainty.

Poast's (2011) study illustrates the point that the absence of systematic, reliable data on failed negotiations is an obstacle not easily overcome. Poast (2011) addresses this problem for one narrow sub-issue area: military alliances. In his context, he can rely on decades of archival research already conducted by historians and draw on a variety of published diplomatic histories to obtain information on members of the population of near-misses. This research design works well for his topic, but is not without its shortcomings despite the relatively rich data environment. For instance, published accounts are mostly European, with other regions of the world not well represented, raising questions about residual non-random selection into the observed population.

More generally, a researcher can enumerate all possible agreements whenever the number of potential parties is finite and whenever having an agreement or not can be coded as a simple binary variable (or even as a multinomial variable). *The key is that the number of possible agreements be finite.* The population becomes impossible to enumerate when agreements have one or more continuous dimensions. Thus, for example, the population of all possible environmental agreements between states cannot be enumerated because environmental agreements have multiple dimensions, many of which are naturally continuous. To pick one relevant case: Agreements to limit greenhouse gas emissions are continuous in the amount of reduction assigned to each party to the agreement *and* in the mechanisms proposed for the reductions *and* in the time frame over which reductions are to occur. Thus, to use formal mathematical jargon, there are uncountably infinitely many possible agreements of this sort even between a single pair of states. Going back to the alliance example, if we are interested in the substantive depth of alliances, we are back in the world of an *uncountably infinite number of possible agreements*. In fact, going further, *at any point in time, a pair of states could replace an alliance agreement with a different one that was substantively shallower or deeper*; taking a very broad view of near-misses, each period in which the states do not replace one agreement with a shallower or deeper one, another infinitely large set of "near-miss" agreements is generated.

In the case where the latent population can be enumerated, the researcher can, in principle, create a data set with an observation corresponding to every observation in the latent population. Of course, the researcher typically does not observe some or all of the characteristics of the latent agreements but usually does observe the characteristics of the parties to the latent agreements, which may allow the use of the statistical strategies Koremenos and Smith outline in their paper.

In cases where the researcher cannot enumerate the population of potential agreements, she must choose one of three alternatives. First, the researcher can abandon the project. This alternative follows naturally from the view that β_1 is really the object of interest and that there is no way to solve the selection problem and thus recover a plausible estimate of β_1, given the absence of statistical tools for handling the case where we cannot enumerate the latent population. Second, the researcher can proceed using only the population of observed agreements while providing strong theoretical and/or empirical reasons for believing that the selection problem does not loom large in the particular context under study. This is the (underused) path of the previous section and the one that applies to the analyses in this book. Third, the researcher can decide that γ_1 is actually the parameter of interest rather than β_1. This strategy works well in the example of how the United States differs from other states in the kind of agreements it ratifies. The research question focuses on outcomes conditional on being observed. Though this strategy looks the same as the second alternative in terms of what gets estimated and reported, it differs in the interpretation placed on the estimates.

Addressing the selection problem

The bivariate normal selection model

The bivariate normal selection model comes into play in cases for which the population of interest does not coincide with the observed population, the correlation between the unobserved components of the outcome and selection equations differs from zero, and the population of interest is enumerable. Koremenos and Smith detail the assumptions, estimation, and identification of this model. Here I only want to summarize and emphasize one point that is relevant to the analysis in Chapter 4: The bivariate normal selection model should not be employed with the same control variables in the selection and outcome equations. The literature offers strong reasons, both theoretical and practical, for instead adding an additional variable to the selection equation but not to the outcome equation. In the terminology of this literature, the variable represents an *exclusion restriction* because the researcher excludes it from the outcome equation while including it in the selection equation.

Variables used as exclusion restrictions must have two very important properties. First, they need to strongly predict observation. Put differently, they need to matter, in both the statistical and substantive senses, in equation (2). This condition has the nice feature that the researcher can easily verify it by checking the magnitude and statistical significance of the coefficient on the exclusion restriction variable (or variables) when estimating (2). The second property is that the exclusion restriction variable does not affect the outcome other than through its effect on whether or not an observation is observed. In formal terms, the exclusion restriction must be uncorrelated with the outcome equation error term, ε. Put differently, the path of simply dropping a variable from the outcome equation while leaving it in the selection equation does not, in most cases, lead to a valid exclusion restriction. Rather, the researcher has to make a case based on theory and/or existing empirical evidence that the excluded variable really does not "belong" in the outcome equation.

In many contexts, the available data may lack a compelling exclusion restriction. In other cases, as in Chapter 4, the theory does not provide a compelling exclusion restriction. That absence does not justify estimation of the bivariate normal model with the same covariates in the selection and outcome equations. It also does not imply that the researcher should toss in the towel. Rather, it means that the researcher should proceed with the sort of sensitivity analysis described next.

Sensitivity analysis

In substantive contexts that lack a plausible exclusion restriction variable, Koremenos and Smith recommend that authors provide a sensitivity analysis along the lines laid out in Altonji, Elder, and Taber (2006). Koremenos and Smith provide the technical details. The basic idea is that, instead of estimating the correlation of the two error terms, $\rho_{\varepsilon\eta}$, various values of this correlation, which necessarily lies in the interval $[-1, 1]$, can be imposed when estimating the two equations jointly. This style of sensitivity analysis represents a generalization of the procedure advocated by Sartori (2003), which focuses solely on the cases where the correlation equals zero, one, or negative one.

A table of estimates based on varying values of $\rho_{\varepsilon\eta}$ clearly indicates the empirical sensitivity of estimates of the parameters of interest to the extent of selection on unobserved variables. Such a table should include as a benchmark estimates corresponding to $\rho_{\varepsilon\eta} = 0$, the case of no selection on unobserved variables into the observed population.

The estimates obtained in any particular substantive context might or might not reveal a substantial amount of sensitivity. If they do not, the researcher can confidently report that her estimates are robust to selection into the observed population based on unobserved variables. In the more likely case where the table reveals substantial sensitivity, the researcher must then apply prior knowledge about the nature and extent of the selection problem, with the goal of narrowing down the range of substantive uncertainty. In many contexts, the researcher will have a pretty clear a priori idea of the likely sign of the bias; this eliminates values of $\rho_{\varepsilon\eta}$ in either $(0, 1)$ or $(-1, 0)$ and will often greatly reduce the amount of uncertainty regarding the parameters of interest.

In other cases, the researcher may even have some idea about the extent of the selection on observed variables problem, perhaps because of strong prior beliefs about the particular unobserved variables generating the correlation and their importance in determining both selection and outcomes. The substantive discussion in Sartori (2003: 117) illustrates the kind of reasoning that researchers should use to justify particular prior beliefs about the correlation.

Summing up

First, the bivariate normal selection model is relevant only to cases wherein the population of interest does not coincide with the observed population, the correlation between the unobserved components of the outcome and selection equations differs from zero, and the researcher can enumerate the population well enough to implement the estimator. Second, even within that set of cases, estimation should proceed only when the researcher can make a compelling case for at least one exclusion restriction variable (i.e., one variable that belongs in the selection equation but not the outcome equation) and that variable has non-trivial predictive power in the selection equation. In the absence of a compelling exclusion restriction, the researcher should conduct and then carefully interpret a sensitivity analysis.

The example of the Comprehensive Test Ban Treaty

The Comprehensive Test Ban Treaty (CTBT) is an instructive case. The CTBT has been adopted by the UN General Assembly, has been ratified by 164 states, but is not in force because China, Egypt, India,

Iran, Israel, North Korea, Pakistan, and the United States have not yet ratified it. The case challenges us to think about how, depending on our research question as well as our assumptions about selection into the observed population, the same agreement could be part of the observed population, part of the latent population, or part of neither.

Underlying the CTBT are some particularly challenging cooperation problems. In this sensitive issue area, abiding by the treaty terms without knowing if other states are abiding by these same terms (the problem of Uncertainty about Behavior) is risky given that at least some actors have incentives to defect (Enforcement problem). The theoretical framework employed in this book, specifically Chapter 9, draws attention to the need for some kind of centralized monitoring system in environments like these. According to the following quote from the US State Department, the verification system in place when the CTBT was ratified by many states but not by the United States and some other powerful states was found lacking in its ability to monitor reliably the actions of other states: "It has been 12 years since our Senate failed to give its advice and consent to the ratification of the CTBT. Lack of support stemmed from two concerns: the verifiability of the Treaty and the continuing safety and reliability of America's nuclear deterrent without nuclear explosive testing."[9]

Thus the CTBT has not entered into force for one or both of the following reasons: (1) The cooperation problem of Uncertainty about Behavior was not adequately resolved or mitigated by the design provision; (2) The agreement was not found to be Pareto-improving from the United States' (and probably others') point of view. If (1) is correct, this case study of a "failed" agreement provides anecdotal evidence in support of the theoretical framework. Importantly, this case does not imply anything about the rationality of the negotiating states; rather, the inability of states to resolve the Uncertainty about Behavior could be attributable to inadequate technology. It is "rational" therefore not to ratify an agreement if one's partners in cooperation might be able to defect without being caught.

Just as interesting, this case calls attention to how changes over time, in this case technological advances, can bring to the table solutions to

---

[9] US Department of State. CTBT Article XIV Conference. Remarks by Ellen Tauscher, Under Secretary for Arms Control and International Security. New York City, September 23, 2011. Available at www.state.gov/t/us/173890. htm [Last accessed July 13, 2015].

problems that were difficult to solve in the past. According to the
US State Department:

The International Monitoring System (IMS) is a worldwide network of
observational technology that will help to verify compliance with and
detect and confirm violations of the Comprehensive Nuclear Test-Ban
Treaty (CTBT).

When complete, the IMS will consist of 337 monitoring facilities. It will be
complemented by an intrusive on-site inspection regime applicable once the
Treaty has entered into force. The CTBTO's [Comprehensive Test Ban
Treaty Organization] experts are confident that their system can aid in the
detection and identification of nuclear explosions anywhere on the planet.

In 1999, there were no certified IMS stations or facilities in place. Today the
IMS is more than 80 percent complete.[10]

Given this technological progress, we can make a theoretically based
prediction about the United States' future behavior regarding
ratification.

   Thus, the COIL framework proves instructive in understanding why
the United States has not ratified the CTBT and thus one of the reasons
the treaty remains a near-miss. It also helps us understand why the
United States' behavior may change (and perhaps the behavior of other
states, too), thereby bringing the treaty into the non-failed observed
population. The identification of a failed treaty thus allowed us to
probe the theoretical framework regarding its explanatory power on
that front.

   The CTBT is also useful in challenging us to think about the
importance of defining the time period before a near-miss agreement is
considered truly failed. As the Bilder quote regarding coffee cooperation
underlines, it often takes time before states understand their interests in
joint cooperation or find the political will to solve their joint problems.
For every agreement in force that is part of the observed population,
there existed a period during which the agreement was not a part of the
observed population. This period could have comprised, for example,
the period before negotiations started, the often-long negotiations
themselves, or the time during which some but not all critical states
have ratified the agreement. With respect to this last "hurdle," often

[10] US Department of State. CTBT: International Monitoring System. Available at
www.state.gov/t/avc/rls/159267.htm [Last accessed July 13, 2015].

the delay is not attributable to the treaty substance or its design, but is due to the domestic institutions in a state or its internal politics. The United States in particular has quite a few veto players when it comes to treaty ratification, given the role of the US Senate in many key treaties, and often there is simply not enough time to consider every international agreement. There are also examples where a lag in ratification is not attributable to the treaty but rather is collateral damage from the broader conflicts between particular political parties, for example, the delayed but eventual ratification of the New START Treaty.

In the case of the CTBT, there is now an understanding according to the State Department, partly due to technological advances, that the CTBT is in the United States' interest:

> With regard to our nuclear deterrent, our extensive surveillance methods and computational modeling developed under the Stockpile Stewardship Program over the last 15 years have allowed our nuclear experts to understand how these weapons work and the effects of aging even better than when nuclear explosive testing was conducted. The United States can maintain a safe and effective nuclear deterrent without conducting nuclear explosive tests.[11]

Twelve years ago, the Senate decided it was not in the United States' interest to ratify the treaty. In other words, it was not in the Pareto-improving set according to that veto player. Now, both time has passed (with the understanding and technology time brings) and a slightly different Senate holds power. Thus at any point the treaty could change categories. The methodological question is, should it be in the latent population until then?

To summarize, the CTBT sheds light on the theoretical model even without being in force. More important for this appendix, the CTBT, because it is likely to be in force eventually, could be considered by some researchers to be a part of the *observed population*. This same treaty could also be considered part of the *latent population* if we define it as treaties that have been discussed, negotiated, and/or approved, if not entered into force. And it could be part of *neither the observed nor latent population* if we consider only treaties that parties consider as

---

[11] See Appendix 3, fn. 9.

potentially Pareto-improving as the population of interest, which is the most plausible for this book given the main research questions.

Subjecting the duration provisions analyses to sensitivity analysis

The choice of the length of a finite duration agreement is conditional on states choosing a finite-duration agreement. That is, states first select into the finite duration set of agreements. Recall from Chapter 4 that the same three variables are hypothesized to affect both states' choice of finite versus indefinite duration agreements and the length of the former if chosen: Uncertainty about the State of the World, Number of Actors, and Preference Heterogeneity. This specification does not include an exclusion restriction, and indeed the COIL data do not contain a plausible exclusion restriction variable. That is, the data contain no theoretically justified variable that I could add to the selection equation that explains when states choose finite versus indefinite agreements and leave out of the outcome equation that explains the length of the finite-duration agreement.

In this situation, a formal sensitivity analysis is called for, and it is incumbent upon the researcher to provide an a priori justification of the likely bias. That is, is there a reason to believe the error terms in the selection equation and outcome equation are positively correlated, negatively correlated, et cetera?

Consider first the selection equation. In addition to the explanatory variables of Uncertainty about the State of the World, Number of actors, and Preference Heterogeneity, what else might affect states' choice to conclude finite or indefinite agreements? Put differently, what might be in the error term? It seems reasonable that something about a negotiator's experience designing other international agreements could factor into whether they are inclined to choose finite versus indefinite agreements. While it is not the thesis of this book, some scholars argue that states follow a template in designing agreements. If other agreements in the issue area have a lot of flexibility incorporated into them, negotiators might be more inclined to choose a finite duration.

Consider now the outcome equation. The same unobserved factors that lead a negotiator to prefer a finite duration agreement are likely to influence their choice for a shorter agreement and vice versa. Thus if a negotiator simply has a philosophy that flexible agreements are superior or has had a lot of experience negotiating flexible agreements or has seen a template where flexibility is key, they will prefer a shorter rather than longer agreement just as they preferred a finite duration agreement to an indefinite duration agreement.

The main point is that the kind of factors that encourage a negotiator to choose a finite duration, such as templates or a general preference for flexibility, will also encourage that same negotiator to make the agreement shorter, given that it is of finite duration. As such, given that the dependent variable in the selection equation is finite or not while the dependent variable in the outcome equation is the length of a finite duration agreement, we would strongly expect the error terms to be negatively correlated.

Are there any countervailing factors? One such factor might be that some negotiators prefer finite duration agreements because they think it is a good idea to force periodic renegotiation, but do not have strong preferences over how long the finite duration should be. The domestic analogue would be a preference for "sunset" provisions in bills that force occasional reconsideration of the issue area by the legislature. Given this additional concern, my prior is that there is a strong negative correlation, most likely somewhere between −0.6 and −0.9, between the two error terms.

Figure A.1 shows how the marginal effects from the selection equation vary as the value of rho (the correlation between the error terms) is fixed at different values. The marginal effects represent average derivatives of the estimated conditional probability of a finite duration agreement with respect to the corresponding independent variable. Because the marginal effects have a clearer substantive interpretation than the probit coefficients, I focus on them in the discussion here; looking at the coefficients instead does not (as one would expect it to not) change the qualitative story.

In Figure A.1, each point in each graph represents the marginal effect of a particular independent variable in the probit equation for whether or not the agreement is of finite duration as part of the two-equation system with the correlation between the two error terms (the rho) fixed at the value indicated on the horizontal axis. Each of the three graphs corresponds to a particular independent variable, but the underlying statistical model is the same across the three graphs for each value of rho. Moving along the horizontal axis reveals how the estimated

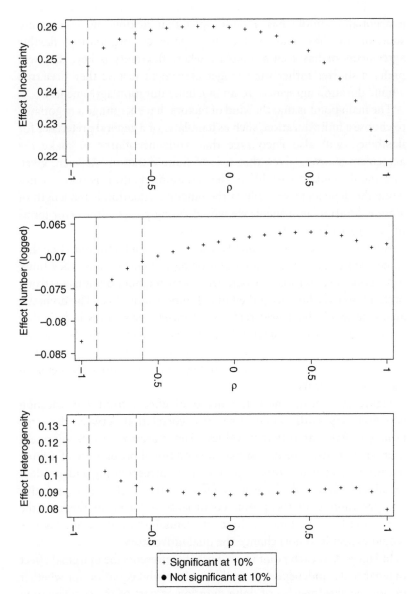

Figure A.1 Sensitivity analysis – finite duration, marginal effects

marginal effect varies as the extent of correlation between the two error terms varies between −1.0 and 1.0 in increments of 0.1.

Similarly, in Figure A.2 each point in each graph represents the coefficient on a particular independent variable in the regression equation for the duration of finite duration agreements as part of the two-equation system with rho fixed at the value indicated on the horizontal axis. The regression coefficients correspond to the selection-corrected equation given the level of selection on unobserved variables represented by each rho. The remainder of the interpretation is the same as for Figure A.1.

In the figures, vertical bars demark the region of rho that corresponds to my prior as developed above. As indicated in the legend of the figure, the plusses correspond to estimates that differ statistically from zero at the ten percent level, whereas circles correspond to estimates that do not differ statistically from zero at that level.

Figures A.1 and A.2 provide evidence on the extent to which the model for the full population of all agreements differs from the model for the observed population of finite duration agreements. In the notation of this appendix, the figures provide evidence on the extent to which the betas differ from the gammas. If the coefficient estimate changes little as rho changes, this implies robustness to selection into the observed population on unobserved variables. If the coefficient estimate changes a lot as rho changes, the substantive conclusion depends on views about this degree of selection. The case of rho equal to zero corresponds to the case of no selection on unobserved variables, in which separate estimation of the length equation yields estimates that apply to the full population of agreements.

Now consider the substantive results, starting with the selection equation in Figure A.1.[12] The top graph in Figure A.1 considers the uncertainty measure. The theory predicts that the probability of a finite duration agreement should increase in the degree of Uncertainty about the State of the World, as indeed I find in the rho = 0 case shown in Table 4.3. The sensitivity analysis indicates the robustness of this finding. The coefficient changes little for negative values of rho,

---

[12] This discussion focuses on the sensitivity of the results from the two-part model rather than on the Tobit results because the two-equation model imposes fewer restrictions on the data.

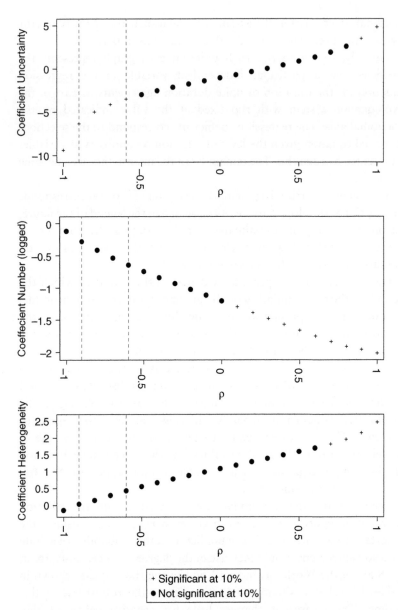

+ Significant at 10%
● Not significant at 10%

Figure A.2 Sensitivity analysis – length of finite duration, coefficient estimates

which I have argued represent the most likely case, and remains positive and statistically significant. For my priors on rho, Uncertainty about the State of the World increases the probability of a finite duration agreement by over 25 percentage points. Even with positive rho, though the magnitude decreases somewhat as rho increases, the estimated marginal effect remains positive, large in magnitude, and statistically significant for all values of rho. Thus no matter what the degree of selection, the findings about the cooperation problem of Uncertainty about the State of the World hold.

The middle graph in Figure A.1 shows the results for the natural log of the Number of participants. Based on the earlier discussion, we would expect the probability of a finite agreement to decrease with the Number of participants. As shown in Table 4.3 for my main results, I do find this pattern in the data. Indeed, I find a negative and statistically significant estimated effect. Recall that the main analysis corresponds to the assumption that rho equals zero. As rho becomes increasingly negative in Figure A.1, the point estimate becomes slightly more negative. Thus, in this case the sensitivity analysis confirms strongly the finding in the main text; in fact, no matter what the degree of selection, the findings about the relationship between Number and finite durations hold.

The bottom graph in Figure A.1 shows the results for the Preference Heterogeneity variable based on UN General Assembly voting (UNGA). In this case, the sensitivity analysis again reveals a stable finding relative to the rho equals zero case presented in Table 4.3 in the main text. As rho becomes increasingly negative, the marginal effect remains positive and statistically significant, with the magnitude increasing a bit for large negative values of rho. For positive values, the marginal effect remains resolutely around 0.09 and statistically significant. These results are stronger with respect to the theoretical prediction of H4-5 than are the ones in the main text.

The sensitivity analysis of the regression equation for the length of finite duration agreements presented in Figure A.2 yields somewhat different findings. The top graph addresses the uncertainty variable. The theory predicts that increasing Uncertainty about the State of the World should reduce agreement duration. The two-part model, with rho equals zero provides a negative but not statistically significant estimate. Moving rho away from zero and toward the negative values I think are most plausible increases the magnitude of the negative effect, which attains statistical significance for values of rho in the region of the prior I argued for above. In stark contrast, for positive values of rho, the estimated coefficient turns positive, and for rho greater than or equal to 0.9 attains statistical significance. In this case, unlike the other variables, the nature of the prior regarding selection into having a finite duration agreement based on unobserved variables really matters. It is worth repeating that a positive correlation between the error terms cannot be theoretically justified; considering this area of the graph is merely a hypothetical exercise. Thus the results regarding Uncertainty about the State of the World are robust to selection.

The middle graph in Figure A.2 presents the results for the variable measuring the Number of participants. Recall that in Table 4.5 I found a positive and statistically significant coefficient estimate of almost 17 years. The sensitivity analysis reveals a very different result. The two-part model, with rho equal to zero, provides a negative and statistically insignificant estimate. Moving rho away from zero and toward the negative values I think are most plausible, the coefficient becomes less negative, remaining statistically insignificant and reaching a magnitude of about zero for rho = -1.0. Within the range of my prior it is both relatively small in magnitude and statistically insignificant. This finding suggests tempering the conclusion in the text. Once one controls for selection, the Number of participants, while encouraging a finite duration agreement, has no effect on the length of that agreement.

The final graph looks at the Preference Heterogeneity variable. Here the estimate is positive but not statistically significant for the rho equals zero case. The same is true, though with a point estimate much closer to zero, for the negative values of rho corresponding to my prior. On the other side of the graph, for positive values of rho, the estimated coefficient is positive and reasonably large, and for rho greater or equal to 0.7 attains statistical significance.

In sum, all three theoretical variables survive the sensitivity analysis with respect to the choice of finite versus indefinite duration; nonetheless, with respect to the length of that duration, only the underlying cooperation problem of Uncertainty about the State of the World retains the predicted sign and statistical significance, with the Number and Preference Heterogeneity variables showing neither substantive nor statistical significance.

Conclusion

This appendix provides a series of steps that all researchers, especially those studying international agreements, should take into account when thinking about selection problems. I describe briefly a set of solutions in cases for which the researcher has made a compelling case that a selection problem does exist. In some cases, the solutions will not always work, but this does not imply that we should not study the related aspect of international agreements; rather, a sensitivity analysis allows researchers to draw some tentative conclusions. Moreover, I have emphasized the importance of theory and evidence in justifying particular choices about how best to address selection problems, sharing the general view of Simmons and Hopkins (2005: 623) that "[c]hoosing to attack selection bias statistically rather than theoretically and empirically may account for selection 'problems' without shedding much light on them." Dealing with selection requires intellectual engagement, not just knowledge of statistics.

More to the point of this book, the appendix makes clear that we should not shoot from the hip when it comes to criticizing scholarship on the basis of an assumed selection bias. Both researchers and their critics must think through the issues laid out in this appendix. It might be the case, as it usually is with respect to the COIL research program as well as similar research programs on international law, that the sample used represents a random subset of the population of interest. The fact that the SALT II agreement[13] is missing from our data sets is not problematic if we are interested in agreement design. SALT II is missing because of the Soviet invasion of Afghanistan, a variable not typically included in theories of agreement design.[14] It might also be the case that the theory being tested is itself conditional on agreements

---

[13] The Strategic Arms Limitation Talks (SALT) II were a series of nuclear arms control negotiations between the United States and the Soviet Union, held between 1972 and 1979. Their objective was to build on the agreements produced by SALT I in 1972, which limited the parties' manufacture of strategic nuclear arms. Both parties signed the SALT II agreement in 1979, but the United States did not ratify it in response to the Soviet invasion of Afghanistan in December 1979. Interestingly, SALT II was for the most part followed despite not having entered in force.

[14] In this case, we can analyze SALT II, and even examine it within the context of bilateral arms control agreements that came before and after, to verify that it was not something about its design or substance that caused it to be "failed."

making it into the observed population, a point nicely illustrated by negotiator Richard Bilder. Agreement design makes sense as a topic only when states realize or decide cooperation is potentially Pareto-improving. Whichever argument is more compelling, the implication is the same: The selection problem is minimal for the questions asked in this book.

References

Abbott, Kenneth W. 1989. "Modern International Relations Theory: A Prospectus for International Lawyers." *Yale Journal of International Law* 14: 335–411.

    1993. "Trust but Verify: The Production of Information in Arms Control Treaties and Other International Agreements." *Cornell International Law Journal* 26 (1): 1–58.

Abbott, Kenneth W., and Duncan Snidal. 1998. "Why States Act through Formal Organizations." *Journal of Conflict Resolution* 42: 3–32.

    2000. "Hard and Soft Law in International Governance." *International Organization* 54 (3): 421–456.

    2013. "Law, Legalization and Politics: An Agenda for the Next Generation of IR-IL Scholars." In *Interdisciplinary Perspectives on International Law and International Relations: The State of the Art*, eds. Jeffrey L. Dunoff and Mark A. Pollack. Cambridge: Cambridge University Press.

Abbott, Kenneth W., Robert O. Keohane, Andrew Moravcsik, Anne-Marie Slaughter, and Duncan Snidal. 2000. "The Concept of Legalization." *International Organization* 54 (3): 401–419.

Allee, Todd, and Clint Peinhardt. 2010. "Delegating Differences: Bilateral Investment Treaties and Bargaining Over Dispute Resolution Provisions." *International Studies Quarterly* 54 (1): 1–26.

Alston, Philip, and James Crawford. 2000. *The Future of UN Human Rights Treaty Monitoring*. Cambridge: Cambridge University Press.

Alter, Karen J. 2013. "The Multiple Roles of International Courts and Tribunals: Enforcement, Dispute Settlement, Constitutional and Administrative Review." In *Interdisciplinary Perspectives on International Law and International Relations: The State of the Art*, eds. Jeffrey L. Dunoff, and Mark A. Pollack. Cambridge: Cambridge University Press.

    2014. *The New Terrain of International Law: Courts, Politics, Rights*. Princeton, NJ: Princeton University Press.

Altonji, Joseph, Todd Elder, and Christopher Taber. 2005. "Selection on Observed and Unobserved Variables: Assessing the Effectiveness of Catholic Schools." *Journal of Political Economy* 113 (1): 151–184.

Arrow, Kenneth J. 1951. *Social Choice and Individual Values*. New Haven, New York/London: J. Wiley/Chapman & Hall.

Aust, Anthony. 1986. "The Theory and Practice of Informal International Agreements." *International and Comparative Law Quarterly* 35 (4): 787–812.

Avant, Deborah D., Martha Finnemore, and Susan K. Sell, eds. 2010. *Who Governs The Globe?* Cambridge: Cambridge University Press.

Axelrod, Robert. 1984. *The Evolution of Cooperation*. New York: Basic Books.

Axelrod, Robert, and Robert O. Keohane. 1985. "Achieving Cooperation under Anarchy: Strategies and Institutions." *World Politics* 38: 226–254.

Baccini, Leonardo. 2010. "Explaining Formation and Design of EU Trade Agreements: The Role of Transparency and Flexibility." *European Union Politics* 11 (2): 195–217.

Bailey, Michael, Anton Strezhnev, and Erik Voeten. "Estimating Dynamic State Preferences from United Nations Voting Data." *Journal of Conflict Resolution*. Forthcoming. Available at SSRN http://ssrn.com/abstract=2330913 [Last accessed June 13, 2015].

Baldwin, Edward, Mark Kantor, and Michael Nolan. 2006. "Limits to Enforcement of ICSID Awards." *Journal of International Arbitration* 23 (1): 1–24.

Barceló, John J. III. 2009. "Burden of Proof, Prima Facie Case and Presumption in WTO Dispute Settlement." *Cornell International Law Journal* 42 (23): 23–43.

Barry, Brian. 1980. "Is it Better to be Powerful or Lucky? Part 2." *Political Studies* 28 (3): 338–352.

Bates, Robert. 1997. *Open-Economy Politics: The Political Economy of the World Coffee Trade*. Princeton, NJ: Princeton University Press.

Bederman, David J. 2010. *International Law Frameworks*. Concepts and Insights Series., 3rd ed. New York: Foundation Press.

Bednar, Jenna. 2011. "The Political Science of Federalism." *Annual Review of Law and Social Science* 7: 269–288.

   2014. "Subsidiarity and Robustness: Building the Adaptive Efficiency of Federal Systems." In *NOMOS LV: Federalism and Subsidiarity*, eds. J. E. Fleming, and J. Levy. New York: New York University Press.

Bennett, D. Scott, and Allan Stam. 2000. "*EUGene*: A Conceptual Manual." *International Interactions* 26: 179–204.

Berman, Paul Schiff. 2006. "Review Essay: 'Seeing Beyond the Limits of International Law'." Review of The Limits of International Law by Jack Goldsmith and Eric Posner. *Texas Law Review* 84 (5): 1265–1306.

Bernheim, Douglas B., and Michael D. Whinston. 1990. "Multimarket Contact and Collusive Behavior." *The Rand Journal of Economics* 21 (1): 1–26.

Betz, Timm, and Barbara Koremenos. 2016. "Monitoring Provisions in International Agreements." In *Oxford Handbook on International Organizations*, eds. Jacob Cogan, Ian Hurd, and Ian Johnstone. Oxford: Oxford University Press.

Bilder, Richard. 1963. "The International Coffee Agreement: A Case History in Negotiation." *Law and Contemporary Problems* 28 (2): 328–391.

Blake, Daniel J. 2013. "Thinking Ahead: Government Time Horizons and the Legalization of International Investment Agreements." *International Organizations* 67 (4): 797–827.

Blake, Daniel J., and Autumn Lockwood Payton. 2014. "Balancing Design Objectives: Analyzing New Data on Voting Rules in Intergovernmental Organizations." *Review of International Organizations* September 2014: 1–26.

Bodansky, Daniel. 1999. "The Legitimacy of International Governance: A Coming Challenge for International Environmental Law." *American Journal of International Law* 93 (3): 596–624.

2013. "Legitimacy in International Law and International Relations." In *Interdisciplinary Perspectives on International Law and International Relations: The State of the Art*, eds. Jeffrey L. Dunoff, and Mark A. Pollack. Cambridge University Press.

Börzel, Tanja A., and Thomas Risse. 2012. "From Europeanisation to Diffusion: Introduction." *West European Politics* 35 (1):1–19.

Bradley, Curtis A., and Jack L. Goldsmith. 2000. "Treaties, Human Rights, and Conditional Consent." *Pennsylvania Law Review* 149 (2): 399–468.

Brewster, Rachel. 2006. "Rule-Based Dispute Resolution in International Trade Law." *Virginia Law Review* 92 (2): 251–288.

Brunnée, Jutta, and Stephen J. Toope. 2010. *Legitimacy and Legality in International Law: An Interactional Account*. Cambridge: Cambridge University Press.

2011. "Interactional International Law: An Introduction." *International Theory*, 3 (2): 307–318.

Buchanan, Allen, and Robert O. Keohane. 2006. "The Legitimacy of Global Governance Institutions." *Ethics and International Affairs* 20 (4): 405–447.

Bueno de Mesquita, Bruce, Alastair Smith, Randolph M. Siverson, and James D. Morrow. 2003. *The Logic of Political Survival*. Cambridge, MA: MIT Press.

Bueno de Mesquita, Bruce and Alastair Smith. 2007. "Foreign Aid and Policy Concessions." *Journal of Conflict Resolution* 51(2): 251–284.

Busch, Marc L. 2000. "Democracy, Consultation, and the Paneling of Disputes under GATT." *Journal of Conflict Resolution* 44 (4): 425–446.

Busch, Marc L., and Eric Reinhardt. 2003. "Developing Countries and General Agreement on Tariffs and Trade/World Trade Organization Dispute Settlement." *Journal of World Trade* 37 (4): 719–735.

Calvert, Randall. 1995. "Rational Actors, Equilibrium and Social Institutions." In *Explaining Social Institutions*, eds. Jack Knight and Itai Sened. Ann Arbor, MI: University of Michigan Press.

Charnovitz, Steve. 2001. "Rethinking WTO Trade Sanctions." *American Journal of International Law* 95 (4): 792–832.

2009. "The Enforcement of WTO Judgements." *Yale Journal of International Law* 34 (2): 558–566.

Chayes, Abram, and Antonia Handler Chayes. 1993. "On Compliance." *International Organization* 47 (2): 175–205.

1995. *The New Sovereignty: Compliance with International Regulatory Agreements*. Cambridge, MA: Harvard University Press.

Chayes, Antonia Handler, Abram Chayes, and Ronald B. Mitchell. 1995. "Active Compliance Management in Environmental Treaties." In *Sustainable Development and International Law*, ed. Winfried Lang. London: Graham and Trotman Ltd.

Choi, Susan. 1995. "Judicial Enforcement of Arbitration Awards Under the ICSID and New York Conventions." *New York University Journal of International Law and Politics* 28 (1): 175–216.

Christakis, Théodore. 2006. "Dénonciation ou retrait dans le cas d'un traité ne contenant pas de dispositions relatives à l'extinction, à la dénonciation ou au retrait – Commentaire de l'article 56 de la Convention de Vienne de 1969 sur le droit des traités." In *Les Conventions de Vienne sur le droit des traités: Commentaire article par article*, eds. Olivier Corten and Pierre Klein. Bruxelles: Ed. Bruylant.

Cogan, Jacob Katz. 2009. "Representation and Power in International Organization: The Operational Constitution and its Critics." *American Journal of International Law* 103 (2): 209–263.

Cohen, Cynthia Price. 1989. "United Nations: Convention on the Rights of the Child." *International Legal Materials* 28 (6): 1448–1476.

Cole, Wade M. 2005. "Sovereignty Relinquished? Explaining Commitment to the International Human Rights Covenants, 1966–1999." *American Sociological Review* 70 (3): 472–495.

Cox, Gary W. 1997. *Making Votes Count: Strategic Coordination in the World's Electoral Systems*. Cambridge: Cambridge University Press.

Cox, Robert W., and Harold Karan Jacobson. 1973. *The Anatomy of Influence; Decision Making In International Organization*. New Haven: Yale University Press.

Dai, Xinyuan. 2002. "Information Systems in Treaty Regimes." *World Politics* 54 (4): 405–436.

Danilenko, Gennady M. 1989. "Outer Space and the Multilateral Treaty-Making Process." *Berkley Technology Law Journal* 4 (2): 217–247.

De Bruyne, Charlotte, and Itay Fischhendler. 2013. "Negotiating Conflict Resolution Mechanisms for Transboundary Water Treaties: A Transaction Cost Approach." *Global Environmental Change* 23 (6): 1841–1851.

De Klemm, Cyrille, and Clare Shine. 1993. "Biological Diversity Conservation and the Law: Legal Mechanisms for Conserving Species and Ecosystems." *IUCN Environmental Policy and Law Paper No. 29.* IUCN, Gland, Switzerland and Cambridge.

Dixon, William J. 1994. "Democracy and the Peaceful Settlement of International Conflict." *American Political Science Review* 88 (March): 14–32.

Donnelly, Jack. 1986. "International Human Rights: A Regime Analysis." *International Organization* 40 (3): 599–642.

    2003. *Universal Human Rights in Theory and Practice*, 2nd Edition. Ithaca, NY: Cornell University Press.

    2008. "The Ethics of Realism." In *The Oxford Handbook of International Law*, eds. Christian Reus-Smit and Duncan Snidal. New York: Oxford University Press.

Dorn, Walter, and Andrew Fulton. 1997. "Securing Compliance with Disarmament Treaties: Carrots, Sticks, and the Case of North Korea." *Global Governance* 3 (1): 17–40.

Downs, George W., and David M. Rocke. 1990. *Tacit Bargaining, Arms Races, and Arms Control.* Ann Arbor, MI: University of Michigan Press.

    1995. *Optimal Imperfection? Domestic Uncertainty and Institutions in International Relations.* Princeton, NJ: Princeton University Press.

Downs, George W., David M. Rocke, and Peter N. Barsoom. 1996. "Is the Good News About Compliance Good News About Cooperation?" *International Organization* 50 (3): 379–406.

Downs, George W., and Michael A. Jones. 2002. "Reputation, Compliance, and International Law." *The Journal of Legal Studies* 31 (1): 95–114.

Drezner, Daniel W. 2003. "The Hidden Hand of Economic Coercion." *International Organization* 57 (3): 643–659.

Duffield, John S. 2003. "The Limits of 'Rational Design.'" *International Organization* 57 (2): 411–430.

Dunoff, Jeffrey L., and Mark A. Pollack. 2013. "International Law and International Relations: Introducing an Interdisciplinary Dialogue." In *Interdisciplinary Perspectives on International Law and International*

Relations: The State of the Art, eds. Jeffrey L. Dunoff and Mark A. Pollack. Cambridge: Cambridge University Press.

Edwards, Richard W. Jr. 1989. "Reservations to Treaties." *Michigan Journal of International Law* 10 (2): 362–405.

Ehrlich, Isaac, and Richard A. Posner. 1974. "An Economic Analysis of Legal Rulemaking." *The Journal of Legal Studies* 3 (1): 257–286.

Fariss, Christopher J. 2014. "Respect for Human Rights has Improved over Time: Modeling the Changing Standard of Accountability." *American Political Science Review* 108 (2): 297–318.

Farrell, Joseph, and Robert Gibbons. 1989. "Cheap Talk Can Matter in Bargaining." *Journal of Economic Theory* 48 (1): 221–237.

Fearon, James D. 1998. "Bargaining, Enforcement, and International Cooperation." *International Organization* 52 (2): 269–305.

Finnemore, Martha, and Kathryn Sikkink. 1998. "International Norm Dynamics and Political Change." *International Organization* 52 (4): 887–917.

Franck, Thomas M. 1990. *The Power of Legitimacy among Nations*. New York: Oxford University Press.

Fudenberg, Drew, David Levine, and Eric Maskin. 1994. "The Folk Theorem with Imperfect Public Information." *Econometrica* 62 (5): 997–1039.

Garvey, Jack I. 1995. "Trade Law and Quality of Life–Dispute Resolution Under the NAFTA Side Accords on Labor and the Environment." *American Journal of International Law* 89 (2):439–453.

Gibler, Douglas M. 2009. *International Military Alliances, 1648–2008*. Washington, DC: CQ Press.

Gibler, Douglas, and Meredith Reid Sarkees. 2004. "Measuring Alliances: The Correlates of War Formal Interstate Alliance Dataset, 1816–2000." *Journal of Peace Research* 41 (2): 211–222.

Giegerich, Thomas. 2012. "Article 56. Denunciation of or Withdrawal from a Treaty Containing No Provision Regarding Termination, Denunciation or Withdrawal." In *Vienna Convention on the Law of Treaties: A Commentary*, eds. Oliver Dörr, and Kirsten Schmalenbach. Berlin, Heidelberg: Springer.

Glendon, Mary Ann. 2001. *A World Made New: Eleanor Roosevelt and the Universal Declaration of Human Rights*. New York, NY: Random House.

Goldsmith, Jack L., and Eric A. Posner. 1999. "A Theory of Customary International Law." *The University of Chicago Law Review* 66 (4): 1113–1177.

2005. *The Limits of International Law*. Oxford; New York: Oxford University Press.

Goldstein, Judith L., Miles Kahler, Robert O. Keohane, and Anne-Marie Slaughter, eds. 2000a. "Legalization and World Politics." *International Organization* 54 (3).

2000b. "Introduction: Legalization and World Politics." *International Organization* 54 (3): 385–399.

Goldstein, Judith L., and Lisa Martin. 2000. "Legalization, Trade Liberalization, and Domestic Politics: A Cautionary Note." *International Organization* 54 (3): 603–632.

Goodman, Ryan. 2002. "Human Rights Treaties, Invalid Reservations, and State Consent." *American Journal of International Law* 96 (3): 531–560.

Grando, Michelle T. 2006. "Allocating the Burden of Proof in WTO Disputes. A Critical Analysis." *Journal of International Economic Law* 9 (3): 615–656.

Green, Jessica F. 2013. *Rethinking Private Authority: Agents and Entrepreneurs in Global Environmental Governance.* Princeton, NJ: Princeton University Press.

Greenhill, Brian, Michael D. Ward, and Audrey Sacks. 2011. "The Separation Plot: A New Visual Method for Evaluating the Fit of Binary Models." *American Journal of Political Science* 55 (4): 990–1002.

Grinspun, Ricardo, and Robert Kreklewich. 1999. "Institutions, Power Relations and Unequal Integration in the Americas: NAFTA as Deficient Institutionality." In *Economic Integration in NAFTA and the EU*, eds. Kirsten Appendini and Sven Bislev. New York: St. Martin's Press.

Guzman, Andrew T. 2006. "The Promise of International Law. Review of 'The Limits of International Law' by Jack Goldsmith and Eric Posner." *Virginia Law Review* 92 (3): 533–564.

2008. *How International Law Works: A Rational Choice Theory.* Oxford; New York: Oxford University Press.

Guzman, Andrew T., and Timothy L. Meyer. 2010. "International Soft Law." *Journal of Legal Analysis* 2 (1): 171–225.

Guzman, Andrew T., and Beth A. Simmons. 2002. "To Settle Or Empanel? An Empirical Analysis of Litigation and Settlement at the World Trade Organization." *The Journal of Legal Studies* 31 (1): 205–235.

Hafner-Burton, Emilie M., Laurence R. Helfer, and Christopher J. Fariss. 2011. "Emergency and Escape: Explaining Derogations from Human Rights Treaties." *International Organization* 65 (4): 673–707.

Haftel, Yoram Z. 2012. *Regional Economic Institutions and Conflict Mitigation. Design, Implementation, and the Promise of Peace.* Ann Arbor, MI: University of Michigan Press. Available at https://muse.jhu.edu/ [Last accessed June 13, 2015].

Haftel, Yoram Z., and Alexander Thompson. 2013. "Delayed Ratification: The Domestic Fate of Bilateral Investment Treaties." *International Organization* 67 (2): 355–387.

Hanmer, Michael J., and Kerem Ozan Kalkan. 2013. "Behind the Curve: Clarifying the Best Approach to Calculating Predicted Probabilities and Marginal Effects from Limited Dependent Variable Models." *American Journal of Political Science* 57 (1): 263–277.

Hansen, Holley E., Sara McLaughlin Mitchell, and Stephen C. Nemeth. 2008. "IO Mediation of Interstate Conflicts: Moving beyond the Global versus Regional Dichotomy." *Journal of Conflict Resolution* 52 (2): 295–325.

Hanson, Arthur J. 2011. "Trilateral Environment and Sustainable Development." *International Journal* 66 (2): 313–331.

Hardin, Russell. 1982. *Collective Action.* Baltimore: Published for Resources for the Future by the Johns Hopkins University Press.

Harrison, John. 2005. "Uniformity, Diversity, and the Process of Making Human Rights Norms." *University of St. Thomas Law Journal* 3 (2): 334–344.

Hathaway, Oona. 2003. "The Cost of Commitment." *Stanford Law Review* 55 (5): 1821–1826.

Hawkins, Darren G., David A. Lake, Daniel L. Nielson, and Michael J. Tierney, eds. 2006. *Delegation and Agency in International Organizations.* Cambridge: Cambridge University Press.

Helfer, Laurence R. 2002. "Overlegalizing Human Rights: International Relations Theory and the Commonwealth Caribbean Backlash against Human Rights Regimes." *Columbia Law Review* 102 (7): 1832–1911.

  2005. "Exiting Treaties." *Virginia Law Review* 91 (7): 1579–1648.

  2006. "Not Fully Committed? Reservations, Risk, and Treaty Design." *Yale Journal of International Law* 31 (2): 367–382.

  2008. "Redesigning the European Court Of Human Rights: Embeddedness as a Deep Structural Principle of the European Human Rights Regime." *European Journal of International Law* 19 (1): 125–159.

  2013. "Flexibility in International Agreements." In *Interdisciplinary Perspectives on International Law and International Relations: The State of the Art*, eds. Jeffrey L. Dunoff and Mark A. Pollack. Cambridge: Cambridge University Press.

Helfer, Laurence R., and Anne-Marie Slaughter. 1997. "Toward a Theory of Effective Supranational Adjudication." *The Yale Law Journal* 107 (2): 273–391.

Henkin, Louis. 1979. *How Nations Behave: Law and Foreign Policy.* New York: Published for the Council on Foreign Relations by Columbia University Press.

1995a. *International Law: Politics and Values* Dordrecht : Martinus Nijhoff.

1995b. "U.S. Ratification of Human Rights Conventions: The Ghost of Senator Bricker." *American Journal of International Law* 89 (2): 341–350.

Hill, Daniel W. 2010. "Estimating the Effects of Human Rights Treaties on State Behavior." *The Journal of Politics* 72 (4): 1161–1174.

Hooghe, Liesbet, and Gary Marks. 2014. "Delegation and Pooling In International Organizations." *The Review of International Organizations* 10 (3): 305–328.

Hufbauer, Gary Clyde, and Gustavo Vega-Cánovas. 2003. "Whither NAFTA: A Common Frontier?" In *The Rebordering of North America*, eds. Peter Andreas and Thomas J. Biersteker. New York: Routlege.

Hurd, Ian. 1999. "Legitimacy and Authority in International Politics." *International Organization* 53 (2): 379–408.

Huth, Paul K., Sarah E. Croco, and Benjamin J. Appel. 2011. "Does International Law Promote the Peaceful Settlement of International Disputes? Evidence from the Study of Territorial Conflicts since 1945." *American Political Science Review* 105 (2): 415–436.

Jackson, John H. 1978. "The Jurisprudence of International Trade." *American Journal of International Law* 72 (4): 747–781.

1992. "Status of Treaties in Domestic Legal Systems: A Policy Analysis." *American Journal of International Law* 86 (2): 310–340.

Jensen, Lloyd. 1974. *Return From The Nuclear Brink: National Interest and the Nuclear Nonproliferation Treaty.* Lexington, MA: Lexington Books.

Johnson, Harry G. 1972 "The International Monetary System and The Rule Of Law." *The Journal of Law and Economics* 15: 277–292.

Jonas, Susanne. 1988. "Contradictions of Guatemala's 'Political Opening'." *Latin American Perspective* 1 (3): 26–46.

2000. "Democratization Through Peace: The Difficult Case of Guatemala." *Journal of Interamerican Studies and World Affairs* 42 (4): 9–38.

Jupille, Joseph, Walter Mattli, and Duncan Snidal. 2013. *Institutional Choice and Global Commerce.* New York: Cambridge University Press.

Kaiser, Karl 1978 "The Great Nuclear Debate: German-American Disagreements." *Foreign Policy* 30 (1): 83–110.

Katzenstein, Peter, and Rudra Sil. 2008. "Eclectic Theorizing in the Study and Practice of International Relations." In *The Oxford Handbook of International Relations*, eds. Christian Reus-Smit, and Duncan Snidal. Oxford, New York: Oxford University Press.

Kaufman, Natalie Hevener. 1990. *Human Rights Treaties and The Senate: A History Of Opposition.* Chapel Hill: University of North Carolina Press.

Kennan, George F. 1951. *American Diplomacy, 1900–1950*. Chicago: University of Chicago Press.

Keohane, Robert O. 1984. *After Hegemony: Cooperation and Discord in the World Political Economy*. Princeton: Princeton University Press.

   1988. "International Institutions: Two Approaches." *International Studies Quarterly* 32 (4): 379–396.

Keohane, Robert O., Andrew Moravcsik, and Anne-Marie Slaughter. 2000. "Legalized Dispute Resolution: Interstate and Transnational." *International Organization* 54 (3): 457–488.

Kleine, Mareike. 2013. "Knowing Your Limits: Informal Governance and Judgment in the EU." *The Review of International Organizations* 8 (2): 245–264.

Koh, Harold Hongju. 1997. "Why do Nations Obey International Law?" *The Yale Law Journal* 106: 2599–2659.

Koremenos, Barbara. 2001. "Loosening the Ties that Bind: A Learning Model of Agreement Flexibility." *International Organization* 55 (2): 289–325.

   2002. "Can Cooperation Survive Changes in Bargaining Power? The Case of Coffee." *The Journal of Legal Studies* 31 (S1): 259–283.

   2005. "Contracting Around International Uncertainty." *American Political Science Review* 99 (4): 549–565.

   2007. "If Only Half of International Agreements Have Dispute Resolution Provisions, Which Half Needs Explaining?" *The Journal of Legal Studies* 36 (1): 189–212.

   2008. "When, What, and Why Do States Choose to Delegate?" *Law and Contemporary Problems* 17 (1): 151–192.

   2013a. "The Continent of International Law." *Journal of Conflict Resolution* 57 (4): 653–680.

   2013b. "Institutionalism and International Law." In *Interdisciplinary Perspectives on International Law and International Relations: The State of the Art*, eds. Jeffrey L. Dunoff and Mark A. Pollack. New York, NY: Cambridge University Press.

   2013c. "What's Left Out and Why? Informal Provisions in Formal International Law." *The Review of International Organizations* 8 (2): 137–162.

   2015. "The Role of State Leadership in the Incidence of International Governance." *Global Policy* 6 (3): 237–246.

Koremenos, Barbara, and Timm Betz. 2013. "The Design of Dispute Settlement Procedures in International Agreements." In *Interdisciplinary Perspectives on International Law and International Relations: The State of the Art*, eds. Jeffrey L. Dunoff and Mark A. Pollack. New York, NY: Cambridge University Press.

Koremenos, Barbara, Charles Lipson, and Duncan Snidal, eds. 2001a. *International Organization, Special Issue: The Rational Design of International Institutions* 55 (4).

2001b. "The Rational Design of International Institutions." *International Organization, Special Issue: The Rational Design of International Institutions* 55 (4): 761–799.

2001c. "Looking Back to Move Forward." *International Organization, Special Issue: The Rational Design of International Institutions* 55 (4): 1051–1082.

Koremenos, Barbara, and Allison Nau. 2010. "Exit, no Exit." *Duke Journal of Comparative & International Law* 21 (1): 81–120.

Koremenos, Barbara, and Duncan Snidal. 2003. "Moving Forward, One Step at a Time." *International Organization* 57 (2): 431–444.

Kramish, Arnold. 1963. *The Peaceful Atom on Foreign Policy.* Published for the Council on Foreign Relations. New York: Harper & Row.

Krasner, Stephen D. 1973. "Business-Government Relations: The Case of the International Coffee Agreement." *International Organization* 27 (4): 495–516.

1983. *International Regimes.* Ithaca: Cornell University Press.

1991. "Global Communications and National Power: Life on the Pareto Frontier." *World Politics* 43 (April): 336–366.

Kreps, David M. 1990. *A Course in Microeconomic Theory.* Princeton, NJ: Princeton University Press.

Krisch, Nico. 2005. "International Law in Times of Hegemony: Unequal Power and the Shaping of the International Legal Order." *European Journal of International Law* 16 (3): 369–408.

Kucik, Jeffrey, and Eric Reinhardt. 2008. "Does Flexibility Promote Cooperation? An Application to the Global Trade Regime." *International Organization* 62 (3): 477–505.

Kunz, Josef L. 1939. "The Problem of Revision in International Law." *American Journal of International Law* 33 (1): 33–55.

Lai, Brian, and Dan Reiter. 2000. "Democracy, Political Similarity, and International Alliances, 1816–1992." *Journal of Conflict Resolution* 44 (2): 203–227.

Lake, David A. 2002. "Progress in International Relations: Beyond Paradigms in the Study of International Institutions." In *Realism and Institutionalism in International Studies,* eds. Michael Brecher and Frank P. Harvey. Ann Arbor: University of Michigan Press.

2010. "Rightful Rules: Authority, Order, and the Foundations of Global Governance." *International Studies Quarterly* 54 (3): 587–613.

Lamare, James W. 1987. "International Conflict ANZUS and New Zealand Public Opinion." *Journal of Conflict Resolution* 31 (3): 420–437.

Leeds, Brett, Jeffrey Ritter, Sara McLaughlin Mitchell, and Andrew Long. 2002. "Alliance Treaty Obligations and Provisions." *International Interactions* 28 (3): 237–260.

Lipson, Charles. 1984. "International Cooperation in Economic and Security Affairs." *World Politics* 37 (October): 1–23.

1991. "Why Are Some International Agreements Informal?" *International Organization* 45 (4): 495–538.

Llamzon, Aloysius. P. 2007. "Jurisdiction and Compliance in Recent Decisions of the International Court of Justice." *European Journal of International Law* 18 (5): 815–852.

Mace, Gordon, and Louis Bélanger. 2004. "What Institutional Design for North America?" In *Free Trade in the Americas: Economic and Political Issues for Governments and Firms* (New Horizons in International Business Series), eds. Sidney Weintraub, Alan M. Rugman, and Gavin Boyd. Northampton, MA: Edward Elgar.

Martin, Lisa. 1992. "Interests, Power and Multilateralism." *International Organization*. 46: 765–792.

2013. "Against Compliance." In *Interdisciplinary Perspectives on International Law and International Relations: The State of the Art*, eds. Jeffrey L. Dunoff and Mark A. Pollack. Cambridge: Cambridge University Press.

Mattli, Walter, and Jack Seddon. 2015. "New Organizational Leadership: Nonstate Actors in Global Economic Governance." *Global Policy* 6 (3). Forthcoming.

McGinnis, Michael D. 1986. "Issue Linkage and the Evolution of International Cooperation." *Journal of Conflict Resolution* 30 (1): 141–170.

McKelvey, Richard D. 1976. "Intransitivities in Multidimensional Voting Models and Some Implications for Agenda Control." *Journal of Economic Theory* 12: 472–482.

Mearsheimer, John J. 1994. "The False Promise of International Institutions." *International Security* 19 (3): 5–49.

Miles, Thomas J., and Eric A. Posner. 2008. "Which States Enter into Treaties, and Why?" *University of Chicago Law & Economics, Olin Working Paper* No. 420; *University of Chicago, Public Law Working Paper* No. 225. Available at SSRN http://papers.ssrn.com/sol3/papers.cfm?abstract_id=1211177 [Last accessed June 24, 2015].

Milgrom, Paul R., Douglass C. North, and Barry R. Weingast. 1990. "The Role of Institutions in the Revival of Trade: The Law Merchant, Private Judges, and the Champagne Fairs." *Economics and Politics* 2: 1–23.

Mitchell, Ronald B. 1998. "Sources of Transparency: Information Systems in International Regimes." *International Studies Quarterly* 42 (1): 109–130.

Mitchell, Ronald B., and Patricia M. Keilbach. 2001. "Situation Structure and Institutional Design: Reciprocity, Coercion, and Exchange." *International Organization* 55 (4): 891–917.

Mitchell, Sara McLaughlin, and Emilia Justyna Powell. 2011. *Domestic Law Goes Global: Legal Traditions And International Courts*. Cambridge: Cambridge University Press.

Moravcsik, Andrew. 2000. "The Origins of Human Rights Regimes: Democratic Delegation in Postwar Europe." *International Organization* 54 (2): 217–252.

2008. "The New Liberalism." In *Oxford Handbook of International Relations*, eds. Christian Reus-Smit and Duncan Snidal. New York: Oxford University Press.

Morrow, James D. 1994. "Modeling the Forms of International Cooperation: Distribution versus Information." *International Organization* 48 (3): 387–423.

2007. "When do States Follow the Laws of War?" *American Political Science Review* 101 (3): 559–572.

Morse, Julia C., and Robert O. Keohane. 2014. "Contested Multilateralism." *The Review of International Organizations* 9 (4): 385–412.

Neumayer, Eric. 2007. "Qualified Ratification: Explaining Reservations to International Human Rights Treaties." *The Journal of Legal Studies* 36 (2): 397–429.

Nietzsche, Friedrich. [1887] 1967. *The Will to Power*. Ed. Walter Kaufmann. New York: Random House.

Norman, George, and Joel P. Trachtman. 2005. "The Customary International Law Game." American Journal of International Law 99 (3): 541–580.

Nye, Joseph S. 1981. "Maintaining a Nonproliferation Regime." *International Organization* 35 (1): 15–38.

Oates, Wallace E. 1999. "An Essay on Fiscal Federalism." *Journal of Economic Literature* 37 (3): 1120–1149.

Olson, Mancur. 1965. *The Logic of Collective Action*. Cambridge, MA: Harvard University Press.

Oneal, John R., and Bruce M. Russett. 1997. "The Classical Liberals Were Right: Democracy, Interdependence, and Conflict, 1950–1985." *International Studies Quarterly* 41 (June): 267–293.

Organski, A. F. K. 1958. *World Politics*. New York: Knopf.

Ostrom, Elinor. 1990. *Governing the Commons: The Evolution of Institutions for Collective Action*. Cambridge: Cambridge University Press.

Oye, Kenneth A. 1986. "Explaining Cooperation under Anarchy: Hypotheses and Strategies." In *Cooperation under Anarchy*, ed. Kenneth A. Oye. Princeton, NJ: Princeton University Press.

Pahre, Robert. 1994. "Multilateral Cooperation in an Iterated Prisoner's Dilemma." *Journal of Conflict Resolution* 38 (2): 326–352.

Palmer, Glenn, Vito D'Orazio, Michael Kenwick, and Matthew Lane. 2015. "The MID4 Data Set: Procedures, Coding Rules, and Description." *Conflict Management and Peace Science.* Forthcoming.

Pauwelyn, Joost. 2001. "The Role of Public International Law in the WTO: How Far Can We Go?" *American Journal of International Law* 95 (3): 535–578.

Pelc, Krzysztof J. 2009. "Seeking Escape: The Use of Escape Clauses in International Trade Agreements." *International Studies Quarterly* 53 (2): 349–368.

Pelc, Krzysztof J., and Johannes Urpelainen. 2015. "When Do International Economic Agreements Allow Countries To Pay To Breach?" *The Review of International Organizations* 10 (2): 231–264.

Pellet, Alain, and Daniel Müller. 2011. "Reservations to Human Rights Treaties: Not an Absolute Evil ..." In *From Bilateralism to Community Interest. Essays in Honour of Judge Bruno Simma,* eds. Ulrich Fastenrath et al. New York: Oxford University Press.

Pevehouse, Jon, Timothy Nordstrom, and Kevin Warnke. 2004. "The Correlates of War 2 International Governmental Organizations Data Version 2.0." *Conflict Management and Peace Science* 21 (2): 101–119.

Poast, Paul. 2012. "Does Issue Linkage Work? Evidence from European Alliance Negotiations, 1860 to 1945." *International Organization* 66 (2): 277–310.

  2013; 2012. "Can Issue Linkage Improve Treaty Credibility?: Buffer State Alliances as a "Hard Case." *Journal of Conflict Resolution* 57 (5): 739–764.

Posner, Eric A., and John C. Yoo. 2005. "Judicial Independence in International Tribunals." *California Law Review* 93 (1): 1–74.

Powell, Emilia Justyna. 2013. "Islamic Law States and the International Court Of Justice." *Journal of Peace Research* 50 (2): 203–217.

Pregelj, Vladimir N. 2005. "The Jackson-Vanik Amendment: A Survey" CRS Report for Congress. Available at www.fas.org/sgp/crs/row/98-545.pdf [Last accessed December 5, 2015]

Putnam, Robert D. 1988. "Diplomacy and Domestic Politics: The Logic of Two-Level Games." *International Organization* 42 (3): 427–460.

Raiffa, Howard. 1982. *The Art and Science of Negotiating.* Cambridge, MA: Harvard University Press.

Rajagopal, Balakrishnan. 2005. "Review of the Limits of International Law by Jack Goldsmith and Eric Posner." *Ethics and International Affairs* 19 (3): 106–109.

Raustiala, Kal. 2005. "Form and Substance in International Agreements." *American Journal of International Law* 99 (3): 581–614.

2006. "Refining the Limits of International Law." *Georgia Journal of International and Comparative Law* 34 (2): 423–444.

Redick, John R. 1981. "The Tlatelolco Regime and Nonproliferation in Latin America." *International Organization* 35 (1): 103–134.

Reynolds, Glenn Harlan. 1995. "The Moon Treaty: Prospects for the Future." *Space Policy* 11 (2): 115–120.

Riker, William H. 1980. "Implications from the Disequilibrium of Majority Rule for the Study of Institutions." *American Political Science Review* 74 (2): 432–446.

Risse, Thomas, and Stephen C. Ropp. 1999. "International Human Rights Norms and Domestic Change." In *The Power of Human Rights*, eds. Thomas Risse, Stephen C. Ropp, and Kathryn Sikkink. Cambridge: Cambridge University Press.

Rosand, Eric. 2003. "Security Council Resolution 1373, the Counter-Terrorism Committee, and the Fight against Terrorism." *American Journal of International Law* 97 (2): 333–341.

Rosendorff, B. Peter, and Helen V. Milner. 2001. "The Optimal Design of International Trade Institutions." *International Organization* 55 (4): 829–857.

Sartori, Anne E. 2003. "An Estimator for some Binary-Outcome Selection Models without Exclusion Restrictions." *Political Analysis* 11 (2): 111–138.

Schabas, William A. 1997. "Reservations to the Convention on the Elimination of all Forms of Discrimination against Women and the Convention on the Rights of the Child." *William & Mary Journal of Women and the Law* 3 (1): 79–112.

Schachter, Oscar. 1977. "The Twilight Existence of Nonbinding International Agreements." *American Journal of International Law* 71 (2): 296–304.

Schloemann, Hannes L., and Stefan Ohlhoff. 1999. "'Constitutionalization' and Dispute Settlement in the WTO: National Security as an Issue of Competence." *American Journal of International Law* 93 (2): 424–451.

Schwartz, Warren F., and Alan O. Sykes. 2002. "The Economic Structure of Renegotiation and Dispute Resolution in the World Trade Organization." *The Journal of Legal Studies* 31 (1): S179–S204.

Scott, Robert. E., and Paul B. Stephan. [2006] 2011. *The Limits of Leviathan: Contract Theory and the Enforcement of International Law*. Cambridge: Cambridge University Press.

Sebenius, James K. 1983. "Negotiation Arithmetic: Adding and Subtracting Issues and Parties." *International Organization* 37 (2): 281–316.

Selznick, Philip. 1949. *TVA and the Grass Roots: A Study in the Sociology of Formal Organization.* Berkeley: University of California Press.

Shaffer, Gregory C., and Mark A. Pollack. 2010. "Hard v. Soft Law: Alternatives, Complements, and Antagonists in International Governance." *Minnesota Law Review* 94 (3): 706–799.

Sheffer, Megan Wells. 2011. "Bilateral Investment Treaties: A Friend or Foe to Human Rights?" *Denver Journal of International Law and Policy* 39 (3): 483–521.

Shepsle, Kenneth A. 1986. "Institutional Equilibrium and Equilibrium Institutions." In *Political Science: The Science of Politics*, ed. Herbert Weisberg. New York: Agathon Press.

Simma, Bruno. 1994. "From Bilateralism to Community Interest in International Law." In *Recueil des Cours (Collected Courses of the Hague Academy of International Law).* Vol. 250. The Hague: Martinus Nijhoff.

Simmons, Beth A. 2009. *Mobilizing for Human Rights. International Law and Domestic Politics.* Cambridge, New York: Cambridge University Press.

2010. "Treaty Compliance and Violation." *Annual Review of Political Science* 13 (1): 273–296.

Simmons, Beth A., and Daniel J. Hopkins. 2005. "The Constraining Power of International Treaties: Theory and Methods." *American Political Science Review* 99 (4): 623–631.

Slaughter Burley, Anne-Marie. 1993. "International Law and International Relations Theory: A Dual Agenda." *American Journal of International Law* 87 (2): 205–239.

Smith, James McCall. 2000. "The Politics of Dispute Settlement Design: Explaining Legalism in Regional Trade Pacts." *International Organization* 54 (1): 137–180.

Snidal, Duncan. 1985. "Coordination versus Prisoners' Dilemma: Implications for International Cooperation and Regimes." *American Political Science Review* 79 (4): 923–942.

Snyder, Scott. 2000. "The Korean Peninsula Energy Development Organization: Implications for Northeast Asian Regional Security Co-operation?" *North Pacific Policy Paper* 3: 1–34.

Stein, Arthur A. 1982. "Coordination and Collaboration: Regimes in an Anarchic World." *International Organization* 36 (2): 299–324.

2008. "Neoliberal Institutionalism." In *Oxford Handbook on International Relations*, eds. Christian Reus-Smit and Duncan Snidal. New York: Oxford University Press.

Steinberg, Richard H. 2002. "In the Shadow of Law or Power?" *International Organization* 56 (2): 339–374.

2013. "Wanted: Dead or Alive – Realist Approaches to International Law." In *Interdisciplinary Perspectives on International Law and International Relations: The State of the Art*, eds. Jeffrey L. Dunoff and Mark A. Pollack. Cambridge: Cambridge University Press.

Stone, Randall W. 2011. *Controlling Institutions: International Organizations and the Global Economy.* New York: Cambridge University Press.

Stone Sweet, Alec, and Thomas L. Brunell. 1998. "Constructing a Supranational Constitution: Dispute Resolution and Governance in the European Community." *American Political Science Review* 92 (1): 63–81.

Swaine, Edward T. 2006. "Reserving." *Yale Journal of International Law* 31 (2): 307–366.

Swenson-Wright, John. 2005. *Unequal Allies? United States Security and Alliance Policy Toward Japan, 1945–1960.* Stanford, CA: Stanford University Press.

Sykes, Alan O. 1991. "Protectionism as a 'Safeguard': A Positive Analysis of the GATT 'Escape Clause' with Normative Speculations." *The University of Chicago Law Review* 58 (1): 255–305.

Szasz, Paul, ed., 1999. *Administrative and Expert Monitoring of International Treaties.* Ardsley, NY: Transnational Publishers.

2002. "The Security Council Starts Legislating." *American Journal of International Law* 96 (4): 901–905.

Tallberg, Jonas, Thomas Sommerer, Theresa Squatrito, and Christer Jönsson. 2013. *The Opening Up Of International Organizations: Transnational Access in Global Governance.* Cambridge: Cambridge University Press.

Tan, Morse. 2005. "Member State Compliance with the Judgments of the Inter-American Court of Human Rights." *International Journal of Legal Information* 33 (3): 319–344.

Thompson, Alexander. 2009. "The Rational Enforcement of International Law: Solving the Sanctioners' Dilemma." *International Theory* 1 (2):307–321.

Thompson, Alexander, and Daniel Verdier. 2014. "Multilateralism, Bilateralism, and Regime Design." *International Studies Quarterly* 58 (1): 15–28.

Tierney, Michael J. 2008. "Delegation Success and Policy Failure: Collective Delegation and the Search for Iraqi Weapons of Mass Destruction." *Law and Contemporary Problems* 71 (2): 283–331.

Tollison, Robert E., and Thomas D. Willett. 1979. "An Economic Theory of Mutually Advantageous Issue Linkage in International Negotiations." *International Organization* 33 (4): 425–449.

Tow, William, and Henry Albinski. 2002. "ANZUS – Alive and Well After Fifty Years." *Australian Journal of Politics & History* 48 (2): 153–173.

Tsebelis, George. 1990. *Nested Games: Rational Choice In Comparative Politics*. Berkley: University of California Press.

Vabulas, Felicity. 2013. "Enhancing Monitoring and Enforcement in IGOs: When and Why States Grant Consultative Status to NGOs." Ph.D. Dissertation. University of Chicago.

Vabulas, Felicity, and Duncan Snidal. 2013. "Organization without Delegation: Informal Intergovernmental Organizations (IIGOs) and the Spectrum of Intergovernmental Arrangements." *The Review of International Organizations* 8 (2):193–220.

van Aaken, Anne. 2014. "Smart Flexibility Clauses in International Investment Treaties and Sustainable Development: A Functional View." *Journal of World Investment and Trade* 15: 827–861.

Verdier, Daniel. 2008. "Multilateralism, Bilateralism, and Exclusion in the Nuclear Proliferation Regime." *International Organization* 62 (3): 439–476.

Verdier, Pierre-Hugues, and Erik Voeten. 2015. "How Does Customary International Law Change? The Case of State Immunity." *International Studies Quarterly* 59 (2): 209–222.

Victor, David G., Kal Raustiala, and Eugene B. Skolnikoff. 1998. *The Implementation and Effectiveness of International Environmental Commitments: Theory and Practice*. Laxenburg, Austria: Cambridge, MA: International Institute for Applied Systems Analysis; MIT Press.

Voeten, Erik. 2012. "Data and Analyses of Voting in the UN General Assembly." Available at SSRN http://ssrn.com/abstract=2111149 [Last accessed June 14, 2015]

von Stein, Jana. 2013. "The Engines of Compliance." In *Interdisciplinary Perspectives on International Law and International Relations: The State of the Art*, eds. Jeffrey L. Dunoff and Mark A. Pollack. Cambridge: Cambridge University Press.

Wallace, Michael, and J. David Singer. 1970. "Intergovernmental Organization in the Global System, 1815–1964." *International Organization* 24 (2): 239–287.

Walt, Stephen M. 1999. "Rigor Or Rigor Mortis? Rational Choice and Security Studies." *International Security* 23 (4): 5–48.

Welsh, Susan B. 1995. "Delegate Perspectives on the 1995 NPT Review and Extension Conference." *The Nonproliferation Review* 2 (3): 1–24.

Wendt, Alexander. 2001. "Looking in the Rearview Mirror: On the Rational Science of Rational Design." *International Organization, Special Issue: The Rational Design of International Institutions* 55 (4): 1019–1049.

Wilson, Robert R. 1934. "Revision Clauses in Treaties since the World War." *American Political Science Review* 28 (5): 901–909.

Winter, Eyal. 1996. "Voting and Vetoing." *American Political Science Review* 90 (4): 813–823.

Wit, Joel. 1999. "Viewpoint: the Korean Peninsula Energy Development Organization: Achievements and Challenges." *The Nonproliferation Review* 6 (2): 59–69.

Wotipka, Christine Min, and Francisco O. Ramirez. 2008. "World Society and Human Rights: an Event History Analysis of the Convention on the Elimination of All Forms of Discrimination against Women." In *The Global Diffusion of Markets and Democracy*, eds. Beth A. Simmons, Frank Dobbin and Geoffrey Garrett. Cambridge: Cambridge University Press.

Young, Oran R. 1991. "Political Leadership and Regime Formation: On the Development of Institutions in International Society." *International Organization* 45 (3): 281–308.

Index